Salt -133 ±131 - Catechumen
Milk & Honey -132 +134 is signed
Milk - p 76

P307 - Rites of RCIA

✷ P315 - Easter tradition
   ✷ Priest conferring
     & returned

Anglican debate
✷ Baptism & Confirmation
  to 20th Century

D0864279

P75 - Roman Rit of Baptism
P87 - East vs West ← w- Removing Sin E Syria
P89 - Serious faults could
        prolong the catechumenat
        for 5-10 or for life
P92 - Controversies & the
        catechumenat
P94 - Syrian 4 & 5 cent
        Lorps, Cyril &
     the 5 mystagogy lectures
   Significance of Baptism
P96 - Syrian Liturgy looks — papers — Easter tradition
   to the West & Renounces
   it (Satan)
P96 — Water = life &
        death. / taking off
        clothes & anointing
P96 - Christ'- Grace instills
        His Divinity in us
P97 mystagogy of receiving
        Eucharist.

P97 Egypt in the 4 & 5 cent
P100 Ancient in 4 th & 5 cent.

P102 - Baptismal Homely of
        St John Chrysostom

P123 - Easter Church - Roman

P130+P131+ what is a "Scrutiny"
P+132 - also a great reference to
        apostolic tradition

Ear & Nostrils - p136, 131
   Gospel effetha, "Be opened"

P140 Holy Spirit - Picture of
   confirmation followed Baptism
   & replaced the part
   Baptismal anointing. This
   occurred around the
   time of Nicea & Constantinople I

The Rites of Christian Initiation
   Possible last Quotes
   P104 - John Chrysostom

P136 – pedalaum in Northern Italy, Milan, Ambrose
P148 – Pre Baptismal ritual for Augustine

P169 – The pre-paschal fast in Hislop

P201 – "Western Disintegration dissolution + reparation" in medieval Initiation
P203 – reparation of Conf. Baptism + Eucharist

Infant Baptism
P213 – Medieval Infant Baptism occured within 1 week of birth – Based on Augustine

P214 – Infant Baptism in France – Middle ages
P155–56 – Augustine: Quam primum (quamprimum)
P215 – Catechumenate disappears in the West for adults
P216 – "rite for the Dying" becomes the "quamprimum" equivalent of Infant Baptism
P220 – Infant Baptism

Catechumenate disappears in the middle ages

Maxwell E. Johnson

The Rites of Christian Initiation

Their Evolution and Interpretation

A PUEBLO BOOK

The Liturgical Press Collegeville, Minnesota

A Pueblo Book published by The Liturgical Press

Design by Frank Kacmarcik, Obl.S.B. Mosaic detail: Arian Baptistry, Ravenna, Italy.

Library of Congress Cataloging-in-Publication Data

Johnson, Maxwell E., 1952–
     The rites of Christian initiation : their evolution and
  interpretation / Maxwell E. Johnson.
          p.   cm.
     "A Pueblo book."
     Includes bibliographical references and index.
     ISBN 0-8146-6011-8 (alk. paper)
     1. Initiation rites—Religious aspects—Christianity—History of
  doctrines.   I. Title.
  BV873.I54   J64   1999
  265'.1'09—dc21   98-12472
                                                           CIP

To
Aelred Tegels, O.S.B.,
Monk, Scholar, Teacher, and Friend,
who, with wit and wisdom,
was one of the first to introduce me to liturgical study,
this book is gratefully dedicated.

THE BAPTISTERY OF THE LATERAN BASILICA

Here a people of godly race are born of heaven;
the Spirit gives them life in the fertile waters.
The Church-Mother, in these waves, bears her children
like virginal fruit she has conceived by the Holy Spirit.

Hope for the kingdom of heaven, you who are reborn in this spring,
for those who are born but once have no share in the life of blessedness.
Here is to be found the source of life, which washes the whole universe,
which gushed from the wound of Christ.

Sinner, plunge into the sacred fountain to wash away your sin.
The water receives the old man, and in his place makes the new man rise.
You wish to become innocent; cleanse yourself in this bath,
whatever your burden may be, Adam's sin or your own.

There is no difference between those who are reborn; they are one,
in a single baptism, a single Spirit, a single faith.
Let none be afraid of the number of the weight of their sins:
those who are born of this stream will be made holy.

—Inscription of Sixtus III, 432–440[1]

---

[1] Translation is adapted from Lucien Deiss, *Springtime of the Liturgy* (Collegeville: The Liturgical Press, 1979) 264.

Contents

Acknowledgments

In addition to the use of several Liturgical Press publications, including those under the Pueblo and Michael Glazier imprints, special thanks are also due to the following for their kind permission to reproduce in this work extended copyrighted extracts of primary texts in English translation and quotations from various authors:

Bishop Collin Buchanan of Grove Books, Ltd., Cambridge, England, for texts and quotations from: Geoffrey Cuming, *Hippolytus: A Text for Students*, GLS 8 (1976); David Holeton, *Infant Communion—Then and Now*, GLS 27 (1981); and Gordon Jeanes, *The Origins of the Roman Rite*, AGLS 20 (1991);

Ms. Mo Dingle of SPCK, London, England, for texts and quotations from: J.D.C. Fisher, *Baptism in the Medieval West* (1965); J.D.C. Fisher, *Christian Initiation: The Reformation Period* (1970); E. C. Whitaker, *Documents of the Baptismal Liturgy* (1970); and John Wilkinson, *Egeria's Travels* (1970);

The editors of *Worship*, Collegeville, Minnesota, for the use of my essay, "Back Home to the Font: Eight Implications of a Baptismal Spirituality," *Worship* 71:6 (November 1997) 482–503, which appears here in an expanded form as Chapter 9, "Back Home to the Font: The Place of Baptismal Spirituality and Its Implications in a Displaced World"; and

The University of Notre Dame Press, Notre Dame, Indiana, for the use of my essay, "Preparation for Pascha? Lent in Christian Antiquity," *Two Liturgical Traditions*, vol. 5: *Passover and Easter*, ed. Paul Bradshaw and Lawrence Hoffman (Notre Dame: University of Notre Dame Press, forthcoming), which appears here in a different form as Chapter 5, "Baptismal Preparation and the Origins of Lent."

Abbreviations

ACC   Alcuin Club Collections

AIRI   Edward Yarnold, *The Awe-Inspiring Rites of Initiation: The Origins of the R.C.I.A.,* 2d ed. (Collegeville: The Liturgical Press, 1994).

ANF   *Ante-Nicene Fathers*

CCSL   *Corpus Christianorum, Series Latina*

DBL   Edward Charles Whitaker, ed., *Documents of the Baptismal Liturgy* (London: SPCK, 1970).

FC   *Fathers of the Church* (Washington, D.C.: Catholic University of America Press, 1946–).

LCC   *Library of Christian Classics* (Louisville: Westminster/John Knox Press).

LW   *Luther's Works* (Philadelphia/Saint Louis)

LWSS   Maxwell E. Johnson, ed., *Living Water, Sealing Spirit: Readings on Christian Initiation* (Collegeville: The Liturgical Press, 1995).

MFC   Message of the Fathers of the Church

MFC 5   Thomas M. Finn, ed., *Early Christian Baptism and the Catechumenate: West and East Syria,* Message of the Fathers of the Church 5 (Collegeville: The Liturgical Press, 1992).

MFC 6   Thomas M. Finn, ed., *Early Christian Baptism and the Catechumenate: Italy, North Africa and Egypt,* Message of the Fathers of the Church 6 (Collegeville: The Liturgical Press, 1992).

NPNF   *Nicene and Post Nicene Fathers*

PG   *Patrologia Graeca*

PL   *Patrologia Latina*

SC   *Sources chrétiennes*

Introduction

Every spring semester for the past several years I have taught a course designed primarily for theology majors entitled "Christian Initiation and Eucharist." Every spring semester I have faced the same problem: What textbook should I use for the Christian initiation section of the course? While the Eucharist, certainly, is both the culminating and repeatable rite of Christian initiation, appropriate textbooks on the evolution and interpretation of the eucharistic liturgy alone are much easier to find than are similar texts on the complete rites of Christian initiation, that is, on baptism and confirmation. Robert Cabié's *History of the Mass*[1] and Gary Macy's *The Banquet's Wisdom: A Short History of the Theologies of the Lord's Supper*,[2] for example, both provide significant selections of primary documents from different periods of Church history as well as helpful interpretive analyses of these documents.

For the specific rites of initiation, however, nothing similar exists at an introductory level. Standard works in the field, such as Aidan Kavanagh's *The Shape of Baptism*,[3] now over twenty years old, his *Confirmation: Origins and Reform*,[4] Gerard Austin's *Anointing with the Spirit: The Rite of Confirmation*,[5] as well as my own recent collection of essays, *Living Water, Sealing Spirit: Readings on Christian Initiation*,[6] can (and should) be read with profit. And yet, while all of these books do

[1] Robert Cabié, *History of the Mass*, trans. Lawrence J. Johnson (Washington, D.C.: Pastoral Press, 1992).

[2] Gary Macy, *The Banquet's Wisdom: A Short History of the Theologies of the Lord's Supper* (New York: Paulist Press, 1992).

[3] Aidan Kavanagh, *The Shape of Baptism: The Rite of Christian Initiation* (New York: Pueblo, 1978).

[4] Aidan Kavanagh, *Confirmation: Origins and Reform* (New York: Pueblo, 1988).

[5] Gerard Austin, *Anointing with the Spirit: The Rite of Confirmation: The Use of Oil and Chrism* (New York: Pueblo, 1985).

[6] Maxwell E. Johnson, ed., LWSS.

make reference to the appropriate historical and liturgical sources, their use necessitates that students also have at their disposal collections of primary liturgical documents. What this means is that, in addition to textbooks like these, collections like E. C. Whitaker's classic *Documents of the Baptismal Liturgy,*[7] now out of print, or Thomas Finn's two-volume *Early Christian Baptism and the Catechumenate,*[8] although limited to the patristic period, and J.D.C. Fisher's *Christian Initiation: The Reformation Period*[9] (also out of print), become "required" texts in the process. In short, then, even an introductory study of the rites of Christian initiation comes to imply that students must have on hand what constitutes a small library of books.

In my introductory essay to *Living Water, Sealing Spirit,* I suggested that the collection of essays be read as a first step toward rewriting a textbook on the history and theology of the rites of Christian initiation.[10] This study is an attempt to do just that. In attempting this, I hope that it will also provide that sought after one-volume text, including both primary and secondary sources, for use in introductory-level courses in the initiation rites. If so, then my annual problem of what to use in such a course is solved, at least for a while.

Although conceived originally with theology majors in mind, this book is by no means intended for well-theologically trained undergraduate students alone. Seminarians and beginning masters-level students in liturgy, it is hoped, will also find this study useful in providing an overall and detailed introduction to the initiation rites. To this end, I have not avoided numerous references to the critical editions of liturgical texts and documents in their original languages. Nor have I avoided references to scholarly studies in modern foreign languages. Similarly, at the end of this book, I have provided a rather lengthy, if select, bibliography on the rites of Christian initiation for those who wish to pursue particular topics of interest further. Those involved in various pastoral ministries, that is, pastors, catechists, directors of liturgy, directors of Christian initiation programs in

---

[7] Edward Charles Whitaker, *Documents of the Baptismal Liturgy* (London: SPCK, 1960).

[8] Thomas M. Finn, *Early Christian Baptism and the Catechumenate: West and East Syria* (Collegeville: The Liturgical Press, 1992).

[9] John Douglas Close Fisher, *Christian Initiation: The Reformation Period* (London: Society for Promoting Christian Knowledge, 1970).

[10] Johnson, LWSS, xii.

parishes, and others may also find this work useful in providing a solid theoretical foundation for their ministries.

As its title clearly indicates, this book is not written from the perspective of anthropology or from what many today refer to as "ritual studies," a discipline that functions together with those of liturgical history and liturgical theology to form the whole field known as "liturgical studies" in general. Nevertheless, it is important to note that the rites of Christian initiation are often interpreted according to what many in the anthropological and ritual studies disciplines have identified as "rites of passage."[11] That is, initiation rites, like those of birth, marriage, entrance into adulthood, specific vocations, and even the funeral rites surrounding death, are those rites by which various communities the world over, since the beginning of time, have celebrated as marking important "passages" from one level of identity and status in a given community or group to another. Such rites, generally, have an overall three-part structure and take place over a predetermined period of time.

stages of initiation

Rites of separation, in which those to be initiated are separated from the community for a time, take place first. This is usually followed by what is called a time of "liminality" or transition, that is, a period "betwixt and between" the initiands' former identity and status and their yet-to-be new identity and status. Several different rites, including, for example, instruction in the customs and traditions of the community, may take place during this liminal period of isolation and transition. The final stage, of course, is that of the initiation or incorporation itself, in which the initiands now enter completely into the life of the community with a new status and identity as full members of that community. Most often, we are told, this final rite of incorporation includes sharing in some kind of ritual meal (e.g., even graduation receptions, wedding banquets, and funeral lunches). Such a process, often quite dramatic and life-threatening in certain aboriginal societies, is commonly viewed in several different cultural contexts as a ritual process of rebirth and/or one of death and

ritual meal at conclusion

[11] Some of the classic anthropological studies of these rites include: Arnold Van Gennep, *The Rites of Passage,* trans. Monika B. Vizedom and Gabrielle L. Caffee (Chicago: University of Chicago Press, 1960), and Victor Turner, *The Ritual Process: Structure and Anti-Structure* (Chicago: Aldine Publishing Co., 1969). Leonel Mitchell's *The Meaning of Ritual* (New York: Paulist Press, 1977) is a very helpful and accessible treatment as well, especially pp. 1–22.

resurrection. Those initiated have "died" to their former way of life and been "resurrected" or "reborn" in another. Even the newly married couple has gone through a process of dying in their single lives so that they might be reborn or resurrected as husband and wife and thus take a new place in society.

Although there is nothing specifically *Christian* about such a ritual process, since early on the Church made use of a similar process to celebrate the initiation of those who, in response to the proclamation of the gospel, the Good News of God's salvation in Christ, have been converted, repented of their sins, and sought incorporation into Christ and the Christian community. The insights of anthropology into what appears to be a rather common human and social process of initiation, then, can be of great help to us in understanding the particular shape of the rites specific to Christian initiation.

Like all human rites of passage, the Christian rites of initiation follow a general pattern consisting of:

(1) entrance to the Catechumenate, a rite of *separation;*
(2) the Catechumenate and eventual "election" for initiation, a liminal time of *transition* and *preparation,* during which those to be initiated are instructed and formed in the teaching and life of the community;
(3) the rites of initiation (baptism, "confirmation," and first communion), rites by which the former catechumens and "elect" are now incorporated fully into the life of the Christian community; and
(4) the period of mystagogy ("explanation of the mysteries"), a continued process of further incorporation or reintegration into the community by explaining what the "mysteries" received signify and what their implications are for ongoing life in the community.

And, significantly, these Christian initiation rites are also often interpreted as rites of "rebirth" (see John 3:5) and "death, burial, and resurrection" (see Romans 6).

As helpful as the insights of anthropology and ritual studies are for understanding the particular structure or shape of the rites of Christian initiation, however, they tell us very little about the actual content and theological interpretation of those rites. Similarly, as one of my former teachers, the late Mark Searle, liked to say, *initiation* rites, as they are generally understood, are about initiating people who *al-*

ready belong in some way to the community into a new level of membership or status within that same community. *Christian* rites of initiation, however, are about conversion and faith. They are about entering a *new* community to which one did *not* belong before, even by birth. The anthropological analogy with the rites of passage, therefore, is only partially true in the case of the Christian rites. The ritual process may be similar, but the contents, goal, and interpretation of that process are not necessarily the same.

While greatly appreciative of the helpful insights of anthropology and ritual studies, this book, of course, is written from the perspective of liturgical texts, history, and theology. Beginning with the New Testament origins of the rites (chapter 1), the next three chapters deal with the further evolution of those rites and related issues within the early Churches of the first few centuries: the pre-Nicene period (chapter 2); and the first major period of liturgical change and renewal in the fourth and fifth centuries in the East (chapter 3) and West (chapter 4). Chapter 5, "Baptismal Preparation and the Origins of Lent," will also appear in a somewhat different form elsewhere.[12] Chapter 6 surveys what has been called for the West the dissolution and disintegration of the rites of Christian initiation within the medieval period. Chapter 7 addresses the changes brought about by the Protestant and Catholic Reformations of the sixteenth century. Chapter 8, the longest chapter of this study, surveys the development, current shape, theological interpretations, and contemporary problems surrounding the initiation rites in some of the churches of today. And the concluding chapter (chapter 9), originally published in a somewhat different form,[13] suggests several implications of a baptismal spirituality for the churches today.

Aided by what I believe is the best of current liturgical scholarship on the evolution and interpretation of the rites of Christian initiation, including, of course, the significant contributions of those "standard works" mentioned above, several chapters present pertinent selections

[12] "Preparation for Pascha? Lent in Christian Antiquity," *Passover and Easter, Two Liturgical Traditions* 5, ed. Paul Bradshaw and Lawrence Hoffman (Notre Dame, Ind.: University of Notre Dame Press, forthcoming).

[13] "Back Home to the Font: Eight Implications of a Baptismal Spirituality," *Worship* 71:6 (1997) 482–504.

either from primary liturgical documents or from authors in the period of history under question. In each case, these selections are followed by a descriptive and interpretive analysis of both the rites and theology presented in the particular document or by the author. Comparative analysis of several documents and/or authors in a particular geographical area or period of history is also provided from time to time as we seek to understand significant developments in the shape of the rites and their theological interpretation.

While much in this study will be quite familiar to those who explore and teach the rites of Christian initiation, this work also offers an occasional critique of traditional scholarship, suggests new ways of looking at some of the classic liturgical sources, and provides a critical but, I hope, fair assessment of selected contemporary rites and their pastoral implications. To this end, this is the first book-length study of the history and theology of Christian initiation which, to my knowledge, attempts to take account of the contemporary advances in scholarship on early Christian liturgical sources pioneered in Paul F. Bradshaw's ground-breaking study *The Search for the Origins of Christian Worship*[14] and the reconstructive insights of Thomas Talley on the early evolution of the liturgical year in his revolutionary *Origins of the Liturgical Year*, with particular regard to his treatment of the development of Lent in relationship to baptism and Easter in light of the distinct Alexandrian liturgical tradition.[15] Previous scholarship tended to make certain assumptions about both liturgical sources and the evolution of the liturgical year that can no longer be held with any degree of certainty.

My approach to the rites of Christian initiation is textual, historical, and theological for a variety of reasons. Thomas Talley has said:

"Our current discussions of pastoral praxis, of theological meaning, or spirituality, and of much more rest finally on the assumption that *we know what we are talking about;* and to know what we are talking

---

[14] Paul F. Bradshaw, *The Search for the Origins of Christian Worship: Sources and Methods for the Study of Early Liturgy* (New York: Oxford University Press, 1992). See also his more recent *Early Christian Worship: A Basic Introduction to Ideas and Practice* (London: SPCK, 1996), especially pp. 1–36 on early Christian initiation.

[15] Thomas Talley, *Origins of the Liturgical Year,* 2d emended ed. (Collegeville: The Liturgical Press, 1991).

about demands knowing much more than can be generated by a mere creativity operating upon data drawn only from the experience of itself."[16]

This is especially the case with the rites of Christian initiation. To draw upon data "only from the experience of itself" in Christian initiation is a dangerous methodology for understanding and interpreting those rites. Our own contemporary Western Christian experience of those rites, for example, is often an experience of rites that have been separated from their original unitive core and integral vision into a disjointed ritual process. Such a separated and disjointed ritual process often includes baptism in infancy, first communion at the "age of reason," and confirmation later in adolescence or early adulthood as a rite of mature faith commitment. Based on our contemporary *experience* we might see that process as normative and proper, as the way it is supposed to be. But if we attend to the evolution and interpretation of those rites throughout the history of the Church we cannot but see those rites today as having become disjointed and disconnected from their source. It is, then, not so much our *experience* of the rites which must be primary in all this, but the evolution and interpretation of those rites themselves that are to shape, challenge, and critique our experience. In other words, here the Christian liturgical tradition as known from the texts of that tradition is primary; our experience of the contemporary use or misuse of that tradition is secondary.

To actually "know what we are talking about" with regard to the rites of Christian initiation, then, means that we have to study history. There is no other way. Robert Taft has said on numerous occasions with regard to liturgy that "those ignorant of history are subject to the latest cliché." Along similar lines he has written that:

"Amidst all the contemporary talk of 'relevance' in matters liturgical it remains my firm conviction that nothing is so relevant as knowledge, nothing so irrelevant as ignorance. So I think that in matters of pastoral relevance there is still something we can learn from comparative liturgical scholarship across a broad range of traditions. . . . One of the great contemporary illusions is that one can construct a

---

[16] Cited in Robert Taft, *Beyond East and West: Problems in Liturgical Understanding* (Washington, D.C.: Pastoral Press, 1984) vii [emphasis added].

liturgical theology without a profound knowledge of the liturgical tradition. So in spite of the (to me) rather perplexing discomfort that many Americans seem to have with history, there can be no theology without it. . . . Christian liturgy is a given, an object, an already existing reality like English literature. One discovers what English literature is only by reading Chaucer and Shakespeare and Eliot and Shaw and the contemporaries. So too with liturgy. If we want to know what Christmas and Chrismation, Eucharist and Easter mean, we shall not get far by studying anthropology or game-theory, or by asking ourselves what we *think* they mean. We must plunge into the enormous stream of liturgical and patristic evidence and wade through it piece by piece, age by age, ever alert to pick up shifts in the current as each generation reaches for its own understanding of what it is we are about."[17]

The pastoral practice of liturgy itself, I am convinced, must also flow from such a historical and theological approach. In a recent book, Dennis Smolarski speaks of the relationship between liturgy and pastoral practice in a way that should be noted carefully by all who are involved in any type of pastoral ministry. Smolarski states:

"The noted French liturgical center is called the *Centre de Pastorale Liturgique de Paris. Pastorale* is the noun and *Liturgique* is the adjective. In English we speak of *pastoral liturgy*. But the French term implies *liturgical pastoral practice*. The liturgy (and its spirit, its history, etc.) forms and informs pastoral practice. We [Americans] tend to think the other way around. We think pastoral concerns are reasons for changing liturgy. The French phrase suggests that liturgy can affect the ways we minister, that the spirit of the liturgy can direct our work. A person should never have to choose between being pastoral or being liturgical, since good liturgy is ultimately pastoral."[18]

Together with an overall textual, historical, and theological approach this book is written from an ecumenical perspective as well. While intended primarily for modern Western Christian readers, an ecumenical approach necessitates that the rites of initiation as they

[17] Ibid., ix–x.

[18] Dennis Smolarski, *Sacred Mysteries: Sacramental Principles and Liturgical Practice* (New York: Paulist Press, 1995) 165.

developed in the Christian East, at least within the first few centuries, be given due attention as well. And although my major concern from the medieval period on will be with Western-Roman Catholic development and theology, my own ecclesial identity as a Lutheran teaching liturgy in a predominantly Roman Catholic setting makes it personally imperative that adequate attention also be given to the insights of the Protestant Reformers in the sixteenth century and to the current shape of the rites of initiation within at least some of the Protestant traditions today (especially the Lutheran and Anglican traditions) within the limits of a primarily North American context. Such an approach, it is hoped, will make this book useful to a wider ecumenical readership.

Before we begin this "plunge into the enormous stream of liturgical and patristic evidence and wade through it piece by piece, age by age," I would be remiss if I did not note here my indebtedness to several people. Almost everything I know about the rites of Christian initiation I learned from two great liturgical scholars: Professor Gabriele Winkler, now the holder of the Chair of *Liturgiewissenschaft* (comparative liturgiology) at the University of Tübingen, Germany; and Professor Paul Bradshaw, professor of liturgy at the University of Notre Dame. As a beginning masters-level student in the School of Theology, Saint John's University, in 1981, it was through Professor Winkler's rites of initiation class that I was introduced by her both to the serious liturgical study of Christian initiation and to the riches of the Christian East, most notably to those of the early Syrian and Armenian traditions. Seven years later, in a 1988 doctoral seminar on Christian initiation in the early Church, under the leadership of Professor Bradshaw, my doctoral dissertation director, I developed a special interest in the early liturgical traditions of Jerusalem and Egypt, leading, ultimately, to a dissertation on a fourth-century Egyptian liturgical document.[19] Indeed, the first time I ever taught a course in the rites of Christian initiation, now almost ten years ago, Professor Bradshaw graciously made available for my use his own lecture notes from a similar course. Not surprisingly, then, especially in chapters 2, 3, 4, and 5 of this study, frequent references are made to

[19] Maxwell E. Johnson, *The Prayers of Sarapion of Thmuis: A Literary, Liturgical, and Theological Analysis,* Orientalia Christiana Analecta 249 (Rome: Pontifico Istituto Orientale, 1995).

the significant writings of both Winkler and Bradshaw. Of course, any use and interpretations I make of their work and contributions, as well as the work of others, remain my own responsibility.

I should also like to acknowledge here several people who have been of immense assistance in the preparation of this book: to my former colleague, Professor Charles Bobertz of the School and Department of Theology, Saint John's University, for his critical reading of and comments on chapter 1; to my Notre Dame colleagues, the Rev. Drs. Michael Driscoll and James White, for their critical reading and comments on several other chapters; to Sister Linda Gaupin of the Diocese of Orlando, Florida, for graciously making available to me several often-ignored French articles on the development of Christian initiation between the seventeenth and early twentieth centuries in Europe; to my graduate assistants, the Rev. Jeffrey Truscott and David Maxwell, for their assistance in research, patient proofreading, and preparation of the index; and to the Rev. Michael Naughton, O.S.B, and Mark Twomey of The Liturgical Press, for their willingness to undertake this project and see it through to its publication under the Pueblo imprint. To all of these I owe an enormous debt of gratitude.

Finally, this study is dedicated to Fr. Aelred Tegels, O.S.B., of Saint John's Abbey, Collegeville, Minnesota. I am one of several people working in some facet of liturgy today who cut their liturgical eye-teeth at a variety of American universities in one of Father Aelred's many introductory graduate-level classes in liturgy called by the foreboding title, "Introduction to Liturgiology." These classes always demonstrated his solid grasp of the liturgical sources and ecumenical scholarship of both East and West in several ancient and modern languages, were spiced with his wonderful and dry sense of humor, and always had an eye oriented to various pastoral implications and applications. By dedicating this book to him I wish to express to him publicly, in this small way, my personal gratitude for his many years of scholarship and teaching.

Chapter 1

The Origins of the Rites of Christian Initiation

"Now the eleven disciples went to Galilee, to the mountain to which Jesus had directed them. When they saw him, they worshiped him; but some doubted. And Jesus came and said to them, 'All authority in heaven and on earth has been given to me. Go therefore and make disciples of all nations, baptizing them in the name of the Father and of the Son and of the Holy Spirit, and teaching them to obey everything that I have commanded you. And remember, I am with you always, to the end of the age'" (Matt 28:16-20).

"Later he appeared to the eleven themselves as they were sitting at the table; and he upbraided them for their lack of faith and stubbornness, because they had not believed those who saw him after he had risen. And he said to them, 'Go into all the world and proclaim the good news to the whole creation. The one who believes and is baptized will be saved; but the one who does not believe will be condemned'" (Mark 16:14-16).

On the basis of these two biblical texts, it would seem that the origins of the rites of Christian initiation are rather clear and obvious. What the churches continue to do today in their initiatory rites have their origins in the explicit command of the risen Jesus, who in his great missionary commissioning of the Church directed his followers to continue a process of evangelization, of making disciples and teaching (catechesis), and of baptizing.

Modern New Testament scholarship on the life and ministry of Jesus, however, urges considerable caution at this point. It is a consensus of contemporary scholars that the above cited passage from Mark's Gospel was not part of Mark's original text, which probably ended at 16:8, but was added at a later point to harmonize with the postresurrection accounts appearing in the other Gospels.[1] Considerable

---

[1] Cf. Morna Dorothy Hooker, *The Gospel According to Saint Mark*, Black's New Testament Commentaries 2 (Peabody, Mass.: Hendrickson Publishers, 1993) 43–8.

doubt has also been raised about the reliability of the precise details in the passage from Matthew 28:16-20. In particular, it is difficult here to reconcile the formulaic-sounding language of "Father, Son, and Holy Spirit" and the special missionary focus on "all nations" with the historical Jesus himself. Since both this type of early trinitarian language and the shift in emphasis from a predominantly Jewish to an almost exclusive Gentile mission seem to reflect later development in the life of the primitive Church, Matthew 28:16-20 is probably not a source for what *Jesus* actually said but represents, rather, the catechetical and liturgical practice of Matthew's own community in the late 80s placed on the lips of Jesus and how that community understood its missionary and evangelical responsibilities.[2] Indeed, if Jesus himself actually commanded baptism "in the name of the Father and of the Son and of the Holy Spirit," it would be quite difficult to understand the numerous references throughout the Acts of the Apostles to baptism simply "in the name of Jesus" (see Acts 2:38) with no indications whatsoever of such trinitarian language.

If the historical reliability of these two texts, which attribute Christian initiation to an explicit dominical command, is questionable, what, then, can we know with some degree of certainty about the origins of these rites from the New Testament? The intent of this chapter is to provide an answer to that question. It will proceed by looking first at Jesus' own meal practices, his "table companionship" with others, as a means of initiating or incorporating people into a special relationship with himself. Second, since the New Testament itself provides several references to Jesus' own baptism in the Jordan River by John the Baptizer, careful attention must be given both to the origins of John's own baptismal practice and to the significance of Jesus' baptism for the ongoing practice and theological interpretation of specifically *Christian* initiation rites. Finally, a survey of the various discernible practices and interpretations of Christian initiation throughout the remainder of the New Testament will be provided. What will become clear is that there is not—even within the New Testament itself—only *one* ritual pattern for the initiation of Christian converts which might be regarded as universally "normative." Rather, from its very origins, Christian liturgical practice reflects considerable variety and multi-formity both in its rit-

---

[2] On all this see George Raymond Beasley-Murray, *Baptism in the New Testament* (Grand Rapids, Mich.: Eerdmans, 1962) 77–92.

ual patterns and in its differing theological interpretations. Nowhere is that diversity and multiplicity of origins more true than in the rites of Christian initiation themselves.

JESUS' "TABLE COMPANIONSHIP" AS AN INITIATION RITE

The late Norman Perrin teaches us that Jesus' own table companionship with "tax collectors and sinners" was "the aspect of Jesus' ministry which must have been most meaningful to his followers and most offensive to his critics."[3] But why was this so? As Nathan Mitchell has written:

"[Jesus] sat at table not as the charming, congenial, ringleted centerpiece of a Rembrandt painting, but as a vulnerable vagrant willing to share potluck with a household of strangers. Normally, a table's prime function is to establish social ranking and hierarchy (by what one eats, how one eats, with whom one eats). Normally, a meal is about social identification, status, and power. . . . But the very *randomness* of Jesus' table habits challenged this system of social relations modeled on meals and manners. . . . It was not simply that Jesus ate with objectionable persons—outcasts and sinners—but that he ate with anyone, indiscriminately. Hence his reputation: He has no honor! He has no shame! . . . [Such] commensality was 'a strategy for building or rebuilding peasant community on radically different principles from those of honor and shame, patronage and clientage.' For Jesus, *healing* (the gift he brings to a home) calls forth *hospitality* (those healed offer refreshment, food and drink, a place at table). . . . The table companionship practiced by Jesus thus recreated the world, redrew all of society's maps and flow charts. Instead of symbolizing social rank and order, it blurred the distinctions between hosts and guests, need and plenty. Instead of reinforcing rules of etiquette, it subverted them, making the last first and the first last."[4]

It is no wonder that Jesus was such a threat to religion, culture, and society alike. Such "table habits," if not watched closely and

[3] Norman Perrin, *Rediscovering the Teaching of Jesus* (New York: Harper & Row, 1976) 102.

[4] Nathan Mitchell, *Eucharist as Sacrament of Initiation*, Forum Essays 2 (Chicago: Liturgy Training Publications, 1994) 89–90.

even curtailed by those in authority, had the potential to transform the world, to subvert the status quo. For this egalitarian, inclusive, challenging, status and role-reversing "table companionship" was nothing other than the concrete sign, prophetic enactment, and very embodiment of the reign of God that Jesus himself proclaimed and for which he was ultimately crucified. Here was anticipated the messianic banquet of the end times (see Isaiah 25), now already joyfully present, in table sharing with the one whom critics labeled both "drunkard and glutton" (Matt 11:19).

What Perrin calls further this "central feature of the ministry of Jesus"[5] remained a primary characteristic of the earliest Christian communities as well, a characteristic witnessed to in the post-resurrection accounts of the Gospels, which closely associate meals with Jesus' post-resurrection appearances (see Luke 24), in Acts (see 2:42, 46), in the New Testament letters (see especially 1 Corinthians 10–11), and in a (probably Syrian) document from the late first or early second century, the *Didache* (9, 10, and 14).[6] Indeed, according to Willy Rordorf, it is the continuation of this joyful table companionship with the crucified, yet risen, Jesus on the first day of the week, called now by the term "Lord's Supper," that eventually led to renaming this day itself the "Lord's Day."[7] Perrin writes:

"In all probability, it was the vividness of the memory of that pre-Easter fellowship between the disciples and the earthly Jesus that provided the pattern for the development of that remarkable sense of fellowship between the early Christians and the risen Lord which is such a feature of primitive Christianity—and which has had such an effect on the Jesus tradition. At all events, we are justified in seeing this table-fellowship as the central feature of the ministry of Jesus; an anticipatory sitting at table in the Kingdom of God and very real celebration of present joy and challenge. Here a great deal of the private teaching of Jesus to his disciples must have had its *Sitz im Leben*—especially the Lord's Prayer must belong here—and here the

---

[5] Perrin, *Rediscovering the Teaching of Jesus*, 107.

[6] On the *Didache* and its interpretation, see below, chapter 2, 35–7.

[7] See Willy Rordorf, *Sunday: The History of the Day of Rest and Worship in the Earliest Centuries of the Christian Church,* trans. A.A.K. Graham (Philadelphia: Westminster Press, 1968).

disciples must have come to know the special way that Jesus had of 'breaking bread' which gave rise to the legend of the Emmaus road (Luke 24:35)."[8]

In reference to the continued meal practices of these earliest Christian communities Nathan Mitchell also notes that:

"Many of the practices and beliefs we modern Christians take for granted were not so obvious to the earliest generations of believers. Among these was the ticklish question of whether Jewish and Gentile Christians could sit down together at the same table. (For many Jews, eating with Gentiles would have meant breaking God's law and becoming unclean.) Was eucharistic dining destined to be a *barrier* separating persons along racial and ethnic lines, or would it become a *bridge* bringing them together? Underlying this question were even more basic questions: Should the Christian community be a closed one, or one that is multicultural, multi-ethnic and racially diverse? Are the disciples of Jesus radically exclusive or inclusive? . . . Christians such as the evangelist Mark came down strongly on the side of *inclusivity,* and they structured their reports of Jesus' meals to support this point of view. In so doing, Mark redefined discipleship and holiness in terms of food. Becoming a disciple, participating in the new kind of holiness envisioned by Jesus, meant taking part in an inclusive table fellowship. It entailed a revolutionary (and highly controversial) understanding of social status and hierarchy. It meant associating with—and offering the reign (presence) of God to—persons who, by the normal standards of Judaism, were wicked. The primary personal and social virtue sought among the members of this newly emergent, culturally/racially/ethnically diversified community was to be *diakonia,* service at table, the work of a slave."[9]

Regarding "initiation" into such a diverse and inclusive "table companionship," however, it is important to underscore the fact that nowhere do the Gospels record anything specific about rites of entrance or preparation for this meal sharing with Jesus. Rather, to use our own now traditional sacramental language, the meal itself was not the *culmination* of initiation but appears, rather, as the *inception,*

[8] Perrin, *Rediscovering the Teaching of Jesus,* 107–8.
[9] Mitchell, *Eucharist as Sacrament of Initiation,* 99–100.

that is, the very *beginnings* of initiation, the "sacrament" *of* initiation, or, *the* rite of incorporation into Christ. Nothing, not even baptism, and certainly nothing like confirmation, were required as preparatory steps. Entrance to the meal of God's reign, anticipated and incarnated in the very life, ministry, and meals of Jesus of Nazareth, was granted by Jesus himself and granted especially to those who were *not* prepared and *not* (yet) converted, to the godless and undeserving, to the impure, and the unworthy. Conversion itself, it seems, was a *consequence* of, not a pre-condition for, such meal sharing. Indeed, one does not earn the labels of "drunkard and glutton," or "friend of tax collectors and sinners" when following prescribed social, religious, or ritual behavior. One earns such labels only by scandalizing the expectations and suppositions of others.

Nevertheless, it is clear that while the meal and table companionship after Jesus' death, resurrection, and ascension did remain distinguishing characteristics of the Christian community (see Acts 2:42), a community which came even to place the banquet table at the architectural center of its assembly places, rites called either *baptisma* (baptism, immersion, or dipping) or *loutron* (bath or washing) came almost immediately to serve as the means of initiation into this community. As early as the first (Christian) Pentecost, Luke describes the following baptismal event:

"Peter said to them, 'Repent, and be baptized every one of you in the name of Jesus Christ so that your sins may be forgiven; and you will receive the Holy Spirit. For the promise is for you, for your children, and for all who are far away, everyone whom the Lord our God calls to him.' So those who welcomed his message were baptized, and that day about three thousand persons were added" (Acts 2:38-39, 41).

The use of such a baptismal or washing ritual as a means of incorporating converts into the newly emerging and developing Christian communities, of course, parallels closely the "baptism of repentance" (Mark 1:4) proclaimed and administered by John the Baptizer at the Jordan River. To this "Johannine" baptism Jesus submitted himself at the beginning of his public ministry and it is this event which provided the foundation and paradigm for the development of specifically *Christian* practices of baptismal initiation. It is to this baptismal rite of John and to the significant event of Jesus' own baptism that we now turn.

JESUS AND BAPTISM

The Baptism of John

That Jesus was baptized by John the Baptizer at the Jordan is asserted or implied in all three of the Synoptic Gospels, each in its own distinct manner: Mark 1:9-11; Matthew 3:13-17; and Luke 3:21-22. But before dealing with this event and its significance, a prior question needs to be addressed. From where did John's baptismal practice itself originate? For this question there is not one clear or certain answer and several theories have been suggested as possibilities. Traditional scholarship has tended toward seeing the origins of John's own practice as stemming either from what was considered to be parallel Jewish "baptismal" rituals performed among the Essene community at Qumran near the Dead Sea or from the tradition of Jewish "proselyte" baptism as an initiatory rite for Gentile converts to Judaism.

Among the Essenes, a first-century quasi-monastic Jewish community that had withdrawn to the desert to live lives of purity in preparation and eschatological expectation for the coming day of the Lord, and whose ritual practices are known to us both from that body of writings called *The Dead Sea Scrolls* and from references in the writings of the pro-Roman, Jewish historian Josephus, it is certainly clear that ritual washings, immersions, or ritual baths were a common practice.[10] Some scholars have not only seen in these ritual washings a close parallel to John's practice but—because John's own lifestyle was so clearly ascetic itself (see Mark 1:6) and his baptismal proclamation also related to a withdrawal into the desert to prepare the way of the Lord (see Mark 1:2-3)—have gone so far as to suggest that John himself may have been a member of this community.[11]

According to Adela Yarbro Collins, however, the dissimilarities between John's baptismal practice and the washings of the Qumran

---

[10] For specific references to the Dead Sea Scrolls and the writings of Josephus, see Gordon Lathrop, "Baptism in the New Testament and Its Cultural Settings," *Worship and Culture in Dialogue*, ed. S. Anita Stauffer (Geneva: Department for Theology and Studies, Lutheran World Federation, 1994) 25–6. On the Dead Sea Scrolls and the Essenes in general see James C. VanderKam, *The Dead Sea Scrolls Today* (Grand Rapids, Mich.: Eerdmans, 1994) 71–120.

[11] For a review of this hypothesis, compare with Hooker, *The Gospel According to Saint Mark*, 41–3.

community are as great as the similarities. That is, while John's baptism appears to be a once-for-all-time ritual of repentance, those washings or immersions at Qumran were repeatable daily washings related to Levitical or ritual purity. In other words, the Essene ritual baths did not constitute an *initiation* into that community but were an ongoing means of maintaining ritual purity for the members of that community. Similarly, the Qumran immersions appear to have been self-administered, while John's was administered by him to those who received it. And, while the community at Qumran was a withdrawn and exclusive community, John the Baptizer not only appeared and baptized in public, but his prophetic message of repentance was directed inclusively to all who heard him.[12]

Furthermore, whatever similarities there may be between the ritual practices of John and the Essenes, Collins adds that such similarities are certainly not unique to them.[13] Rather, in the context of first-century Judaism there are numerous examples of the use of water for the practice of ritual washing and/or bathing. Gordon Lathrop has recently summarized this context, saying that:

"Ancient Jewish and Christian sources of at least the second century list a variety of groups who seem to be identified by their accent on repeated and central washings: the daily baptizers, the Masbotheans, the Sabaeans, the Banaim, the morning bathers. Two ancient texts [i.e., the *Sybilline Oracles* 4:65 and the *Life of Adam and Eve* 6–11], recently identified as most likely Jewish first-century writings, give central importance to full-body washing in a river. And some scholars believe the root baptizing traditions of the much later Mandeans of Mesopotamia must be traced to the Transjordan during the time of the origins of Christianity. . . . New Testament texts . . . point to washing traditions among the Pharisees (Mark 7:3-4) and Jewish purification rites requiring a large amount of water in stone jars (120–180 gallons; John 2:6). What is more, archeological evidence also points toward a considerable interest in bathing at about this time. Cisterns with stairways that seem to be designed for full-body bathing and that utilize, at least in part, an

[12] Adela Yarbro Collins, "The Origin of Christian Baptism," LWSS, 40–1.
[13] Ibid., 41.

unbroken access to fresh rainwater, are found in considerable numbers at Jerusalem, Jericho, Herodium, Masadah, and at Qumran itself as well as elsewhere."[14]

It has thus become very difficult to maintain the position that a particular cause and effect relationship exists between the ritual water practices of the Essenes and the baptismal rite of John.

As noted above, along with the attempt to see the origins of John's baptism among the Essenes, scholars have also sought those origins in the Jewish practice of "proselyte" or convert baptism. But here again there is little certain or solid evidence for such a cause and effect connection or relationship. While Jewish proselyte baptism is similar to that of John's in that it was a once-for-all ritual administered to someone by another and signified a type of inner conversion or transformation (i.e., repentance), explicit documentary evidence for such a practice is actually too late (late first or early second century at the earliest) to conclude with any degree of certainty that John derived his own practice from it.[15] Aidan Kavanagh, therefore, is undoubtedly correct when he writes that:

"On the matter of practice, New Testament evidence linking Christian baptism to proselyte baptism is not only lacking, but what evidence there is points instead toward Jesus' own baptism by John the Baptist in the Jordan as the prototype of Christian practice. In the scriptural accounts of the Baptist's teaching, there is no hint of a death-resurrection theme, no initiatory motif, and no trace of proselyte baptism's admission of a convert to the sacrificial cult of Israel. John's emphases dwell rather upon prophetic expectations of the divine cleansing to be consummated by the work of the promised Messiah in a time of greatly heightened eschatological hope. John's baptism of repentance is preparatory for the messianic work. It is not a means for making gentiles Jews, as was proselyte baptism, nor is it wholly bounded by the bathing ablutions of the Essene ascetics at Qumran. It is its own distinctive thing, subsequently viewed by New Testament authors as the opening of a new order of things without actually being included in it. John's baptism is in water: it will give

[14] Lathrop, "Baptism in the New Testament and Its Cultural Settings," 27–8.
[15] For the various theories related to the practice and meaning of Jewish proselyte baptism see Collins, "The Origin of Christian Baptism," 41–6.

9

way to another baptism by One who will baptize with Holy Spirit and with a judgment finer than fire."[16]

In other words, rather than seeing John's baptismal practice as having been derived from a specific Jewish type it is more likely the case that both Jewish proselyte baptism and the baptism of John are parallel developments stemming from a common source or context.

If neither Jewish proselyte baptism nor the Essene ritual washings are the actual source for John's baptismal practice, from where, then, does it ultimately derive? Given that overall first-century context of the increasing ritual use of water for various purifications within Judaism, noted above by Collins and Lathrop, the presence of a charismatic and prophetic "baptizer" like John is probably not all that surprising. Kavanagh's comment that "John's emphases dwell . . . upon prophetic expectations of the divine cleansing to be consummated by the work of the promised Messiah in a time of greatly heightened eschatological hope," together with a number of Old Testament prophetic texts, which speak of God's new creation and restoration as beginning with a divine washing away of sin (e.g., Isa 1:16-17 and Ezek 36:25-28), suggest that John's "baptism of repentance" was a ritually enacted prophetic sign which anticipated the very coming of God in human history and the ultimate cleansing with water which would inaugurate the new creation of God itself.[17] This was no repeatable immersion of ritual or cultic purity. Nor was John's baptism a way to make Jewish converts out of Gentiles. What John proclaimed, anticipated, and ritually enacted, in typical prophetic fashion, was the dawning of God's decisive intervention in history, the beginning of God's cleansing, restoration, and transformation of God's people. Even the specific *Jordan River* location for John's baptismal practice is significant in this regard. The Jordan River itself was "ritually unclean," and so hardly fitting for a rite of Jewish "purification."[18] Rather, its significance lies in its historical connotations for Israel. For, just as centuries before Israel

---

[16] Aidan Kavanagh, *The Shape of Baptism: The Rite of Christian Initiation* (New York: Pueblo, 1978) 10.

[17] See Collins, "The Origin of Christian Baptism," 46-7.

[18] See Werner Georg Kümmel, *The Theology of the New Testament According to Its Major Witnesses: Jesus-Paul-John*, trans. John E. Steely (Nashville: Abingdon Press, 1973) 29.

had entered the Promised Land of Canaan by a dramatic crossing of the Jordan River under Joshua's leadership (see Joshua 3–5), so now, at the dawn of a new age, it is precisely to the necessity of a new Jordan experience as a (trans)formative event that John points.[19] Although undoubtedly influenced by the watery and eschatologically expectant context of his own day, it becomes increasingly possible to assert that John's own baptismal practice was not directly dependent upon any other previously known rituals at all. Instead, the baptismal rite at the Jordan to which Jesus himself submits may have been a practice that originated with John the Baptizer himself.

The Baptism of Jesus at the Jordan

The Gospel narratives of the life and ministry of Jesus of Nazareth, as especially Mark's version makes clear (Mark 1:1-11), all begin with Jesus' own baptism by John at the Jordan. While both Matthew and Luke preface their narration of this event with distinct infancy (Matthew 1–2; Luke 1:1–2:20) and childhood (Luke 2:21ff.) accounts, and John begins his version with the hymnic prologue about the eternal Word becoming flesh (John 1:1-18), these are but prolegomena which anticipate events to occur only later in the context of Jesus' death and resurrection and serve here to set the stage for the actual beginning of the "Gospel" at the Jordan.[20] In Acts Luke himself points to Jesus' baptism by John as this "beginning," when, to Cornelius and others gathered in Caesarea, the Apostle Peter says:

"You know the message he [God] sent to the people of Israel, preaching peace by Jesus Christ—he is Lord of all. That message spread throughout Judea, *beginning in Galilee after the baptism that John announced:* how God anointed Jesus of Nazareth with the Holy Spirit and with power; how he went about doing good and healing all who were oppressed by the devil, for God was with him" (Acts 10:36-38, emphasis added).

[19] See Lathrop, "Baptism in the New Testament and Its Cultural Settings," 30–1.

[20] On the role and interpretation of the infancy narratives in Matthew and Luke see Raymond Brown, *The Birth of the Messiah* (Garden City, N.Y.: Doubleday, 1977). For a shorter version see Raymond Brown, *An Adult Christ at Christmas* (Collegeville: The Liturgical Press, 1978).

Within the narration of the event of Jesus' baptism in the Synoptic Gospels, however, it is clear that Matthew, Mark, and Luke each have their own distinctive emphases and points of view. As a careful reading of the following parallel texts from these synoptic accounts helps to demonstrate, Matthew, Mark, and Luke are not simply narrating an event in the life of Jesus but are interpreting this event and its theological meaning for their own respective communities.

Matthew 3:13-17	Mark 1:9-11	Luke 3:21-22
Then Jesus came from Galilee to John at the Jordan, to be baptized by him. John would have prevented him, saying, "I need to be baptized by you, and do you come to me?" But Jesus answered him, "Let it be so now; for it is proper for us in this way to fulfill all righteousness." Then he consented. And when Jesus had been baptized, just as he came up from the water, suddenly the heavens were opened to him and he saw the Spirit of God descending like a dove and alighting on him. And a voice from heaven said, "This is my Son, the Beloved, with whom I am well pleased."	In those days Jesus came from Nazareth of Galilee and was baptized by John in the Jordan. And just as he was coming up out of the water, he saw the heavens torn apart and the Spirit descending like a dove on him. And a voice came from heaven, "You are my Son, the Beloved; with you I am well pleased."	Now when all the people were baptized, and when Jesus also had been baptized and was praying, the heaven opened, and the Holy Spirit descended upon him in bodily form like a dove. And a voice came from heaven, "You are my Son, the Beloved; with you I am well pleased."

That Jesus was, indeed, baptized by John the Baptizer in the Jordan River at the beginning of his public ministry is one of those few events in the life of the historical Jesus of Nazareth on which modern New Testament scholars tend to agree. Whatever other specific historical details of Jesus' life and teaching(s) may be uncertain or questionable, scholars are at a consensus in asserting that Jesus' baptism by John is a historical fact.[21] Not only is there multiple attestation to it in the New Testament (i.e., the Synoptic Gospels, John, and Acts), but the fact that such an event would have been quite embarrassing to the primitive Christian communities for a number of reasons adds to its historical credibility. First, Jesus' submission to John's "baptism of repentance for the forgiveness of sins" would challenge the early christological claim that Jesus was one who "knew no sin" (2 Cor 5:21) and was "without sin" (Heb 4:15). Second, and more importantly, to have Jesus submit to John the Baptizer in this way would seem to imply a certain subordination of Jesus to John himself. That is, it would tend to make Jesus of Nazareth a disciple or follower of John. In spite of these potential problems of casting doubt on Jesus' sinlessness and implying his subordination to John, that the Gospel writers were obviously compelled to narrate the event of Jesus' baptism speaks highly in favor of its historicity. If Jesus' baptism had not happened there would have been no reason whatsoever for the New Testament writers to include references to it. In fact, it would have been easier for their portrayal of Jesus had such an event *not* taken place.

The problem of this relationship between Jesus and John the Baptizer is reflected in the synoptic accounts themselves. While Mark simply tells the story of Jesus' baptism, both Matthew and Luke add what can only be considered as further theological reflection upon that story. Matthew, for example, handles the apparent problem of Jesus' subordination to John by introducing here a dialogue between them about who should be baptizing whom and resolves any ongoing tension about whether John or Jesus is the greater of the two by asserting that Jesus' baptism is "proper . . . in this way to fulfill all righteousness." For his part, Luke deals with this issue by conveniently having John the Baptizer already arrested by Herod and placed in prison (Luke 3:20) before describing Jesus' baptism itself.

---

[21] On this see Kilian McDonnell, "Jesus' Baptism in the Jordan," *Theological Studies* 56 (1995) 209; and Kilian McDonnell, *The Baptism of Jesus* (Collegeville: The Liturgical Press, 1996).

From the way in which Luke shapes his account, the reader could be left wondering whether it was actually John—or someone else—who baptized Jesus. Whatever the precise relationship between Jesus and John the Baptizer may have been historically, it is certainly the point of the New Testament narratives of Jesus' baptism, as well as other texts treating the preaching and practice of John (i.e., Matt 3:1-12; Mark 1:1-8; and Luke 3:1-20), to emphasize John's subservient role as "forerunner" vis-à-vis Jesus. In this way, although there is no denying that Jesus, indeed, was baptized by John, this "messenger," who is the greatest of those "born of women" (Matt 11:11), is not the Messiah himself (Luke 3:15; John 1:25) but merely the one sent to prepare the way for the Messiah's arrival in history.

To say that Jesus' baptism by John at the Jordan was a historical event is not to say that the Gospel accounts of this event constitute an objective record of what actually took place. Rather, the evangelists have painted here a rather biased theological portrait which reflects, of course, their own Easter faith in the identity of the crucified and risen Christ. It is from this faith perspective that the evangelists proclaim this identity of Christ, the beloved Son of God, as revealed now already at the Jordan and, hence, draw attention to the significance of this event for Christian faith, life, and practice.

The theological key to the synoptic accounts of Jesus' baptism is the descent of the Holy Spirit upon him, whether "like a dove" or "in bodily form like a dove," and the message of the divine voice which identifies him as the beloved Son of God. New Testament scholars such as Oscar Cullman,[22] Joachim Jeremias,[23] and others have long noted that the message proclaimed at this event—"You are [this is] my Son, the Beloved; with you [with whom] I am well pleased"—is a combination of two important Old Testament texts related to the identity and coronation of kings in ancient Israel (Ps 2:7) and to the identity and vocation of that one known as the "Suffering Servant" in the songs or poems of that sixth-century B.C.E. prophet called Deutero-Isaiah (Isa 42:1). Psalm 2:7 reads, "You are my son; today I have begotten you"; Isaiah 42:1 states, "Here is my servant, whom I

---

[22] See Oscar Cullmann, *The Christology of the New Testament,* rev. ed., trans. Shirley C. Guthrie and Charles A. M. Hall (Philadelphia: Westminster Press, 1963) 51–82.

[23] Joachim Jeremias, *New Testament Theology: The Proclamation of Jesus* (New York: Scribner, 1971) 43–55.

uphold, my chosen in whom my soul delights." By combining these two texts, one which deals with the king (i.e., the "messiah," or "anointed one" in Hebrew; "christos," or "Christ" in Greek) and another which deals with this servant of God, who, as Deutero-Isaiah makes clear, will be "wounded for our transgressions, crushed for our iniquities" (Isa 53:5), the divine voice at Jesus' baptism proclaims Jesus' identity not as a glorious and powerful Messiah, who comes in wrath, fire, and judgment, as John the Baptizer had proclaimed, but, rather, as a "suffering Messiah," the "suffering servant," who will "give his life as a ransom for many" (Mark 10:45). In this way, then, scholars have seen this baptismal event at the Jordan to have "vocational" significance for Jesus' own life and ministry. From this point on, the Gospel accounts narrate the unfolding story of Jesus as one which leads, inescapably, to his cross. For this end he had been baptized, toward this end he had begun his journey at the Jordan, and to follow him as his disciple means a sharing in his baptism and cross as well (see Mark 10:38).

That the Holy Spirit should be associated so clearly with this Jordan event is also significant. John the Baptizer had proclaimed, "I baptize you with water for repentance. . . . He will baptize you with the Holy Spirit and fire" (Matt 3:11). And here in Jesus' own baptism *is* that Holy Spirit. Indeed, it is the presence and gift of this Holy Spirit that distinguish Jesus' own and subsequent Christian baptism from that of John. The synoptic accounts of Jesus' baptism, then, are not simply about what happened to Jesus at the Jordan River. They are about what happens in *Christian* baptism, in general, namely, the very gift of the Holy Spirit inseparably associated with that baptism, who therein brings about the new birth of God's beloved "sons and daughters," in whom God is well pleased. Again, as the Apostle Peter said in his baptismal invitation on the first Pentecost, "Repent, and be baptized every one of you in the name of Jesus Christ so that your sins may be forgiven; and you will receive the Holy Spirit" (Acts 2:38).

This focus on baptismal birth by the Holy Spirit is made even more explicit in a textual variant to Luke 3:22 in a number of good Greek manuscripts of Luke's Gospel. While scholars generally prefer the above-noted reading of Luke 3:22, "You are my Son, the Beloved; with you I am well pleased," the variant reading consists of the direct citation of Psalm 2:7, "You are my son; today I have begotten you." Given the strong manuscript support for this, it is quite possible that this textual variant was the original Lucan reading which later copyists changed in order to harmonize Luke's account with those of Matthew and Mark and, more importantly, to avoid the possibility of suggesting either that Jesus was adopted by God or somehow only "became" God's Son at the Jordan. Nevertheless, in a mid-second-century Gospel harmony called the *Diatessaron*, written by the Syrian Christian Apologist Tatian,[24] Psalm 2:7 is quoted as the content of the message of the divine voice at Jesus' baptism. Similarly, while John the Baptizer's preaching had referred to Jesus' baptizing with "the Holy Spirit and fire," the *Diatessaron* refers to fire blazing in the Jordan itself when Jesus was baptized. Until the fifth century, when it was replaced by the four Gospels themselves, the *Diatessaron* of Tatian was the standard text of the Gospels within Syriac-speaking Christianity. It should be no surprise, then, as we shall see in the next chapter,[25] that in the early Syrian Christian tradition not only is Christian initiation understood as a pneumatic (i.e., Holy Spirit oriented) "new birth" rite in imitation of Jesus' own baptismal "birth" in the Jordan, but Psalm 2:7 plays an important role as an interpretative key for understanding the theology of this rite. And, it will be noted, the presence of fire, a powerful biblical image of the divine presence, also makes its appearance in an initiation context within early liturgical texts from this Syrian tradition.

Jesus and Baptism in the Fourth Gospel

The significance of the synoptic portrayal of Jesus' baptism and its influence on the development of the rites of Christian initiation within early Christianity cannot be overemphasized.[26] To this, however, must be joined the equally important witness of the Fourth Gospel, the Gospel of John. Like Matthew and Luke, the author of the Fourth Gospel also treats the relationship between John the Baptizer and Jesus in a unique manner. But unlike the Synoptic Gospels, except possibly Luke, in which John baptizes Jesus and is arrested and imprisoned before Jesus' public ministry begins, the Fourth Gospel nowhere indicates that Jesus is baptized at all and has the ministry of both John and Jesus taking place at the same

[24] For a text of Tatian's *Diatesseron* see ANF, vol. 10, 43–129.
[25] See below, chapter 2, 34–50.
[26] See above, note 21.

time (see John 3:22-23). That Jesus came to John at the Jordan is noted (John 1:28-29) but, rather than describe his baptism, the following is reported:

"The next day he [John] saw Jesus coming toward him and declared, 'Here is the Lamb of God who takes away the sin of the world! This is he of whom I said, "After me comes a man who ranks ahead of me because he was before me." I myself did not know him; but I came baptizing with water for this reason, that he might be revealed to Israel.' And John testified, 'I saw the Spirit descending from heaven like a dove, and it remained on him. I myself did not know him, but the one who sent me to baptize with water said to me, "He on whom you see the Spirit descend and remain is the one who baptizes with the Holy Spirit." And I myself have seen and have testified that this is the Son of God'" (John 1:29-34).

As in the Synoptic Gospels, the Fourth Gospel also presents John the Baptizer as subordinated to Jesus and uses this Jordan event to underscore both the coming of the Holy Spirit to Jesus and, now through John the Baptizer's own testimony, rather than by means of a divine voice, Jesus' identity as suffering servant (i.e., sacrificial "lamb") and Son of God. But by not narrating the event of Jesus' baptism itself there is no way in the Fourth Gospel in which Jesus can appear to play a subordinate role to John the Baptizer at all. Rather, from the very beginning of this Gospel, John the Baptizer, who is clearly neither the Messiah, Elijah, nor a prophet (John 1:19-21), is completely subordinated to Jesus as the one whose purpose it is to testify to the true light of the world (John 1:6-9).

Even more intriguing in this Fourth Gospel is that, three times (!), Jesus himself is reported to have baptized others as part of his public ministry:

"After this Jesus and his disciples went into the Judean countryside, and he spent some time there with them and baptized" (John 3:22). Jesus

"They [John's disciples] came to John and said to him, 'Rabbi, the one who was with you across the Jordan, to whom you testified, here he is baptizing, and all are going to him'" (John 3:26).

"Now when Jesus learned that the Pharisees had heard, 'Jesus is making and baptizing more disciples than John'—although it was not

Jesus himself but his disciples who baptized—he left Judea and started back to Galilee" (John 4:1-3).

Since the qualifying phrase in John 4:2—"although it was not Jesus himself but his disciples who baptized"—is generally regarded by New Testament scholars as a later addition to the text of the Fourth Gospel,[27] the possibility is raised here that these references to Jesus' own baptizing practice may actually reflect a historical reminiscence. That is, like John the Baptizer himself, the historical Jesus of Nazareth may once have been a "baptizer" as well. Adela Yarbro Collins has recently drawn attention to this possibility, saying it is probable that:

"The gospel of John is more accurate than the Synoptics on this point, because there is no plausible theological reason why the tradition that Jesus and his disciples once baptized would be invented. The practice of Christian baptism did not need such support. If there were followers of the Baptist around who rivalled the Christians for whom the gospel was written, the information that Jesus had imitated John would provide them with ammunition against the independence and authority of Jesus. A further argument in favour of . . . reliability . . . is that the report of Jesus' baptizing creates a problem for the evangelist. In 1:33 Jesus was presented as the one who baptizes with holy spirit. But the description in chapters 3–4 does not imply that Jesus' baptism was different in kind from John's. According to 7:39, the spirit is given only after Jesus' 'exaltation.' The appropriate conclusion seems to be that the gospel of John is historically accurate on this point and that the authors of the other gospels were unaware of, or suppressed, the tradition that Jesus baptized."[28]

Collins argues further that such baptizing practices on the part of the historical Jesus would easily explain why it was that the early Christian communities themselves continued to initiate new converts by means of baptism. There would be, thus, a clear and direct continuity in practice between John the Baptizer, Jesus, and the New Testament churches. Indeed, the baptism to which Peter invites those who heard his sermon on the first Pentecost ("Repent, and be baptized

[27] See Raymond Brown, *The Gospel According to John I–XII* (Garden City, N.Y.: Doubleday, 1966) 164–5.
[28] Collins, "The Origin of Christian Baptism," 48–9.

every one of you . . . so that your sins may be forgiven," Acts 2:38), even if now given "in the name of Jesus" for the reception of the Holy Spirit, parallels closely the type of baptism of repentance proclaimed and administered by John at the Jordan, received by Jesus according to the Synoptic Gospels, and, according to the Fourth Gospel, administered by Jesus and his disciples during his own ministry.[29] If such an interpretation is correct, it may even shed light on a possible historical core behind the baptismal command placed on the lips of the risen Lord in Matthew 28:16-20. That is, while the specific details of this account—i.e., the trinitarian language and "all nations" mission emphasis—may well reflect the post-Easter situation of the primitive Church rather than that of Jesus, the attribution of an explicit baptismal command to him may be Matthew's way of underscoring that the roots of Christian baptism do go back to Jesus' own practice and that there is, indeed, some kind of continuity between the Church's baptismal practice and that of the historical Jesus himself.

Theologically, as well, it is important to note that the context of the references to Jesus' baptizing practice in the Fourth Gospel is precisely a discussion of the meaning of baptism itself. Immediately before the first report of Jesus and his disciples baptizing in Judea (3:22) comes a significant conversation between Jesus and Nicodemus regarding the necessity of one being "born from above" (3:4) in order to see and enter the reign of God. And the manner of this divine birth is explicitly stated as accomplished through "water and Spirit" (3:5), that is, through baptism. Whether this particular conversation is historical or not, the theological understanding of baptism as a "new birth through water and the Holy Spirit" presented herein certainly reflects the meaning of *Christian* baptism within the Johannine community. The crucified and risen Jesus, who breathes the Holy Spirit on the disciples gathered together in the upper room in Jerusalem on the first Easter night (John 20), is the one who truly "baptizes with the Holy Spirit." As noted above, this understanding of baptism as a divine and pneumatic birth from above, combined with the similar implications for baptism from the synoptic accounts of Jesus' own baptism, will become a central focus and paradigm for the practice and interpretation of Christian baptism especially within the Syrian, and some other, early Christian liturgical traditions.

[29] Ibid., 49.

Before leaving the witness of the Fourth Gospel, it is necessary to consider one other possible—and intriguing—initiation allusion or practice among at least some members of the Johannine community. This possible allusion is reflected in the unique Fourth Gospel account of Jesus' washing of the disciples' feet at the Last Supper (John 13:1-20). Many Western Christians today, of course, know this rite only as an annual occurrence in conjunction with the opening liturgy of the Paschal Triduum on Holy or Maundy Thursday evening, where, after the reading of John 13 and the homily or sermon, it is ritually enacted as a dramatic parable by the presiding minister and representatives of the liturgical assembly. Most would certainly interpret the meaning of this liturgical act in a manner similar to that provided already by John 13:12ff., that is, as a parable of servanthood and service in imitation of Christ's own servanthood.

As we know from later liturgical sources, however, a footwashing rite called the *Pedilavium* does become an important part of the rites of Christian initiation in a number of different places such as Milan, North Africa, Spain, Gaul, and Syria.[30] Because of this, questions are surely raised as to whether its origins might also have an initiatory meaning and context and whether this is reflected or alluded to already in the account of John 13. In a recent and very convincing article,[31] Martin Connell subjects the received Greek text of John 13:1-20 and its variant readings to a detailed literary, text-critical, and redactional analysis and concludes that the original narrative comprised only verses 6-10, that is:

"[Jesus] came to Simon Peter, who said to him, 'Lord, are you going to wash my feet?' Jesus answered, 'You do not know now what I am doing, but later you will understand.' Peter said to him, 'You will never wash my feet.' Jesus answered, 'Unless I wash you, you have no share with me.' Simon Peter said to him, 'Lord, not my feet only but also my hands and my head!' Jesus said to him, 'One who has bathed does not need to wash, except for the feet, but is entirely clean. And you are clean, though not all of you.'"

[30] See below, chapter 3, 114, and chapter 4, 136–7.
[31] Martin F. Connell, "*Nisi Pedes,* Except for the Feet: Footwashing in the Community of John's Gospel," *Worship* 70:4 (1996) 20–30.

To this "original narrative," argues Connell, the final redactor(s) of the Fourth Gospel added a supplement (vv. 12-20) which reinterpret the footwashing along the lines of servanthood and humility. No such interpretation, however, is present anywhere in verses 6-10. To the contrary, there it appears as a necessary rite ("If I do not wash you . . .") done, like baptism elsewhere, in order to give the recipient a participatory "share" in Christ himself.

Within this "original narrative" Connell thus sees reflected the possibility that among some of the early communities that made up the intended audience of the Fourth Gospel[32] it was not baptism (as in the synoptic or "Petrine" led communities) but *footwashing* that constituted the rite of initiation. He writes:

"Might not the footwashing itself, especially as this is captured in 13:6-10, have been the initiatory rite of some Johannine communities? Might it not have been the rite of sanctification which wiped away one's sin or, to take from the Gospel, 'made one entirely clean'? Recall the text's 'Unless I wash you, you have no share with me' (13:8), and 'One who has bathed does not need to wash, except for the feet' (13:10). With these verses the footwashing takes on far more gravity than any of the same Gospel's few references to baptism."[33]

That such an initiation rite would come to be reinterpreted either as a supplement to baptism, as it does appear within some liturgical traditions, or as a rite signifying the humble servant character of the Church, as it tends to function liturgically today, is perfectly logical. Whatever the fringe nature and identity of the early Johannine communities and their relationship with the more dominant synoptic-based or Petrine-led churches once may have been, it is well known that, ultimately, at least part of the Johannine community—along with its Gospel—came into communion with these other churches. In so doing, its own unique theological traditions and structures of "apostolic" leadership, symbolized by the "Beloved Disciple" throughout

[32] On the nature and identity of these "Johannine" communities see Raymond Brown, *The Community of the Beloved Disciple: The Life, Loves, Hates of an Individual Church in New Testament Times* (New York: Paulist Press, 1979). See also Raymond Brown, *The Churches the Apostles Left Behind* (New York: Paulist Press, 1984).

[33] Connell, *"Nisi Pedes,* Except for the Feet," 24.

the Fourth Gospel, became either excised or made subservient to those of the other communities as the Fourth Gospel itself is further redacted along these interpretive lines.[34] If this is what happened in the relationship between the synoptic and Johannine communities in terms of theology and leadership, then Connell is absolutely correct in suggesting that a similar process may also have taken place with regard to Johannine liturgical and sacramental rites. Footwashing does not go away but, at most, it remains either as a mere supplement to baptism or as an occasional dramatic rite demonstrating Christian service and humility.

The most intriguing implication of Connell's contribution to this footwashing text is that it makes the question of the New Testament origins of Christian initiation even more complex than has been assumed previously. If Connell is correct about footwashing being the rite of Christian initiation within the Johannine communities, it means that from the beginning of Christianity there is variety and diversity not only in the theological interpretations of Christian initiation but in the very rites of initiation themselves. In other words, the possibility is raised that some Christian communities initiated new converts by a John the Baptizer-type of baptism, others by a footwashing, and perhaps even others by rites (e.g., handlaying and/or anointings) no longer clearly known to us. But both practices are attributed in the Gospels to the authority of Jesus himself, who not only *was* baptized by John in the Jordan, according to the Synoptics, but possibly baptized others himself, and commanded his followers to do likewise. Or, is the so-called "editorial insertion" in John 4:2 ("it was not Jesus . . . but his disciples who baptized") actually closer to the truth, after all? Was it only Jesus' disciples who baptized, because Jesus himself washed feet?

CHRISTIAN INITIATION IN THE NEW TESTAMENT COMMUNITIES

Rites of Initiation in the New Testament Communities

However diverse the precise origins of the rites of Christian initiation may be, from the first Pentecost on (Acts 2) it became, at least, the dominant tradition of the early Churches to initiate new converts to the Christian faith through a ritual process which included a bap-

---

[34] On this, see the references cited above, note 32.

tismal washing of some sort. Georg Kretschmar is certainly correct in asserting that "there is no apostolic norm in a bare immersion, without accompanying rites (nor is it probable that any such thing ever existed)."[35] But the problem with the numerous references and allusions to baptismal rites throughout the New Testament is that it is not often clear what these "accompanying rites" may have been. It is possible that there was some sort of preliminary period of instruction (or catechesis) for new converts, but, apart from the brief chariot ride discussion between Philip and the Ethiopian eunuch leading to the latter's baptism (Acts 8:26-40), we know nothing about it or the extent of what such teaching may have been. Similarly, it is quite likely that the rite would have included some kind of profession of faith in Jesus Christ in one form or another but, again, *explicit* baptismal professions of faith are lacking in the New Testament. Or, with regard to possible pre- or postbaptismal rites of anointing with oil, possibly suggested by references to having been anointed and sealed by the Holy Spirit (2 Cor 1:22; Eph 1:13; 1 John 2:20) and to God's servants having been marked with this "seal on their foreheads" (Rev 7:3), we simply do not know whether a literal initiatory practice is being described or a metaphorical interpretation of initiation is intended.[36] While an actual liturgical practice could certainly have suggested such a metaphor,[37] the fact that Acts 10:38 describes Jesus as having been "anointed . . . with the Holy Spirit and with power" at his own baptism, where no Gospel account specifies anything of the sort, might tend to argue more toward a metaphorical meaning in these other passages as well.

One "accompanying rite" described in the New Testament with some detail, however, is a postbaptismal rite of handlaying, which is interpreted in relationship to the giving of the Holy Spirit. Acts 8:14-17 tells of certain Samaritan converts who, having received baptism "in the name of the Lord Jesus," had not received the Holy Spirit. Only when the apostles Peter and John laid hands on them and prayed for the Holy Spirit did that Spirit finally come to them. Similarly, in

[35] Georg Kretschmar, "Recent Research on Christian Initiation," LWSS, 33.

[36] See Paul Bradshaw, *The Search for the Origins of Christian Worship* (New York: Oxford University Press, 1992) 41.

[37] See also Kavanagh, *The Shape of Baptism,* 26ff., who argues that more ritual weight should be given to such New Testament anointing references.

Acts 19:1-7 we read of twelve disciples in Ephesus who had not received (or even heard of) the Holy Spirit, but had been baptized only with John the Baptizer's "baptism of repentance." In response to Paul, they are baptized "in the name of the Lord Jesus," and then, through the laying on of Paul's hands, they too receive the Holy Spirit.

If, in the light of a much later Western (but only *Western*) split between baptism and what will come to be called "confirmation,"[38] such a postbaptismal rite seems clear and obvious, the interpretation of Acts 8:14-17 and 19:1-7 are anything but clear and obvious. Some scholars have assumed that what is described in these two events reflects a general two-stage ritual pattern of Christian initiation in the primitive communities with baptism followed immediately by a pneumatic handlaying rite.[39] Such a two-fold ritual pattern may even be reflected in Luke's account of Jesus' own baptism (Luke 3:21-22), where the Holy Spirit comes upon Jesus only *after* he was baptized and while he was praying.[40] Although the Holy Spirit was a life-giving reality related to the forgiveness of sins bestowed in baptism, according to these scholars, Luke's understanding is that the Spirit is a prophetic force only loosely connected to baptism and the gift of this prophetic or ecstatic Spirit is thus ritualized by means of a different rite.[41] Other scholars would find such an interpretation to be anachronistic, that is, reading back into the New Testament a ritual pattern known only on the basis of later practice. Alternatively, these scholars have tended to underscore the apparent exceptional contexts and situations of both Acts 8 and 19. The account in Acts 8 is concerned with the conversion and Christian initiation of *Samaritans*, whose

[38] See below, chapters 3 and 4.

[39] Compare with Thomas Marsh, *Gift of Community: Baptism and Confirmation* (Wilmington, Del.: Michael Glazier, 1984). But see the response to Marsh in Frank Quinn, "Confirmation Reconsidered: Rite and Meaning," LWSS, 219–37. For a discussion of all the pertinent baptismal texts in Luke-Acts, see also Kilian McDonnell and George T. Montague, *Christian Initiation and Baptism in the Holy Spirit* (Collegeville: The Liturgical Press, 1991) 23–41.

[40] Compare with the discussion of this in McDonnell and Montague, *Christian Initiation and Baptism*, 24–5.

[41] Compare with Marsh, *Gift of Community*, 27–67; and Gerard Austin, *Anointing with the Spirit: The Rite of Confirmation: The Use of Oil and Chrism* (New York: Pueblo, 1985) 6–9.

conversion and initiation came about not by or under the direction of the Jerusalem apostles, but through the mission of Philip. So, by having the apostles Peter and John go to Samaria to lay hands on these converts, Luke is underscoring one of his key emphases throughout the Acts of the Apostles. That is, all Christian missionary work must somehow be subordinated to or ratified by the apostles in Jerusalem themselves. Along similar lines, the context and situation in Acts 19:1-7 concerns those who had received only *John's* baptism, not *Christian* baptism. Such situations as these can hardly be seen as reflecting some sort of normative pattern, but, rather, specific and unique occasions.[42]

It is undoubtedly true that in some primitive communities handlaying rites were used to ritualize the gift of the Holy Spirit in Christian initiation. The exceptional situations in Acts 8 and 19, however, do suggest that one should not generalize here toward some kind of universal ritual practice in the primitive Church. These two texts probably tell us very little about "normal" initiation practices in the apostolic period. Indeed, if postbaptismal pneumatic handlaying was an "apostolic" initiatory practice, one would expect to find it as a universal feature within the later initiation rites of both East and West. But, as we shall see, such is certainly not the case.

Furthermore, Acts 8 and Acts 19 are not the only places in Acts that treat the relationship between Christian baptism and the Holy Spirit. Not only does Peter's Pentecost sermon (Acts 2:38) imply no separate postbaptismal handlaying rite for the gift of the Holy Spirit, but Acts 10:44-48 tells of the Holy Spirit coming upon Gentiles in Caesarea during another of Peter's sermons even *before* they are baptized. In fact, it is this very *prebaptismal* gift of the Holy Spirit which comes to serve as the basis *for* their subsequent and immediate baptism. Peter says here: "'Can anyone withhold the water for baptizing these people who have received the Holy Spirit just as we have?' So he ordered them to be baptized in the name of Jesus Christ" (Acts 10:47-48). Something similar is described regarding the initiation of Paul in Acts 9, after his sight-losing Damascus road experience. That is, Paul's sight is not only restored but the Holy Spirit comes upon him through the laying on of Ananias' hands (Acts 9:17) *before* he is baptized (Acts 9:18).

[42] See McDonnell and Montague, *Christian Initiation and Baptism*, 31–9; and Austin, *Anointing with the Spirit*, 7–9.

The most that we can assume on the basis of these few baptismal events described in Acts, then, is that, for the earliest Christians, baptism and Holy Spirit were bound together inseparably. In some places no ritual act other than baptism itself was used to ritualize this gift. In others there was quite possibly the addition of "accompanying rites" such as the postbaptismal handlaying we see on these occasions in Acts (see also Heb 6:2), or in still others perhaps some kind of anointing with oil, which might be implied by other New Testament texts. It is even possible that the sequence of the coming of the Holy Spirit *before* baptism in the case of the Gentiles in Caesarea and Paul himself in Damascus reflects yet another pattern of Christian initiation within some early communities. Indeed, a number of scholars have suggested that 1 John 5:7-8 ("There are three that testify; the Spirit and the water and the blood . . .") is an allusion to a such a ritual sequence of initiation with the gift of the Holy Spirit ritualized somehow first, and then followed by baptism ("water") and first communion ("the blood").[43] But whether the Holy Spirit comes before, during, or after baptism, the point is that baptism and Holy Spirit are seen as closely united. Since, for some reason, the gift of the Holy Spirit was absent from the baptism of the Samaritans in Acts 8 and from those who received only the baptism of John in Acts 19 this anomalous situation had to be remedied by the apostles themselves so that this normal relationship between baptism and Holy Spirit would be (re)connected.

If we are unclear about the existence or precise identity, frequency, and normativity of "accompanying rites" to baptism in the New Testament churches, we are equally unclear about a number of details regarding the rite of baptism itself in this early period. At least three questions are suggested: How were the earliest Christian baptisms administered? What words were used in the conferring of baptism? Were infants baptized in the time of the New Testament?

How were the earliest Christian baptisms administered? In her book on the architecture and meaning of baptismal fonts S. Anita Stauffer notes that there have been four different modes of conferring baptism throughout history:

[43] See E. C. Ratcliff, "The Old Syrian Baptismal Tradition and Its Resettlement under the Influence of Jerusalem in the Fourth Century," *Studies in Church History* 2 (1965) 19–37; and Bradshaw, *The Search for the Origins of Christian Worship*, 165–6.

(1) *submersion,* also called *dipping,* in which the candidate is completely submerged under the baptismal waters;

(2) *immersion,* in which the candidate stands or kneels in rather shallow water and the water is either poured over the head of the candidate or the candidate's head itself is pushed partially into the water;

(3) *affusion,* in which water is poured over the head of the candidate; and

(4) *aspersion,* in which the baptismal candidate is merely sprinkled with water.[44]

The earliest modes of baptism were probably either submersion or immersion but it is often difficult to tell which was preferred. When Paul compares baptism to the Christian's death and burial in Christ (Rom 6:3-11), for example, it is quite likely that he has the mode of submersion in mind. But evidence from early iconographic depictions of Jesus' own baptism by John show immersion as the mode, and what archaeological evidence there is of specific Christian baptismal spaces reveals rather shallow fonts in which submersion would have been extremely difficult. At the same time, while the practices of affusion and aspersion became increasingly common only later in the history of the (Western) Church, when the majority of baptismal candidates were infants, there is some evidence for the practice of both of these modes in the early Church as well. In other words, we do not know enough about specific baptismal practices within the various New Testament communities to suggest that one mode of baptismal administration was normatively practiced over another. *matter + form*

   What words were used in the conferring of baptism? Western Christians have inherited from medieval scholasticism a sacramental theology which defines valid sacraments generally as the combination of proper "matter" (i.e., water) and "form" (i.e., the trinitarian formula: "I baptize you in the name of the Father and of the Son and of the Holy Spirit"). Because of this, it has been natural to view the baptismal command of the risen Lord in Matthew 28:16-20 as indicating that such a "formula" for baptism was already in use in Matthew's community in the late first century. Or, with regard to the phrase

[44] S. Anita Stauffer, *On Baptismal Fonts: Ancient and Modern,* Alcuin/GROW Liturgical Study 29–30 (Bramcote/Nottingham: Grove Books, 1994) 9–10.

"baptism in [or 'into'] the name of Jesus" (or "Lord Jesus," or "Lord Jesus Christ"), frequently occurring throughout the book of Acts, it has been natural to assume also that something like "I baptize you in the name of Jesus" functioned as a specific baptismal formula within the communities of Luke-Acts.

Both assumptions may well be accurate but, again, anachronism should be avoided here. Explicit liturgical evidence for the use of a baptismal formula within baptismal rites is known only later in both East[45] and West, and for that matter, only much later in the West.[46] Concerning either of these phrases in the New Testament, then, it is quite possible that they are intended not as liturgical formulas at all but as theological or catechetical interpretations of the very *meaning* of baptism itself. That is, to be baptized "in" or "into the name of Jesus" is to be baptized into Christ, to be associated as closely as possible with Christ himself as the very mediator of God's salvation.[47] Similarly, to be baptized into Christ is to receive the Holy Spirit, who creates a new relationship between the baptized and God and enables the newly baptized to address God, in the words of Jesus, as "Abba, Father" (Gal 4:6-7). Hence, to be baptized "in the name of the Father and of the Son and of the Holy Spirit" at this stage of liturgical development need be nothing other than what Aidan Kavanagh has called a "theological declaration"[48] of the new relationship which baptism establishes between the baptized and God, a relationship signified in the paradigmatic story of Jesus' own baptism in the Jordan, where his identity as "Son" in relationship to both "Father" ("You are [This is] my Son, the Beloved") and "Holy Spirit" is proclaimed.

Were infants baptized in the time of the New Testament? Specific answers to this question have often been based on the confessional positions of those who give them. Traditionally, those who deny the propriety of baptizing infants have noted (correctly) that there are no references to infant baptism anywhere in the New Testament, while those who defend the practice argue that it is possible, if not probable, that infants were baptized from the very beginnings of the

---

[45] See below, chapters 2 and 3, 37, 86, 104, and 122.

[46] See below, chapter 6, 183.

[47] See Collins, "The Origin of Christian Baptism," 50–2.

[48] Kavanagh, *The Shape of Baptism,* 22.

Church.[49] Since references to the baptism of entire "households" do occur in the New Testament (Acts 16:15; 18:8; 1 Cor 1:16) it is *possible* that infants were included here as well. But these references are silent on the specific question of infants and an argument from silence is always the most difficult kind either to defend or refute.

We do know that at least some early Christian traditions did initiate infants and children at a date early enough for the practice to be considered traditional already by the late second century.[50] Nevertheless, within the New Testament period itself the primary candidate for Christian initiation would have been an adult. Based primarily, again, on descriptions of baptism from Acts, Aidan Kavanagh conveniently summarizes the general pattern of the Christian initiation of adults in the New Testament as following a four-step sequence:

"First . . . the proclamation of the gospel . . . always precedes baptism. . . . Second, the normal response of those who hear the gospel proclaimed is expected to be conversion to faith in the exalted Lord. . . . Third, the gospel proclaimed and believed usually results in the water bath itself. . . . Fourth, there are the events that follow water baptism. . . . [That is,] what apostolic proclamation, conversion, and baptism in water and Spirit—the whole initiatory process—resulted in was life in a Spirit-filled community living by apostolic teaching, in unity with apostolic witnesses of the risen Lord who is exalted and now become life-giving Spirit for his people, through eucharistic prayer at home and petitionary prayer in the synagogue. The regular postbaptismal events at this period are not a series of specific liturgical 'completions' of an only partial water rite, but full and robust engagement in the Church itself: a whole new ethic and way of life. . . . Here is the common ground

---

[49] The classic debate along such confessional lines is between Kurt Aland, *Did the Early Church Baptize Infants?* trans. G. R. Beasley-Murray (Philadelphia: Westminster Press, 1963), and Joachim Jeremias, *The Origins of Infant Baptism: A Further Study in Reply to Kurt Aland* (Naperville, Ill.: A. R. Allenson, 1963). Today, however, the debate about the role of infant baptism takes place within rather than across denominational boundaries. See Paul F. X. Covino, "The Postconciliar Infant Baptism Debate in the American Catholic Church," LWSS, 327–49.

[50] See below, chapter 2, 65–6.

that serves as articulation point for all the multivalent practices that enter the initiatory continuum."[51]

With regard to any regular "accompanying rites," the age of baptismal candidates, and even the very mode of conferring baptism itself, therefore, the New Testament leaves us with many more questions than answers. Unfortunately, we do not know enough, beyond the rather general description of the sort provided above by Kavanagh, to say with absolute certainty what the regular shape of the rites of initiation was within the primitive Christian communities. What we see in the New Testament, instead, are a number of distinct theological interpretations of the experience of becoming a Christian.

Theological Interpretations of Initiation in the New Testament
Whatever the particular rites employed in the Christian initiation of new converts in the primitive communities may have been, it is clear from the New Testament that the *meaning* of initiation itself was understood in a variety of different ways. These numerous ways include: forgiveness of sins and the gift of the Holy Spirit (Acts 2:38); new birth through water and the Holy Spirit (John 3:5; Titus 3:5-7); putting off of the "old nature" and "putting on the new," that is, "being clothed in the righteousness of Christ" (Gal 3:27; Col 3:9-10); initiation into the "one body" of the Christian community (1 Cor 12:13; see also Acts 2:42); washing, sanctification, and justification in Christ and the Holy Spirit (1 Cor 6:11); enlightenment (Heb 6:4; 10:32; 1 Peter 2:9); being "anointed" and/or "sealed" by the Holy Spirit (2 Cor 1:21-22; 1 John 2:20, 27); being "sealed" or "marked" as belonging to God and God's people (2 Cor 1:21-22; Eph 1:13-14; 4:30; Rev 7:3); and, of course, being joined to Christ through participation in his death, burial, and resurrection (Rom 6:3-11; Col 2:12-15).
Paul Bradshaw has noted that "this variation in baptismal theology encourages the supposition that the ritual itself may also have varied considerably from place to place."[52] And if not already present in some places, these theological interpretations will certainly give rise to specific ritual practices later. Literal anointings with oil, for example, will develop in all early Christian liturgical traditions to express ritually the gift, anointing, and seal of the Holy Spirit in

[51] Kavanagh, *The Shape of Baptism*, 20–3.
[52] Bradshaw, *The Search for the Origins of Christian Worship*, 46–7.

initiation. Putting off the old nature and being clothed with the new nature of Christ (Gal 3:27) will eventually be expressed by prebaptismal strippings of clothes and postbaptismal clothings in new white garments. Either connected to an anointing or not, the mark of God's ownership of the newly initiated will come to be signified by various signings or consignations with the cross. Enlightenment will be expressed by the use of baptismal candles or tapers. And the baptismal font and waters will come to be interpreted as either or both womb (John 3:5) and tomb (Romans 6), grave and mother. Given the rich variety of New Testament interpretations of Christian initiation, it was only inevitable that the rites themselves would evolve in this way. That is, a rich biblical theology such as this would seem to call for an equally rich liturgical expression and practice.

Of all these New Testament interpretations, however, two will stand out with particular emphasis in the evolving life of the Church: Christian initiation as new birth through water and the Holy Spirit (John 3:5ff.), and Christian initiation as being united with Christ in his death, burial, and resurrection (Rom 6:3-11). The first of these finds its foundation in Jesus' own baptism by John in the Jordan; the second, of course, in the ultimate completion of that baptism in his death on the cross. While these two interpretations need not be mutually exclusive, and, indeed, will be brought ultimately to a kind of synthesis later in the history of the Church, each one by itself will serve as the dominant interpretation of Christian initiation within specific early liturgical traditions. Not surprisingly, then, it is around these two primary interpretations that all the other New Testament images and metaphors as particular ceremonies will eventually tend to cluster.

CONCLUSION

This chapter began with a discussion of Jesus' inclusive, egalitarian, table companionship "with tax collectors and sinners" as the primary way in which Jesus himself ritually enacted and invited others, indeed, all, to share already in the great banquet of the reign of God drawing near. If, as we have seen, the witness of the Fourth Gospel is historically accurate about Jesus as a baptizer himself, then it is quite possible that Jesus and his disciples did, in fact, baptize others into this table companionship. Or, if there were any prerequisite rites of entrance, perhaps Jesus' own manner of initiation into such table community was the servant rite of footwashing as a sign of the kind of table service, ministry, and hospitality that those who sat at table with him would be expected to offer to others.

Whatever Jesus' own initiatory practices may have been, however, Jesus himself was baptized by John in the Jordan at the beginning of his public ministry, and, at least, since the first Pentecost, the normal pattern of initiation into that continuation of Jesus' table companionship called Church has been some form of baptism "in water and the Holy Spirit." And, like Jesus' own eating practices themselves, this rite of Christian initiation into Christ and his table has been radically inclusive, open to all as the very place where those customary human (and sinful) distinctions between people based on race or ethnicity, social status, or gender are transcended by the new eschatological (end-time) creation, the radical new humanity of the Second Adam, God's Son and servant, Jesus the Christ. Paul writes of this new situation brought about by God's salvific act in Christ and mediated through baptism, saying:

". . . for in Christ Jesus you are all children of God through faith. As many of you as were baptized into Christ have clothed yourselves with Christ. There is no longer Jew or Greek, there is no longer slave or free, there is no longer male and female; for all of you are one in Christ Jesus" (Gal 3:26-27).

It is to the evolution of these great equalizing rites of death, burial, new life, and new creation in Christ and their theological interpretation throughout the history of the Church that the following chapters are devoted.

Chapter 2

Christian Initiation in the Pre-Nicene Period

The first verse of the popular hymn by John Oxenham (1852–1941), "In Christ There Is No East or West," reads:

"In Christ there is no east or west,
In him no south or north,
But one great fellowship of love
Throughout the whole wide earth."[1]

Such a text certainly underscores the transcultural unity of baptismal faith in Christ, that radical unity of faith that cuts across all ethnic, social, and racial categories. Indeed, as Paul writes in Ephesians, there is "one Lord, one faith, and one baptism" (Eph 4:5) into this "great fellowship of love." But in the study of the evolution and interpretation of Christian liturgy it becomes clear immediately that in Christ there is, and always has been, both an "East and a West," just as it is becoming increasingly evident that there is also a distinct south and north within Christianity, with greater attention today being given to the unique theologies, spiritualities, and devotional practices indigenous to and emerging from the peoples of Central and South America. Because of such geographical and cultural distinctions, the "one baptism" of the Church has always been expressed by means of a variety of different liturgical practices and interpretations within the distinct Christian churches.

To study the evolution and interpretation of the rites of Christian initiation, then, is to engage in a study of multiculturalism and liturgical inculturation and adaptation from the very beginning of the Church's history as the "one baptism" takes shape within differing ecclesial contexts. The rites of Christian initiation, we might say, plunge people into an ecclesial reality which is decidedly diverse and

[1] Cited from *The Collegeville Hymnal* (Collegeville: The Liturgical Press, 1990) hymn 650.

multicultural by definition, a Church *Catholic* or *universal* comprised of various and distinct geographical, cultural, ethnic, and linguistic Christian communities. This is not simply a characteristic or fad of our modern age which thinks it alone has somehow discovered multi-culturalism and its importance as characteristics of human social life. Rather, already in the Church of the first three centuries we meet several differing Christian groups: the early Syriac-speaking Christians of East Syria living in what is modern day Iraq and Iran; the Greek-speaking Christians of West Syria centered in Antioch of Syria and in the Jerusalem of Syro-Palestine; the Greek and Coptic-speaking Christians of Egypt; the Latin-speaking members of the North African churches; and the (undoubtedly) multi-linguistic groups which made up the Christian communities living in Rome. As in the New Testament itself, therefore, we should not expect to find only *one* practice and theology of initiation in this period of the Church's history before the Council of Nicea (325 C.E.) but great diversity both within the rites themselves as well as in their theological interpretations.

This chapter provides a selective overview of the rites of Christian initiation and their theological interpretation within the Christian churches of the first three centuries. Descriptions and interpretations of those rites as they appear both from the few extant liturgical documents as well as in specific authors from Syria, Egypt, North Africa, and Rome will be presented and analyzed. However, because it has often been customary within liturgical scholarship to view the evidence of the Syrian and Egyptian East through the eyes of a presumed normative North African and/or Roman West, and, consequently, to discount any liturgical or theological diversity encountered therein as aberrations or departures from this supposed "norm," the witnesses of early East and West Syria and Egypt will be presented first. In this way it is hoped that each of these ancient liturgical traditions, including those of North Africa and Rome, might be viewed in their own right, according to their own unique and distinctively characteristic ritual patterns and theological emphases.

PART I: CHRISTIAN INITIATION
IN THE PRE-NICENE EAST

East and West Syria
    As noted above, early "Syrian" Christianity is generally described as either "East" or "West" Syrian, designations related not only to

geography but to several other factors as well. On the one hand, East Syrian Christianity, centered in the region of Nisibis (Nusyabin, Syria) and in Edessa (Urfa, Turkey), beyond the borders and influence of the dominant Roman Empire, retained a strongly Semitic (Jewish) flavor in its thought and expression. It is characterized by the use of the Syriac language (a dialect of the Aramaic spoken by Jesus himself), a fondness for poetry and rich biblical symbolism in its rites and theology, and a pronounced theology of the Holy Spirit.

West Syrian Christianity, on the other hand, centered primarily as it was in Antioch, the very seat of Roman government throughout the Near East in this era, was not only Greek-*speaking* but also Greek or Hellenistic in its thought and expression. That is, the West Syrian Christianity of the Mediterranean coastline was much more oriented to and shaped by the dominant Greco-Roman culture and its philosophical schools than was its East Syrian counterpart in the inner regions of Syria.[2] These distinctions between East and West Syria will become especially important in the next chapter, when the rites of initiation throughout the Christian East will be seen to undergo a dramatic revision within the context of various changes occurring in the fourth and fifth centuries. For the purposes of this chapter, however, it is enough to speak of early "Syrian" rites in general without specifying whether they belong more properly to either East or West Syria.

The Didache. Unknown to modern Christians until its discovery in 1873 and subsequent publication by the Greek Metropolitan of Nicomedia, Philotheos Bryennios, in 1883, the *Didache,* or "The Teaching of the Lord to the Gentiles through the Apostles," dates from either the late first or early second century in Syria.[3] Compiled originally in Greek and based, undoubtedly, on a number of different sources, this document, the first of its kind in history, is a manual or "church order" of sixteen chapters designed to offer directions for the worship and life of an early Christian congregation. Chapter 7 of this important document provides us with the earliest description of the

[2] See the introductions to both West and East Syrian Christianity provided by T. M. Finn, MFC 5, 29–32 and 111–5.

[3] On issues related to the date and provenance of this document and for a discussion of "church order" literature in general see Paul Bradshaw, *The Search for the Origins of Christian Worship* (New York: Oxford University Press, 1992) 80–110, esp. 84–6.

rites of Christian initiation we have beyond those given in the New Testament itself:

"7.1. Regarding baptism. Baptize as follows: after first explaining all these points . . . , 'Baptize in the name of the Father and of the Son and of the Holy Spirit' [Matt 28:19], in running water. 2. But if you have no running water, baptize in other water; and if you cannot in cold, then in warm. 3. But if you have neither, pour water on the head three times 'in the name of the Father and of the Son and of the Holy Spirit.' 4. Before the baptism, let the baptizer and the candidate for baptism fast, as well as any as are able. Require the candidate to fast one or two days previously."[4]

Before this all too brief description of the baptismal rite, the Didachist, as the editor or compiler of this document is called, has prefaced six chapters containing a "catechism" called "The Two Ways" (of death and life) consisting of "catechesis" (i.e., instruction) on the moral life of Christians. Based on the Decalogue (the Ten Commandments) and on a number of Jesus' sayings from the Sermon on the Mount (Matthew 5–6) and other Gospel passages,[5] this "Two Ways" catechism seems to function in the *Didache* as prebaptismal catechesis for adult converts to Christianity. Presumably, then, these are the "points" referred to in *Didache* 7 which are to be "explained" prior to baptism. Similarly, it should be noted that chapter 9 of the *Didache* makes it clear that baptism is a necessary prerequisite for participation in the Eucharist.

What emerges from this early document is a developing ritual pattern or process of Christian initiation consisting of various stages and/or steps:

(1) a period of prebaptismal catechesis, the duration of which the *Didache* does not indicate;

(2) an immediate preparation for the rites themselves consisting of a one- or two-day fast on the part of the minister, the candidate(s), and, ideally, the whole community;

[4] The best critical edition of the Greek text of the *Didache* is that of Willy Rordorf and André Truillier, eds., *La doctrine des douze apôtres*, SC 248 (Paris: Cerf, 1978). The English translation above is from J. Kleist, trans., *Didache* 1–7, Ancient Christian Writers 6 (New York: Newman Press, 1948), as cited in MFC 6, 36.

[5] For text of *Didache* 1–6 see MFC 5, 33–6.

(3) the celebration of the rite of baptism itself, preferably by means of either submersion or immersion, which may be accompanied by the trinitarian formula, though it is unclear here if an actual "formula" is intended; and *mystagogy*

(4) ongoing participation in the Eucharist, though it is not clear from the document if "first communion" functioned as the culmination of the baptismal rite itself.

As such, this four-fold ritual pattern corresponds in broad outline to what we have seen in the previous chapter to be the regular sequence for adult initiation in the New Testament period described by Aidan Kavanagh. That is, the proclamation of the gospel leads to some kind of response of faith and conversion, which, in turn, leads also to the rite of baptism and, following baptism, to an ongoing life of faith within the community.[6]

There is, however, a great deal that the *Didache* does *not* tell us about the initiation rites. In addition to those elements noted above (i.e., the duration of prebaptismal catechesis, whether the trinitarian language is a reference to a baptismal "formula," and whether the baptismal rite culminated immediately in the Eucharist), the *Didache* also does not indicate any preferred day or season for baptism, is silent about what sort of profession of faith may have been expected from the baptismal candidates, offers no information about the "ministers" of baptism, and makes no reference whatsoever to any sort of additional rites that may have accompanied baptism itself. Equally absent from this document is any definitive theological interpretation of or reflection on the meaning of baptism. Unfortunately, then, the information provided about the rites of Christian initiation by the *Didache* is only of the most general kind.

The witness of Justin Martyr. Born near the beginning of the second century in Flavia Neapolis (the ancient city of Sichem) within Syro-Palestine (Samaria), Justin, the great Christian philosopher and Apologist, lived and taught in the city of Rome during the reign of Emperor Antoninus Pius (138–61 C.E.), where he and six of his students were ultimately martyred in ca. 165 C.E. While normally reckoned as a witness to the evolution of the *Roman* liturgy, Justin's witness is included here under the Syrian rites not only because of

---

[6] See above, 29–30.

37

his origins but, as we shall see, because his particular *theology* of Christian initiation has much more in common with what is known to be characteristic of early Syrian theology in general. Indeed, among Justin's students at Rome was the famous Tatian, the editor of the *Diatesseron,* that early Gospel harmony referred to in the previous chapter,[7] which came to serve as the principal Gospel text for the Syrian churches until the fifth century.

For the purposes of the evolution and interpretation of Christian initiation, chapters 61 and 65 of Justin's *First Apology,* his *apologia* or "defense" of the Christian faith, addressed to Emperor Antoninus Pius in ca. 148 C.E., are extremely important.

"(*Chapter 61*): Lest we be judged unfair in this exposition, we will not fail to explain how we consecrated ourselves to God when we were regenerated through Christ. Those who are convinced and believe what we say and teach is the truth, and pledge themselves to be able to live accordingly, are taught in prayer and fasting to ask God to forgive their past sins, while we pray and fast with them. Then we lead them to a place where there is water, and they are regenerated in the same manner in which we ourselves were regenerated. In the name of God, the Father and Lord of all, and of our Savior, Jesus Christ, and of the Holy Spirit, they then receive the washing with water. For Christ said: 'Unless you be born again, you shall not enter the kingdom of heaven' (John 3:5). . . . In order that we do not continue as children of necessity and ignorance, but of deliberate choice and knowledge, and in order to obtain in the water the forgiveness of past sins, there is invoked over the one who wishes to be regenerated, and who is repentant of his sins, the name of God, the Father and Lord of all. . . . This washing is called illumination, since they who learn these things become illuminated intellectually. Furthermore, the illuminated one is also baptized in the name of Jesus Christ, who was crucified under Pontius Pilate, and in the name of the Holy Spirit, who predicted through the prophets everything concerning Jesus.

"(*Chapter 65*): After thus baptizing the one who has believed and given his assent, we escort him to the place where are assembled those whom we call brethren, to offer up sincere prayers in common

[7] See above, 15.

38

for ourselves, for the baptized person, and for all other persons wherever they may be, in order that, since we have found the truth, we may be deemed fit through our actions to be esteemed as good citizens and observers of the law, and thus attain eternal salvation. At the conclusion of prayers we greet one another with a kiss. Then, bread and chalice containing wine mixed with water are presented to the one presiding over the brethren. He takes them and offers praise and glory to the Father of all, through the name of the Son and of the Holy Spirit, and he recites lengthy prayers of thanksgiving to God in the name of those to whom he granted such favors. At the end of these prayers and thanksgiving, all present express their approval by saying 'Amen.' This Hebrew word, 'Amen' means 'So be it.' And when he who presides has celebrated the Eucharist, they whom we call deacons permit each one present to partake of the Eucharistic bread, and wine and water; and they carry it also to the absentees."[8]

On the one hand, Justin's text tells us only a little more than what we have seen already in the *Didache*. Apart from similar references to prebaptismal catechesis and fasting on the part of the baptismal candidates, to baptism itself as administered at "a place where there is water," and to similar omissions about "ministers," preferred days, or any accompanying rites, Justin's witness is clear that the culmination of initiation is understood to be a complete participation in the liturgical life of the community (i.e., the "prayers in common," and the "kiss"), especially in its Eucharist. In addition, his use of what appears to be credal language in reference to the name of God "invoked" at baptism (i.e., "the Father and Lord of all . . . Jesus Christ, who was crucified under Pontius Pilate, and . . . the Holy Spirit, who predicted through the prophets everything concerning Jesus") may be an indication of the kind of profession of faith made by the candidate at the time of baptism[9] or it may be simply Justin's way of referring to a formula recited by the one who baptizes.

On the other hand, unlike the *Didache*, Justin *does* offer a theological interpretation of the meaning of baptism. For Justin, baptism is not only for the forgiveness of sins, but it is, primarily, a ritual of "new birth" and/or "regeneration" along the lines of John 3:5, as

[8] English translation from FC 6, as cited in MFC 6, 38–40.
[9] On this see John Norman Davidson Kelly, *Early Christian Creeds*, 3d ed. (New York: D. McKay Co., 1972) 70–6.

39

well as a *photismos,* an "illumination" or "enlightenment," an understanding of baptism consistent with one who is, after all, a Christian philosopher, and one that will continue to be characteristic of Eastern Christianity in general. As a ritual of "new birth" through water and the Holy Spirit, however, it is clear from elsewhere in Justin's writings that his dominant baptismal paradigm is Jesus' own baptism by John in the Jordan River. In his famous *Dialogue with Trypho* (ca. 1?), the oldest extant Christian apology in relationship to Judaism, Justin refers to Jesus' baptism saying:

"When Jesus had gone to the river Jordan, where John was baptizing, and when He had stepped into the water, a fire was kindled in the Jordan; and when He came out of the water, the Holy Ghost lighted on Him like a dove, [as] the apostles of this very Christ of ours wrote. Now, we know that he did not go to the river because He stood in need of baptism, or of the descent of the Spirit like a dove; . . . but . . . the Holy Ghost . . . *for man's sake* . . . lighted on Him in the form of a dove, and there came at the same instant from the heavens a voice . . . 'Thou art My Son: this day have I begotten Thee'; [the Father] saying that His generation would take place for men, at the time when they would become acquainted with Him: 'Thou art My Son; this day have I begotten thee.'"[10]

Kilian McDonnell, in his recent study of the role of Jesus' baptism in the developing theology of the early Church, writes that:

"For Justin . . . the baptism of Jesus is the messianic manifestation of who this person is, a messianic sign given to the Church. Also unmistakably clear is the relationship between Christ receiving the Spirit at his baptism and Christians receiving the Spirit at theirs. . . . In a word, Justin is attempting to show that at birth, at the baptism, and finally at the crucifixion, through the signs of power and his true identity, Christ was demonstrating the plan of salvation. However, in the mysteries that reveal the identity of the Christ, the baptism has certain precedence because it was at the Jordan that humankind 'first realized who he was,' more precisely, the Messiah. The Jordan event is the first sign."[11]

---

[10] *Dialogue with Trypho,* 88, ANF 1, 243–4; emphasis added.

[11] Kilian McDonnell, *The Baptism of Jesus in the Jordan: The Trinitarian and Cosmic Order of Salvation* (Collegeville: The Liturgical Press, 1996) 43–4.

According to Justin, therefore, Christian baptism is a birth ritual modeled on Jesus' own baptism in the Jordan, where Christians become by adoption what Christ is by nature: sons and daughters begotten by God through water and the Holy Spirit.

Didascalia Apostolorum. The type of baptismal theology articulated by Justin Martyr is even more clearly expressed in the early-third-century Syrian church order known as the *Didascalia Apostolorum,* or "The Catholic Teaching of the Twelve Holy Apostles and Disciples of our Savior." Modeled on the *Didache* and originally composed in Greek by a Syrian bishop in the region of Antioch, presumably, the *Didascalia* is extant only in much later Syriac and incomplete Latin translations.[12] Of its twenty-six total chapters two, in particular, provide significant information on the rites of Christian initiation, with other references scattered here and there throughout the document.

"*(Chapter 9):* . . . the bishop, through whom the Lord gave you the Holy Spirit and through whom you have learned the word and have known God, and through whom you have been known of God, and through whom you were sealed, and through whom you became children of the light, and through whom the Lord in baptism, by the imposition of the hand of the bishop, bore witness to each one of you and uttered his holy voice, saying: *You are my son: today I have begotten you.*[13]

"*(Chapter 17):* In the first place, when women go down into the baptismal water: those who go down into the water ought to be anointed by a deaconess with the oil of anointing; and where there is no woman at hand, and especially no deaconess, he who baptizes must of necessity anoint the woman who is being baptized. But where there is a woman, and especially a deaconess, present, it is not fitting that women should be seen by men, but with the imposition of hand you

[12] The most recent critical edition with English translation is that of Arthur Vööbus, *The Didascalia Apostolorum in Syriac,* Corpus Scriptorum Christianorum Orientalium 401, 402, 407, 408 (Louvain: Secretariat du CSCO, 1979). See also Sebastian Brock and Michael Vasey, eds., *The Liturgical Portions of the Didascalia,* Grove Liturgical Study 29 (Bramcote, Nottingham: Grove Books, 1982).

[13] Text adapted from DBL, 12.

should anoint the head only. As of old priests and kings were anointed in Israel, so do you likewise, with the imposition of hand, anoint the head of those who receive baptism, whether you yourself baptize, or you tell the deacons or presbyters to baptize, let a woman, a deaconess, anoint the women, as we have already said. But let a man pronounce over them the invocation of the divine names in the water."[14]

In these two chapters not only do we see an emphasis upon the role of the bishop and other "orders" in the process of Christian initiation (e.g., presbyters and deacons, including a necessary baptismal role assigned to what should be translated as *women* deacons, not "deaconesses"), but here is presented a ritual sequence which includes:

(1) a *prebaptismal* anointing of the head with oil, accompanied by an imposition of the bishop's hand;
(2) a citation of Psalm 2:7 ("You are my son . . ."), apparently recited as a formula to accompany this handlaying and anointing;
(3) a full body anointing of the candidate administered by the appropriate ministers; and
(4) baptism itself accompanied by the "invocation of the divine names," presumably some version of a baptismal formula.

That this ritual was preceded by some form of catechesis under the bishop's direction is indicated from chapter 9 above (e.g., "through whom you have learned the word and have known God . . .") as well as from chapter 10: ". . . when the heathen desire and promise to repent, saying 'We believe,' we receive them into the congregation so that they may hear the word, but do not receive them into communion until they receive the seal and are fully initiated."[15]

Similarly, that this rite led to participation in the Eucharist is not only indicated by this same text from chapter 10 but also by another place in chapter 9, where bishops are described as those who, following baptism, "allowed you to partake of the holy eucharist of God, and made you partakers and joint heirs of the promise of God."[16]

What is most intriguing, of course, is that the *Didascalia* does not indicate the existence of any postbaptismal ceremonies other than

---

[14] Brock and Vasey, *The Liturgical Portions of the Didascalia*, 22.
[15] Ibid., 12.
[16] Ibid.

participation in the Eucharist. Rather, the major concern of this document is with the *prebaptismal* anointing(s), and particularly with the prebaptismal anointing of the candidate's head. Theologically and ritually, it is *this* liturgical act, interpreted *messianically* in relationship to the anointing of priests and kings in ancient Israel and accompanied by the citation of Psalm 2:7 (the textual variant of Luke 3:22 in the account of Jesus' own baptism in the Jordan), which receives the primary emphasis within the overall initiation rite. Before we can deal adequately with this sequence and interpretation, however, it is necessary to look at a rather unique collection of documents containing a number of other early Syrian initiation texts, where the same ritual patterns are described and where the same theological interpretations of this new birth event are presented.

Apocryphal Acts of the Apostles. Coming probably from the city of Edessa in East Syria in the second and third centuries, and existing in both Syriac (originally) and Greek versions, is a collection of texts recounting the legendary missionary adventures or *Acts* of various apostles. This collection is generally referred to as the *Apocryphal Acts of the Apostles* and includes stories about Peter, Paul, and others. It is within the *Acts of Judas Thomas*, describing the work of the apostle Thomas in evangelizing India, and the *Acts* or *History of John, the Son of Zebedee*, recounting the apostle John's alleged missionary activity in Ephesus, where significant descriptions of initiation rites are provided. Although these *Acts* are not to be interpreted as accurate portrayals of first-century apostolic work by any means, their importance here comes from their probable depiction of the initiation rites as reflecting the time period in which these *Acts* were composed, a depiction which generally corroborates what we have already seen in the *Didascalia Apostolorum* above.

The *Acts of Judas Thomas* are particularly rich in initiation materials with five different baptismal events described. Here, in the interest of space, only two of these will be presented: "The Baptism of Gundaphorus," from chapters 25–7 of the Syriac version, and "The Baptism of Sifur," from chapters 132–3 of the Syriac version.

"*(Chapters 25–7 [Syriac]):* And they begged of him that they might receive the *sign,* and said to him: 'Our souls are turned to God to receive the *sign* for we have heard that all the sheep of that God whom you preach are known to him by the *sign.*' Judas said to them: 'I too rejoice, and I ask of you to partake of the Eucharist and of the blessing

43

of this Messiah whom I preach.' And the king gave orders that the bath should be closed for seven days, and that no man should bathe in it. And when the seven days were done, on the eighth day they three entered into the bath by night that Judas might baptize them. And many lamps were lighted in the bath. . . . And when they had entered into the bath-house, Judas went in before them. And our Lord appeared unto them, and said to them: 'Peace be with you, my brothers.' And they heard the voice only but the form they did not see, whose it was, for until now they not been baptized. And Judas went up and stood upon the edge of the cistern, and poured oil upon their heads, and said: 'Come, holy name of the Messiah; come power of grace, which is from on high: [Greek version: Come, compassionate *mother*. Come, communion of the male. Come, *she* that reveals the hidden mysteries] come, perfect mercy; come, exalted gift; come, sharer of the blessing; come, revealer of hidden mysteries; come, *mother* of seven houses, whose rest was in the eighth house; come, messenger of reconciliation, and communicate with the minds of these youths; come Spirit of holiness, and purify their reins and their hearts.' And he baptized them in the name of the Father and of the Son and of the Spirit of holiness. And when they had come up out of the water, a youth appeared to them, and he was holding a lighted taper; and the light of the lamps became pale through its light. And when they had gone forth, he became invisible to them; and the Apostle said: 'We were not even able to bear Your light, because it is too great for our vision.' And when it dawned and was morning, he broke the Eucharist.[17]

"*(Chapters 132–3 [Syriac]):* And Sifur the general said to him: 'I and my daughter and my wife will henceforth live purely, in one mind and in one love; and we beg that we may receive the *sign* [of baptism] from your hands.' . . . And he [Judas] began to speak of baptism, and said: 'This is the baptism of the remission of sins; this is the bringer forth of new men; this is the restorer of understandings, and the mingler of soul and body, and the establisher of the new man in the Trinity, and which becomes a participation in the remission of sins. Glory to you, hidden power of baptism. Glory to you, hidden

---

[17] Text adapted from DBL, 13–4 [emphasis added]. For the Greek additions to this text, which probably were in the original Syriac version as well, see DBL, 16–7.

power, that communicates with us in baptism. Glory to you, power that is visible in baptism. Glory to you, you new creatures, who are renewed through baptism, who draw nigh to it in love.' And when he had said these things, he cast oil upon their heads and said: 'Glory to you, beloved fruit. Glory to you, name of the Messiah. Glory to you, hidden power that dwells in the Messiah.' And he spoke, and they brought a large vat, and he baptized them in the Name of the Father and the Son and the Spirit of holiness. . . . And when they were baptized and had put on their clothes, he brought bread and wine."[18]

A similar description of the rites is given in the account of "The Baptism of the Priests of Artemis" in Ephesus in the *Acts of John*, a text, which in its present state, it should be noted, is probably a *fourth-century retranslation* into Syriac from a now lost Greek version.[19]

"And when the font was prepared, the procurator commanded, and oil was brought. Then St John arose, and prayed, and said: 'Glory be to You, Father and Son and Spirit of holiness, forever, Amen.' And they answered after him, 'Amen.' And he said: 'Lord God Almighty, let Your Spirit of holiness come, and rest and dwell upon the oil and upon the water; and let them be bathed and purified from uncleanness; and let them receive the Spirit of holiness through baptism; and henceforth let them call you "Our Father who art in Heaven." Yes, Lord, sanctify this water with your voice, which resounded over the Jordan and pointed out our Lord Jesus as with the finger, saying, "This is my beloved Son in whom I am well pleased, hear him." You are here who was at the Jordan. Yes, I beseech you, Lord, reveal yourself here before this assembly who have believed on you with simplicity, and let the nations of the earth hear that the city of Ephesus was the first to receive your gospel before all cities, and became a second sister to Urhai [Edessa] of the Parthians.' And in that hour fire blazed forth over the oil, and the wings of the angels were spread forth over the oil; and the whole assembly was crying out, men and women and children, 'Holy, holy, holy, Lord Almighty, of whose

[18] Text adapted from DBL, 15 [emphasis added].
[19] On this see Gabriele Winkler, "Nochmals zu den Anfängen der Epiklese und des Sanctus im Eucharistischen Hochgebet," *Theologisches Quartalschrift* 74:3 (1994) 220–1.

praises heaven and earth are full.' And straightway the vision was taken away. . . . And the priests fell down on their faces and wept. And St John drew nigh and raised them up, and they said: 'We believe in the Name of the Father and the Son and the Spirit of holiness, and we will never know aught else.' And John drew near, and washed them clean of the soot [which they wore in token of grief], and anointed them with oil, and baptized them in the Name of the Father and the Son and the Spirit of holiness, for the forgiveness of debts and the pardon of sins. And St John said to the procurator: 'Command that they go and fetch fine white bread and wine.'[20]

On the basis of these three examples, not only do we encounter an overall ritual sequence of anointing, baptism, and Eucharist, but, again, as in the *Didascalia Apostolorum* above, the very high point of the entire baptismal rite appears to be this prebaptismal anointing of the head. In fact, this anointing is so important that it is accompanied by either lengthy epicleses (invocations) of the Holy Spirit, doxologies of praise, visions of angels (whose wings are spread over the oil just as the six-winged Seraphim cover the divine presence in Isa 6:2), the communal chanting of the Sanctus from Isaiah 6:3, or by the reference to fire blazing over the oil just as it did in the Jordan, according to both the biblical text known to Justin Martyr and the *Diatessaron*, at Jesus' own baptism.

There is no better guide to the interpretation of this early Syrian tradition of Christian initiation than Gabriele Winkler, who has devoted several important publications to critical analyses of these rites, their historical development, and their theological meaning and implications.[21] While liturgical scholars had debated long and hard about the absence of any postbaptismal ceremonies in these texts and about the precise meaning of the prebaptismal anointing(s),[22] it is Winkler's great and convincing contribution to assert that in this early Syrian tradition:

[20] Text adapted from DBL, 23.

[21] See especially Gabriele Winkler, "The Original Meaning of the Prebaptismal Anointing and Its Implications," LWSS, 58–81; and Gabriele Winkler, *Das armenische Initiationsrituale*, Orientalia Christiana Analecta 217 (Rome: Pont. Institutum Studiorum Orientalium, 1982).

[22] For a survey of these debates see Bradshaw, *The Search for the Origins of Christian Worship*, 163–7.

"Christian baptism is shaped after Christ's baptism in the Jordan. As
Jesus had received the anointing through the divine presence in the
appearance of a dove, and was invested as the Messiah, so in Christian baptism every candidate is anointed and, in connection with this
anointing, the gift of the Spirit is conferred. Therefore the main theme
of this prebaptismal anointing is the entry into the eschatological
kingship of the Messiah, being in the true sense of the word assimilated to the Messiah-king through this anointing. . . . The anointing
of the priest-king of the old covenant prefigured the anointing of the
Messiah. Jesus is revealed as the Messiah-King at the Jordan through
the descent of the Spirit in the appearance of a dove. What happened
at the Jordan is dramatically reinvoked in the earliest Syriac documents. . . . It is also no longer puzzling why the anointing, and not
the immersion in the water, forms the central part of baptism in the
early Syriac sources. . . . The description of Christ's baptism culmi-
nates in the appearance of the dove and the divine voice. This event,
and not the actual descent into the water, is emphasized by Matthew,
Luke and Mark. Furthermore, in John (1:32-33) Jesus is explicitly depicted as the one who baptizes with the Spirit, in contrast to John's
baptism with water. . . . In the process of ritualization, therefore, it
was the anointing that became, in Syria, the first and only visible gesture for the central event at Christ's baptism: his revelation as the
Messiah-King through the descent of the Spirit."[23]

So significant is this prebaptismal anointing in the early Syrian tradition
that its Syriac term, *rushma,* translated correctly as "sign" or "mark," becomes the way to refer to the whole of Christian initiation. To be initiated into Christ, then, is to be assimilated by the Holy Spirit into the life
pattern of the anointed one (the meaning of the term "Christ") himself;
to be a "Christian" is to be, literally, an "anointed one."
    There are a number of other elements in these early Syrian sources
that call for additional comment. First, there is no indication in any of
these sources as to a preferred day or season for the celebration of the
rites of Christian initiation. But with Jesus' own baptism in the Jordan
and the "new birth" theology of John 3:5 functioning as the models
for interpreting the rites, and with the absence of any reference to Romans 6, we can be quite certain that this early tradition did not know

[23] Winkler, "The Original Meaning of the Prebaptismal Anointing," 71–2.

paschal (Easter) baptism. If any day was preferred it most likely would have been January 6, the feast of the Epiphany, which was, initially, in the Eastern churches, the celebration of Jesus' "beginnings," that is, his birth in Bethlehem *and* his "birth" in the Jordan, later reduced in focus to only his baptism, after the acceptance of the Western feast of Christmas on December 25 in the late fourth century.[24]

Second, while some of these texts do refer to a time of prebaptismal catechesis, none of them indicate how long or how formalized such a process may have been. A clue to the length of this catechumenal process in early Syria, however, may be provided by a much later baptismal rite (ninth/tenth century) from the Armenian Church in which the following rubric (ritual direction) appears:

"The Canon of Baptism when they make a Christian. Before this it is not right to admit him into the church. Hands shall have been laid on him beforehand, *three weeks* or more before the baptism, in time sufficient for him to learn from the Wardapet [instructor] both the faith and the baptism of the church."[25]

Since Armenia itself was initially evangelized by Syria, most notably, according to tradition, by the Syrian-educated Gregory the Illuminator (consecrated as a bishop, and, hence, as the first Armenian *Catholicos*, in ca. 302), it is only natural to expect liturgical correlation between Syria and Armenia in this early period of development.[26] According to Winkler, in fact, the earliest extant Armenian sources (including Gregory the Illuminator's own catechism or *Teaching*,[27] the famous *Agathangeli historia* [the mid-fifth-century history of Armenian Christianity by Agathangelos], and several structural and other parallels in the above noted Armenian baptismal ritual) show a ritual shape and interpretation of Christian initiation which closely parallel those of the early Syrian tradition.[28] It is quite possible, then, that this

---

[24] On this see Thomas Talley, *The Origins of the Liturgical Year,* 2d ed. (Collegeville: The Liturgical Press, 1986) 121–47.

[25] Text adapted DBL, 60 [emphasis added].

[26] On the evangelization of Armenia, the first "Christian nation," see the helpful summary in McDonnell, *The Baptism of Jesus in the Jordan,* 37–8.

[27] For an abridged version of this catechism see MFC 5, 197–206.

[28] For specific details see Winkler, *Das armenische Initiationsrituale,* and Winkler, "The Original Meaning of the Prebaptismal Anointing," 59–62.

Armenian rubric calling for at least "three weeks" of instruction before baptism reflects a traditional length of prebaptismal catechesis within early Syria.

Third, along with a theological understanding of the rite of Christian initiation as a ritual of new birth in water and the Holy Spirit in imitation of Jesus' own baptism in the Jordan, it is not without significance that in this early Syrian tradition the word for Spirit, *ruah*, is feminine and that early Syriac texts refer to the Holy Spirit as "Mother" and invoke her as such in the context of both initiation and Eucharist.[29] Along similar lines, Joseph Chalassery directs our attention to what he calls an "unusual analogy" between the Holy Spirit and the woman deacon in the *Didascalia Apostolorum*. Quoting the *Didascalia* he writes:

"'. . . the bishop sits for you in the place of God Almighty. But the deacon stands in the place of Christ, and you should love him. The deaconess, however, shall be honored by you *in the place of the Holy Spirit*.' This comparison between the deaconess and the Holy Spirit shows how the ancient Syrian-Christian mind conceived the Holy Spirit as the feminine dimension of God."[30]

And, closely related to these feminine characteristics of the Holy Spirit and women deacons is the fact that within this Syrian tradition as well the baptismal font itself is customarily referred to in a number of different authors as a "womb."

Finally, the centrality and influence of the event of Jesus' baptism in the Jordan within this tradition should not be under-emphasized whatsoever. Not only was it *the* paradigm for understanding the new birth of Christian initiation in the early Syrian tradition but, again, according to Winkler, Jesus' baptism, especially with regard to the descent of the Holy Spirit at that Jordan event, was recognized as an article of faith within early Syriac and Armenian credal statements.[31]

---

[29] For additional texts see Winkler, "Nochmals zu den Anfängen der Epiklese und des Sanctus im Eucharistischen Hochgebet," 214–31.

[30] Joseph Chalassery, *The Holy Spirit and Christian Initiation in the East Syrian Tradition* (Rome: Mar Thoma Yogam, 1995) 22.

[31] See Gabriele Winkler, "Eine bemerkenswerte Stelle im armenischen Glaubensbekenntnis: Credimus et in Sanctum Spiritum qui descendit in Jordanem et proclamavit missum," *Oriens Christianus* 63 (1979) 130–62; and

That is, prior to the doctrinal shifts brought about in the context of the fourth-century trinitarian controversies leading, ultimately, to what we now know as the Nicene Creed, as well as those within the later fifth-century christological controversies,[32] the profession of faith in the Holy Spirit within this early tradition included explicit reference to the baptism of Jesus. In what she calls the "ancient stratum" of this profession Winkler points to the following Armenian text: "We also believe in the Holy Spirit, uncreated and perfect, who spoke in the law, the prophets, and the gospels, *who descended into the Jordan,* and proclaimed the Sent One, and dwelt in the saints."[33] Such credal references to the baptism of Jesus and the descent of the Spirit, she notes, go back as far as Ignatius of Antioch in the late first century and, at least among Armenian Christians, continue in use within baptismal professions of faith, in Eucharistic Prayers, and in other forms of liturgical prayer. In other words, faith in the Holy Spirit who descends at Jesus' baptism in the Jordan is a constitutive element in the trinitarian faith and profession of the early Syrian and Armenian churches. In this way, then, the event of the baptism of Jesus itself becomes in this tradition the very revelation of the doctrine of the Trinity.

Egypt

According to ancient tradition, the conversion of Egypt was due to the missionary work of St. Mark the Evangelist, whose Gospel came to be the primary Gospel read in the Egyptian liturgy and whose name became attached both to the Patriarchate of Alexandria (i.e., The See of St. Mark) and to the once-dominant Egyptian eucharistic liturgical tradition (i.e., the Liturgy of St. Mark). Whether this tradition is accurate or not, recent scholarship on the origins and evolution of Egyptian Christianity would date its presence in Alexandria quite early (ca. 50 C.E.), reaching "Egypt from Palestine in a form strongly influenced by Judaism," and in close relationship with the

---

Gabriele Winkler, "A Remarkable Shift in the Fourth-Century Creeds: An Analysis of the Armenian, Syriac, and Greek Evidence," *Studia Patristica* 17:3 (1982) 1396–401. Winkler's work here is conveniently summarized by McDonnell, *The Baptism of Jesus in the Jordan,* 29–49, esp. 38ff.

[32] See below, 110–1.

[33] Winkler, as cited by McDonnell, *The Baptism of Jesus in the Jordan,* 38; emphasis added.

Hellenistic Judaism which had long characterized the Jewish community of Alexandria.[34] Greek-speaking in origin and centered in Alexandria in the north ("Lower Egypt"), so many converts had been made among the native peoples of the south ("Upper Egypt") by the third century that the Scriptures were already being translated into Coptic and the liturgy was being celebrated in Coptic.

We do not know a great deal about the rites of Christian initiation in Egypt during this period of the first three centuries. But, from the little that is actually known, it would seem that the closest liturgical and theological parallels are with the early Syrian tradition described above. Our sources here are the writings of Clement of Alexandria (ca. 150–215 C.E.) and Origen of Alexandria (ca. 185–253 C.E.). Unfortunately, neither of these authors give us complete descriptions of either the prebaptismal catechumenate or of the specific rites themselves.

Clement of Alexandria. Clement of Alexandria, born in Athens (ca. 150 C.E.), was to become in ca. 190 the successor of his own teacher, the Sicilian-born Pantaenus, the first known leader of a famous theological school at Alexandria. Although this Alexandrian school is sometimes called a "catechetical school," and while unbaptized "catechumens" and others might certainly have been numbered among its students, this "school" was more of a philosophical and theological academy than it was an institute for prebaptismal or catechumenal instruction. Indeed, Clement himself had already become a Christian before coming to Alexandria to study under Pantaenus.

In one of his writings, however, Clement may be a witness to a rather lengthy process of prebaptismal catechesis in Egypt when he writes in his *Stromata* (or *Miscellanies*) II.18:

[34] Colin H. Roberts, *Manuscript, Society, and Belief in Early Christian Egypt* (New York: Oxford University Press, 1979) 49ff. For other works on early Egyptian Christianity see Birger A. Pearson and James E. Goehring, eds., *The Roots of Egyptian Christianity* (Philadelphia: Fortress Press, 1968), and C. Wilfred Griggs, *Early Egyptian Christianity: From Its Origins to 451 C.E.* (Leiden/New York: E. J. Brill, 1989). On the rites of Christian initiation in Egypt see Georg Kretschmar, "Beiträge zur Geschichte der Liturgie, inbesondere der Taufliturgie, in Ägypten," *Jahrbuch für Liturgik und Hymnologie* 8 (1963) 1–54; Paul Bradshaw, "Baptismal Practice in the Alexandrian Tradition: Eastern or Western?" LWSS, 82–100; and Maxwell Johnson, *Liturgy in Early Christian Egypt,* Alcuin/GROW Liturgical Study 33 (Cambridge: Grove Books, 1995) 7–16.

". . . husbandmen derived advantage from the law in such things. For it orders newly planted trees to be nourished *three years* in succession, and the superfluous growths to be cut off, to prevent them being loaded and pressed down; and to prevent their strength being exhausted from want, by the nutriment being frittered away, enjoins tilling and digging round them, so that [the tree] may not, by sending out suckers, hinder its growth. And it does not allow imperfect fruit to be plucked from immature trees, but *after three years, in the* fourth year; dedicating the first-fruits to God after the tree has attained maturity. This type of husbandry may serve as *a mode of instruction,* teaching that we must cut the growths of sins, and the useless weeds of the mind that spring up round the vital fruit, till the shoot of faith is perfected and becomes strong. For in the fourth year, since there is need of time to him that is being catechized, the four virtues are consecrated to the God, the third alone being already joined to the fourth, the person of the Lord."[35]

Because another early Christian document, the so-called *Apostolic Tradition,* ascribed to Hippolytus of Rome (ca. 217 C.E.), *does* have a reference to "three years" of catechumenal instruction,[36] scholars have often concluded that the overall length of the prebaptismal catechumenate both in Egypt and Rome, if not universally throughout the early Church, lasted three years. But arguing against such an interpretation for Egypt is the early-fourth-century Egyptian church order known as the *Canons of Hippolytus* (ca. 336 C.E.).[37] Recognized today as the earliest derivative of this *Apostolic Tradition,* this church order contains no reference whatsoever to a three-year catechumenate. Instead, *Canons of Hippolytus* 12 states that "during *forty days* they [the catechumens] are to hear the word and if they are worthy they are to be baptized."[38] If Clement's agricultural image is to be taken as a literal reference to three years of prebaptismal catechesis, it is odd that *nowhere* else in the early Egyptian liturgical tradition is this corroborated. A three-year period of *penance* for sins committed *after*

[35] ANF 2, 368; emphasis added.
[36] See below, 79.
[37] For the text see Paul Bradshaw, ed., *The Canons of Hippolytus,* Alcuin/GROW Liturgical Study 50 (Bramcote, Nottingham: Grove Books, 1987).
[38] Ibid., 19; emphasis added.

baptism seems to be known by Peter II, patriarch of Alexandria, at the turn of the third century,[39] but, as we shall see below, what evidence there is for the prebaptismal catechumenate in Egypt shows it limited to a rather inclusive period of forty days in duration. Clement's reference, then, is most likely a metaphor used to underscore the necessity of Christian maturity and virtue rather than as an indication of a literal period of time.

Nevertheless, as in the early Syrian tradition, Clement's clear references to Christian initiation in Egypt point to a similar theological understanding based on the event of Jesus' own baptism in the Jordan. In language reminiscent of the Syrian documents above, Clement writes in his *Paedagogus (The Instructor)* 6:25 and 26:

"25. But do not find fault with me for claiming that I have such knowledge of God. This claim was rightfully made by the Word, and he is outspoken. *When the Lord was baptized, a voice loudly sounded from heaven, as a witness to him who was beloved: 'You are my beloved Son; this day have I begotten you.'* . . .

"26. This is what happens with us, whose model the Lord made himself. When we are baptized, we are *enlightened;* being *enlightened,* we become *adopted sons* [see Gal 4:5]; becoming *adopted sons,* we are made perfect; and becoming perfect, we are made divine. 'I have said,' it is written, 'you are gods and all the sons of the Most High' [Ps 81:6]. This ceremony is often called 'free gift' [Rom 5:2, 15; 7:24], 'enlightenment' [Heb 6:4; 10:32], 'perfection' [Jas 1:7; Heb 7:11], and 'cleansing' [Titus 3:5; Eph 5:26]—'cleansing,' because through it we are completely purified of our sins; 'free gift,' because by it punishments due to our sins are remitted; *'enlightenment,'* since by it we behold the wonderful holy light of salvation, that is, it enables us to see God clearly; finally, we call it 'perfection' as needing nothing further, for what more does he need who possesses the knowledge of God?"[40]

That Jesus' own baptism by John in the Jordan is Clement's primary model for interpreting Christian baptism is further expressed by his

---

[39] See Canon 1 of the *Canons of Peter of Alexandria,* ANF 6, 269. It may be that such a period for postbaptismal penance ultimately suggested a similar length for the prebaptismal catechumenate such as we see in the *Apostolic Tradition.*

[40] Text from FC 23, as cited in MFC 6, 186 [emphasis added].

use of the Old Testament typology of the Israelites crossing the Jordan under Joshua (= Jesus) into the Promised Land (see Joshua).[41] Similarly, in *Stromata* I.21 Clement witnesses to an early Egyptian celebration on January 6, Epiphany or Theophany, of the "birth" of Christ, which some (i.e., the followers of the Gnostic teacher Basilides) celebrate as the festival of Jesus' baptism, a festival which even included an all-night vigil.[42] Whether Clement himself knew this festival of Jesus' baptism on January 6 as a practice in his own particular community is not known. But the content of Epiphany as it developed within the Egyptian liturgical tradition will certainly be that of Jesus' baptism. As recent scholarship on the liturgical year has demonstrated, the early Egyptian church began each new year in January with the sequential reading of the Gospel of Mark, a Gospel which begins not with narratives of Jesus' conception and birth, but with the preaching of John the Baptizer and Jesus' own baptism by him (see Mark 1:1-11).[43]

Clement of Alexandria is also an important witness to another unique Alexandrian practice in Christian initiation and, again, this is closely related to the use of the Gospel of Mark within this tradition. In a letter called the *Mar Saba Clementine Fragment,* extant only in fragmentary form and yet widely accepted today as authentic Clement, Clement addresses a certain Theodore regarding a *mystikon euangelion* (a "mystic" or "secret" gospel), which contains certain additions to the Gospel of Mark, and which, in Clement's opinion, Mark himself added to his Gospel after coming to Alexandria from Rome.[44] These additions, notes Clement, were to be read "only to those who are being initiated into the great mysteries."[45] Between the canonical Mark 10:32-34 and Mark 10:35-45 (where Jesus refers to the disciples sharing in his "baptism" and drinking his "cup") this "Clementine" version of Mark inserts a narrative about Jesus "initiating" a Lazarus-like figure he had raised from death six days earlier:

---

[41] *Ecologae propheticae* 5–6 in O. Stählin, *Die Griechischen christlichen Schriftsteller der ersten drei Jahrhunderte,* 17 (Berlin: 1909)135–55.

[42] ANF 2, 333.

[43] On this see Talley, *The Origins of the Liturgical Year,* 117ff.

[44] This document was discovered by Morton Smith in Mar Saba (near Jerusalem) in 1958 and was subsequently analyzed and edited by him appearing as *Clement of Alexandria and a Secret Gospel of Mark* (Cambridge, Mass.: Harvard University Press, 1973).

[45] Ibid., 446, as cited by Talley, *The Origins of the Liturgical Year,* 207.

"And they come to Bethany. And a certain woman whose brother had died was there. And, coming, she prostrated herself before Jesus and says to him, 'Son of David, have mercy on me.' But the disciples rebuked her. And Jesus, being angered, went off with her into the garden where the tomb was, and straightway a great cry was heard from the door of the tomb. And going near Jesus rolled away the stone from the door of the tomb. And straightway, going in where the youth was, he stretched forth his hand and raised him, seizing his hand. But the youth, looking upon him, loved him and began to beseech him that he might be with him. And going out of the tomb they came into the house of the youth, for he was rich. And after six days Jesus told him what to do and in the evening the youth comes to him, wearing a linen cloth over his naked body. And he remained with him that night, for Jesus taught him the mystery of the kingdom of God. And thence, arising, he returned to the other side of the Jordan."[46]

Because much later Coptic tradition preserves a memory that in the early Egyptian Church baptisms were conferred on the sixth day of the last week of a six-week (or *forty* day) fast, the day on which this tradition also claims that Jesus was to have baptized his disciples, Thomas Talley concludes that it was on this day that the above passage would have been read to the candidates as part of their initiation. Similarly, with "The beginning of the Gospel of Jesus Christ, the Son of God" (Mark 1:1) through his baptism by John (Mark 1:9-11) read as the Gospel on January 6, the forty-day or six-week fast, in strict imitation of Jesus' own postbaptismal fast in the wilderness (see Mark 1:12-13), began immediately as a time for the prebaptismal instruction of catechumens. This period, claims Talley, would have been marked by the sequential Sunday readings of Mark's Gospel organized in such a way that the "secret gospel" would have naturally occurred within the context of the rites of initiation themselves at the end of the forty days.[47] While such an interpretation may seem rather speculative, it is interesting to note, as does Talley, that in the later (tenth-century) lectionary of Constantinople, still used today in those churches of the Byzantine Rite, the Gospel readings for the Sundays

---

[46] Ibid., 447, as cited by Talley, *The Origins of the Liturgical Year,* 207–8.

[47] For a shorter version of Thomas Talley's argument see his "The Origin of Lent at Alexandria," *Worship: Reforming Tradition* (Washington, D.C.: Pastoral Press, 1990) 87–112.

in Lent follow a sequential reading of Mark until the Saturday before Palm Sunday when, on this day called "Lazarus Saturday," the Gospel reading (John 11:1-45) narrates Jesus' raising of Lazarus from the dead. Such a text, in Talley's opinion, is but the "canonical equivalent" to the above story in the *Mar Saba Clementine Fragment*.[48]

Origen of Alexandria. Like Clement, his teacher and predecessor in the theological school at Alexandria, the great biblical exegete and commentator, preacher, and influential philosophical theologian, Origen of Alexandria, also used the Jordan event of Jesus' own baptism as his primary model for interpreting Christian initiation. In several of his writings, but especially in his *Commentary on Joshua*,[49] Origen, again like Clement, makes frequent reference to Israel's crossing of the Jordan under Joshua as an Old Testament allegory for Christian baptism. While St. Paul already used the Exodus from Egypt in a similar way (see 1 Cor 10:1-5), Origen sees in the Exodus crossing of the Red Sea a typology of one's entrance into the catechumenate. French Patristics scholar Jean Laporte summarizes Origen's approach, saying:

"The image of the crossing of the Red Sea, and of leaving Egypt for the desert where the people of Israel is trained by Moses and taught in the Law, becomes in Origen, as it was in Philo [of Alexandria], a symbol of purification from the passions, and of the catechumenate. . . . The Apostle Paul sees in the Exodus from Egypt a figure of the purification of baptism. Origen accepts this Pauline tradition . . . [but] prefers to spread the interpretation of baptism over two crossings instead of one. The first is the crossing of the Red Sea, and the second is the crossing of the Jordan. The first is closer to the renunciation of catechumens to idolatry, and leads them to instruction in the Law and its purifying influence. It is baptism, indeed, but in some regard superficial, fragile, still in need of the guidance of Moses. . . . The second crossing is that of the Jordan, the 'river which rejoices the City of God,' a symbol of Christ. Baptism now becomes deep and serious, and focuses on the mystery of Christ. . . . We mortify our members, and we are renewed, regenerated by the

[48] Ibid., 211–4.
[49] SC 71. I am unaware of any English translations of this important commentary.

Spirit of God. Origen likes to relate this baptism in the Jordan to the 'second circumcision' accomplished by Joshua after the crossing. This 'second circumcision,' or 'circumcision of the heart,' removes the impurities which prevent the edification of the 'new man' with his 'internal senses' and his ability to see God. With the baptism in the Jordan we are already living in the heavenly Kingdom in its eschatological reality. . . . Joshua removed from the sons of Israel the 'shame of Egypt,' and 'he was exalted.' Our Joshua—Jesus—in the mystery of baptism, in the exaltation of the cross, removes from our hearts the 'shame of Egypt,' i.e., the servitude of the flesh, which is far more difficult to uproot."[50]

Because a number of scholars have assumed that Origen knew in Alexandria the tradition of Easter baptism along with its Romans 6 interpretation as the baptized's participation in Christ's death, burial, and resurrection,[51] it is extremely important that Origen's primary baptismal model of the Jordan with its theology of rebirth and regeneration be underscored. To be sure, Origen is the first and *only* Eastern theologian to refer to the text of Romans 6 in relationship to Christian baptism in the first four centuries. Indeed, he not only refers to this in several works,[52] but even writes a *Commentary on Romans* itself.[53] As Kilian McDonnell has recently demonstrated, however, Origen's frequent use of this Pauline interpretive image "does not mean that he has abandoned the previous tradition that took the baptism of Jesus as its primary paradigm."[54] Not at all. Nor does Origen's use of this model imply that he knew Easter baptism in the

[50] John Laporte, "Models from Philo in Origen's Teaching on Original Sin," LWSS, 113–5. For more on Origen's baptismal theology see also C. Blanc, "Le Baptême d'après Origène," *Studia Patristica* 11 (1972) 113–24; H. Crouzel, "Origène et las structure du sacrement," *Bulletin de littérature ecclesiastique* 2 (1962) 81–92; Jean Daniélou, *Bible and Liturgy,* Liturgical Studies 3 (Notre Dame, Ind.: University of Notre Dame Press, 1956) 99–113; and Jean Daniélou, *Origen,* trans. Walter Mitchell (New York: Sheed and Ward, 1955) 52–61.

[51] Compare with MFC 6.

[52] For select texts in English see MFC 6, 195ff.

[53] PG XIV. Again, I am unaware of any English translations of this commentary.

[54] McDonnell, *The Baptism of Jesus in the Jordan,* 203.

Egyptian tradition. Rather, what Origen does theologically is to combine the traditional emphasis on the dominant event of Jesus's baptism with the theology of Romans 6. But even in doing so, the Jordan itself, both as baptism *and* as a symbol for Christ himself, remains a primary model in his overall approach.[55]

There are three more points that need to be noted in Origen's treatment of Christian initiation. First, regarding the rite of baptism itself, Origen witnesses to a credal interrogation of baptismal candidates (i.e., "Do you believe in God, . . ." etc.) as the profession of faith within the context of baptism. And while Clement of Alexandria does refer to baptismal anointing in general, it is quite possible that prior to the mid fourth century there was only a *prebaptismal* anointing in Egypt, similar to the initiation practice of the early Syrian tradition. For baptism, notes Origen even in his *Commentary on Romans,* is in "the Holy Spirit and the water," and, in his *Homilies on Leviticus,* he says that "the unction of chrism and the baptism have continued in you undefiled."[56] If Origen intends this as a reference to the ritual sequence of baptism, it is significant that both the anointing and the gift of the Holy Spirit come *before* the washing of baptism itself.

Second, in his *Homilies on Leviticus* Origen refers to various fasting practices in the church of his day, saying:

"They fast, therefore, who have lost the bridegroom; we having him with us cannot fast. Nor do we say that we relax the restraints of Christian abstinence; for we have the *forty days consecrated to fasting,* we have the fourth and sixth days of the week, on which we fast solemnly."[57]

Unfortunately, Origen does not indicate *when* these forty days of fasting are to take place. But this reference, combined with that of the early-fourth-century *Canons of Hippolytus* 12, noted above, that "during *forty days* they [the catechumens] are to hear the word and if they are worthy they are to be baptized," as well as other early and later Egyptian references,[58] suggest that this "forty days consecrated to

---

[55] See ibid., 203–6. See also Laporte, "Models from Philo in Origen's Teaching on Original Sin," 116–7, n. 88.

[56] For references see Bradshaw, "Baptismal Practice," 97.

[57] English translation from Talley, *Origins,* 192; emphasis added.

[58] See below, 170–1.

fasting," if not yet clearly prebaptismal in orientation in Origen's time, was certainly an indigenous Egyptian practice which would lend itself to such use in the very near future. This intriguing and ambiguous reference, then, *may* offer *some* support for the unique Egyptian forty-day post-Epiphany period of prebaptismal catechesis.

Finally, unlike any of the sources we have noted so far in this study, Origen is a witness to the existence of infant baptism in the third century. Such a practice, he writes in his *Commentary on Romans*, was "received from the apostles" themselves. While this, of course, is impossible to prove, the fact that Origen sees infant baptism as an "apostolic custom" certainly points to it as a long standing tradition within his own Alexandrian church. Further, in his *Homilies on Leviticus* he states that "while the church's baptism is given for the remission of sin, it is the custom of the Church that baptism be administered even to infants. Certainly, if there were nothing in infants that required remission and called for lenient treatment, the grace of baptism would seem unnecessary."[59] Some have seen in this rationale Origen's acceptance of the theology of "original sin" inherited from Adam, such as will be developed in Western Christianity in Augustine of Hippo.[60] Jean Laporte has shown, however, that for Origen it is not so much "sin" that needs remission in the case of infants but, rather, a kind of "defilement" or "stain" attached to the impure blood of birth that calls for purification. Even Jesus himself, who had no personal sin, needed *this* sort of cultic purification (see Luke 2:27), according to Origen.[61]

Although the sources for the rites of Christian initiation in Egypt are neither as numerous nor as clear as they are for the early Syrian tradition, it would appear that both of these traditions shared a great deal in common. Such common elements include:

(1) a relatively short catechumenal period of possibly "three weeks" (Syria) or "forty days" (Egypt) in total length;
(2) a theological understanding of Christian initiation as "new birth," "regeneration," and "adoption" through water and the Holy Spirit (John 3:5), modeled on Jesus' own baptism, where the voice of God declared him as the beloved Son, "begotten" by God in the Jordan;

---

[59] *Homilies on Leviticus* 8.3, as cited by Johannes Quasten, *Patrology*, vol. 2 (Westminster: Newman Press, 1964) 83.

[60] On this, see below, 153–5.

[61] Laporte, "Models from Philo in Origen's Teaching on Original Sin," 112–3.

(3) a ritual sequence which focuses on the prebaptismal anointing (at least in Syria and possibly in Egypt) as the Holy Spirit's assimilation of the baptismal candidate to the messianic priesthood and kingship of Christ;

(4) a ritual sequence in which no postbaptismal ceremonies are present other than participation in the Eucharist; and

(5) an Epiphany-based rather than Easter-based celebration.

It is the presence of such common elements in these two important early Christian traditions that leads Georg Kretschmar to claim that, with regard to Christian initiation, Syria and Egypt shared a common "root relationship."[62]

PART II: THE PRE-NICENE WEST

North Africa

From the Syriac, Greek, and Coptic-speaking churches of the early Christian East we move westward to the very cradle of Latin Christianity in the early North African church, centered on the important Mediterranean sea port and metropolis of Carthage. Although North African Christianity disappears from sight after the Arab invasions of the late seventh century, it is hard to overestimate the importance and influence of this tradition for Western Christianity in general during the first few centuries of the Church's history. From important and influential writers such as Tertullian (155–ca. 220 C.E.), Cyprian of Carthage (ca. 200–258 C.E.), and later in the fourth century the renowned Augustine of Hippo, North African Christianity gave to the West a Latin theological vocabulary (e.g., words like *trinitas* [trinity], *persona* [person], *substantia* [substance], and *sacramentum* [sacrament or "oath"]) and an overall interpretation of Christianity that is still quite influential today.

Concerning the rites of Christian initiation in the North African tradition of the early to mid third century, we are fortunate to have enough material by which a fairly complete description of the rites themselves can be offered. Further, other important information about the overall theological interpretation of those rites, the preferred day(s) for baptism in this tradition, the role of infant baptism, and a particular third-century controversy between North Africa and Rome

[62] Kretschmar, "Beiträge zur Geschichte der Liturgie," 36, 47–8.

over the question of "re-baptism" is provided. What we discover both in the rites and their interpretation is a liturgical tradition ritually and theologically quite distinct from what we have seen in Syria and Egypt. If to modern Western readers this North African ritual pattern and its theological interpretation seem much more familiar and comfortable, this is due, in no small way, to the manner in which Western sacramental practice and theology have been shaped ever since.

Tertullian. "But we, little fishes, after the example of our IXΘΥΣ Jesus Christ, are born in water, nor have we safety in any other way than by permanently abiding in water."[63] So writes the Christian convert, expert lawyer, and possibly presbyter, Quintus Septimius Florens Tertullianus, or Tertullian, in the introduction to his *De baptismo (On Baptism)*, the earliest treatise on baptism ever written in the history of the Church (ca. 198–200 C.E.).[64] Both in this treatise, which perhaps also served as a series of prebaptismal addresses to catechumens in Carthage, as well as in several other of his writings, Tertullian provides us with valuable details on the structure and interpretation of the rites of Christian initiation within the North African church of his day. According to his descriptions,[65] those rites had the following pattern:

(1) catechumenate of an unspecified length and an immediate preparation for baptism;
(2) prayer of sanctification invoking the Holy Spirit on the baptismal waters;
(3) affirmation of a renunciation of "the devil and his pomp and his angels," previously done, apparently, at some point within the assembly "under the bishop's control" or "hand" (*sub antitistis manu*);
(4) three-fold interrogatory profession of faith in the water (with "interrogations rather more extensive than our Lord has prescribed in the gospel") connected with a three-fold submersion or immersion;
(5) postbaptismal anointing with oil ("chrism");
(6) signing with the cross;

---

[63] ANF 3, 669.

[64] On Tertullian, his writings, and his theology see J. Quasten, *Patrology*, 246–340.

[65] The following outline is based on the texts from Tertullian's various writings as they are printed in DBL, 7–10.

(7) handlaying "in benediction, inviting and welcoming the Holy Spirit";

(8) Eucharist, which included the reception "of a compound of milk and honey."

Such, for Tertullian, is the ritual process by which "Christians are made, not born."

Theologically, as well, Tertullian offers significant interpretations of the various stages of this process outlined above. Those who are at the point of their immediate preparation for baptism are urged "to pray, with frequent prayers, fastings, bendings of the knee, and all-night vigils, along with the confession of all their sins," so that they might imitate "the baptism of John" (*De baptismo* 20).[66] The prayer of sanctification over the baptismal waters invokes the Holy Spirit, he says, so that all water used for baptism might "absorb the power of sanctifying," and acquire a "healing power by an angel's intervention" (see John 5:4) in order that "the spirit" of those being baptized "is in those waters corporally washed while the flesh is in those same waters spiritually cleansed" (*De baptismo* 4).[67] The one *postbaptismal* anointing—whether of the head or entire body of the candidate is unclear—is interpreted by him in line with the Old Testament tradition of the anointing of priests:

"Ever since Aaron was anointed by Moses, there was a custom of anointing them for priesthood with oil out of a horn. That is why [the high priest] is called a christ, from 'chrism' which is [the Greek for] 'anointing': and from this also our Lord obtained his title, though it had become a spiritual anointing, in that he was anointed with the Spirit by God the Father" (*De baptismo* 7).[68]

And the imposition or laying on of the presider's hand "in benediction, inviting and welcoming the Holy Spirit," is understood by Tertullian *not* in relationship to the various accounts in the New Testament Acts of the Apostles (e.g., Acts 8:14-17) but, rather, according to the Old Testament narrative of the patriarch Jacob blessing his grandsons (Gen 48:8-22). He writes:

[66] Ibid., 9.
[67] Ibid., 7.
[68] Ibid., 8.

"This too is involved in that ancient sacred act in which Jacob blessed his grandsons, Joseph's sons, Ephraim and Manasseh, by placing his hands interchanged upon their heads, turned transversely upon themselves in such a manner as to make the shape of Christ, and at that early date to prefigure the blessing that was to be in Christ" (*De baptismo* 8).[69]

On the relationship between this postbaptismal imposition of the hand and gift of the Holy Spirit it is extremely important to note that already in the early-third-century North African West a kind of theological distinction and/or separation is beginning to be made between the water bath and the gift of the Holy Spirit. While the rite that he describes is certainly a unitive and integral one in that the imposition of the hand and Spirit gift are not separated from the water bath by any interval of time, Tertullian couldn't be clearer that it is with this postbaptismal imposition that the Holy Spirit is most closely associated. He writes: "Not that *in* the waters we obtain the Holy Spirit; but in the water, under (the witness of) the angel, we are cleansed, and prepared *for* the Holy Spirit" (*De baptismo* 6).[70] Here, then, in comparison with the early Syrian (and possibly Egyptian) tradition comes the most obvious distinction in rite and interpretation between early Eastern and Western Christianity. While in the Syrian East, as we have seen, the Holy Spirit was associated with the *prebaptismal* anointing as the great *rushma* or "sign" of one's baptismal assimilation by the Spirit to the Messiah-Christ, here in North Africa the prebaptismal *and* baptismal rites themselves are viewed as rites of purification and cleansing in *preparation* for the *postbaptismal* blessing or gift of the Holy Spirit.

This, however, is not the only difference to be noted. Tertullian certainly knows the importance of the event of Jesus' own baptism for Christian baptismal theology. Not only are those preparing for their immediate baptism urged by him to imitate the "baptism of John" by confessing their sins, but he must also have had the event of Jesus' baptism in mind when, in the context of describing the postbaptismal anointing, he refers to Christ as having been "anointed with the Spirit by God the Father" (*De baptismo* 7). In another writing, in fact, Tertullian

---

[69] Ibid.
[70] ANF 3, 672.

clearly relates even the name of "Christ" to his own baptism, saying, "He is called Christ from the sacrament (*sacramentum*) of anointing."[71] Nevertheless, that Jesus' baptism is not a crucial paradigm for his overall theology of baptism is surely indicated by the following list of preferred days or seasons for its appropriate celebration:

"The Passover [i.e., Easter] provides the day of most solemnity for baptism, for then was accomplished our Lord's passion, and *into it we are baptized*. . . . After that, Pentecost is a most auspicious period for arranging baptisms, for during it our Lord's resurrection was several times made known among the disciples, and the grace of the Holy Spirit first given. . . . For all that, every day is a Lord's day: any hour, any season, is suitable for baptism. If there is any difference of solemnity, it makes no difference to the grace."[72]

Here (even if only by allusion rather than direct citation) is clearly articulated the beginnings in the West of a dominant Romans 6 theology of baptism as the candidate's participation in the death, burial, and resurrection of Christ. While this, of course, does not prove that paschal (Easter) baptism was already a normative practice within the North African church of his own day, Tertullian's allusion to Romans 6 and his preference for Easter and the fifty days of the Easter season (i.e., this "most auspicious period" known as "Pentecost"; the "fifty") as appropriate baptismal occasions will become widespread throughout both East and West in the following centuries. Clearly, with Tertullian we are in a different world, ritually and conceptually, than we are with the authors and documents of Syria and Egypt.

Furthermore, while the early Syrian East, perhaps as early as the *Didache*, already knew the use of an indicative baptismal formula— "I baptize you in the name . . ."—in the conferral of baptism, Tertullian witnesses to a three-fold interrogation and response as the "form" of this rite. That is, after responding "I believe" to each of three credal questions (i.e., "Do you believe in God the Father, . . . in Jesus Christ, . . . and in the Holy Spirit . . . ?") the baptismal candidate was submersed or immersed each time into the baptismal waters. "Thrice are we baptized into each of the three persons at each of

[71] *Against Praxeas* 28, as cited by McDonnell, *The Baptism of Jesus in the Jordan*, 115.

[72] DBL, 9; emphasis added.

64

the several names," writes Tertullian (*Adversus Praxean*, 20).[73] Although this kind of interrogation may also have been a part of the early Egyptian tradition, as we have seen, such will be the way in which baptism itself is administered for several centuries within Western Christianity.

He was against Infant Baptism

Finally, Tertullian is the first known witness to the custom of infant baptism in the Church, a practice he does not like. In a strong and rather modern-sounding protest that actually serves to demonstrate its obvious and widespread acceptance in North Africa, including the existence of sponsors or godparents, he says:

Tertullian - on Infant Baptism

"It follows that deferment of baptism is more profitable, in accordance with each person's character and attitude, and even age: and especially so as regards children. For what need is there, if there really is no need, for even their sponsors to be brought into peril, seeing they may possibly themselves fail of their promises by death, or be deceived by the subsequent development of an evil disposition? It is true our Lord says, *Forbid them not to come to me* [Matt 19:14]. So let them come when they are growing up, when they are learning, when they are being taught what they are coming to: let them be made Christians when they have become competent to know Christ. Why should innocent infancy come with haste to the remission of sins? Shall we take less cautious action in this than we take in worldly matters? Shall one who is not trusted with earthly property be entrusted with heavenly? Let them first learn how to ask for salvation, so that you may be seen to have given to one that asketh" (*De baptismo* 18).[74]

Because Tertullian knows well the problems associated with the forgiveness of serious postbaptismal sin—a once in a lifetime(!) possibility after baptism consisting of a lengthy period of public penance before reconciliation with the Church[75]—his concern here, undoubtedly,

---

[73] Ibid.

[74] Ibid., 8–9.

[75] On the early history of what came to be known as the system of "canonical penance," long before the custom of individual sacramental confession and absolution became known, see James Dallen, *The Reconciling Community: The Rite of Penance* (Collegeville: The Liturgical Press, 1986). Tertullian's own treatise, *De paenitentia* (On Penance) is itself the earliest document describing this process in detail. See ANF 3, 657–68.

is to spare both children and their sponsors from any eventual need to undertake what was a rather harsh penitential discipline. And since those serious sins included both fornication and adultery it is not only children but also unmarried adults that Tertullian seeks to spare. "With no less reason," he continues, "ought the unmarried also to be delayed until they either marry or are firmly established in continence" (*De baptismo* 18).[76] That Tertullian's protest here against the baptism of infants and the unmarried was ignored, however, is easily demonstrated by subsequent history.

Cyprian of Carthage. Cyprian, the great bishop of Carthage and influential leader of North African Christianity from 248 C.E. through both the Decian and Valerian persecutions until his martyrdom on September 14, 258 C.E., is a significant witness primarily to the theology of Christian initiation in the early Church. What is known from him of the rites of Christian initiation themselves tends to parallel closely the ritual pattern we saw above in Tertullian. In fact, the only additional information about the rites that Cyprian provides is that:

(1) the oil or "chrism" used for the one postbaptismal anointing is consecrated or "sanctified" on the altar within the context of the Eucharistic Liturgy (*Letter 70, to Januarius*, 2);[77]
(2) the question, "Dost thou believe in eternal life and remission of sins through the holy church?" (*Letter 70, to Januarius*, 1), was part of the baptismal interrogations; and
(3) it is to the *bishops* that the newly baptized are immediately brought in order that "by our prayers and by the imposition of the hand [they might] obtain the Holy Spirit, and [be] perfected with the Lord's seal [*signaculo dominico*]" (*Letter 73, to Jubaianus*, 9).[78]

Concerning the last of the above additions, two crucial aspects are to be noted. First, Cyprian's reference to "the Lord's seal" or "sign," in light of a discussion about it in another of his works,[79] is certainly to be interpreted here as a signing with the cross, or "consignation," of the foreheads of the newly baptized at the conclusion of the

---

[76] DBL, 9.
[77] Ibid., 11.
[78] Ibid.
[79] See his treatise entitled, *To Demetrianus*, 22, in ANF 5, 476.

bishop's handlaying ceremony. In comparison to the rite described by Tertullian, where this signing is said to take place between the post-baptismal anointing and the imposition of the hand, Cyprian is a witness to change and further development within the North African rite. Second, when stating that it is bishops who perform the post-baptismal rites of handlaying and "sealing," Cyprian also becomes the first writer in the early Church to cite the Acts 8 event of Peter and John laying hands on the Samaritan converts as justification for this practice.[80] Postbaptismal rites of handlaying and consignation explicitly connected to the ministry of bishops and justified theologically by appeals to apostolic precedent on the basis of Acts 8 will have a long and influential history in the evolution and interpretation of the rites of Christian initiation in the West.

Cyprian's theology of Christian initiation is significant and influential in other areas as well. With regard to infant baptism, for example, Cyprian is a staunch defender of it. While Tertullian protested strongly against the practice, it fell to Cyprian to offer the beginnings of a theological rationale *for* it. In response to a bishop Fidus, who apparently had argued on the basis of Jewish circumcision that infants should not be baptized until they were eight days old, Cyprian reports the decision of a recent synod, saying:

"If anything could hinder men from obtaining grace, their more heinous sins might rather hinder those who are mature and grown up and older. But again, if even to the greatest sinners, and to those who had sinned much against God, when they subsequently believed, remission of sins is granted—and nobody is hindered from baptism and from grace—how much rather ought we to shrink from hindering an infant, who being lately born, has not sinned, except in that, being born of the flesh according to Adam, he has contracted the contagion of the ancient death at its earliest birth, who approaches the more easily on this very account to the reception of the forgiveness of sins—that to him are remitted, not his own sins, but the sins of another. And therefore, dearest brother, this was our opinion in council, that by us no one ought to be hindered from baptism and from the grace of God, who is merciful and kind and loving to all" (*Epistle* 64).[81]

---

[80] See the full text of his *Letter 73, to Jubaianus,* 9, in ANF 5, 349.
[81] ANF 5, 354.

To this Cyprian adds his own support for the almost immediate baptism of infants: "We think [baptism] is to be even more observed in respect of infants and newly-born persons, who on this very account deserve more from our help and from the divine mercy, that immediately, on the very beginning of their birth, *lamenting and weeping, they do nothing else but entreat.*"[82]

Cyprian's appeal to the cries of newly-born babies aside, what is significant in the above text is that it shows the *beginnings* of a theology of original sin in relationship to baptism based on the inheritance of that sin from Adam. To be precise, however, what is inherited, according to Cyprian, is "the contagion of the ancient *death* at *its* earliest birth," rather than "original sin" per se. Furthermore, since this "sin" is still that of another (i.e., of Adam) and not their own, infants themselves remain innocent.

Closely related to his defense of infant baptism is the fact that Cyprian is also the first undisputed witness to the practice of baptized infants—like adults—also receiving communion both at the conclusion of the baptismal rite (i.e., as their "first communion") and as a subsequent and regular practice as they participate in the ongoing liturgical life of the community. In an important study of "infant communion" in the history of the Western churches, Canadian Anglican scholar David Holeton provides the following summary of Cyprian's theology:

"Cyprian gives us what appears to be an already developed theology of the practice as well as several illustrations of infant communion. First, he bears witness to the coupling of John 3:5 ('Unless a man be born again of water and the Spirit . . .') and John 6:53 ('Unless you eat the flesh of the Son of Man . . .') as a single *logion* in the *traditio fidei,* establishing what is necessary for participation in the Christian community. Infants are as capable of baptism as are adults and share equally in the divine gift given in baptism. Having thus been baptized in the Spirit the newborn drink thereon from the Lord's cup, and are thus both 'baptized and sanctified' (*'baptizandum et sanctificandum'*). It is baptism and eucharist which establish membership in the Christian community. Membership in the community thereafter depends, for Cyprian, on continued participation in the

---

[82] Ibid. [emphasis added].

eucharist. . . . [F]or Cyprian the eucharist is as necessary for the Christian as is baptism, and for both sacraments age is unimportant. Baptism and the eucharist are inseparable and for Cyprian it is the eucharist that creates the Christian community. To abandon the eucharist is to abandon the community and to abandon either is to abandon Christ."[83]

Such a practice and theological understanding, as we shall see in subsequent chapters, continues still today in the churches of the Christian East and was maintained in the Latin West as well for at least the first millennium.

Finally, Cyprian of Carthage is important also for the role he played in an important third-century controversy with Stephen, bishop of Rome (254–7 C.E.), over the question of the appropriate liturgical rites to be used for the reconciliation of heretics and schismatics who sought to return to the unity of the Church. This controversy, it seems, was precipitated initially by what is referred to as the "Novatianist Schism," a split in the church at Rome resulting in a rather puritanical and exclusivist Christian sect of "Novatianists" which refused to readmit to communion any who had lapsed (i.e., denied the Christian faith) during the recent Decian persecution of 250 C.E. Established in opposition to the church of Rome and its duly elected bishop Cornelius in 251 C.E., who permitted the reconciliation of those who had lapsed after a period of penance, this sect, under the leadership of its own bishop, Novatian, saw itself as the only legitimate Church. Excommunicated, rightly or wrongly, as "heretical," the continued existence of a Novatianist church raised the question of the validity of the sacraments administered by those outside the unity of the Church and it is within this context that the real controversy arose.

In several of his letters, Cyprian follows the traditional teaching of the North African church[84] and stresses the invalidity of baptism given by heretics and schismatics alike. Baptism administered outside

---

[83] David Holeton, *Infant Communion: Then and Now*, Grove Liturgical Study 27 (Bramcote, Nottingham: Grove Books, 1981) 5.

[84] See Tertullian, *De baptismo* 15, ANF 3, 676. For a recent study of the rebaptism controversy in the time of Cyprian see J. P. Burns, "On Rebaptism: Social Organization in the Third-Century Church," *Journal of Early Christian Studies* 1:4 (1993) 367–403.

of unity with the Catholic Church was invalid and so had to be repeated for those seeking to come back into unity because:

(1) "the Church alone has the living water, and the power of baptizing and cleansing man" (*Letter 69, to Magnus,* 3);[85]
(2) the "remission of sins cannot be given except by the holy Church" (*Letter 69, to Magnus,* 7);[86]
(3) heretics "have not the Holy Spirit," and so cannot give what they do not have (*Letter 69, to Magnus,* 11);[87]
(4) only those in authority in the Church founded on Peter and his power of binding and loosing are able to baptize and give the remission of sins (*Letter 73, to Jubaianus,* 2);[88] and
(5) there is simply "no salvation out of the Church," not even on the basis of confession (i.e., confessing the faith publicly in the face of persecution) and martyrdom (*Letter 73, to Jubaianus,* 21).[89]

So strong, in fact, is Cyprian's insistence on this proper and necessary ecclesiological context of baptism that "he can no longer have God for his Father, who has not the Church for his mother" (*De unitate ecclesiae,* "On the Unity of the Church," 5).[90]

Cyprian is careful not to call what he considers the "necessary" baptism of heretics and schismatics a "re-baptism." Since baptism itself did not exist outside of the Church, "those who come thence are not *re-baptized* among us, but are baptized" (*Letter 71, to Quintus,* 1).[91] But it is on this point that Cyprian and Stephen enter a profound disagreement, a disagreement that seriously threatened to break off communion between the churches of North Africa and Rome. Geoffrey Willis writes that "the Church of Rome took the more liberal view that baptism administered in the name of the Blessed Trinity, and with the intention of incorporating a man into the Church, was valid even if administered by heretics and schismatics."[92] At Rome itself, those bap-

---

[85] ANF 5, 398.
[86] Ibid., 399.
[87] Ibid., 400.
[88] Ibid., 380.
[89] Ibid., 384.
[90] Ibid., 423.
[91] Ibid., 388.
[92] Geoffrey Willis, *Saint Augustine and the Donatist Controversy* (London: SPCK, 1950) 147–8.

tized in schism or heresy, were merely received back into communion, as in the reconciliation of apostates and penitents, by the imposition or laying on of hands by the bishop. They were not (re-)baptized. Stephen is so adamant about this as the practice to be followed, a practice based, in his opinion, on the authority of St. Peter the Apostle himself, that he threatens breaking off communion with the North African church if they continue in this "innovative" manner.

For his part, however, Cyprian's arguments were based on the decisions of the Council of Carthage (220 C.E.), presided over by his immediate predecessor Agrippinus. This council had decided in favor of "re-baptism" and this is the traditional view that Cyprian vigorously defends. Under Cyprian's leadership, in fact, three other councils were held at Carthage in order to discuss this matter further (one in 255 C.E. and two in 256 C.E.). And, in spite of Stephen's threats, the North African tradition of "re-baptism" was upheld. In Cyprian's own words at this third and final council on the subject: "According to evangelical and apostolic testimony, heretics, who are called adversaries of Christ and Antichrists, when they come to the Church, must be baptized with the one baptism of the Church, that they may be made of adversaries, friends, and of Antichrists, Christians."[93] These words of Cyprian were the sacramental and doctrinal norm for the North African church. As there was only *one* Church there could only be *one* baptism. Even if properly celebrated and administered elsewhere, it could not and did not exist outside of unity with the one Church.

While history shows that it was the view of Stephen and the church of Rome that ultimately triumphed in this controversy, the problem remained unresolved in the life times of both Cyprian and Stephen (+ 257) themselves, both of whom suffered martyrdom during the Valerian persecution. Furthermore, as we shall see, the early North African tradition of requiring re-baptism for heretics and schismatics will return with a vengeance in the fourth century and beyond in what is called the "Donatist Controversy" during the episcopate of Augustine of Hippo.

Rome

In light of the liturgical sources and documents we have from other traditions in early Christianity, it is frustrating that the evidence for the evolution and interpretation of the rites of Christian initiation

[93] "The Seventh Council of Carthage under Cyprian," ANF 5, 572.

71

within the highly important and influential church of Rome during the first three centuries is so limited. Justin Martyr's mid-second-century description of those rites in his *First Apology* 61 and 65, written in Rome and addressed to the emperor, as we have seen,[94] is probably general enough in its details to present a universal outline of the baptismal ritual, even if his particular theology of baptism appears to be more Syrian than Western in orientation. But, apart from Justin's brief description, the only other undisputed evidence we have for this early period is a reference in an early-third-century *Commentary on Daniel*, written by a Hippolytus of Rome, who, like Novatian above, was a schismatic, rigorist, and conservative bishop set up in opposition to the current bishop of Rome, Callistus (217–22 C.E.). In commenting on Daniel 13:15, Hippolytus writes:

"On that day [the pasch] the bath is prepared in the Garden for those who are burning and the Church . . . is presented to God as a pure bride; and faith and charity, like her [Susanna's] companions, prepare the oil and the unguents for those being washed. What are the unguents but the commandments of the Word? What is the oil but the power of the Holy Spirit, with which, like perfume, believers are anointed after the bath?"[95]

While this might not appear as much, Hippolytus *does* witness here to the custom of paschal (Easter) baptism at Rome in the early third century and to the fact that the rite of baptism there did include a postbaptismal anointing. Such, as we have seen, are characteristics of the North African rites as well.

The (so-called) Apostolic Tradition, ascribed to Hippolytus of Rome (ca. 215 C.E.). The name of Hippolytus of Rome, however, is most important because of another document which has been ascribed to him frequently by contemporary scholars, i.e., the so-called *Apostolic Tradition, a church* order of forty-three chapters concerned with various liturgical rites and other ecclesiastical issues.[96] Of these forty-three

---

[94] See above, 37–41.

[95] SC 14, 100. English translation by Paul Bradshaw, "'*Diem baptismo sollemniorem*': Initiation and Easter in Christian Antiquity," LWSS, 138.

[96] The critical edition is that of Bernard Botte, *La Tradition apostolique de saint Hippolyte* (Münster Westfalen: Aschendorffsche, 1963). See also Jean

chapters, chapters 15–21 deal with the catechumenate and the rites of
Christian initiation.

According to this document, those who wish to become catechumens (i.e., "hearers of the word") are presented to the "teachers" by
their "sponsors," who must testify about the manner of their life and
their motives in seeking to become Christians (ch. 15). A section follows (ch. 16) outlining several crafts and professions which are considered to be forbidden, such as brothel keepers, idol makers, actors,
teachers, charioteers, gladiators, pagan priests, soldiers, magistrates,
magicians, charmers, astrologers, unfaithful concubines, men who
keep concubines, and prostitutes and others involved in what are
considered to be sexually perverse practices. Only after those involved in such crafts and professions agree to renounce them are
they admitted into the catechumenate.

"Catechumens shall continue to hear the word for three years" (ch.
17), during which time they are to pray by themselves in the liturgical assembly, apart from the faithful. They are not to participate in
sharing the kiss of peace at the conclusion of prayer, "for their kiss is
not yet holy" (ch. 18). Rather, at the end of prayer, they are dismissed
from the assembly by the teacher, whether ordained or lay, with a rite
consisting of an imposition of hands (ch. 19). At the end of this
"three-year" catechumenal process, "those who are to receive baptism are chosen" (ch. 20). During this final period of immediate
preparation they are now examined again as to the quality and conduct of their lives while catechumens ("Have they honoured the wid-
ows? Have they visited the sick? Have they done every kind of good
work?" [ch. 20]). From the time of their election until the day of their
baptism, an unspecified period of time in the text, they are to be exorcized daily by the teachers, and, finally, by the bishop himself "in

---

Michel Hanssens, *La Liturgie d'Hippolyte* (Rome: Pont. Institutum Orientalium
Studiorum, 1959), and Gregory Dix, ed., *The Treatise on the Apostolic Tradition
of St. Hippolytus of Rome* (Ridgefield, Conn.: Morehouse Publishers, 1992). The
best available English translation, which is regularly cited in this chapter, is
that of Geoffrey J. Cuming, *Hippolytus: A Text for Students,* Grove Liturgical
Study 8 (Bramcote, Nottingham: Grove Books, 1976). With Paul Bradshaw
and L. Edward Phillips I am involved in the preparation of new edition of
this document with commentary, forthcoming from Fortress Press in the
Hermeneia commentary series.

order that he may know whether he is pure" (ch. 20). At this point, from the middle of chapter 20 through the end of chapter 21, the document presents us with the following detailed account of the rites themselves:[97]

"(Chapter 20): Those who are to be baptized should be instructed to bathe and wash themselves on the Thursday. And if a woman is in her period, let her be put aside, and receive baptism another day. Those who are to receive baptism shall fast on the Friday. On the Saturday those who are to receive baptism shall be gathered in one place at the bishop's decision. They shall all be told to pray and kneel. And he shall lay his hand on them and exorcize all alien spirits, that they may flee out of them and never return into them. And when he has finished exorcizing them, he shall breathe on their faces; and when he has signed their foreheads, ears, and noses, he shall raise them up.

"And they shall spend the whole night in vigil; they shall be read to and instructed. Those who are to be baptized shall not bring with them any other thing, except what each brings for the eucharist. For it is suitable that he who has been made worthy should offer an offering then.

"(Chapter 21): At the time when the cock crows, first let prayer be made over the water. Let the water be flowing in the font or poured over it. Let it be thus unless there is some necessity; if the necessity is permanent and urgent, use what water you can find. They shall take off their clothes. Baptize the little ones first. All those who can speak for themselves shall do so. As for those who cannot speak for themselves, their parents or someone from their family shall speak for them. Then baptize the men, and lastly the women, who shall have loosened all their hair, and laid down the gold and silver ornaments which they have on them. Let no one take any alien object down into the water.

"And at the time fixed for baptizing, the bishop shall give thanks over the oil, which he puts in a vessel: one calls it 'oil of thanksgiving.' And he shall also take other oil and exorcize it: one calls it 'oil of exorcism.' And a deacon takes the oil of exorcism and stands on the

[97] Text cited from Cuming, *Hippolytus,* 17–22.

priest's left; and another deacon takes the oil of thanksgiving and stands on the priest's right. And when the priest takes each one of those who are to receive baptism, he shall bid him renounce, saying: I renounce you, Satan, and all your service and all your works. And when each one has renounced all this, he shall anoint him with the oil of exorcism, saying to him: Let every spirit depart from you. And in this way he shall hand him over naked to the bishop or the priest who stands by the water to baptize. In the same way a deacon shall descend with him into the water and say, helping him to say: I believe in one God, the Father almighty. . . . And he who receives shall say, according to all this: I believe in this way. And the giver, having his hand placed on his head, shall baptize him once. And then he shall say: Do you believe in Christ Jesus, the Son of God, who was born from the holy Spirit from the Virgin Mary, and was crucified under Pontius Pilate, and died, and rose again on the third day alive from the dead, and ascended into heaven, and sits at the right hand of the Father, and will come to judge the living and the dead? And when he has said, 'I believe,' he shall be baptized again. And he shall say again: Do you believe in the holy Spirit and the holy Church and the resurrection of the flesh? Then he who is being baptized shall say, 'I believe,' and thus he shall be baptized a third time.

"And then, when he has come up, he shall be anointed from the oil of thanksgiving by the presbyter, who says: I anoint you with holy oil in the name of Jesus Christ.

"And so each of them shall wipe themselves and put on their clothes, and then they shall enter into the church.

"And the bishop shall lay his hands on them and invoke, saying: Lord God, you have made them worthy to receive remission of sins through the laver of regeneration of the holy Spirit: send upon them your grace, that they may serve you according to your will; for to you is glory, to Father and Son with the holy Spirit in the holy Church, both now and to the ages of ages. Amen.

"Then, pouring the oil of thanksgiving from his hand and placing it on his head, he shall say: I anoint you with holy oil in God the Father almighty and Christ Jesus and the holy Spirit. And having signed him on the forehead, he shall give him a kiss and say: The Lord be with you. And he who has been signed shall say: And with your spirit.

"So let him do with each one. And then they shall pray together with all the people: they do not pray with the faithful until they have carried out all these things. And when they have prayed, they shall give the kiss of peace.

"And then the offering shall be presented by the deacons to the bishop; and he shall give thanks over the bread for the representation, which the Greeks call 'antitype,' of the body of Christ; and over the cup mixed with wine for the antitype, which the Greeks call 'likeness,' of the blood which was shed for all who have believed in him; and over milk and honey mixed together in fulfillment of the promise which was made to the fathers, in which he said, 'a land flowing with milk and honey,' in which also Christ gave his flesh, through which those who believe are nourished like little children, making the bitterness of the heart sweet by the gentleness of his word; and over water, as an offering to signify the washing, that the inner man also, which is the soul, may receive the same thing as the body. And the bishop shall give a reason for all these things to those who receive.

"And when he breaks the bread, in distributing fragments to each, he shall say: The bread of heaven in Christ Jesus. And he who receives shall answer: Amen.

"And if there are not enough presbyters, the deacons also shall hold the cups, and stand by in good order and reverence: first, he who holds the water; second, the milk; third, the wine. And they who receive shall taste of each thrice, he who gives it saying: In God the Father Almighty. And he who receives shall say: Amen. And in the Lord Jesus Christ. (Amen). And in the holy Spirit and the holy Church. And he shall say: Amen. So shall it be done with each one.

"When these things have been done, each one shall hasten to do good works and to please God and to conduct himself rightly, being zealous for the Church, doing what he has learnt and advancing in piety.

"We have handed over to you in brief these things about holy baptism and the holy offering, for you have already been instructed about the resurrection of the flesh and the other things as it is written. But if there is anything else which ought to be said, the bishop shall say it privately to those who have received baptism. Unbelievers must not get to know it, unless they first receive baptism. This is

76

the white stone of which John said, 'A new name is written on it, which no one knows except him who receives the stone.'"

In broad outline, at least, the above description of the initiation rites from this *Apostolic Tradition* shows a ritual pattern quite similar to what we saw in the third-century North African liturgical tradition above. Such similarities include a blessing of the baptismal waters, a renunciation of Satan, a profession of faith in an interrogatory form connected closely with the submersion or immersion itself, a postbaptismal anointing, a handlaying prayer associated with the bishop, a consignation, and a culminating participation in the Eucharist, which includes even the cup(s) of milk and honey, which Aidan Kavanagh has referred to as "a gustatory icon of the promised land."[98] A comparison of the forbidden crafts and professions in chapter 16 with a number of Tertullian's writings would also show a common early Christian attitude about morality with many of the same crafts and professions dismissed by him as highly inappropriate for Christians.[99] And, the references to "those who cannot speak for themselves" in chapter 20 would seem to indicate as well that, as in Cyprian, infants are among the candidates for Christian initiation in this community.

It would seem, then, that chapters 15–21 of this *Apostolic Tradition* do present us with a ritual shape and general content highly consistent with what is known of Western liturgical practice elsewhere in the early to mid third century. Where it differs most obviously from what we have seen in North Africa is in the specific contents of the postbaptismal handlaying prayer by the bishop and in the additional second anointing by the bishop at the end of this prayer. And yet a postbaptismal ritual structure consisting of an anointing by a presbyter, a prayer with imposition of hands by the bishop, and a second anointing by the bishop with consignation is precisely the pattern of the postbaptismal rites as they will develop in Rome. As such, there would appear to be little basis for disagreeing with the traditional scholarly opinion that this document reflects the practice of the *Roman* church at the time of Hippolytus himself.

[98] Aidan Kavanagh, "A Rite of Passage," *The Three Days: Parish Prayer in the Paschal Triduum*, Gabe Huck (Chicago: Liturgy Training Publications, 1981) 110.

[99] Cf. *De idolatria* (On Idolatry), ANF 3, 61–78; *De corona* (The Chaplet or Crown), ANF 3, 93–104; and *De spectaculis* (The Shows), ANF 3, 79–92.

But can we be so certain of this? Some familiarity with the various textual problems in the history of the document can be of great assistance here. The *Apostolic Tradition* does not exist as an early and complete text anywhere. While written originally in Greek, only a few fragments of the Greek text appear elsewhere in Christian literature of the fourth century. But *none* of these fragments contain the materials on the catechumenate or the initiation rites. The earliest version of the document we possess is a Latin translation in a late-fifth-century manuscript from Verona, Italy, which scholars generally believe represents a mid-fourth-century text (ca. 350 C.E.). Unfortunately, however, this Latin translation is not complete, with "one gap . . . of six pages, and two gaps of two pages each."[100] Whatever the original Greek text of the *Apostolic Tradition* may have been, then, we simply do not know. And even if the original Greek text reflected early-third-century *Roman* practice we cannot be certain that this Latin translation itself does not reflect subsequent development and expansion beyond what the Greek would have been. Similarly, a *translation*, especially of church order materials, a genre of "living literature" notorious for *prescribing* as well as describing practice,[101] does not necessarily equal immediate adoption and liturgical use. Beyond this earliest extant Latin version, it is important to be aware that translations of the document also appear in Sahidic Coptic (eleventh-century manuscript), Arabic (fourteenth-century manuscript), Ethiopic (fifteenth-century manuscript), and Bohairic Coptic (nineteenth-century manuscript). Hence, scholars have had to depend on these "Oriental" versions, as well as on possible parallels in other early Christian literature (e.g., the *Canons of Hippolytus*), in order to attempt a reconstruction of what the original text might have been.

These textual problems have a direct relationship to the catechumenate and the rites of Christian initiation in the document. Since chapters 15 through the first baptismal interrogation in the middle of chapter 21 fall into the gaps in the fifth-century Latin version, as does the material coming immediately after the distribution of communion in chapter 21, what we "know" of the catechumenate and the first part of the initiation rites in this so-called *Apostolic Tradition* is actu-

---

[100] Cuming, *Hippolytus*, 6.

[101] On this see Bradshaw, *The Search for the Origins of Christian Worship*, 80–110.

ally supplied from the much later Oriental versions. While much of this, as we have seen, is paralleled in the writings of Tertullian, especially the materials related to forbidden crafts and professions, other elements in these chapters do not correspond to such an early historical context. For example, the earliest undisputed parallel we have to the "three-year catechumenate" of chapter 17 is a similar reference in a late-fourth-century Syrian document known as the *Apostolic Constitutions* (ca. 381 C.E.). Recall here from above that in *Canons of Hippolytus* 12, based on *some* version of *Apostolic Tradition* 17 available in the early fourth century, the reference is not to "three years" but, rather, "forty days" of catechesis. And, at the same time, clear references to "daily exorcism" as part of final preparation for baptism (ch. 20) and prebaptismal anointings with an "oil of exorcism" (ch. 21) also find their parallel only within fourth-century documents. Although none of this proves that such practices could not have existed in the Roman church of the early third century, the lack of parallels in other texts of the same time period should make us rather cautious about assuming uncritically that they did.

As we have seen, traditional scholarship, represented especially by Gregory Dix and Bernard Botte, claimed that this *Apostolic Tradition*, as reconstructed from the various extant manuscripts and editions, was an early-third-century document "written" by Hippolytus of Rome himself (ca. 215 C.E.). Contemporary work on this document, however, is challenging strongly these earlier and widely-held conclusions.[102] Concerning the rites of initiation, in particular, Paul Bradshaw has recently surveyed the work of a few scholars who have argued that the initiation materials actually reflect at least two different sources, a possibly older Roman core (focusing on the role of the bishop) and a later North African source (with more detailed instructions regarding the roles of presbyters and deacons) which were conflated to produce the final form of the text.[103] Bradshaw himself goes

---

[102] Cf. M. Metzger, "Nouvelles perspectives pour la prétendue *Tradition apostolique*," *Ecclesia Orans* 5 (1988) 241–59; M. Metzger, "Enquêtes autour de la prétendue *Tradition apostolique*," *Ecclesia Orans* 9 (1992) 7–36; and M. Metzger, "A propos des règlements écclesiastiques et de la prétendue *Tradition apostolique*," *Revue des sciences religieuses* 66 (1992) 249–61.

[103] See Paul F. Bradshaw, "Re-dating the Apostolic Tradition: Some Preliminary Steps," *Rule of Prayer, Rule of Faith: Essays in Honor of Aidan Kavanagh, O.S.B.*, ed. John Baldovin and Nathan Mitchell (Collegeville: The Liturgical

beyond this and suggests that in addition to specific "sources," which may have been used or conflated in the development of the text, there were possibly three distinct stages in its evolution.

First, the earliest text of the initiation rites in this document, according to Bradshaw, would probably have been something like the following:

"At the time when the cock crows, first let prayer be made over the water. Let the water be (pure and) flowing [in the font or poured over it].[104] Let it be thus unless there is some necessity; if the necessity is permanent and urgent, use what water you can find. They shall take off their clothes. Baptize the little ones first. All those who can speak for themselves shall do so. As for those who cannot speak for themselves, their parents or someone from their family shall speak for them. Then baptize the men, and lastly the women, who shall have loosened all their hair, and laid down the gold and silver ornaments which they have on them. Let no one take any alien object down into the water.

"As he who is to be baptized is descending into the water, let him who baptizes him say thus [as he lays his hand upon him], 'Do you believe in God the Father omnipotent?' And let the one being baptized say, 'I believe.'[105] And the giver . . . shall baptize him once. And

---

Press, 1996) 3–17. Bradshaw surveys the contributions of Jean Paul Bouhot, *La confirmation, sacrement de la communion ecclésiale* (Lyon: Editions du Chalet, 1968) 38–45, R. Cabié, "L'ordo de l'Initiation chrétienne dans la 'Tradition apostolique' d'Hippolyte de Rome," *Mens concordet voci, pour Mgr. A. G. Martimort* (Paris: Desclee, 1983) 543–58, and Victor Saxer, *Les rites de l'initiation chrétienne du IIe au VIe siécle* (Spoletto: Centro italiano di studi sullálto Medioevo, 1988) 118–9.

[104] According to Bradshaw, the specific reference to a "font" probably reflects "later terminology," since both the *Canons of Hippolytus* and the *Testamentum Domini*, a late-fourth- or early-fifth-century Syrian church order also derived in part from the *Apostolic Tradition*, only speak of "pure and flowing water."

[105] This part of the text, following Bradshaw's suggested reconstruction, is taken from the version preserved in the *Testamentum Domini*, according to the translation of Grant Sperry-White, *The Testamentum Domini: A Text for Students*, Alcuin/GROW Liturgical Study 19 (Bramcote, Nottingham: Grove Books, 1991) 28.

then he shall say: 'Do you believe in Christ Jesus, the Son of God . . . ?'
And when he has said, 'I believe,' he shall be baptized again. And he
shall say again: 'Do you believe in the holy Spirit . . . ?' Then he who
is being baptized shall say, 'I believe,' and thus he shall be baptized a
third time.

"And so each of them shall wipe themselves and put on their clothes,
and then they shall enter into the church. . . . And then they shall
pray together with all the people: they do not pray with the faithful
until they have carried out all these things. And when they have
prayed, they shall give the kiss of peace."

If his suggested reconstruction here of an earlier stratum in the text
is correct, there is no reason why this part of *Apostolic Tradition* 21
could not have been in existence already in the mid to late second
century. As Bradshaw notes, such a rite would have some parallel
both to the baptismal instructions in *Didache* 7 and to the description
of the baptismal rites and credal formulae noted by Justin Martyr in
his *First Apology.*

Second, the next stage in this evolution would have been the addition of those ceremonies assigned to the bishop alone, namely: the
postbaptismal prayer with the imposition of hands, the episcopal
anointing, the kiss, and the greeting ("The Lord be with you") of the
neophyte ("newly born" or "newly baptized"). Third, and finally, the
more detailed instructions pertaining to presbyters and deacons (e.g.,
the prebaptismal rites of blessing of oils, renunciation, and anointing
with "exorcised oil," and the presbyteral postbaptismal anointing)
would have been the last elements added to produce the final form
of the text. Bradshaw writes: "Not only does the more detailed character of these instructions suggest that they belong to a later date, but
we have no other evidence for the use of oil for prebaptismal exorcism prior to the middle of the fourth century." Consequently, he
concludes that "the resultant composition" of *Apostolic Tradition* 21,
most likely completed by ca. 325, "is . . . not a single coherent rite as
practiced by a particular local church but a conflation of different traditions from different periods, and very probably different places."[106]

One of the major problems with interpreting the rites of initiation in
this document has been the precise contents of the bishop's handlaying

---

[106] Bradshaw, "Re-dating the Apostolic Tradition," 12.

prayer in chapter 21. No one reading the *Latin* text of this prayer, as printed above, would automatically conclude that the prayer—or the bishop's anointing, for that matter—is related to the giving of the Holy Spirit, as is stated for a similar gesture and prayer in the North African sources we have seen. Rather, the Latin version of the bishop's prayer for the imposition of hands on the neophyte is a prayer not for the gift of the Holy Spirit but for *grace:* "send upon them your grace, that they may serve you according to your will." And the operating assumption in this prayer is that the gift of the Holy Spirit is not subsequent to baptism but already given in and connected to the water rite itself: "Lord God, you have made them worthy to receive remission of sins through the laver of regeneration of the holy Spirit." It is here where the problems begin. Instead of stating "Lord God, you have made them worthy to receive remission of sins through the laver of regeneration of the holy Spirit" all of the Oriental versions omit "of the holy Spirit." And, before continuing with the petition for grace, all of these versions add something like: "make them worthy to be filled with [your] Holy Spirit."[107] In other words, by asking explicitly for the Holy Spirit in this prayer, all of the Oriental versions of *Apostolic Tradition* more closely parallel the evidence provided by both Tertullian and Cyprian for North Africa.

In the history of scholarship there has been a long debate over whether the Latin text is corrupt here and whether the explicit language about the bestowal of the Holy Spirit, in addition to grace, in the Oriental versions is to be preferred. Gregory Dix, for example, was so convinced of the corrupt nature of the Verona Latin at this point that, while normally following the Latin text throughout his edition, he based his English translation of *this* prayer upon the Oriental versions and entitled the entire section, "Confirmation."[108] Along similar lines, Bernard Botte suggested that a line referring to the gift of the Holy Spirit in this prayer had been left out here from either the Verona Latin translation or the Greek original.[109] But the scholarly evaluation of the Latin text has changed since the work of both Dix and Botte. G.W.H. Lampe, for example, noted that there are no grammatical problems with the Latin at this point and that the

[107] DBL, 6.
[108] Dix, *The Treatise on the Apostolic Tradition of St. Hippolytus of Rome,* 38.
[109] Botte, *La Tradition apostolique de saint Hippolyte,* 53.

text as it stands translates quite clearly.[110] It is the Latin text of this prayer that Geoffrey Cuming translated in his edition.[111] And, more recently, Aidan Kavanagh has argued strongly for the reliability of the Latin, saying:

"While it is true that translations of *[Apostolic Tradition]* in other languages such as Arabic and Ethiopic render the 'Lord God' prayer as an epiclesis of the Holy Spirit, these texts are very much later than the Verona Latin version, which was done c. 350; the Arabic and Ethiopic versions date from the thirteenth century, over nine centuries later. The probability is strong that these later translations represent a development . . . on this matter which was unknown when the document was written and the Verona translation was made. . . . The text of the 'Lord God' prayer in the Verona translation clearly associates the Holy Spirit with *baptism*, the 'bath of regeneration of the Holy Spirit,' in complete harmony with Titus 3.5 and John 3.5. *[Apostolic Tradition]* is not alone in this. Later Western baptismal allusions make similar associations."[112]

In the subsequent development of the *Roman* rites of Christian initiation a handlaying prayer like this, together with a second anointing, will become closely associated with the gift of the Holy Spirit and will be reserved exclusively to the bishop. Similarly, this episcopal rite, in time, will break off from the unitive rite of Christian initiation as a whole and become a separate sacramental rite called "confirmation." But the explicit *Roman* evidence for the association of this prayer and anointing with both the Holy Spirit and the bishop, as we shall see, comes to us only in the second decade of the *fifth* century. What, then, does this bishop's rite signify in the *Latin* text of this document?

Aidan Kavanagh has argued that these episcopal rites of handlaying and anointing in *Apostolic Tradition* 21 reflect only the traditional structure of what may be termed an episcopal *missa*, that is a "dismissal" of

---

[110] See Geoffrey W. H. Lampe, *The Seal of the Spirit* (London: SPCK, 1967) 138–41.

[111] Cuming, *Hippolytus*, 20.

[112] Aidan Kavanagh, *Confirmation: Origins and Reform* (New York: Pueblo, 1988) 47. See also his "Confirmation: A Suggestion from Structure," LWSS, 148–58.

various categories of people from the liturgical assembly (e.g., catechumens and penitents) as was known to happen frequently in
Christian antiquity. Various groups of people, before leaving the
liturgical assembly, would go before the bishop and receive, often by
a handlaying rite, his blessing. In the case of Christian initiation in
Apostolic Tradition, just as these newly baptized had often been "dismissed" from both catechetical instruction and from liturgical gatherings by a rite which included the laying on of hands (see ch. 19), so
now, according to Kavanagh, they are again dismissed by means of a
similar ritual structure, but this time the "dismissal" is *from* the baptismal bath *to* the eucharistic table. While later this dismissal rite
would develop theologically into a postbaptismal conferral of the
Holy Spirit and be ultimately separated from baptism itself, the origins of what will be this later "confirmation" rite are *structural* rather
than theological.[113]

Kavanagh's intriguing view has not been received without criti-
cism. Paul Turner has questioned his understanding of these episcopal acts as constituting an actual "dismissal." While dismissals do
happen frequently in early Christian liturgy, they are not dismissals
from one liturgical rite into another but tend to take place only at the
conclusion of liturgical rites. To have such a *missa* right in the very
center of a rite, as Kavanagh maintains here, would thus be quite un-
characteristic in relation to the dismissal rites that are actually known
to us. Alternatively, Turner suggests that these episcopal acts of
handlaying and anointing should be viewed as "the first public gesture of ratification for the bishop and the faithful who did not witness the pouring of water," as it is quite clear that both baptism and
the presbyteral anointing happened at a place outside of the assembly itself.[114] In other words, this unit of the bishop's handlaying
prayer and anointing constitutes a rite of "welcome" rather than dismissal, a rite by which those newly born of water and the Holy Spirit
are now welcomed officially into the eucharistic communion of the
Church. And they are welcomed there by the chief pastor of the community, the bishop, who now prays for God's grace to guide them in
order that they might be faithful to what their baptism has already

[113] Kavanagh, "Confirmation: A Suggestion from Structure," 148.
[114] P. Turner, "The Origins of Confirmation: An Analysis of Aidan Kavanagh's Hypothesis," LWSS, 255.

made them to be. According to the Latin version of this document, the bishop's acts of handlaying and anointing have nothing explicit to do with the Holy Spirit because the Holy Spirit is connected to baptism itself.

Before leaving the *Apostolic Tradition,* one more thing should be noted. Since chapter 20 refers to the rites of initiation taking place at cockcrow on Sunday after an all-night Saturday vigil, it has often been assumed that it is the paschal (Easter) Vigil that is intended. While this *may,* in fact, be the case, the document does not say so explicitly. Not only were vigils a rather common practice in early Christianity, but chapter 33 of *Apostolic Tradition* refers to the annual celebration of Easter without any reference, whatsoever, to the rites of Christian initiation. While Hippolytus of Rome himself, like Tertullian and Cyprian, certainly knew paschal baptism, there is no evidence that the author of this text did. The most we can conclude, then, is that the rites were celebrated on Sundays.

What, then, may we say with certainty about the rites of Christian initiation and their interpretation in the Church at Rome in the first three centuries? Unfortunately, we cannot say a great deal. Apart from a couple of undisputed references (e.g., Justin Martyr and the *real* Hippolytus of Rome), much depends upon the authorship, location, and date of this so-called *Apostolic Tradition.* Given the close relationship between early Roman and North African Christianity in general, however, it is probably safe to assume that their liturgical practices were quite similar, and later Roman evidence would tend to confirm that general similarity. Nevertheless, beyond this probability we have to be content with knowing far less than has often been assumed.

CONCLUSION

This short study of the rites of Christian initiation in the pre-Nicene churches of East and West has shown considerable variety both in ritual structure and theological interpretation. At least three different ritual patterns have suggested themselves. As the following comparative chart demonstrates, first, as in Syria, and possibly in Egypt, we have seen a ritual structure consisting of anointing, baptism, and Eucharist. Second, as in North Africa, we have observed a ritual process of baptism, anointing, handlaying, and Eucharist. And third, as possibly in early Rome, and certainly in later Rome, we have noted an evolving pattern of baptism, anointing, handlaying, and a second postbaptismal anointing culminating in the Eucharist:

TABLE 2.1

Rites	Didache	Justin Martyr	Syrian Documents	Egypt	North Africa (Tertullian/Cyprian)	Rome (?) (Apostolic Tradition)
Preparation	Instruction in the "Two Ways" Two days of fasting in immediate preparation	Instruction in the "truth" Preparatory fasting and prayer	Catechesis (possibly three weeks in length)	Possibly "40 days" of catechesis after "Epiphany"; associated with Jesus' temptation	Catechesis of unspecified length; included vigils, fasting, prayer	Three-year catechumenate Election to baptism Immediate preparation; included fasting, prayer, daily exorcism
Prebaptismal			Anointing(s) as the high point of the rite associated with the gift of the Holy Spirit	Anointing associated with the Holy Spirit	Sanctification of the waters Renunciation	Blessing of water and oils Renunciation of Satan Anointing/exorcism
Baptism Proper	Baptism in "running water" with trinitarian formula	"Regenerated" and "enlightened" with possible interrogations	Baptism with trinitarian "formula": "new birth," "adoption"; possible use of Ps 2:7	"Regeneration" and "new birth," associated with crossing of the Jordan; formula or interrogation	Baptism connected to three-fold interrogation and profession of faith	Baptism connected to three-fold interrogation and profession of faith
Postbaptismal		Led to the assembly for common prayers and kiss			Anointing Handlaying related to Holy Spirit Consignation (Cyprian)	Anointing by presbyter Handlaying prayer for "grace" by bishop Anointing by bishop with consignation
Eucharist	Only for the baptized	Eucharist as culmination	Eucharist as culmination	Unclear if Eucharist was immediate culmination	Included "milk and honey"	Included "milk and honey"

Theologically as well, these various ritual patterns are interpreted according to differing dominant models. In early Syria and Egypt, the Jordan event of Jesus' baptism by John is the central paradigm. Together with the "new birth" theology of John 3:5 Christian initiation was interpreted as the means by which new converts became adopted as children of God and assimilated by the Holy Spirit to the life of the Messiah, Jesus Christ. The high point of the initiation ritual, at least in early Syria, is the prebaptismal anointing as the very *rushma* or sign of this new reality and identity. Alternatively, in North Africa, and possibly also in early Rome, the primary metaphor for baptism is that of Romans 6, the newly baptized's participation in the death, burial, and resurrection of Christ. As such, any prebaptismal rites tend to be associated with purification (North Africa) and even exorcism (compare with *Apostolic Tradition*) in preparation for the cleansing of the waters of baptism and the connected or subsequent gift of the Holy Spirit. In the East, we might say, the prebaptismal rites are oriented toward the reception of the *Holy* Spirit, while in the West the prebaptismal rites are oriented toward the expulsion of *evil* spirits.

Such differing theological emphases also have implications for how the catechumenate itself was structured and carried out. As we have seen for early Syria and Egypt, the catechumenate does not appear to be highly structured or formalized. In the early West, however, the catechumenal process seems to be quite formal and quite structured with rather detailed and specific instructions for catechumens and sponsors alike and with the *possibility* that it took three years to complete. Nevertheless, in both East and West, the overall purpose of the catechumenate appears to be that of formation in Christian living, of forming disciples of Christ, rather than training in doctrinal content.

In light of these various rites and interpretations, it is probably only natural to ask which of them is the "original" from which the others derived. And, given the Syriac-speaking, Semitic-oriented tradition of the Syrian East, it is also natural to assume that it is the early Syrian tradition which represents the original baptismal pattern. But we should be cautious about assuming any "original" pattern or original theological interpretation at all. Both approaches, a Jordan-based ritual of new birth and adoption and a paschal-based ritual of death and resurrection, come to us from the apostolic Church of the New Testament era. And along these lines, the words of Georg Kretschmar are most appropriate: "The triadic pattern of baptismal bath / imposition of hands / Eucharist is a venerable Western tradition, traceable indeed back into apostolic times—but we have no right to regard it as the sole normative structure of Christian initiation. *The plurality of possibilities is itself apostolic.*"[115]

Such an apostolic "plurality of possibilities," however, will tend to become hidden under the developing liturgical homogeneity of the fourth and fifth centuries. It is with this development that the next two chapters are concerned.

---

[115] Kretschmar, "Recent Research," LWSS, 33; emphasis added.

Chapter 3

Initiation in the Christian East During the Fourth and Fifth Centuries

In his important book on the development of the adult catechumenate in the early Church, Michel Dujarier writes that:

"The peace of Constantine, inaugurated in 313, marks an important turning point in the history of the Church. From an illegal religion, Christianity became legally tolerated, and this position was soon transformed into one of privileged liberty. The Christians rejoiced, and rightly so, in being able to profess their faith without being harassed. But this change brought with it grave new pastoral problems, especially when it became the official religion instead of being only a permitted religion."[1]

Scholars have often identified one of these pastoral problems to be the decline of an authentic catechumenate, presumably involving years of general preparation geared toward expressing and fostering a real conversion, in favor of what had previously been the period of final preparation, a limited period now consisting of six to eight weeks' duration, or shorter, as the season of Lent developed.[2] Thus, so it has been thought, the Church now had to accomplish in a short period of time what previous centuries had taken several years to do.

It is certainly true that after the conversion of Constantine, large numbers of people wanted to join the Church and not always for the right reasons. Defective motivations for "converting" to Christianity included the desire to marry a Christian, as well as political or economic gain in a society having become increasingly "Christianized." *Confessor* And, since it was thought that the forgiveness of sins which baptism

---

[1] Michel Dujarier, *A History of the Catechumenate: The First Six Centuries* (New York: Sadlier, 1959) 78.

[2] On the development of Lent and its relationship to the catechumenate, specifically, see chapter 5 below.

conveyed could only be obtained once, with the exception of the one-time postbaptismal penitential process known as "canonical penance," there was a widespread tendency to delay baptism as long as possible in order to be more sure of winning ultimate salvation. Even Constantine himself, who, according to tradition, suggested the word *homoousios* ("consubstantial" or "one in Being") at the Council of Nicea (325 C.E.) as the proper term to describe the relationship between God the Father and God the Son, was not baptized until he was on his deathbed. Because entry into the catechumenate assured one's status as a Christian, postponement of baptism itself became a common practice in this period.

The exact length of the prebaptismal catechumenate in pre-Nicene Christianity, however, is not known with any degree of certainty. As we saw in the previous chapter, *Apostolic Tradition* 17 does indicate that the catechumenate may have lasted for as long as three years, depending upon the worthiness of the individual catechumen. Many, assuming that *Apostolic Tradition* reflects early-third-century Roman liturgical practice, have concluded from this that the length of pre-baptismal preparation in *the* pre-Nicene Church was three years in duration. But this single reference is not corroborated anywhere in liturgical texts before the late-fourth-century *Apostolic Constitutions* (ca. 381 C.E.). And the early-fourth-century *Canons of Hippolytus* 12, clearly based on some version of the *Apostolic Tradition* 17, mentions only an exclusive forty-day baptismal preparation period.[3] Outside of these liturgical documents the earliest parallel with *Apostolic Tradition* 17 about a lengthy catechumenal period in the early Church is Canon 42 of the early-fourth-century Council of Elvira (ca. 305 C.E.), which specifies a *two-year* general catechumenate. While Dujarier interprets this as a reduction or "relaxation of discipline" in relationship to previous centuries, the fact of the matter, as he himself notes, is that this same council mandates that serious faults could prolong the catechumenate to *three years* (Canon 4), five years (Canon 73), or even to the end of one's life (Canon 73).[4] Similarly, the Council of Nicea itself (325 C.E.) also sought to ensure that a period of adequate preparation for baptism be provided in order to guarantee that the transition from pagan to Christian life not be as abrupt as apparently

[3] See above, 79.
[4] Dujarier, *A History of the Catechumenate*, 69.

it had been previously.[5] In Canon II of Nicea, for example, specific reference is made against ordaining bishops and presbyters too soon after their conversion and with only a small amount of prebaptismal instruction.[6] And Canon XIV of Nicea requires that catechumens who had "fallen" were to spend, significantly, *three years* as catechumens before being admitted to immediate prebaptismal preparation.[7]

Apart from *Apostolic Tradition* 17, a concern for the length of baptismal preparation expressed in terms of several years appears throughout the Church only in the fourth century. While *Apostolic Tradition* 17, then, *may* reflect an early-third-century context, the more logical conclusion is that it also belongs to an overall *fourth*-century context and is quite possibly an addition to the text of *Apostolic Tradition* itself. In any event, the traditional and widely held assumption that the pre-Nicene Church knew a general catechumenate of three years' duration is one that should be received with due caution. At the same time, the notion that in the aftermath of Constantine the Church now had to accomplish in a short period of time what previous centuries had taken several years to do, also appears less certain. It is, after all, within this fourth-century context that we begin to hear about the need for extended prebaptismal catechesis most clearly. This, of course, does not mean that this fourth-century concern for length is not, somehow, in continuity with what went before. It only means that we are uncertain about it before the fourth century.

In other words, whatever may have been the actual state of the length and content of the general catechumenate in pre-Nicene Christianity, in the wake of mass "conversions" within the so-called "Golden Age" of the fourth century, the real development of the catechumenate itself is the result of the Church seeking to ensure that its sacramental/baptismal life would have some kind of integrity when authentic conversion and properly motivated desire to enter the Christian community could no longer be assumed on the part of the candidates. In his short book on monasticism, British historian David Knowles describes this period saying:

"The conversion of Constantine [brings about] the swift transformation of the Church from a persecuted and fervent sect into a ruling

---

[5] Ibid.
[6] NPNF 14, second series, 10.
[7] Ibid., 31.

and rapidly increasing body, favoured and directed by the emperor, membership of which was a material advantage. In the sequel, the standards of life and the level of austerity were lowered and the Christian Church became what it has in large measure remained ever since, a large body in which a few are exceptionally devout, while many are sincere believers without any pretension to fervour, and a sizeable number, perhaps even a majority, are either on their way to losing the faith, or retain it in spite of a life which neither obeys in all respects the commands of Christ nor shares in the devotional and sacramental life of the Church with regularity."[8]

In such a context, an organized prebaptismal catechumenate as we see developing throughout this period becomes an absolute necessity. Nevertheless, it must be noted as well that this organized catechumenate represents both the rise and fall of the catechumenal process itself, a process which will eventually disappear with the great increase in infant baptisms and especially with the theological justification for infant baptism later.

It is not only the catechumenate, however, that receives its most definitive form in these centuries. The prebaptismal, baptismal, and postbaptismal rites themselves also begin to take on numerous elements surely designed to heighten dramatically the experience and emotions of those being initiated, elements of the rites as well as the Creed and Our Father often kept secret from the baptismal candidates until after they had experienced or received them solemnly. While in an earlier time this *disciplina arcani* ("discipline of the secret") would probably have been a practical necessity in a world largely hostile to Christianity, such an emphasis now, according to Georg Kretschmar, was due more to dramatic effect and tension, to impress upon the candidates the seriousness of the step they were taking.[9]

The question is often raised in this context as to whether or not the Church of this period was consciously borrowing from the numerous contemporary Greco-Roman mystery religions available to it from the wider culture. Edward Yarnold answers this question in the following manner:

[8] David Knowles, *Christian Monasticism* (New York: McGraw Hill, 1969) 12.
[9] Georg Kretschmar, "Die Geschichte des Taufgottesdienstes in der alten Kirche," *Leitourgia: Hanbuch des evangelischen Gottesdienstes* 5 (Kassel, 1970) 1–348.

"The answer perhaps is that the rites themselves were hardly influenced but the explanation given of them began to emphasize the element of mystery and fear. . . . One wonders whether Constantine was responsible for this development. In his gradual conversion from Sun-worship (presumably tinged with Mithraism) to Christianity, he seems to have wanted his temple at Jerusalem [i.e., the Holy Sepulchre which he built] to be the Christian equivalent of a mystery shrine. Eusebius' account of Constantine's baptism in 337, written shortly after the event, contains several terms borrowed from the vocabulary of the mysteries. It was at Jerusalem that the veneration of the Christian sacred objects (the cross, Calvary, the tomb) began and apparently the practice of mystagogic catechesis began here too. Cyril [of Jerusalem] applied to his sermons the name *mystagogia*, with all its pagan associations."[10]

Such is the overall developmental context in which the authors and liturgical sources in this and the following chapter should be read.

THE SYRIAN TRADITIONS

From the evidence supplied by fourth- and fifth-century West Syrian sources (i.e., Cyril of Jerusalem, the pilgrim Egeria, the *Apostolic Constitutions,* John Chrysostom, and Theodore of Mopsuestia), it is clear that the earlier Syrian rites undergo a complete transformation in the fourth century which resulted in a reorganization and theological reinterpretation of the rites of initiation from the period of catechetical preparation all the way through postbaptismal mystagogy. The best way to illustrate this, of course, is from the available texts themselves; the most striking example of this transformation of rites is the evidence from the Jerusalem liturgy.

Jerusalem

Cyril of Jerusalem. From Cyril, the renowned bishop of Jerusalem from ca. 350–87 C.E., we possess an abundance of texts related to the rites of Christian initiation as they were celebrated in the mid- to

[10] AIRI, 66. See also Anscar Chupungco, "Baptism in the Early Church and Its Cultural Settings," *Worship and Culture in Dialogue,* ed. S. Anita Sauffer (Geneva: Department for Theology and Studies, Lutheran World Federation, 1994) 39–56.

late-fourth-century Jerusalem church. To those called *photizomenoi* ("those to be enlightened") Cyril presented during Lent an introductory lecture (the *procatechesis*) and a series of eighteen prebaptismal catecheses focusing primarily (lectures 4–18) on the contents and meaning of the Creed.[11] During Easter Week Cyril presented a series of five *mystagogical catecheses*[12] (catechetical lectures on the "mysteries") to the newly baptized (the neophytes) on the meaning of the rites of Christian initiation they had received and experienced at the Easter Vigil only a few days before. Cyril provides a rationale for his pedagogical approach, saying in his first *mystagogical catechesis*: "I knew well that visual testimony is more trustworthy than mere hearsay, and therefore I awaited this chance of finding you more amenable to my words, so that out of your personal experience I could lead you into the brighter and more fragrant meadow of Paradise on earth."

As the following excerpts from his *mystagogical catecheses* demonstrate, Cyril describes the process of Christian initiation itself as a close imitation, an image or icon, of the saving events in the life of Christ.[13] That is, the stripping of the candidate signifies the nakedness of Christ on Calvary, the prebaptismal anointing joins the candidate to the cross, and the three immersions or submersions in the font imitate Jesus' three days in the tomb. After baptism, Cyril's paradigm changes from Christ's passion and burial to that of his baptism in the Jordan. In other words, for Cyril, the rite of initiation itself has become for the candidate a dramatic ritual enactment of the salvific events themselves:

[11] Critical edition is PG 33. For an English translation see NPNF 7, second series.

[12] Critical edition in Greek with French translation is Saint Cyril, *Catéchèses Mystagogiques*, ed. Auguste Piédagnel, trans. Pierre Paris, SC 126 (Paris: Editions du Cerf, 1966); the translation below is adapted from AIRI, 70–85. For another Greek text with English translation see *St. Cyril of Jerusalem's Lectures on the Christian Sacraments*, ed. F. L. Cross (Crestwood, N.Y.: St. Vladimir's Press, 1977).

[13] On this see E. J. Cutrone, "Cyril's Mystagogical Catecheses and the Evolution of the Jerusalem Anaphora," *Orientalia Christiana Periodica* 44 (1978) 52–64; John Baldovin, *The Urban Character of Christian Worship: The Origins, Development, and Meaning of Stational Liturgy*, Orientalia Christiana Analecta 228 (Rome: Pont. Institutum Studiorum Orientalium, 1987) 45–104; and John Baldovin, *Liturgy in Ancient Jerusalem*, Alcuin/GROW Liturgical Study 57 (Bramcote, Nottingham: Grove Books, 1989).

you began by entering th' room · *face westward toward Satan* · *Westward*

"(*Mystagogical Catechesis* 1.2): You began by entering the outer room
of the baptistery. You faced westward, heard a voice commanding
you to stretch out your hand, and renounce Satan as though to his
face. . . . (1.4): . . . you are told to stretch out your hand, and to address the devil as if he were before you: *I renounce you, Satan. I will*
tell you now, for you need to know, why you face westward. The *repe*
west is the quarter from which darkness appears to us; now the devil
is darkness, and wields his power in darkness. So we look to the
west as a symbolic gesture, and renounce the leader of shadow and
darkness. . . . (1.5): The second phrase you are instructed to recite is:
and all your works. The works of Satan are all wickedness; this you
must also renounce, for when one escapes a tyrant, one surely es- *renounced*
capes his weapons as well. So every form of sin is numbered *Satan*
amongst the devil's works. . . . (1.6): Next you say: *and all your*
pomp. The devil's pomp is the mad world of the stage, horse-racing,
hunting, and all such futility. (1.7): Also included in the pomp of the
devil are the meat, loaves, and other offerings suspended during the
festivals in honour of idols, and polluted by the invocation of abom-
inable demons. . . . (1.8): Your next words are: *and all your worship*.
The devil's worship is prayer in pagan temples, honour paid to life-
less idols, kindling lamps and burning incense by fountains or rivers
. . . , and similar rites. So do not practise them. Augury, divination,
watching for omens, wearing amulets, writing on leaves, sorcery and
other such evil practices are the worship of the devil. These, then,
you must avoid. . . .

"(1.9): . . . when you renounce Satan, you trample underfoot your *renounced*
entire covenant with him, and abrogate your former treaty with Hell.
The gates of God's Paradise are open to you, that garden which God
planted in the east, and from which our first parent was expelled for
his transgression. When you turned from west to east, the region of
light, you symbolized this change of allegiance. Then you were told
to say: *I believe in the Father, the Son, and the Holy Spirit, and in one bap-*
tism of repentance.

"(2.2): Upon entering [the inner room of the baptistery] you took off *taking off*
your clothing, and this symbolised your stripping off of 'the old na- *clothes*
ture with its practices.' Stripped naked, in this too you were imitating *pulling*
Christ naked on the cross, who in his darkness 'disarmed the princi- *of*
palities and powers' and on the wood of the cross publicly 'tri- *Christ*
umphed over them.'

95

"(2.3): Next, after removing your garments you were rubbed with exorcised oil from the hair of your head to your toes, and so you became sharers in Jesus Christ, who is the cultivated olive tree. . . . The exorcised oil, then, symbolised your partaking of Christ's richness; it is the token which drives away every trace of the enemy's power.

"(2.4): Then you were conducted by the hand to the holy pool of sacred baptism, just as Christ was conveyed from the cross to the sepulchre which stands before us. Each person was asked if he believed in the name of the Father and of the Son and of the Holy Spirit. You made the confession that brings salvation and submerged yourselves three times in the water and emerged: by this symbolic gesture you were secretly re-enacting the burial of Christ three days in the tomb. . . . In one and the same action you died and were born; the water of salvation became both tomb and mother for you. What Solomon said of others is apposite to you. On that occasion he said: 'There is a time to be born and a time to die,' but the opposite is true in your case—there is a time to die and a time to be born. A single moment achieves both ends, and your begetting was simultaneous with your death. . . . (2.5): What a strange and astonishing situation! We did not really die, we were not really buried, we did not really hang from a cross and rise again. Our imitation was symbolic, but our salvation a reality. . . . (2.7): . . . For Christ really died, his soul really was separated from his body; he really was buried, for his holy body was wrapped in pure linen. In his case all these events really occurred; but in your case there was a likeness of death and suffering, but the reality, not the likeness, of salvation.

"(3.1): Christ bathed in the river Jordan, and having invested the waters with the divine presence of his body, he emerged from them, and the Holy Spirit visited him in substantial form, like coming to rest on like. In the same way, when you emerged from the pool of sacred waters you were anointed in a manner corresponding with Christ's anointing. . . . (3.3): But be sure not to regard the myron [oil] merely as ointment. Just as the bread of the Eucharist after the invocation of the Holy Spirit is no longer just bread, but the body of Christ, so the holy myron after the invocation is no longer ordinary ointment but Christ's grace, which through the presence of the Holy Spirit instils his divinity into us. It is applied to your forehead and organs of sense [i.e., ears, nostrils, and chest] with a symbolic meaning; the body is anointed with visible ointment, and the soul is sanctified by the holy, hidden Spirit."

In the next two catecheses Cyril devotes his attention to the meaning of the Eucharist (*Mystagogical Catechesis* 4) and to the structure of the Eucharistic Liturgy (*Mystagogical Catechesis* 5) as it was celebrated in the church of his day. Significantly, he provides the neophytes with explicit instructions on how to receive holy communion.

"(*Mystagogical Catechesis* 5.21): So when you come forward . . . make your left hand a throne for your right since your right hand is about to welcome a king. Cup your palm and receive in it Christ's body, saying in response *Amen*. Then carefully bless your eyes with a touch of the holy body, and consume it, being careful to drop not a particle of it. (5.22): After partaking of Christ's body, go to receive the chalice of his blood. Do not stretch out your hands for it. Bow your head and say *Amen* to show your homage and reverence, and sanctify yourself by partaking also of Christ's blood. While your lips are still moist with his blood, touch it with your hands and bless your eyes, forehead, and other organs of sense. Then await the [post-communion] prayer, and give thanks to God who has counted you worthy of such mysteries."

Egeria. Egeria (sometimes referred to as Etheria, Aetheria, and even Sylvia), the late-fourth-century Spanish pilgrim to Egypt and the Middle East, gives us an observer's view of the catechumenal process, the rites of Christian initiation, and the week of postbaptismal mystagogy as these existed in Jerusalem probably toward the end of Cyril's episcopate there (ca. 381–4 C.E.). In her travel diary, called the *Peregrinatio Egeriae* ("Pilgrimage of Egeria"), she writes:

"(Chapter 45): I feel I should add something about the way they instruct those who are to be baptized at Easter. Names must be given in before the first day of Lent, which means that a presbyter takes down all the names before the start of the eight weeks for which Lent lasts here. . . . Once the priest has all the names, on the second day of Lent at the start of the eight weeks, the bishop's chair is placed in the middle of the Great Church, the Martyrium [i.e., the Holy Sepulchre], the presbyters sit in chairs on either side of him, and all the clergy stand. Then one by one those seeking baptism are brought up, men coming with their [god]fathers and women with their [god]mothers.

As they come in one by one, the bishop asks their neighbours questions about them: 'Is this person leading a good life? Does he respect his parents? Is he a drunkard or a boaster?' He asks about all the serious human vices. And if his inquiries show that anyone has not committed any of these misdeeds, he himself puts down his name; but if someone is guilty he is told to go away, and the bishop tells him that he is to amend his ways before he may come to the font.

"(Chapter 46): They have here the custom that those who are preparing for baptism during the season of the Lenten fast go to be exorcized by the clergy first thing in the morning, directly after the morning dismissal in the Anastasis. As soon as that has taken place, the bishop's chair is placed in the Great Church, the Martyrium, and all those to be baptized, the men and the women, sit round him in a circle. . . . His [the bishop's] subject is God's Law; during the forty days he goes through the whole Bible, beginning with Genesis, and first relating the literal meaning of each passage, then interpreting its spiritual meaning. He also teaches them at this time all about the resurrection and the faith. And this is called *catechesis*. After five weeks' teaching they receive the Creed, whose content he explains in the same way as he explained the Scriptures, first literally and then spiritually. . . . At nine o'clock they are dismissed from Catechesis, and the bishop is taken with singing straight to the Anastasis. So the dismissal is at nine, which makes three hours' teaching a day for seven weeks. But in the eighth, known as the Great Week, there is no time for them to have their teaching if they are to carry out all the services. . . . So when seven weeks have gone by . . . the bishop comes early into the Great Church, the Martyrium. His chair is placed at the back of the apse, behind the altar, and one by one the candidates go up to the bishop, men with their [god]fathers and women with their [god]mothers, and repeat the Creed to him. When they have done so, the bishop speaks to them all as follows: 'During these seven weeks you have received instruction in the whole biblical Law. You have heard about the faith, and the resurrection of the body. You have also learned all you can as catechumens of the content of the Creed. But the teaching about baptism itself is a deeper mystery, and you have not the right to hear it while you remain catechumens. Do not think it will never be explained; you will hear it all during the eight days of Easter after you have been baptized. But so long as you are catechumens you cannot be told God's deep mysteries.'

"(Chapter 38): They keep their paschal vigil like us, but there is one addition. As soon as the 'infants' have been baptized and clothed, and left the font, they are led with the bishop straight to the Anastasis. The bishop goes inside the screen and after one hymn says a prayer for them. Then he returns with them to the church, where all the people are keeping the vigil in the usual way.

"(Chapter 47): Then Easter comes, and during the eight days from Easter Day to the eighth day . . . the newly baptized come into the Anastasis, and any of the faithful who wish to hear the Mysteries; but, while the bishop is teaching, no catechumen comes in, and the doors are kept shut in case any try to enter. The bishop relates what has been done, and interprets it, and, as he does so, the applause is so loud that it can be heard outside the church. Indeed the way he expounds the mysteries and interprets them cannot fail to move his hearers."[14]

Antiochia (The Region of Antioch)

What we see in Cyril of Jerusalem and the travel diary of Egeria is closely paralleled by the ritual and theological developments taking place in the region of Antioch. Here our sources include:

(1) the late-fourth-century church order known as the *Apostolic Constitutions* (ca. 381 C.E.), a document of eight books based in part on the *Didache, Didascalia Apostolorum,* and, significantly, the *Apostolic Tradition;*
(2) the catecheses of John Chrysostom (i.e., "John the Golden Mouthed"), while he was still a presbyter in Antioch (ca. 388–90 C.E.); and
(3) the catecheses of Theodore of Mopsuestia, ordained as a presbyter at Antioch (ca. 383 C.E.) and as bishop of Mopsuestia (ca. 392–428 C.E.), a small city about one hundred miles northeast of Antioch.

While there is enough parallel between all of these documents so as to enable us to recognize their belonging to the same overall "family"

---

[14] Critical edition in Latin with French translation is Egeria, *Égerie: Journal de voyage,* ed. Pierre Maraval, trans. Manuel C. Díaz y Díaz, SC 296 (Paris: Editions du Cerf, 1982). The above English translation is adapted from *Egeria's Travels,* trans. John Wilkinson (London: SPCK, 1971).

of rites—usually called either "West Syrian" or "Antiochene"—several significant differences do emerge in comparison with Cyril and Egeria. Certainly one difference to be noted here is that the baptismal lectures delivered by Chrysostom and Theodore were given *before* the rites themselves and so, unlike Cyril in his postbaptismal *mystagogical catecheses*, dealt with the meaning of the sacraments already in a prebaptismal context. Nevertheless, as Yarnold notes, it is Chrysostom and Theodore, primarily, who speak most often of the "awesome aspect of the rites."[15]

The Apostolic Constitutions (ca. 381 C.E.)[16]

"(3.16): You . . . O bishop . . . shall anoint the head of those that are being baptized, whether men or women, with the holy oil, for a type of the spiritual baptism. After that, either you, O bishop, or a presbyter under you, calling and naming over them the solemn invocation of the Father and Son and Holy Spirit, shall baptize them in the water; and let a deacon receive the man and a deaconness the woman, that so the conferring of this inviolable seal may take place with a becoming decency. And after that, let the bishop anoint with chrism those that have been baptized.

"(3.17): This baptism therefore is given into the death of Jesus [Rom 6:8]: the water is instead of the burial, and the oil instead of the Holy Spirit; the seal instead of the cross; the chrism is the confirmation of the confession; . . . the descent into the water the dying together with [Christ]; the ascent out of the water the rising again with [him]. (3.18): . . . let him that is baptized be free from all iniquity; one that has left off to work sin, the friend of God, the enemy of the devil, *the heir of God the Father, the joint-heir with his Son* [Rom 8:17]; one that has renounced Satan and his demons and deceits; chaste, pure, holy, beloved of God, the son of God, praying as a son to his father, and saying, as from the common congregation of the faithful, thus; Our Father [etc.].

"(7.22): Now concerning baptism, O bishop, or presbyter . . . first anoint the person with holy oil, and afterward baptize him with

---

[15] AIRI, 66.

[16] Critical edition in Greek with French translation is *Les Constitutions Apostolique*, vol. 3, trans. Marcel Metzger, SC 336 (Paris: Editions du Cerf, 1987). The above English translation is adapted from DBL, 30–5.

water, and finally seal him with chrism; that the anointing with oil may be a participation of the Holy Spirit, and the water a symbol of the death, and the chrism a seal of the covenants. . . . But before baptism, let him that is to be baptized fast. (7.39): Let him . . . who is to be taught the knowledge of piety be instructed before his baptism in the knowledge of the unbegotten God, the understanding of his only begotten Son, the certainty of the Holy Spirit. . . .

"(7.41): Let . . . the candidate for baptism declare thus in his renunciation: 'I renounce Satan, and his works, and his pomps, and his service, and his angels, and his inventions, and all things that are under him.' And after his renunciation let him in his Act of Adherence [Syntaxis] say: 'And I adhere to Christ. . . .'

renounces Satan

"(7.43): Him [God] . . . let the priest even now call upon in baptism, and let him say: Look down from heaven and sanctify this water and give it grace and power, that so he that is baptized, according to the command of your Christ, may be crucified with him, and may die with him, and may be buried with him, and may rise with him to the adoption which is in him, that he may be dead to sin and live to righteousness. (7.44): And after this, when he has baptized him in the Name of the Father and of the Son and of the Holy Spirit, let him anoint him with chrism. (7.45): After this let him stand up, and pray that prayer which the Lord taught us. But, of necessity, he who is risen again ought to stand up and pray, because he that is raised stands upright. Let him, therefore, who has been dead with Christ, and is raised up with him, stand up.

"(8.22): Those that first come to the mystery of godliness, let them be brought to the bishop or to the presbyters by the deacons, and let them be examined as to the causes wherefore they come to the word of the Lord; and let those that bring them exactly inquire about their character, and give them their testimony. . . . [Here follows a lengthy treatment of crafts and professions based on the *Apostolic Tradition*] Let him who is to be a catechumen be a catechumen *for three years*; but if any one be diligent, and has a good-will to his business, let him be admitted: for it is not the length of time, but the course of life, that is judged."[17]

---

[17] English translation from ANF 7, 494–5.

John Chrysostom[18]

"(*Baptismal Homily* II.11): As you know, baptism is a burial and a resurrection: the old self is buried with Christ to sin and the new nature rises from the dead 'which is being renewed after the image of its creator.' We are stripped and we are clothed, stripped of the old garment which has been soiled by the multitude of our sins, clothed with the new that is free from all stain. What does this mean? We are clothed in Christ himself. St. Paul remarks: 'As many of you as were baptized into Christ have put on Christ.'

"(II.12): Since you are on the threshold of the time when you are to receive these great gifts, I must now teach you, as far as I can, the meaning of each of the rites, so that you may go from here with knowledge and a more assured faith. So you need to know why it is that after the daily instruction we send you off to hear the words of the exorcists. This rite is neither a simple . . . nor a pointless [one]. You are about to receive the heavenly King into your house. So those who are appointed for this task, just as if they were preparing a house for a royal visit, take you on one side after our sermon, and purify your minds by those fearful words, putting to flight all the tricks of the evil one, and so make the house fit for the presence of the King. For no demon, however fierce and harsh, after these fearful words and the invocation of the universal Lord of all things, can refrain from flight with all speed. . . . (II.14): Such is the effect of these marvellous, awesome words and invocations. But something else is made known to us by the outward attitude—the bare feet and the outstretched hands. Just as those who suffer bodily captivity show by the appearance they present their dejection . . . so do those men who have been captives of the devil. As they are about to be freed from his tyranny and go beneath the yoke that is easy, first of all they remind themselves by their appearance of their previous situation. . . .

"(II.18): Now consider once again the posture of captivity. The priests who introduce you first of all tell you to kneel down and pray with your hands raised to heaven, and by this attitude of body recall to your mind the one from whom you have been delivered and the

---

[18] Critical edition in Greek with French translation is A. Wenger, *Jean Chrysostome: Huit Catéchèses Baptismales*, SC 50 (Paris: Editions du Cerf, 1957). The above English translation is adapted from AIRI, 152–64.

other whom you are about to join. After that the priest approaches
each in turn and demands your contracts and confessions and instructs each one to pronounce those fearful and awesome words: *I renounce you, Satan.* . . . (II.20): . . . The priest then instructs you to
say, *I renounce you, Satan, your pomp, your worship and your works.* . . .

"(II.21): Have you seen the terms of the contract? After the renunciation of the Evil One and all the works he delights in, the priest instructs you to speak again as follows: *And I pledge myself, Christ, to
you.*

Covenant

"(II.22): Then once you have made this covenant . . . by which you
pledge yourself to Christ, you are now a soldier and have signed on
for a spiritual contest. Accordingly, the bishop anoints you on the
forehead with spiritual myron, placing a seal on your head and saying: *N. is anointed in the name of the Father, the Son, and the Holy Spirit.*
(II.23): It is for this reason that the bishop anoints you on your forehead and marks you with the seal, to make the devil turn away his
eyes. He does not dare to look at you directly because he sees the
light blazing from your head and blinding his eyes. From that day
onwards you will confront him in battle, and this is why the bishop
anoints you as athletes of Christ before leading you into the spiritual
arena."

From another series of Chrysostom's baptismal homilies we learn
that this renunciation *(apotaxis)* and Act of Adherence *(syntaxis)* took
place, apparently, on Good Friday.[19] He continues:

"(II.24): Then after this at the appointed hour of the night, he strips
you of all your clothes, and as if he were about to lead you into
heaven itself by means of these rites, he prepares to anoint your
whole body with this spiritual oil so that his unction may armour all
your limbs and make them invulnerable to any weapons the Enemy
may hurl.

"(II.25): After this anointing he takes you down into the sacred waters, at the same time burying the old nature and raising 'the new
creature, which is being renewed after the image of the creator.' Then
by the words of the priest and by his hand the presence of the Holy

---

[19] See DBL, 36.

Spirit flies down upon you and another man comes up out of the font, one washed from all the stain of his sins, who has put off the old garment of sin and is clothed in the royal robe.

"(II.26): As the priest pronounced the words, *N. is baptized in the name of the Father and of the Son and of the Holy Spirit,* he plunges your head into the water and lifts it up again three times. . . . He does not say, 'I baptize N.,' but rather, 'N. is baptized.' This shows that he is only the minister of the grace and merely lends the hand since he has been ordained for this by the Spirit. It is the Father, Son, and Holy Spirit, the indivisible Trinity, who bring the whole rite to completion.

"(II.27): As soon as they come up from those sacred waters all present embrace them, greet them, kiss them, congratulate and rejoice with them, because those who before were slaves and prisoners have all at once become free men and sons who are invited to the royal table. For as soon as they come up from the font, they are led to the awesome table which is laden with all good things. They taste the body and blood of the Lord and become the dwelling place of the Spirit; since they have put on Christ, they go about appearing everywhere like angels on earth and shining as brightly as the rays of the sun."

Theodore of Mopsuestia. We are fortunate that Theodore of Mopsuestia begins each of his five extant homilies on the rites of Christian initiation with a short synopsis or summary of what he is about to say in more detail in the body of his homily. For the purposes in this study, direct citation of the introductory synopses from his *Baptismal Homilies* II and III, together with some additional information supplied from elsewhere in the texts where necessary, will be sufficient.

"(*Baptismal Homily* II: Synopsis): You stand again on sackcloth, barefooted, with your outer garment removed and your hands stretched out to God in the attitude of prayer. First you fall on your knees, holding the rest of your body upright. Then you say, 'I renounce Satan, all his angels, all his works, all his service, all his vanity and all his worldly enticements. I pledge myself by vow, I believe and I am baptized in the name of the Father, of the Son and of the Holy Spirit.' Kneeling on the ground, but with the rest of your body upright, you look to heaven and stretch out your hands in the attitude of prayer. The bishop, wearing light, shining vestments of linen, signs your forehead with the oil of anointing, saying: 'N. is signed in the name of the Father and of the Son and of the Holy Spirit.' Your sponsor, standing behind you, spreads a linen stole over your head and raises you to your feet."[20]

With regard to the sackcloth upon which the baptismal candidates stand and kneel, Theodore understands this as a part of the rites of exorcism. He comments on this, saying: "you stand also on garments of sackcloth so that from the fact that your feet are pricked and stung by the roughness of the cloth you may remember your old sins."[21] And, concerning the linen stole spread over the head of the candidate after the renunciation of Satan and act of adherence to Christ, he says:

"To begin with, you stand naked, like prisoners and slaves; but when you receive the sign [i.e., the *prebaptismal* anointing], you spread the linen cloth over your head to symbolize the freedom to which you are called, for this is the decoration that free men wear both indoors and out (II.19)."[22]

He continues:

"(*Baptismal Homily* III: Synopsis): Then you come forward to be baptized. First you strip completely; then you are anointed all over with the oil of anointing in the prescribed manner. The bishop begins the ceremony with the words: 'N. is anointed in the name of the Father and of the Son and of the Holy Spirit.' Then you go down into the water that has been blessed by the bishop. The bishop stands and lays his hand on your head saying: 'N. is baptized in the name of the Father and of the Son and of the Holy Spirit.' He wears the same vestments as before. He lays his hand on your head with the words, 'In the name of the Father,' and while pronouncing them pushes you down into the water. If you were free to speak at this moment you would say, 'Amen.' You bow down under the water, then lift up

---

[20] Critical editions in *Theodorus, Les Homélies Catéchétiques de Théodore de Mopsuestia*, trans. Raymond Tonneau and Robert Devreesse, Studi e Testi 145 (Vatican City: Biblioteca apostolica vaticana, 1949). The English translation above is from AIRI, 168.

[21] Text from DBL, 45.

[22] AIRI, 179.

your head again. Meanwhile the bishop says, 'and of the Son,' and guides you with his hand as you bend into the water as before. When you raise your head, the bishop says, 'and of the Holy Spirit,' pressing you down into the water again with his hand. Then you come up out of the font and put on a dazzling garment of pure white. The bishop comes to you and puts a seal on your forehead saying: 'N. is sealed in the name of the Father and of the Son and of the Holy Spirit.'"[23]

For Theodore, as for Cyril of Jerusalem above, baptism is interpreted as both a rite of new birth and a rite of participation in the death and burial of Christ.[24] Like Chrysostom, the use of the passive formula ("N. is baptized . . ."), both for anointing and baptizing, is also defended by Theodore on the basis that God alone is the cause of the many benefits in baptism.[25] And, while it is clear that Theodore relates the postbaptismal "sealing" to the gift of the Holy Spirit, again like Cyril of Jerusalem, in ritual imitation of the sequence of Jesus' own baptism in the Jordan, it is by no means clear that Theodore himself knew the presence of a postbaptismal anointing at this point in the rite.[26]

Theodore's remaining baptismal homilies are concerned with the Eucharistic Liturgy as he knew it in Mopsuestia. He indicates that participation in the Eucharist was the culmination of the baptismal rite by saying: "When you have undergone the sacramental birth of baptism in this way, you will come forward to receive the food of immortality, the food that will be in keeping with your birth" (*Baptismal Homily* III.29).[27]

The West Syrian documents compared. The rites of Christian initiation as described by these three great mystagogues, together with the witness of the *Apostolic Constitutions*, are, indeed, quite similar in their

---

[23] Ibid., 180.

[24] See ibid., 181–4.

[25] See ibid., 189–95.

[26] See ibid., 198–200. Unfortunately, the text of AIRI, 198, entitles this rite "The Final Anointing" and so tends to prejudice the argument here. Nevertheless, see the helpful discussion and review of the relevant literature on 198–9, n. 65.

[27] Ibid., 200.

overall shape and theological interpretation. In distinction to the primary characteristics of the earlier Syrian tradition discussed in the previous chapter, all of these late-fourth- and early-fifth-century documents show that:

(1) the final preparation of catechumens for baptism now takes place during the forty days of Lent and appears to have included not only daily catechesis but daily exorcism as well;

(2) the Easter vigil has become in the East the prime time for the rites of initiation themselves, and that the central paradigm for interpreting baptism is now Romans 6 (participation in the death and burial in Christ), although the earlier emphasis on the "new birth" theology of John 3 still operates to some extent;

(3) the prebaptismal rites have been transformed from a pneumatic to an exorcistic emphasis with the prebaptismal anointing(s) gradually becoming related to preparation for athletic and even military-like contests with evil; and

(4) the explicit reference to the gift of the Holy Spirit gradually shifts from a prebaptismal or baptismal (Chrysostom) location to a post-baptismal one (Theodore and Cyril), and becomes associated with the addition of a postbaptismal anointing (Cyril).

On this last point, however, it is important to note that in none of these documents has the prebaptismal anointing completely lost its earlier emphasis and meaning. In *Apostolic Constitutions* 7.22, which, like Cyril, already witnesses to a postbaptismal anointing, the prebaptismal anointing itself is still understood as being performed so "that the anointing with oil may be a participation of the Holy Spirit." And, while Cyril is the first witness after *Apostolic Tradition* 21 to the use of "exorcised oil" for the prebaptismal anointing,[28] that anointing itself is not only for exorcism but it is seen as the means by which the candidates now become "sharers in Jesus Christ, who is the cultivated olive tree" (*Mystagogical Catechesis* 2.3). What we see here, then, are rites in obvious transition and development.

[28] It is important to recall here that, apart from Cyril and other *fourth-century* documents, we have no evidence which would corroborate the use of "exorcised oil" for the prebaptismal anointing in *Apostolic Tradition* 21. Such lack of evidence might suggest that such a reference in *Apostolic Tradition* 21 is a later addition to the text. See above, 79.

Furthermore, while a Romans 6 paschal theology certainly dominates the writings of these mystagogues with regard to the act of baptism itself, it is the event of Jesus' own baptism that functions, at least for Cyril and Theodore, as the dominical warrant for the now *postbaptismal* ritualization of the gift of the Holy Spirit. In other words, both death, burial, and resurrection in Christ *and* new birth through water and the Holy Spirit based on the Jordan event become synthesized and held together theologically. As Cyril of Jerusalem says it: "in one and the same action you died and were born; the water of salvation became both tomb and mother for you" (*Mystagogical Catechesis* 2.4).

Why, however, does such a transformation of the early Syrian rites take place in this fourth- and fifth-century context? Several theories have been suggested. With the exception of Origen in the third century, the Pauline paradigm of baptismal death and resurrection in Christ (Romans 6) "seemingly had fallen through a hole in the memory of the early Church."[29] In part this was perhaps due, as traditional scholarship has supposed, to the appeal of Paul's overall theology within various heretical (Marcion and Gnostic) circles.[30] But whatever the reason for this absence of Pauline thought generally throughout the first three centuries, it is, certainly, the recovery of this theology that characterizes Christian initiation in the fourth- and fifth-century East. Kilian McDonnell points to the "mass accession" of converts to the Church in the late fourth century and suggests that:

"to accommodate this new flood of converts, some may have thought that Romans 6:4 offered possibilities the Jordan event did not. For all—Jews, Gentiles, catechumens, Christians—death is a more primary anthropological event, a weightier universal experience, more threatening, rooted deep in the archaeology of dread, tapping unconscious forces of great power. In symbol, drama, and imagination, it makes the Jordan event seem almost decorative. The pastoral and liturgical possibilities of death and resurrection, to-

[29] Kilian McDonnell, *The Baptism of Jesus in the Jordan: The Trinitarian and Cosmic Order of Salvation* (Collegeville: The Liturgical Press, 1996) 183.

[30] On this see Walter Bauer, *Orthodoxy and Heresy in Earliest Christianity*, ed. Robert A. Kraft and Gerhard Krodel (Philadelphia: Fortress Press, 1971) 219ff.; and André Benoît, *Le baptême chrétien au second siècle: La théologie des pères* (Paris: Presses Universitaires de France, 1953) 227.

gether with the call to radical conversion implicit in it, may have been too much to resist."[31]

Closely related to this recovery is another factor as well. Again, as McDonnell notes:

"Only at this time was it noted that in the Gospel narratives the Spirit descends on Jesus only *after* he had ascended out of the Jordan. . . . If baptism is a going down into the death and resurrection of Jesus, then the Spirit and the gifts of the Spirit cannot be imparted before that sacramental experience of dying and rising. Calvary comes before Pentecost. The Spirit and the gifts of the Spirit cannot logically be given in a prebaptismal anointing. The imparting of the Spirit, therefore, is . . . transferred to later in the baptismal rite."[32]

Regarding this same Pauline focus on death and resurrection in baptism and the introduction of a postbaptismal anointing, E. C. Ratcliff pointed to the topography of Jerusalem—i.e., the discovery of the holy places associated with Christ's passion and death and the great Constantinian basilicas built at those places—as fostering an interest in following and reproducing liturgically the path of the historical Jesus, especially in his suffering and death.[33] The Liturgy of Jerusalem, then, began to follow the sequence of the economy of salvation and was becoming understood now as a dramatic and allegorical reenactment of historical redemption. Hence, an anointing after baptism, associated with the gift of the Holy Spirit, was adopted first in Jerusalem and from there it spread elsewhere in the Christian East.

Bernard Botte linked the introduction of this postbaptismal anointing associated with the Holy Spirit to the ritual practices used in the reconciliation of heretics.[34] In the East such were not rebaptized when they sought to return to the Church, but were only anointed. This

---

[31] McDonnell, *The Baptism of Jesus in the Jordan,* 231–2.

[32] Ibid., 230.

[33] E. C. Ratcliff, "The Old Syrian Baptismal Tradition and Its Resettlement under the Influence of Jerusalem in the Fourth Century," *Studies in Church History* 2 (1965) 19–37.

[34] Bernard Botte, "Post-Baptismal Anointing in the Ancient Patriarchate of Antioch," *Studies in Syrian Baptismal Rites,* ed. Jacob Vellian, Syrian Churches Series 6 (Kottayam: J. Vellian, 1973) 63–71.

practice, according to Botte, then led to the addition of a postbaptismal anointing within the initiation rite itself.

Others have suggested that we need to look more closely at the various doctrinal controversies in the fourth and fifth centuries. It seems clear that these controversies over trinitarian and christological issues, brought about initially by Arianism, had a role to play in the transformation of Syrian initiation rites. Similarly, the introduction of the feast of Christmas on December 25, for example, brings with it a focus on the incarnation, the birth of Jesus in the flesh, rather than the older unitive emphases of Epiphany on baptism and incarnation, centered primarily on the event of the baptism of Jesus, his "spiritual" birth in the Jordan. This event, along with what in the Syrian East was a preference for the direct citation of Psalm 2:7 ("you are my Son, this day I have begotten you"), was subject to an "adoptionist interpretation." That is, if Jesus *became* God's Son at his baptism, was he not God's Son before that event? Was he, then, only a human being who was "adopted" by God at the Jordan? Consequently, in the interests of maintaining an "orthodox" view of the identity of Christ against heretical interpretations, it was perhaps inevitable that there would be a conscious movement away from what was considered now to be a dangerous theology associated with Jesus' baptism toward a more paschal or Romans 6 approach.[35]

As we shall see in more detail in chapter 5, it is only after the Council of Nicea (325 C.E.) that we can note with certainty the existence of "Lent" as a forty-day period of preparation for penitential and catechumenal preparation before Pascha (Easter). The implication of this may certainly be that part of the Nicean decision was the determination of Pascha itself as the preferred baptismal day in the East, with forty days of preparation for baptism, already, as we have seen, associated in Egypt with Jesus' own temptation, now universally imposed on the churches of East and West as the period *before* Easter. In other words, while paschal baptism is probably quite early for Rome and North Africa (at least by the third century), the Council of Nicea makes it the baptismal day for the East as well. Here, then, based on Nicene orthodoxy and the centrality of both the incarnation of the Word and what is often called today the "paschal mystery" of

[35] See Thomas Talley, *The Origins of the Liturgical Year,* 2d ed. (Collegeville: The Liturgical Press, 1986) 134–41.

Christ's death, resurrection, and gift of the Spirit, there is a dramatic shift taking place throughout the eastern part of the Roman Empire. If a particular tradition has not celebrated initiation at Easter the chances are that the operative theology of baptism in that tradition is not paschal in orientation. But now, after Nicea, the theology of Christian initiation will move increasingly to a paschal mystery focus suggested by Romans 6.

Closely related to this is also the specific development of a theology of the Holy Spirit itself. In the fourth-century the "Semi-Arians" (*tropikoi* and Pneumatomachians) and orthodox defenders disputed over the relationship between the Holy Spirit to the Father and the Son; these disputes led to an increased emphasis upon the role of the Holy Spirit in doctrine and liturgy. Here, for example, we begin to see more clearly the development of explicit epicleses of the Holy Spirit within the blessing of water in baptism or in the developing Eucharistic Prayers, asking, as we see already in Cyril of Jerusalem, that the Spirit might now "consecrate" the water or the eucharistic gifts. In fact, an emphasis upon the divinity of the Holy Spirit in this period is argued by great theologians such as Athanasius of Alexandria[36] and Basil of Caesaria[37] on the basis of the "divine works" that the Spirit does. And central among these divine works is that Christians are baptized not only in the name of the Father and the Son but also of the Holy Spirit! If, then, like the Father and the Son the Holy Spirit also baptizes, the Holy Spirit must also be divine. At the Council of Constantinople (381 C.E.) this emphasis upon the divine gifts and activity of the Holy Spirit leads to the phrase, "We believe in the Holy Spirit, the Lord and giver of life, who proceeds from the Father. With the Father and the Son he is worshiped and glorified. . . ."

Gabriele Winkler, however, has suggested another theory altogether. Winkler looks closely at the rites themselves and argues that this transition comes about due to:

". . . the inner change of dynamics within the ritual itself. Once baptism moved away from its original essence, being the *mimesis* of the event at the Jordan, and shifted at the same time toward a cathartic

---

[36] See C.R.B. Shapland, trans., *The Letters of Athanasius Concerning the Holy Spirit* (London: Epworth Press, 1951).

[37] See D. Anderson, ed., *St. Basil the Great on the Holy Spirit* (Crestwood, N.Y.: St. Vladimir's Press, 1980).

principle, it was inevitable that all rites that preceded baptism proper became subordinated to a process of thorough cleansing. The catharsis slowly became an indispensable condition for the coming of the Spirit. Consequently, only after intensive purification and the washing away of sins could the Spirit enter the heart of the baptized."[38]

Winkler sees this "inner change" reflected in several places even within the Syrian *Apocryphal Acts* summarized in the previous chapter. In those passages from the *Acts of Thomas* which contain a prebaptismal anointing of the head *as well as* a full body anointing (see also the *Didascalia* above), the emphasis in the rite is already moving from a pneumatic assimilation of the candidate to the messianic kingship of Christ (symbolized by the anointing of the head as in the Old Testament) to purification, healing, and cleansing. A further step in this direction is to be seen in Chrysostom, Cyril, and Theodore, where this prebaptismal anointing is becoming exorcistic and associated with a combat and struggle against evil. It was inevitable, then, that this "inner change" from Spirit (anointing of the head) to cleansing and purification (full body anointing) would result ultimately in a reinterpretation of the prebaptismal rites. And when this happens the Holy Spirit, inevitably, comes to be associated with the postbaptismal rites.

Nevertheless, it is quite possible, of course, that all of these things—the topography of Jerusalem, the reconciliation of heretics, and changes within the inner dynamics of the rite—contributed to bring about these transitions. Nor ought we ignore the fact that such "Western" appearing things, such as a formal catechumenate accompanied by frequent exorcisms and other purificatory elements, initiation at Easter with the adoption of Pauline death-burial imagery, and above all the postbaptismal anointing, generally turn up in the East first—not surprisingly—in Jerusalem, where pilgrimages, like that of Egeria, brought Eastern and Western Christianity face to face.

East Syria

As we have seen, within the region of West Syria in the fourth and fifth centuries the earlier Syrian rites of Christian initiation undergo a dramatic shift and transition. Within the inner regions of Syria, how-

---

[38] Winkler, "The Original Meaning of the Prebaptismal Anointing and Its Implications," LWSS, 78, n. 63.

ever, that is, *East* Syria, the earlier structure and theology of those rites is more clearly maintained. Although our evidence for this period indicates that paschal baptism along with its Romans 6 interpretation does become important, it is significant that it does not play the same dominating role with regard to either the structure or understanding of the initiation rites in this tradition. Indeed, a post-baptismal anointing does not even enter the East Syrian rites of Christian initiation until the mid-*seventh*-century liturgical reforms of patriarch Isho'yabh III (ca. 650–60 C.E.)![39]

For the period of the fourth and fifth centuries our sources are the richly symbolic poetic homilies and hymns of the great East Syrian Fathers, Aphrahat the "Persian Sage" (+ after 345 C.E.), Ephrem the "Harp of the Spirit" (306–70 C.E.), and Narsai (399–502 C.E.). What can be gleaned from their various writings clearly demonstrates a ritual structure of Christian initiation in close continuity with the Syrian pattern we have seen earlier, a pattern consisting of prebaptismal anointing(s), baptism itself, and participation in the Eucharist.

Aphrahat. Like Clement of Alexandria and Origen in the early Egyptian tradition, Aphrahat also points to Israel crossing the Jordan river under Joshua (Joshua 3) as a model for interpreting baptism:

"(*Demonstration* XI.11–12): They find life who are circumcised in their hearts and who circumcise themselves a second time on the true Jordan, the baptism of the forgiveness of sins. Joshua the son of Nun circumcised the people a second time with knives of stone when he and his people crossed the Jordan. Joshua (Jesus) our redeemer a second time circumcised the peoples who believed in him with the circumcision of the heart, and they were baptised and circumcised with 'the knife which is his word that is sharper than the two-edged sword' (Heb. 4:12). Joshua the son of Nun led the people across to the Land of promise; and Joshua our redeemer promised the land of the living to whoever passed through the true Jordan, believed, and circumcised the foreskin of his heart. . . . Blessed are those whose hearts are circumcised from the foreskin and who are born through water, the second circumcision, for they are inheritors with Abraham."[40]

---

[39] On this see Joseph Chalassery, *The Holy Spirit and Christian Initiation in the East Syrian Tradition* (Rome: Mar Thoma Yogam, 1995) 88, n. 249.

[40] Ibid., 42.

It is also significant that Aphrahat sees the institution of Christian baptism as resulting from Jesus' washing of the feet at the Last Supper in John 13 (*Demonstration* XII.10): "Our redeemer washed the feet of his disciples on the night of the paschal sacrifice, (which is) the mystery of baptism. You should know, my beloved, it was on this night that our redeemer gave the true baptism."[41]

Is it possible that Aphrahat is a witness here to the practice of foot washing as a part of the East Syrian rites of initiation in the mid fourth century? While this is a strong possibility,[42] all we know with certainty about those rites in Aphrahat's day is the ritual sequence implied in the following statement (*Demonstration* XII.9): "After he circumcises his heart from evil deeds, then he progresses to baptism, the fulfillment of the true circumcision, is joined with the people of God, and added to the body and blood of the Messiah."[43] For Aphrahat, as for Ephrem below, this "circumcision of the heart" is quite possibly a reference to the prebaptismal anointing itself.

Ephrem. In the great metrical homiletic hymns of Ephrem we note several allusions to the rites of initiation and their interpretation within the life of the fourth-century East Syrian Church. Although it is clear that Ephrem knows paschal baptism, his interpretation is anything but paschal in orientation.

"(*Hymns on Virginity* 7.5): A royal portrait is painted with visible colors, and with oil that all can see is the hidden portrait of our hidden King portrayed on those who have been signed: on them baptism, that is, in travail with them in its womb, depicts the new portrait, to replace the image of the former Adam [1 Cor 15:45] who was corrupted; it gives birth to them with triple pangs, accompanied by the three glorious names, of Father, Son and Holy Spirit.

"(7.6): This oil is the dear friend of the Holy Spirit, it serves him, following him like a disciple. With it the Spirit signed priests and anointed kings; for with the oil the Holy Spirit imprints his mark on his sheep. Like a signet ring whose impression is left on wax, so the hidden seal of the Spirit is imprinted by oil on the bodies of those who are anointed in baptism; thus are they marked in the baptismal mystery.

---

[41] Ibid., 44.

[42] See Gabriele Winkler, "Confirmation or Chrismation?" LWSS, 204.

[43] Chalassery, *The Holy Spirit and Christian Initiation*, 50.

"(7.8): The priesthood ministers to this womb as it gives birth; anointing precedes it, the Holy Spirit hovers [Gen 1:2] over its streams, a crown of Levites surrounds it, the chief priest is its minister, the angels rejoice at the lost who in it are found [Luke 15:10]. Once this womb has given birth, the altar suckles and nurtures them: her children eat straight away, not milk, but perfect Bread.[44]

"(*Hymns on the Church* 36.3): The river in which he was baptized conceived him again symbolically; the moist womb of the water conceived him in purity, bore him in chastity, made him ascend in glory."[45]

Even the fire enkindled in the Jordan, long associated in the Syrian tradition with Jesus' baptism, finds its place in Ephrem (*Hymns on the Faith* 10.17): "See, Fire and Spirit in the womb that bore you! See, Fire and Spirit in the river where you were baptized! Fire and Spirit in our Baptism; in the Bread and the Cup, Fire and Holy Spirit!"[46]

Narsai. In a manner quite similar to that of Theodore of Mopsuestia, Narsai witnesses to a synthesis of Jordan new birth and paschal death imagery in his interpretation of initiation. The rite that Narsai knows, however, does not appear to have the developing postbaptismal rites present in Theodore.

While Narsai witnesses to the fact that the prebaptismal section of the rite had become somewhat exorcistic in the late fifth and early sixth centuries (e.g., renunciation of Satan, the candidate kneeling naked on sackcloth, etc.), his own interpretation of the prebaptismal anointing still suggests the early Syrian approach:

"(*Homily 22: On Baptism*): This power the oil of anointing imparts: not the oil, but the Spirit that gives it power. The Spirit gives power to the unction of the feeble oil, and it waxes firm by the operation that

---

[44] Ephrem, *Hymns on Virginity, The Harp of the Spirit: Eighteen Poems of Saint Ephrem,* trans. Sebastian Brock (London: Fellowship of St. Alban and St. Sergius, 1983), as cited in MFC 5, 154–5.

[45] Ephrem, *Hymns on the Church,* in S. Brock, "St. Ephrem on Christ as Light in Mary and in the Jordan: Hymni de Ecclesia 36," *Eastern Churches Review* 7 (1975) 137–44, as cited in MFC 5, 158.

[46] Ephrem, *Hymns on the Faith,* in S. Brock, "A Hymn of St. Ephrem to Christ on the Incarnation, the Holy Spirit, and the Sacraments," *Eastern Churches Review* 3 (1970) 142–50, as cited in MFC 5, 163.

is administered in it. By its firmness it makes firm the body and the faculties of the soul, and they go forth confidently to wage war against the Evil One. The sign of his Name the devils see upon a man; and they recoil from him in whose name they see the Name of honour. The Name of the Divinity looks out from the sign on the forehead: and the eyes of the crafty one are ashamed to look on it."[47]

And, although the theology of Romans 6 is operative as well, the traditional Syrian focus on baptism as "new birth" is still Narsai's dominant paradigm:

"(Homily 21: On the Mysteries of the Church and on Baptism): He verily dies by a symbol of that death which the Quickener of all died; and he surely lives with a type of the life without end. Sin and death he puts off and casts away in baptism, after the manner of those garments which our Lord departing left in the tomb. . . . As a babe from the midst of the womb he looks forth from the water; and instead of garments the priest receives him and embraces him. He resembles a babe when he is lifted up from the midst of the water; and as a babe everyone embraces and kisses him. Instead of swaddling clothes they cast garments upon his limbs, and adorn him as a bridegroom on the day of the marriage-supper. . . . Mystically he dies and is raised and is adorned; mystically he imitates the life immortal. His birth [in Baptism] is a symbol of that birth which is to be at the end, and the conduct of his life of that conversation which is [to be] in the Kingdom on high."[48]

EGYPT

As in West Syria, a similar process of change and transition appears to have taken place in the Egyptian liturgical tradition in the fourth and fifth centuries.[49] What liturgical documents there are for Egypt in this period—that is, primarily, the *Canons of Hippolytus* (ca.

[47] DBL, 54. Homilies 21 and 22 in the collection of Narsai's works are incorrectly numbered. Their enumeration should have been reversed, i.e., 21 is actually 22 and 22 actually 21.

[48] Ibid., 55–6.

[49] For discussions of the rites of Christian initiation in the Egyptian tradition see Georg Kretschmar, "Beiträge zur Geschichte der Liturgie, insbesondere der Taufliturgie, in Aegypten," *Jahrbuch für Liturgik und Hymnologie* 8 (1963) 1–54; Paul Bradshaw, "Baptismal Practice in the Alexandrian Tradi-

336 C.E.) and the *Prayers of Sarapion of Thmuis* (ca. 350 C.E.), a collection of thirty prayers ascribed to a bishop in northeastern Egypt, who was a close friend of Athanasius and Antony[50]—show the presence of a postbaptismal anointing associated with the Holy Spirit and some evidence that initiation was coming to be interpreted along the lines of a Romans 6 approach. Nevertheless, traces of the earlier Egyptian ritual pattern and theological interpretation summarized in the previous chapter are certainly discernible in these texts as well.

We have already seen in the *Canons of Hippolytus,* for example, that the entire catechumenate itself was restricted to a forty-day period of prebaptismal preparation.[51] And, whereas other Eastern traditions tended to make use of several scrutinies (examinations of the lifestyle of the baptismal candidates) and performed "daily" exorcisms throughout the period of final baptismal preparation, *Canons of Hippolytus* 19 refers to a *single* scrutiny—without exorcism—sometime before the day of baptism itself:

"(*Canons of Hippolytus* 19): The catechumen, when he is baptized, and he who presents him attests that he has been zealous for the commandments during the time of his catechumenate, that he has visited the sick or given to the needy, that he has kept himself from every wicked and disgraceful word, that he has hated vainglory, despised pride, and chosen for himself humility, and he confesses to the bishop that [takes] responsibility for himself, so that the bishop is satisfied about him and considers him [worthy] of the mysteries, and that he has become truly pure, then he reads over him the Gospel at that time, and asks him several times, 'Are you in two minds, or under pressure from anything, or driven by convention? For nobody mocks the kingdom of heaven, but it is given to those who love it with all their heart.'"[52]

---

tion," LWSS, 82–100; and Maxwell E. Johnson, *Liturgy in Early Christian Egypt,* Alcuin/GROW Liturgical Study 33 (Bramcote, Nottingham: Grove Books, 1995) ch. 2.

[50] See Maxwell Johnson, *The Prayers of Sarapion of Thmuis: A Literary, Liturgical, and Theological Analysis,* Orientalia Christiana Analecta 249 (Rome: Pontifico Instituto Orientale, 1995).

[51] See above, 79. See also chapter 5, below.

[52] Paul Bradshaw, ed., *The Canons of Hippolytus,* Alcuin/GROW Liturgical Study 50 (Bramcote, Nottingham: Grove Books, 1987) 21.

Similarly, there is no indication that the rites of Christian initiation were celebrated at Easter or that this catechumenal period corresponded to a pre-Easter lenten season. Indeed, in Egyptian Christianity the rites of Christian initiation and Easter were never viewed as necessarily or closely related.

Along with other Syrian-type elements in the Egyptian rites, such as an *apotaxis* and *syntaxis*,[53] and the probable use of a baptismal *formula* having replaced an earlier interrogative pattern,[54] traces of a similar Syrian-type emphasis upon the Holy Spirit the prebaptismal anointing remain present as well. Didymus the Blind (313–98 C.E.), the Alexandrian teacher and ascetic, wrote in his treatise on the Holy Trinity that "in the name of the Father and of the Son and of the Holy Spirit were we both sealed and baptized" in that order.[55] And in Prayer 15 of Sarapion's collection, the prayer for the consecration of the prebaptismal oil, the overall emphasis on the prebaptismal anointing appears to be on re-creation and healing.[56] The relevant section of this prayer reads:

"And we anoint with this oil those who approach this divine rebirth, imploring that our Lord Christ Jesus may work in it and reveal healing and strength-producing power through this oil, and may heal their soul, body, spirit. . . . And, when they have been molded again through this oil and purified through the bath and renewed in the Spirit, they will be strong enough to conquer . . . and so be bound and united to the flock of our Lord and Savior Jesus Christ and inherit the promises to the saints."[57]

And, in Prayer 10 of this same collection, a prayer recited either before or after the prebaptismal anointing as the candidate now entered

[53] See ibid., 22, and Johnson, *The Prayers of Sarapion of Thmuis*, 57, 126–34.

[54] On this see E. Lanne, "La confession de foi baptismale à Alexandrie et à Rome," *La liturgie expression de la foi,* ed. A. M. Triacca and A. Pistoia, Bibliotheca "Ephemerides Liturgicae" Subsidia 16 (Rome: C.L.V.-Edizioni liturgiche, 1979) 23.

[55] *De Trinitate* 2.15.

[56] See Bradshaw, "Baptismal Practice in the Alexandrian Tradition," 92.

[57] Johnson, *The Prayers of Sarapion of Thmuis*, 63.

into the actual place of baptism, there is an emphasis upon the Holy Spirit:

"Lover of humanity, benefactor, savior of all who have made conversion toward you, be merciful to this your servant. Guide him to the new birth with your right hand. Let your only-begotten word guide him to the bath. Let his new birth be honored; let it not be empty of your grace. Let your holy word be present and let your holy Spirit be with him to drive away and cast out every temptation."[58]

Closely related to an emphasis upon the role of the Holy Spirit in a prebaptismal context is a theological understanding of baptism as "new birth" (John 3) and the event of Jesus' own baptism in the Jordan as the primary model for this. This too, as the above quotations from Sarapion's prayers indicate, also remains a characteristic of the Egyptian tradition in the fourth century. But nowhere is this Jordan emphasis made more clear than in Sarapion's Prayer 7 for the blessing or sanctification of the baptismal waters:

"Look now from heaven and gaze upon these waters and fill them with holy spirit. Let your inexpressible word come to be in them. Let it change their operation and make them generative, being filled with your grace, so that the mystery now being accomplished may not be found empty in those being born again, but may fill with divine grace all those who go down and are baptized. Lover of humanity, benefactor; spare that which is made by you, save the creature which was made by your right hand, and mold all who are born again of your divine and inexpressible form, so that through being formed and born again they may be able to be saved and be made worthy of your kingdom. *And as your only-begotten word, when he descended upon the waters of the Jordan made them holy, so also now let him descend into these.* Let him make them holy and spiritual in order that those who are baptized may no longer be flesh and blood but spiritual and able to give worship to you."[59]

In spite of these traces of an earlier ritual and theology, however, both the *Canons of Hippolytus* (Canon 19) and the *Prayers of Sarapion of*

[58] Ibid., 57.
[59] Ibid., 55; emphasis added.

Thmuis (Prayer 16), as noted above, do contain postbaptismal anointings. In Sarapion's collection, especially, this postbaptismal anointing with "chrism" is associated explicitly with the "gift" and "seal" of the Holy Spirit.[60] These documents, however, may simply be the *first* witness to the addition of postbaptismal anointing in the Egyptian tradition, and it must be recalled here that since the *Canons of Hippolytus* themselves are certainly dependent upon the *Apostolic Tradition,* they undoubtedly reflect the influence of that document within Egypt. Georg Kretschmar[61] and Paul Bradshaw both have pointed to various legends in later Coptic literature that appear to point back precisely to the fourth century as a time of liturgical innovation within Egypt, particularly with regard to the introduction of this postbaptismal anointing. Bradshaw writes:

"The 'Book of the Chrism' contains two legends concerning the origin of the postbaptismal anointing. The first asserts that its use was traditional at Alexandria, the chrism itself having been obtained from the embalming of Jesus, but that it eventually fell into neglect and the supply of chrism disappeared, so that Athanasius had to write to the bishop of Rome and to the patriarchs of Antioch and Constantinople asking them to compose prayers to read over the baptismal oils, Basil being credited with the composition of those adopted. The second legend . . . maintains that it was Theophilus who originated the use of chrism. He received from an angel the order to bring balsam trees from Jericho, plant them, extract the balsam and cook the spices, and to do this 'on the Friday of the sixth week in the monastery of St Macarius, if possible, if not at Alexandria, according to the rite which the angel had made known. He wrote about it to all the patriarchs.'"[62]

While such legends are not historically reliable as providing a trustworthy description of what actually took place, they do suggest, notes Bradshaw, that there is some memory preserved here which looks at the postbaptismal anointing as a fourth-century addition to the rites. For the prestigious patriarchate of Alexandria to ask Rome or Antioch for chrism, as these legends claim, would have been

---

[60] Ibid., 65.
[61] Kretschmar, "Beiträge zur Geschichte," 43ff.
[62] Bradshaw, "Baptismal Practice in the Alexandrian Tradition," 97.

quite embarrassing and, thus, may suggest that this anointing did, indeed, enter the Egyptian tradition from elsewhere. Similarly, to attribute the introduction of chrism to Theophilus (patriarch of Alexandria from 385–412 C.E.) also underscores a fourth-century context.

What happened in the Syrian tradition with regard to the various shifts in rite and interpretation, therefore, might also be true for Egypt in this same time period. That is, in spite of certain indigenous traditions, such as the forty-day period of baptismal preparation and what appears to be a firm resistance to Easter baptism,[63] Egypt also appears to have experienced the introduction of a postbaptismal anointing associated with the gift and seal of the Holy Spirit. With that develops a new understanding of the prebaptismal rites as rites of preparation, exorcism, and purification *for* the gift of the Spirit and, at least, some shift in focus away from baptism as new birth to the Pauline emphasis on baptism as death and/or burial in Christ. Even Sarapion's Prayer 15, the prayer of consecration of the prebaptismal oil, tends to point in that direction when it asks that the anointing

"may heal their soul, body, spirit from every sign of sin and lawlessness or *satanic taint,* and by his own grace may grant forgiveness to them so that, *having no part in sin [or dying to sin], they will live in righteousness.* And, when they have been molded again through this oil and *purified through the bath* and renewed in the Spirit, they will be strong enough to *conquer against other opposing works and deceits of this life* which come near them."[64]

CONCLUSION

In spite of several distinctions in *some* ritual detail and theological interpretation, the rites of initiation in the fourth- and fifth-century Christian East, with the notable exception of East Syria, show a remarkable degree of commonality across ecclesial and geographical lines. The following chart demonstrates the degree to which such homogeneity appears to have been achieved within the shape of the rites themselves in this period:

[63] On this, see below, 169–72.
[64] Johnson, *The Prayers of Sarapion of Thmuis,* 63; emphasis added.

Chart 3.1

Cyril	Chrysostom	Theodore	East Syria	Egypt
		PREBAPTISMAL RITES		
Renunciation	Renunciation	Renunciation	Renunciation	Renunciation
Syntaxis (?)	Syntaxis	Syntaxis	Syntaxis	Syntaxis
Anointing (head)	Anointing (head)	Anointing (head)		Anointing
Stripping	Stripping	Stripping		
Anointing (body)	Anointing (body)	Anointing (body)		
		BAPTISM PROPER		
Interrogations				
Baptism	Baptism (formula)	Baptism (formula)	Baptism (formula)	Baptism (formula)
		POSTBAPTISMAL RITES		
Anointing with chrism		Kiss		Anointing with chrism
White garment (?)	Radiant garment vesting			
		Signing		
Station at Tomb (only in Egeria)				
	Kiss			
Eucharist	Eucharist	Eucharist	Eucharist	Eucharist

Together with the above details of the rites, other common ways of interpreting these rites also developed throughout the East in these centuries. As we have seen throughout this chapter, such interpretative elements include:

(1) the adoption of paschal or *Easter* baptism and the season of Lent as the time of final baptismal preparation for the *photizomenoi* or *competentes;*

(2) the use of scrutinies and exorcisms throughout the period of final baptismal preparation;

(3) the development of specific rites called *apotaxis* (renunciation) and *syntaxis* (adherence) as demonstrating a "change of ownership" for the candidates;

(4) the development of ceremonies like the solemn *traditio symboli* and *redditio symboli*;

(5) the reinterpretation of the prebaptismal anointing as a rite of exorcism, purification, and preparation for combat;

(6) the use of Romans 6 as the dominant metaphor for interpreting the baptismal submersion or immersion; and

(7) the introduction of a postbaptismal anointing associated with the gift of the Holy Spirit.

In relationship to the earlier Eastern or Syrian pattern of Christian initiation, summarized in the previous chapter, it is abundantly clear that some significant transitions have taken place. Such transitions were to become permanent in the Christian East. Whoever was the first in the East to rediscover the Romans 6 interpretation of baptism, and wherever the postbaptismal anointing with chrism was first added to the rites of initiation, it is clear that both were copied by others throughout the Eastern Christian world. Even within East Syria we have seen that both Easter baptism and a Romans 6 interpretation exercise some degree of influence.

While not every author summarized in this chapter witnesses to the inclusion of a postbaptismal anointing (e.g., Chrysostom and Theodore), it is this anointing with chrism that will come to be interpreted in the East as the very "Seal of the Holy Spirit," a direction already taken by Cyril of Jerusalem. As the rites themselves appear to demonstrate, then, the ritualizing of the initiatory gift of the Holy Spirit in this time period gradually migrates from a prebaptismal location (the earlier Syrian and, possibly, Egyptian position), to the water bath itself (Chrysostom), and, finally, to a postbaptismal context (Theodore and Cyril). And there, connected to the postbaptismal anointing with chrism, the gift of the Holy Spirit will remain.

It should be noted, however, that nowhere in the documents analyzed in this chapter is this postbaptismal gift of the Holy Spirit related explicitly to the physical presence of the bishop at the rites of Christian initiation. That is, while the bishop may be mentioned on occasion as the presider of the *entire* rite, there develops no explicit

requirement in the East, other than the necessity of the bishop consecrating the chrism, that certain rites, like the postbaptismal anointing,
are reserved to him. Rather, even if a presbyter presided at the rites
he administered baptism, chrism, and first communion all together.
This, as we shall see in the following chapter, is a fundamental distinction between the Christian East and certain churches within the
Christian West.

Chapter 4

Initiation in the Christian West During the Fourth and Fifth Centuries

The evolution of the rites of Christian initiation in the West during the fourth and fifth centuries is located in the same general historical and cultural context outlined at the beginning of the previous chapter. None of that needs to be repeated here.

One significant difference that occurs in describing and interpreting the Western rites, however, is that, unlike the numerous catechetical and mystagogical sources available for the Christian East, only the single witness of Ambrose of Milan's catecheses is available for the West. In other words, we do not know, unfortunately, what a Leo I or an Innocent I might have said to the newly baptized during Easter Week. This means that for the West we are dependent upon other types of literature, such as letters, canons from various local councils, passing references to Christian initiation in other treatises and documents, and later liturgical sources in order to reconstruct what the ritual practice may have been in this period. Nevertheless, the Western sources available to us *do* provide us with enough evidence to enable us to reconstruct both the overall shape of the rites and their interpretation. In particular, as we shall see, the theological interpretation of Christian initiation in the West, especially in North Africa, thanks to the controversies faced by Augustine of Hippo, emerges with great clarity.

ROME

Unfortunately, we have no liturgical texts for Christian initiation from the Church of Rome during this period of history.[1] In order to

---

[1] Much of this section on Rome and North Italy is based on my recent article, "The Postchrismational Structure of *Apostolic Tradition* 21, the Witness of Ambrose of Milan, and a Tentative Hypothesis Regarding the Current Reform of Confirmation in the Roman Rite," *Worship* 70:1 (1996) 16–34.

reconstruct what may have taken place it is necessary to depend upon references in other literature of the period. Two documents, both from the late fourth century, have sometimes been cited as evidence for the Roman rites of initiation. In his *Altercation of a Luciferian with an Orthodox*, Jerome (ca. 342–420 C.E.) witnesses to a practice of bishops imposing hands on and praying for the Holy Spirit for those neophytes, in rural areas, who had been baptized by presbyters and/or deacons in the absence of bishops.[2] Jerome himself, however, does not think much of this practice and suggests that it was being done "more to the honour of the ministry [episcopate] than for the principle of necessity."[3] And a fragment called the *Mai Fragment*, reflecting an Arian argument against Orthodoxy by citing orthodox liturgical texts, refers to the formula of *a* postbaptismal anointing, saying: "The God and Father of our Lord Jesus Christ, who granted you regeneration by water, himself anoints you with the Holy Spirit and the rest."[4] But it is by no means clear if either of these documents actually reflect specifically *Roman* liturgical practice. If they do, it is significant to note that neither refers clearly to the structure of *both* episcopal handlaying and (second) episcopal anointing known from *Apostolic Tradition* 21.

Our best witnesses to the Roman rites in this period are four important letters from the late fourth through the end of the fifth century which give us some insight into the evolving ritual pattern. Written as responses from bishops and others in Rome to particular questions concerning specific aspects of the rites, none of these letters, unfortunately, gives us a complete or detailed picture of those rites as a whole. Nevertheless, the information they provide is invaluable in trying to reconstruct their overall ritual shape and interpretation in this tradition.

Among these four letters, two of them provide us with only *some* small pieces of information about the catechumenate and the preferred day for baptism at Rome. First, a late-fourth-century *Letter of*

---

[2] For an English translation see Gordon Jeanes, ed. and trans., *The Origins of the Roman Rite*, Alcuin/GROW Liturgical Study 20 (Bramcote, Nottingham: Grove Books, 1991) 19–20.

[3] Ibid., 20.

[4] Ibid., 41. Whatever the phrase "and the rest" may have included, Jeanes is certainly correct here in interpreting this address to the neophyte as following the pattern of the first postbaptismal anointing and not the subsequent episcopal anointing of the Roman rite. See 41, n. 4.

Pope Siricius to Himerius of Terragona in Spain (ca. 384–5 C.E.)[5] refers to the enrollment of the electi before the beginning of Lent—*ante quadraginta* ("before the forty")—and to daily prayer, fasting, and exorcism throughout the time of preparation for Easter baptism. Not only is this one of the first references to a forty-day, pre-paschal Lent that we have in the West, but it indicates also that exorcisms were part of baptismal preparation at Rome. What is not clear in this letter, however, is whether or not Siricius is referring here to the "election" of former "catechumens" for baptism or if by now at Rome enrollment in the catechumenate and election to baptism have become synonymous events. Second, reference to baptismal preparation and exorcism occurs also at the end of the fourth-century in a document called the *Canones ad Gallos,* that is, "Canons to the Gauls" (ca. 400 C.E.), a collection of Roman responses to various inquiries from Gallican bishops. In Canon 8 of these responses, concerned with the frequency and use of "exorcized oil" during the baptismal preparation period, we read that "if the chrism poured upon the head imparts its grace to the whole body, in the same way also if he who is scrutinized *at the third scrutiny* is touched with the oil only once and not many times, God [nevertheless] acts upon his [whole] life."[6] Here we see our *first* clear indication of the *Roman* use of "exorcised oil" within the rites after the witness of the *Apostolic Tradition,* and that the Roman tradition has come to know *three* scrutinies during the period of final preparation for baptism. Lent as the time of final preparation for baptism, the use of exorcisms combined with anointings, and the practice of at least three scrutinies during Lent will remain characteristics of the Roman rite for centuries to come.

The two remaining letters for this period confirm what we see in Siricius' *Letter* and the *Canones ad Gallos.* In addition to this they provide us with some further detail about the shape of the initiation *rites* themselves.

The Letter of Pope Innocent I to Decentius of Gubbio (March 19, 416 C.E.)
In response to obvious confusion on the part of Bishop Decentius of Gubbio, a city about one hundred miles north of Rome, concerning

---

[5] Joannes Dominicus Mansi, *Sacrorum conciliorum nova et amplissima collectio,* III (Florence: 1759–98) 656B.
[6] DBL, 229; emphasis added.

who might administer what postbaptismal rites and where, Innocent I (bishop of Rome from 402–17 C.E.) writes:

"About the signing of the newly baptized: it is quite clear that no one may perform it except the bishop. For although presbyters are priests (*sacerdotes*), they do not have the highest degree of the priesthood (*pontificatus*). It is not only the custom of the Church which demonstrated that the signing and the gift of the Holy Spirit is restricted to bishops (*pontifices*), but the passage in the Acts of the Apostles which declares that Peter and John were sent to give the Holy Spirit to those already baptized. For when presbyters baptize, whether in the absence of a bishop or in his presence, they may anoint the baptized with chrism (provided that it is consecrated by the bishop) but they do not sign the forehead with this same oil. That is reserved to the bishops when they give the Spirit, the Paraclete."[7]

This important letter is our *first* undisputable witness to the practice of an episcopal handlaying and (second) postbaptismal anointing as parts of the *Roman* Rite. While the structure is obviously similar to *Apostolic Tradition* 21, here this unit is closely associated not only with the bishop but with the explicit giving of the Holy Spirit. Similarly, if no bishop is present at the rites of baptism, these postbaptismal rites are to be supplied later when a bishop can be present.

If the Latin translation of *Apostolic Tradition* reflects the middle of the fourth century (ca. 350 C.E.), then, sometime between the middle of that century and March 19, 416, it appears that the episcopal prayer of *Apostolic Tradition* 21, or a prayer very much like it, became pneumatic in orientation and remained so in the continual evolution of the Roman rites of initiation.[8] An episcopal, postbaptismal handlaying prayer invoking the Holy Spirit does appear later in the Roman tradition. Within the *Gelasian Sacramentary*, an early-seventh-century Roman presider's book for the Eucharist and other sacramental rites, the relevant prayer reads:

"God almighty, Father of our Lord Jesus Christ, who granted regeneration to your servants by water and the Holy Spirit, and who have

---

7 Jeanes, *The Origins of the Roman Rite,* 44–5.
8 See Aidan Kavanagh, *Confirmation: Origins and Reform* (New York: Pueblo, 1988) 59ff.

given them forgiveness of all their sins, send on them, Lord, your Holy Spirit the Paraclete, and give them the Spirit of wisdom and understanding, the Spirit of counsel and might, the Spirit of knowledge and godliness, fill them with the Spirit of the fear of God, in the name of our Lord Jesus Christ, with whom you live and reign, God forever with the Holy Spirit for ever and ever. Amen."[9]

Given Innocent's focus on the Holy Spirit in relationship to the bishop's postbaptismal ceremonies, it is quite possible that he is pointing to the existence of such a prayer already in the early part of the fifth century. Nevertheless, prior to his letter, we simply do not know what the postbaptismal rites looked like at Rome. And the difficult question, therefore, is whether or not this *structure* of prayer with episcopal imposition and the anointing reflects traditional *Roman* practice or represents a new development in the Roman initiation rites based on or adapted from something like the Latin version of *Apostolic Tradition* 21 itself.

With regard to the necessary role of the bishop underscored by Innocent in these postbaptismal rites, Aidan Kavanagh has suggested that Innocent's claim should be interpreted as pontifical "propaganda rather than a serene and objective articulation of doctrine" within the early-fifth-century Roman church. He writes:

"Communications in Italy were being disrupted by barbarian invasions at this time, and Rome itself had been sacked by the Visigoths in 410, a catastrophe which shocked the world. . . . An indigenization of Christianity in Roman forms of language and art was under way in order to fill the vacuum caused by the withdrawal of imperial administration and Christian urbanity eastward to Constantinople after 330. The church of the left behind laid claim to Rome's classical heritage, shorn of its paganism, as one of its own reasons to be the unique source of culture and religion in a West facing dark days. Latin language, art, and architecture were being Christianized and were beginning to flourish under strong popes like Damasus, Leo, and Gregory, who dedicated themselves to making Roman Christianity paradigmatic for the West. . . . One aspect of this effort in the face of appalling odds was the latinizing, stabilizing, and commending influence of Roman liturgical procedures to the church outside the

---

[9] English translation from Jeanes, *The Origins of the Roman Rite*, 17.

City. This is what Innocent is doing in his letter to the bishop of Gubbio. . . . Innocent is adamant that only bishops are involved. The reason for this is twofold. *Implicitly* it enhances the bishop's unique and indispensable role as the focus of unity in churches beset by the disintegrating effects of barbarian violence. . . . *Explicitly* Innocent requires episcopal hegemony . . . on the precedent of Acts 8."[10]

It should not be concluded automatically, however, that Innocent's letter to Decentius effected any immediate changes in how the rites of initiation were celebrated within the Roman tradition. Some seventy years later Pope Gelasius I (492–6 C.E.) also writes that presbyters were forbidden "to boldly take on themselves the things reserved to the episcopal degree: not to seize for themselves the faculty of making chrism nor of applying the pontifical consignation,"[11] a sure sign that presbyters were continuing to do both. Similarly, almost *one hundred* years later, Pope Gregory I (590–604 C.E.), although supporting the "traditional" prohibition against presbyters conducting these rites, says, "if any are troubled at all by this, we concede that where bishops are absent, *even presbyters ought to anoint the baptized with chrism on their foreheads.*"[12] Therefore, in spite of Innocent's firm insistence on the physical presence of the bishop for the celebration of these rites, outside of the city of Rome, where bishops were not in similar abundance, there remained, obviously, long-lasting confusion about the actual "need" for the presence of bishops for these rites and, hence, the continuation of presbyters themselves presiding at the whole rite. And it is this that Gregory I actually supports! Nevertheless, with Innocent's letter to Decentius, we see the real beginnings of what will come to be called in the Western Church the "sacrament of *confirmation,*" normally administered only by bishops either as a part of the "baptismal" rite or after some interval later.

The Letter of John the Deacon to Senarius (ca. 500 C.E.)
Apart from the following letter, we know nothing about either John the Deacon or Senarius. John, apparently, was a deacon in the Church of Rome during the troubled pontificate of Pope Symmachus (498–514

[10] Kavanagh, *Confirmation,* 56–7.
[11] Text in Paul Turner, *Sources of Confirmation: From the Fathers through the Reformers* (Collegeville: The Liturgical Press, 1993) 56.
[12] Ibid., 58; emphasis added.

C.E.); Senarius, possibly a member of the Roman nobility, addressed a series of questions to him about different aspects of Roman initiatory practice. In his response, John offers the following important information, giving us a glimpse of the overall shape both of the catechumenal process and the initiation rites at Rome on the eve of the sixth century:

"2. . . . you also ask what a scrutiny is, and why infants are scrutinized three times before Easter, and what benefit accrues to them by the concern and requirement of these scrutinies, and so forth.

what is a scrutiny

"3. . . . There is no doubt that, until born again in Christ, one is held bound by the power of the devil. Indeed, [one thus bound] should not approach the grace of the saving bath, unless, renouncing him [the devil] as part of the early rudiments of faith, one is extricated from his snares. In consequence, it is required that [candidates] enter first the schoolroom of the catechumens. . . . *Catechesis* is the Greek for 'instruction.' [Catechumens] are instructed through the church's ministry, by the blessing of the one who lays his hand [on their heads]. . . . [A catechumen], therefore is exorcised by exsufflation that with the devil put to flight, entry may be prepared for Christ our Lord. . . . [Next] the catechumen is signed with blessed salt, for just as all flesh is preserved healthy by salt, so the mind, drenched and driven by the waves of the world, is held on course by the salt of wisdom and of the preaching of God's word. . . .

"catechesis"
"catechumen"
Salt +"
p

"4. And so, by his own efforts and those of others, the person . . . now merits to receive the words of the creed handed down by the apostles. As a result, one who had just borne the name 'catechumen' is now called 'competent' or 'elect.' . . . Then follows what church custom called scrutinies. For we thoroughly test their hearts concerning faith to determine whether, since the renunciation of the devil, the sacred words [of the creed] have become fixed in their minds fastened themselves. . . . When it becomes clear from their replies that it is so . . . their ears and also their nostrils are touched with holy oil. The ears are touched [especially] because faith enters the mind, just as the apostle says: 'Faith comes by hearing, and hearing by the word of God' [Rom 10:17]. Thus, the ears, protected by a kind of holy wall, will admit nothing noxious to entice them back.

"competent" or "elect"
"scrutinies" — a church custom
Holy oil to ears and nostrils

"5. . . . The anointing of the nostrils signifies also that [the nostrils], with the oil blessed in the name of the Savior, are to be led to his

— Ears + nostrils

faith enters through the ear (Rom 10:17) + Faith enters through the mind
led to his odor by Spiritus its sweetness

131

spiritual odor by a certain inexpressible sweetness [perceived by their] inner sense. . . .

"6. Next, their breast, the seat and dwelling place of the heart, is anointed with the consecrated oil. . . . Then when either the elect or the catechumens have progressed in the faith through these spiritual vehicles, so to speak, then it is also necessary to be consecrated in the baptism of the unique bath. For in this sacrament one is baptized by triple immersion. . . . Then he is vested in a white garment, and his head is anointed with the unction of sacred chrism, so that the [newly] baptized may understand that in his person the kingdom and the priestly mystery have met. . . . For a fuller expression of the image of the priesthood, the head of the reborn is covered with a linen cloth. For the priests of that [ancient] time always wore a certain mystical covering on the head. . . . [T]hey wear white garments so that, although the ragged dress of ancient error has darkened the infancy of their first birth, the garment of the second birth may symbolize the garment of glory, so that attired in a wedding garment the [newly baptized] may approach the table of the heavenly bridegroom as a new person.

"7. . . . all these things are done even to infants, who by reason of their age understand nothing. Thus, you need to realize that by being sponsored by their parents or others, it is necessary that their salvation should come through other people's profession, since their damnation came by another's fault.

"12. You ask why milk and honey are [mixed] in the most sacred cup and offered with the Paschal Sabbath [the vigil Mass on Holy Saturday]. . . . This kind of rite is offered to the newly baptized, then, so that they may realize that only they, who share the Body and Blood of the Lord, shall receive the land of promise."[13]

Several parallels are to be noted here both with Tertullian and Cyprian in North Africa and the *Apostolic Tradition* in chapter 2 (i.e., prebaptismal exorcisms, paschal baptism, the presence of a postbaptismal anointing, the use of milk and honey in the giving of first communion, and the explicit mention of the participation of infants in *all* of the rites).

---

[13] Critical edition is André Wilmart, ed., *Epistola ad Senarium, Analecta reginensia,* Studi e Testi 59 (Vatican City: Biblioteca apostolica Vaticana, 1933) 170–9. The above translation is taken from MFC 6, 85–9.

With the *Canones ad Gallos* John confirms the presence of three scrutinies of the electi or *competentes* during the final period of baptismal preparation before Easter. In addition, John refers to the use of salt as part of the rite of becoming a catechumen as well as to an anointing of the ears, nostrils, and breast of the candidate during the scrutinies.

What is lacking in John's rather full description, however, is any mention of the postbaptismal rites underscored by Innocent and Gelasius I above. While no information from chapters 8 through 11 is included in the selection printed above, nothing about these rites is contained in those chapters. Chapter 8 does refer to the necessity of the bishop consecrating the chrism used for the postbaptismal anointing described in chapter 6, but not to the bishop performing an imposition of hands with prayer or administering a second anointing. Rather, the rites of initiation that John describes pass from baptism to the postbaptismal rites of being vested in a white garment and anointed with chrism and, immediately, to the reception of first communion during the baptismal Eucharist.

John, however, certainly *does* know the existence of the episcopal ceremonies of handlaying and (second) chrismation but questions their need. In chapter 14, in fact, when asked about the necessity of these ceremonies with regard to salvation, he responds by saying that all that is necessary is given already in the rites as he has described them.[14] Such reluctance on his part to advocate for these episcopal ceremonies would seem, again, to underscore at the end of the fifth century, and in spite of past papal directives to the contrary, that the rites of Christian initiation even at Rome itself had not yet become synthesized into a single dominant pattern.

The Rites of Christian Initiation at Rome

On the basis of the above letters, a picture of the overall shape of the rites of Christian initiation at Rome in this time period can be delineated. While variations in detail, including the absence or presence of the episcopal handlaying and anointing, can be discerned, the following general picture of those rites emerges:

(1) enrollment in the catechumenate of an unspecified length, with rites such as the giving of blessed salt, followed by a period of instruction,

[14] See MFC 6, 89.

during which rites of exorcism and exsufflation were frequently done;

(2) election to baptism, with the final baptismal preparation for the elect or *competentes* encompassing the forty days of Lent;

(3) three "scrutinies" were performed during this period of final preparation. On the basis of other evidence it seems certain that these three scrutinies corresponded to the third, fourth, and fifth Sundays of Lent;[15]

(4) prebaptismal anointing(s) of the senses;

(5) baptism itself by triple immersion;

(6) vested in white;

(7) postbaptismal anointing on the crown of the newly baptized's head with chrism, associated with the priesthood of Christ and administered by a presbyter;

(8) handlaying prayer and second anointing with chrism by the bishop *in frontem* (on the newly baptized's forehead), associated with the gift of the Holy Spirit; and

(9) reception of First Communion, including the cup of milk and honey.

With regard to the cup of milk and honey, the "Leonine," or Verona "Sacramentary," a sixth-century compilation of various prayers for the celebration of the Eucharist, refers to this as well in its collection of prayers for Pentecost.[16] Nevertheless, this document is our final reference to this practice, a practice which must have ceased in the Roman tradition shortly after the witness of John the Deacon itself.

As noted previously, the above outline does not give us a complete picture of Christian initiation at Rome in these centuries. While John tells us that the Creed was given to the elect at some point before the three scrutinies, none of the documents summarized above inform us about the *redditio symboli*, the *traditio* or *redditio* of the Our Father, the precise wording used in the administration of the anointings, handlaying prayer, or exorcisms, and whether or not a particular formula had yet developed at Rome in the administration of baptism itself. Nevertheless, the general outline presented above is consistent with what we know to be the later Roman liturgical pattern. It is this pattern, especially within the episcopal postbaptismal rites, that will be-

[15] On this, see below, chapter 5.
[16] See DBL, 153–4.

come, at least theoretically, the normative pattern for Christian initiation in the Latin West.

NORTH ITALY

ambroy 4ct Century

Ambrose of Milan

In the explanations of Christian initiation given within his two mystagogical catecheses, *De Sacramentis* and *De Mysteriis* (both of which are dated ca. 380–90 C.E.),[17] the great Ambrose, late-fourth-century bishop of Milan, provides us with valuable information on the shape of the rites and the theology of Christian initiation outside of Rome itself.

While there is little evidence of the entire catechumenal process in his writings, by Ambrose's time the final preparation of the *competentes* lasted throughout Lent. We also know that: (1) Ambrose himself gave daily addresses on Christian morals when the deeds of the patriarchs or the book of Proverbs were read; (2) sermons called *de Abraham* were delivered to those "proceeding to the grace of the Lord"; (3) a *traditio symboli* took place on Palm Sunday; and (4) the Lord's Prayer was delivered only *after* initiation itself.

What is extremely interesting, however, is that according to Ambrose himself in *In Expos, Ev. Luc. 4.76*, the enrollment of *competentes* did not take place at the beginning of Lent but, rather, on the feast of Epiphany (January 6), a custom which is also attested by Maximus of Turin (near Milan). It is possible that we have here, then, a connection with Alexandrian practice and perhaps also an indication that at some point in its history Milan itself knew a baptismal day and season of preparation unrelated to Easter.[18]

Beyond these few references to the catechumenate Ambrose gives us the following details of the Milanese rites of his day:[19]

"(*De Sacramentis* I.2): So what did we do on Saturday? The opening, of course. The mysteries of the opening were celebrated when the

---

[17] Critical editions in Latin with French translations in Bernard Botte, *Ambroise de Milan. Des Sacraments, Des mystéres. Explication du symbole*, SC 25 (Paris: Editions du Cerf, 1961).

[18] On this see Paul Bradshaw, *The Search for the Origins of Christian Worship* (New York: Oxford University Press, 1992) 180.

[19] The following passages of *De Sacramentis* are taken from Jeanes, *The Origins of the Roman Rite*, 9–10.

bishop touched your ears and nostrils.[20] What does this mean? In the gospel, our Lord Jesus Christ, when a deaf and dumb man was brought to him, touched his ears and mouth, his ears because he was deaf, his mouth because he was dumb, and said, 'Effetha,' a Hebrew word which means, 'Be opened.' And so the bishop touched your ears to open them to the words of the bishop and what he was to say.

"(I.4): We came to the baptistery. You entered, you were anointed. . . . You were anointed as Christ's athlete. . . .

"(I.5): When you were asked, 'Do you renounce the devil and his works?' what did you reply? 'I renounce.' 'Do you renounce the world and all its pleasures?' What did you reply? 'I renounce.'

"(II.16): You came to the font. You went down into it. . . .

"(II.20): You were asked, 'Do you believe in God the Father almighty?' You said 'I believe,' and you were immersed. . . . Again you were asked, 'Do you believe in our Lord Jesus Christ and in his cross?' You said, 'I believe' and you were immersed. . . . A third time you were asked, 'Do you believe also in the Holy Spirit?' You said, 'I believe,' and you were immersed a third time.

"(II.24): So you were immersed, you came to the bishop. What did he say to you? He said, 'God the Father almighty, who granted you regeneration of water and the Spirit and has forgiven you all your sins, himself anoints you to everlasting life.'

"(III.4): You came out of the font. What followed? You heard the reading. The bishop girded himself . . . and washed your feet.

"(III.5): We know that the church of Rome does not have this custom. We follow her pattern and form in everything; however, she does not have this custom of the footwashing.

"(III.8): There follows the spiritual seal of which you heard in the lesson today. After the font there remains the 'perfecting,' when the Holy Spirit is poured down at the bishop's invocation, 'the Spirit of

---

[20] Note that in John the Deacon, above, this was a "closing" of the senses rites rather than "opening."

136

wisdom and understanding, the Spirit of counsel and strength, the Spirit of knowledge and godliness, the Spirit of holy fear.'

"(III.11): What happens after this? You can approach the altar."

As we see, Ambrose claims to be following the customs of the Church of Rome in everything except for the unique Milanese rite of the *pedilavium,* a rite he justifies on the basis of the apostle Peter himself. Does this mean, then, that the postbaptismal rites known and described by him for Milan parallel those known and used at Rome in the same time period? The implication would seem to be that they are, since Ambrose nowhere attempts to defend an alternate practice.

The problem, however, is that the way in which Ambrose describes these postbaptismal rites is not all that clear. The structure certainly *appears* to be the same as *Apostolic Tradition* 21. Even his description of the spiritual seal in relationship to Isaiah 11:2-3 seems to parallel the prayer presumably known already by Innocent I.

Here, however, one must proceed with the utmost caution. As Pamela Jackson has demonstrated, Ambrose's spiritual seal is "elusive," and we simply do not know "what ritual action—*if any*—accompanied the bishop's prayer."[21] Aidan Kavanagh suggests that it may have been simply a general prayer for the neophytes or a concluding prayer for the entire rite.[22] And, to muddy the waters even further, whatever this spiritual seal may have been for Ambrose, later sources for the Milanese or "Ambrosian" liturgical tradition (e.g., the tenth-century *Ambrosian Manual*[23] and the twelfth-century *Ordo of Beroldus*[24]) have no corresponding rites beyond the one postbaptismal anointing and *pedilavium.*

---

[21] Pamela Jackson, "The Meaning of 'Spiritale Signaculum' in the Mystagogy of Ambrose of Milan," *Ecclesia Orans* 7 (1990) 94. Jackson suggests (93) that Ambrose "understood the rite not so much as a discrete effective sign, but more as a 'symbolic overflow' of what had just occurred in the font. Associating various dimensions of salvation with specific ritual actions still vivid in the neophytes' sense-memory would not only enable Ambrose's hearers to have a clearer understanding of the manifold aspects of God's grace in their lives, but also serve as a kind of mnemonic device enabling the neophytes to remember them years after their sacramental experience."

[22] Kavanagh, *Confirmation,* 55.

[23] DBL, 133–47.

[24] Ibid., 147–52.

The facts, therefore, are these:

(1) Ambrose claims to be describing a rite which, other than the *pedilavium*, does not depart from that used in the Church at Rome;
(2) Ambrose witnesses to an immediate postbaptismal anointing which parallels, structurally, the first anointing in Roman practice and cites an anointing formula here which parallels what is present in later Roman practice; and
(3) Ambrose refers to something he calls the spiritual seal, which, again, appears to correspond structurally to the episcopal handlaying prayer of *Apostolic Tradition* 21, and what we saw above in Innocent I and Gelasius I.

However:

(4) we do not have a clue about any gesture or ritual act associated with this spiritual seal in Ambrose; and
(5) the later Milanese liturgical tradition preserves nothing of this spiritual seal in its initiation rites.

How, then, are we to interpret Ambrose's claim that the rite he describes is no different from that used in Rome? At least three possibilities suggest themselves:

(1) Ambrose knows that the Roman postchrismational rite is actually different from that of Milan so he is attempting to make the Milanese rite *sound* as "Roman" as possible by using his episcopal freedom to cite a Roman prayer for the sevenfold-Spirit as a concluding prayer for the rite; or
(2) the rite in Ambrose's Milan was identical to that in Rome, which already had both an episcopal handlaying prayer and second chrismation, and Ambrose's spiritual seal should thus be interpreted similarly as a handlaying prayer with second chrismation, a unit which, for whatever reason, disappeared from Milanese usage later on; or
(3) the Roman rite itself had already moved in a pneumatic direction with the handlaying prayer, but it had either not yet adopted a second episcopal anointing or had done so only recently. And Ambrose either knew it as a recent innovation or did not know it at all. Consequently, his spiritual seal corresponds structurally only to the postchrismational handlaying prayer of the Roman rite and Ambrose is, thus, a witness that at Rome it was a prayer for the gift of the seven-

fold *Spirit.* But whether Ambrose's similar prayer included any accompanying ritual gesture cannot be known.

Of these three possibilities, the first is similar to that suggested above by Kavanagh, a possibility finding some support in later Gallican liturgical sources, where a final prayer for the neophytes, following either the single postbaptismal chrismation or the *pedilavium,* often concludes the whole initiation rite.[25] Ambrose, of course, *may* have been doing something similar in Milan, but we have no hard evidence that he was. The second possibility is actually a fairly traditional argument,[26] but, like the first, it too is little more than conjecture without any supporting evidence. If Milan once had a postbaptismal structure equivalent to what would become "confirmation" in the Roman rite, why would it disappear later, especially in the medieval period when everyone else is adopting the Roman structure? What then of the third possibility?

While the third possibility is also highly speculative in nature, and based more on an argument *ex silentio* than upon hard data, the following fact remains: Ambrose, who is so careful to describe other aspects of the initiation rites in detail, becomes so ambiguous here. And, when this is coupled with the paucity of sources corresponding to the Roman rites of initiation prior to the middle of the fourth century, both Ambrose's claim that Milan does not depart from Rome in this context and his ambiguity regarding what appears to be a significant portion of those rites in ca. 380–90 C.E. becomes quite suggestive. Could it be, indeed, that the Roman rite in this time period is itself ambiguous because the very elements by which that rite will come to be distinguished from all other non-Roman Western rites—i.e., the episcopal handlaying and subsequent episcopal anointing—have not yet fully developed beyond a handlaying prayer for the gift of the Holy Spirit, a rite to which Jerome possibly also refers in his *Altercation* in the 380s? Is, then, Innocent I's reference to the episcopal chrismation as a "custom of the Church" actually a reference to a practice relatively unknown at Rome before the mid to late fourth century, a practice which is becoming both pneumaticized theologically and

[25] See below, chapter 5, 198.
[26] See Leonel Lake Mitchell, *Baptismal Anointing,* ACC 48 (London: SPCK, 1966) 85–91.

integrated ritually into the Roman rite only in the last quarter of that century?

As we have seen, the fourth century in general was an era in which postbaptismal rites throughout the Christian world were added to rites that did not have them already. The rites which were added— most often, at least in the East, a single postbaptismal chrismation— were those associated with the conferral of the gift or seal of the Holy Spirit. Something similar, then, must have happened in Rome as well but there the pneumatic focus became attached not specifically to an anointing but to an episcopal handlaying prayer. Since the years between the Councils of Nicea (325 C.E.) and Constantinople (381 C.F.) were years of intense pneumatological debate and doctrinal dispute and consensus regarding the Holy Spirit, such ritual development is perfectly logical. Almost everyone in the fourth century is receiving a postbaptismal anointing into their initiation rites, except East Syria, of course, and the churches of North Africa and Rome where a single postbaptismal anointing was already in existence. But what is unique about Rome in this context is that Rome *alone* comes to adopt a *second* postbaptismal anointing, one reserved exclusively to the bishop as the concluding act of his pneumatic handlaying prayer.

Ambrose, therefore, may indeed be a credible witness to the Roman rite of his day. He knows the Roman rite and reflects that rite as far as he is able. But what he knows and reflects is a developmental stage in what will ultimately become the final form of that rite. In other words, Ambrose's spiritual seal and citation of a prayer are not references to an anointing but, more likely, to the pneumatically-oriented handlaying prayer of the Roman rite. If Ambrose had any ritual gesture for his spiritual seal, then the most likely one would be an imposition of hands. But *whatever* he may have been doing at Milan between the *pedalavium* and the Eucharist, it is quite clear that this spiritual seal as a particular ceremony does not remain an integral part of the Milanese or "Ambrosian" initiation rites.

Other Witnesses to the North Italian Rites

A detailed treatment of other Italian rites in this time period is not all that necessary. It will suffice to note that both [Pseudo] Maximus of Turin and Zeno of Verona, contemporaries of Ambrose of Milan, refer to initiation rites quite similar to those known by Ambrose— including also for Maximus, at least enrollment of the "elect" on Epiphany and the postbaptismal *pedalavium*—in their respective locales.[27] What is most significant here is that neither Maximus nor Zeno demonstrates any familiarity with a postbaptismal rite equivalent to the location of Ambrose's spiritual seal. Rather, any "sealing" or "consignation" gestures appear to be connected to the postbaptismal anointing itself, as in the *Mai Fragment* referred to above.[28] Outside of Rome, then, the rites of Christian initiation within North Italy appear to be rites that never knew or contained anything similar to the episcopal postbaptismal ceremonies of handlaying and (second) chrismation defended and advocated by Innocent I and Gelasius I within the Roman tradition. As we shall see below, a pattern similar to North Italy is encountered also in the Western liturgical traditions of Spain and Gaul.

SPAIN AND GAUL

As is the case elsewhere, no liturgical texts of initiation rites are available from Spain[29] or Gaul for the fourth and fifth centuries. On the basis of later "Gallican" and "Mozarabic" liturgical sources, however, it appears that the rites themselves in this period would have resembled more closely those of West Syria and northern Italy than those of Rome. A famous description by Gregory of Tours (ca. 594 C.E.) of the baptism of Clovis on Christmas Day (!) at Reims in 496 or 498 C.E., the barbarian king who was to become the leader of a new kingdom known as France, would tend to support this parallel.[30] While Gregory of Tours' account does not give us as many details as we would like for the fifth century beyond references to Clovis being baptized in the name of the Trinity and anointed immediately thereafter, vestiges of elements like the traditional distinction between catechumens and *competentes,* the use of salt in the rite of enrollment,

---

[27] See Bradshaw, *The Search for the Origins of Christian Worship,* 180; and Mitchell, *Baptismal Anointing,* 152–4.

[28] See Gordon Jeanes, ed. and comp., *The Day Has Come! Easter and Baptism in Zeno of Verona,* ACC 73 (Collegeville: The Liturgical Press, 1995) 179–86 and 206ff.

[29] The standard study for Spain is T. Akeley, *Christian Initiation in Spain, c. 300–1100* (London: Darton, Longman & Todd, 1967).

[30] On this see the recent article by my colleague Michael Driscoll, "The Baptism of Clovis and French Baptismal Consciousness," *Proceedings of the North American Academy of Liturgy* (Valparaiso, Ind.: The Academy, 1997) 133–46.

exorcisms and scrutinies during the period of final preparation, the *traditio symboli* on Palm Sunday, a single postbaptismal anointing, an imposition of hands (Spain), and the *pedilavium* (Gaul) appear in the writings of Isidore of Seville (+ 636 C.E.)[31] and Ildefonse of Toledo (+ 667 C.E.)[32] for Spain and in several "Gallican" liturgical books of the eighth century. In addition, several local councils held during the course of the fourth and fifth centuries in Spain and Gaul do provide us with valuable information on some aspects of the development of those rites. Particularly significant is the fact that it is in these local councils where we first encounter the word "confirmation" (*confirmare* or *perficere*) used in reference to particular rites associated with the ministry of bishops.

Spain

The Council of Elvira, 305 C.E.

"*(Canon 38):* Travelers abroad or those in an area far from a church may baptize a faithful catechumen placed in the necessity by sickness, if the bath is unbegun and the catechumen is not a bigamist. If the catechumen survives, they lead him or her to the bishop, that the catechumen may profit through the laying on of hands."[33]

"*(Canon 48):* It was agreed to change the custom which has grown up, namely, that those who are baptized shall not make any payment, so the priest not appear to be charging for what he himself has received freely. Also, the feet of those baptized shall not be washed by priests or clerics."[34]

"*(Canon 77):* If any deacon governing the people baptizes some without the bishop or presbyter, the bishop will have to perfect [*perficere*] them through the blessing. If they leave this world beforehand, under the faith in which they believed, they are able to be justified."[35]

---

[31] See DBL, 109–11.

[32] See ibid., 111–5.

[33] Mansi, *Sacrorum conciliorum*, II.12, 18. Translation adapted from Turner, *Sources of Confirmation*, 53–4.

[34] Translation is adapted from DBL, 223.

[35] Mansi, *Sacrorum conciliorum*, II.18. Translation adapted from Turner, *Sources of Confirmation*, 54.

The First Council of Toledo, 398 C.E.

"*(Canon 20):* Although almost everywhere it is held that no one may make chrism but a bishop, nevertheless, since in some places or provinces presbyters are said to make chrism, it is agreed from this day that no one else but the bishop may make chrism and send it throughout the diocese. Thus in individual churches deacons or sub-deacons are appointed for the bishop before the day of Easter, that chrism made by the bishop, destined for the day of Easter, may appear. Certainly it is permitted for a bishop to make chrism at any time; but without the knowledge of a bishop practically nothing should be done. But it is established that when the bishop is absent, a deacon may not use chrism, but a presbyter may. But if the bishop is present, the presbyter may use it if this has been ordered by the bishop himself."[36]

Gaul

The First Council of Arles, 314 C.E.

"*(Canon 8 or 9):* Concerning Africans who use their own law to rebaptize, it is agreed that if people come to the Church from a heresy, the African faithful may ask them for the creed. If the faithful discern that the inquirers were baptized into the Father, the Son, and the Holy Spirit, only let the hand be imposed on them that they may receive the Holy Spirit. But if when asked for the creed they do not know this Trinity, let them be baptized."[37]

The First Council of Orange, 441 C.E.

"*(Canon 2):* By no means should *any minister* who accepts the duty of baptizing proceed without chrism, because it is agreed among us to be *chrismated once.* However, at confirmation *[in confirmatione],* the priest *[sacerdos,* i.e., bishop] will be reminded about those who were not chrismated in baptism, when some necessity appeared. For among certain ministers of this chrism, it is nothing but a blessing [or, *chrism can only confer its blessing once*], not to foreshadow anything, *but that a repeated chrismation not be held necessary.*"[38]

---

[36] Mansi, *Sacrorum conciliorum,* III.1002. Translation from Turner, *Sources of Confirmation,* 74–5.

[37] CCSL 148.10–11. Translation from Turner, *Sources of Confirmation,* 87.

[38] CCSL 148.78. Translation adapted from Turner, *Sources of Confirmation,* 49; emphasis added. See also the translation in DBL, 228.

The Rites of Christian Initiation According to These Councils

Apart from references to the possibility of lay people baptizing in cases of necessity and the use of the *pedilavium* at some point in the rite, the overall importance of these councils lies in what they have to say about the development of the postbaptismal rites, the use of chrism, and the number of chrismations within those postbaptismal rites. As the Councils of Elvira and Toledo make clear, presbyters, obviously, were not only consecrating the chrism to be used in baptism but, within late-fourth-century Spain, deacons themselves were performing the postbaptismal anointing. By underscoring that only the bishop can "make" or consecrate chrism, then, these councils were attempting to put an end to both of those situations, although there is no question here about presbyters themselves as the appropriate ministers of the entire rite.

With regard to the use of *"confirmare"* or *"perficere"* in relationship to the bishop within these documents, we must proceed cautiously. The situations referred to in the texts above all appear to be "exceptional" or extraordinary cases, rather than a regular part of a standard ritual pattern. That is, only in extraordinary situations, such as emergency baptisms (Elvira 38, 77), the reconciliation of heretics (Arles 9), or when chrism had been unavailable or, for some other reason, the chrismation after baptism was omitted (Orange 2), is the bishop then required to do something in addition to what had taken place in baptism itself.

What this "something" is that the bishop was to do, however, is not all that clear from these documents. According to Gabriele Winkler,[39] followed by Aidan Kavanagh[40] and Gerard Austin,[41] the phrase *in confirmatione* ("at confirmation") in Orange 2 above, refers, primarily, to a *visit* of the bishop to the parishes of his diocese, who on those occasions "confirmed" or ratified what had already been done by the presbyter or deacon. That is, it is not the newly baptized but the *sacramental ministry* of the local presbyter or deacon which is *confirmed* by the bishop's visit.

Any liturgical acts the bishop may have actually done on such visits would most likely vary according to the particular situations he en-

---

[39] Gabriele Winkler, "Confirmation or Chrismation?" LWSS, 210–4.

[40] Kavanagh, *Confirmation*, 66–7.

[41] Gerard Austin, *Anointing with the Spirit: The Rite of Confirmation: The Use of Oil and Chrism* (New York: Pueblo, 1985) 13.

countered. If a deacon, rather than a presbyter, had performed the baptism, the bishop would "perfect" this baptism through a "blessing," possibly the imposition of the bishop's hands on the newly baptized (Elvira 38, 77). If a presbyter had performed all of the initiation rites, including the postbaptismal chrismation, it is possible that the bishop did not perform any liturgical act whatsoever at this "confirmation" visit (Toledo 20, Orange 2). Alternatively, if that postbaptismal chrismation had been omitted by the presbyter this was supplied by the bishop (Orange 2). Hence, it is quite possible these fourth- and fifth-century councils are directing bishops to "perfect," "complete," or "confirm" baptisms done by presbyters or deacons as a matter of pastoral oversight rather than regular sacramental ministry.

Concerning the postbaptismal chrismation in Orange 2, it is important to underscore the fact that it is to a *single* and not double chrismation that reference is made. That is, bishops are to supply this *single* chrismation *"in confirmatione"* only if it had not been done already at baptism itself. In other words, this council, by asserting that "chrism can confer its blessing *once*," thus seems to be protecting the unitive nature of the Gallican initiation rites, which knew only *one* postbaptismal anointing. Either presbyters were chrismating and then presenting the newly baptized for another chrismation by the bishop, or some bishops, in imitation of Roman practice (?), were adding a second anointing with chrism *in confirmatione*, and the First Council of Orange is attempting to put an end to that questionable and "unnecessary" practice.

A Famous Sermon on Pentecost

It is possible that the above references in the Spanish and Gallican councils to *confirmare* or *perficere* do refer to an episcopal act of postbaptismal handlaying associated with the gift of the Holy Spirit.[42] As we have seen previously, it was in this same time period that Jerome (ca. 342–420 C.E.) knew of bishops who imposed hands on and prayed for the Holy Spirit for neophytes, in rural areas, who had been baptized in the absence of bishops.[43] Furthermore, we do have one Gallican text that clearly refers to a separate postbaptismal imposition of

---

[42] See Frank Quinn, "Confirmation Reconsidered: Rite and Meaning," LWSS, 219–37.

[43] See above, 126.

hands as, presumably, a regular part of the rites of Christian initiation, a fifth-century (or later?) Pentecost homily, attributed to a Bishop Faustus of Riez. Faustus was a fifth-century south Gallican bishop who, although revered there as a saint for his defense of orthodoxy against Arianism, was actually a semi-Pelagian in his theology of grace.[44] Whatever the date of this homily and whoever its author was—both are disputed[45]—the key part of this homily, based on a division between baptism and "confirmation," as an *imposition of hands* by the bishop, is the following statement which will become classic in Western theology of confirmation:

"What the imposition of the hand bestows in confirming individual neophytes, the descent of the Holy Spirit gave people then in the world of believers. . . . The Holy Spirit, who descends upon the waters of baptism by a salvific falling, bestows on the font *a fullness toward innocence,* and presents *in confirmation an increase for grace.* And because in this world we who will be prevailing must walk in every age between invisible enemies and dangers, *we are reborn in baptism for life, and we are confirmed after baptism for the strife. In baptism we are washed; after baptism we are strengthened.* And although the benefits of rebirth suffice immediately for those about to die, nevertheless the helps of confirmation are necessary for those who will prevail. Rebirth in itself immediately saves those needing to be received in the peace of the blessed age. Confirmation arms and supplies those needing to be preserved for the struggles and battles of this world. But the one who arrives at death after baptism, unstained with acquired innocence, is confirmed by death because one can no longer sin after death."[46]

---

[44] See L. A. Van Buchem, *L'Homélie Pseudo-Eusébienne de Pentecôte: L'origine de la confirmation en Gaule Méridionale et l'interprétation de ce rite par Fauste de Riez* (Nijmegen: Drukkerij Gebr. Janssen, 1967). On Pelagianism see below, 153–5.

[45] I tend to agree with Winkler, "Confirmation or Chrismation?" 214–6, against Van Buchem, that it is actually a later text than mid fifth century. Indeed, because of the clear separation between baptism and "confirmation" in the text, it appears to be justifying the Carolingian import and imposition of the Roman rites of initiation into the liturgy of Gaul in the early Middle Ages, not within the time period of the mid fifth century.

[46] CCSL 101.37f. Translation from Turner, *Sources of Confirmation*, 35–6; emphasis added.

How widespread or normative this kind of rite was in fifth-century Gaul is not known. What should be noted, however, is that, presumably, this handlaying rite took place at some interval after the Gallican rites of initiation themselves had been performed. Nevertheless, as we shall see further below,[47] the later Gallican and Mozarabic rites which have been preserved display no liturgical trace of anything like an additional or separate episcopal act of handlaying or chrismation as part of those traditions.

NORTH AFRICA

Augustine of Hippo

The influence of Augustine of Hippo (354–430 C.E.) on sacramental theology in Western Christianity cannot be overemphasized.[48] After about thirty-three years as a "catechumen," although not an active or faithful one by any means, Augustine eventually became one of the *competentes*, while teaching in Milan, and was baptized by Ambrose himself at the Easter Vigil in 387 C.E. Four years later he was ordained a presbyter at Hippo in North Africa and in 395 C.E. became that city's bishop, where he remained until his death.

Augustine does not tell us too much about the particular rites of initiation that he knew and experienced. What he does tell us indicates that the North African rites of his day were similar to the other non-Roman Western rites we have seen already. With regard to initiation, then, Augustine's primary importance is in his theological thought about what constitutes a "valid" sacrament and in his development of the relationship of sin to baptism, particularly in the case of the initiation of infants. Both of these topics, as we shall see, were hammered out in the midst of serious controversies in the North African Church of his day.

The North African Rites of Initiation in the Time of Augustine

What we know of the North African rites of Christian initiation in the late fourth and early fifth centuries shows numerous parallels to those of Milan and with what we assume were the rites of initiation also in Gaul and Spain. References in both Augustine and the Third

---

[47] See chapter 6, 189–94, 197–201.
[48] On Augustine himself, see Peter Brown's excellent biography, *Augustine of Hippo* (Berkeley: University of California Press, 1967).

Council of Carthage (397 C.E.) refer to *salt* being given to catechumens.[49] In fact, in Augustine's famous *Confessions* he writes of having been made a catechumen as a small child, saying: "For while yet a boy I had heard of the eternal life promised in the lowliness of our Lord God condescending to our proud minds: I was signed with his cross and seasoned with his salt from my mother's womb."[50]

Augustine also knew several penitential practices associated with the final preparation of candidates for baptism such as fasting, exorcisms, the wearing of hair shirts, and assembly at vigils. As in Milan, the North African rites also seem to have known the ceremony of the *Pedilavium*, but here it functioned as a *prebaptismal* ceremony done on Holy Thursday. In North Africa as at Rome, there were, apparently, three scrutinies during this final preparation period, including on two separate occasions the *traditio symboli* and the delivery of the Our Father, with the *redditio symboli* within the context of initiation itself. In North Africa, at least, these scrutinies could be quite severe. Based on several scattered references in Augustine and elsewhere, Thomas Finn gives the following description of a North African scrutiny:

"In the eerie light of first dawn the candidates stood barefoot on the coarse animal skins (*cilicium*), naked and with head bowed. Invoking the power of Christ and the Trinity, voicing vituperative biblical condemnations of Satan, and imposing hands, the exorcist hissed in the faces of competents, preemptorily commanding the Evil One to depart. There followed a physical examination to determine whether any of the competents showed evidence of a disease, which signaled the continued inhabitation of Satan. Granted that they passed scrutiny, the competents, each in her or his own voice, then renounced Satan, his pomps, and his service."[51]

Concerning the rites themselves, a late-fourth-century North African bishop, Optatus of Milevi (ca. 370 C.E.) refers to three "sacraments" or "mysteries" in the celebration of initiation: baptism, the sacrament of oil, the sacrament of the imposition with hands. He writes:

[49] On Augustine and the rites of Christian initiation in general see the recent and detailed study of William Harmless, *Augustine and the Catechumenate* (Collegeville: The Liturgical Press, 1995).

[50] *Confessions* I.11, DBL, 100.

[51] MFC 6, 155.

148

"The heaven is open. When God anoints him the spiritual oil at once comes down under the form of a dove and sits upon his head and pours over him; the oil is spread asunder; whence he began to be called Christ, for he was anointed by God the Father; and lest he should seem to lack the imposition of a hand, the voice of God was heard from the cloud, saying . . ."[52]

Augustine himself refers to the postbaptismal anointing with chrism as a sacrament like baptism itself. It is associated with the person of Christ and is a sign of our participation in him. A royal and priestly anointing, it is also related to the newly baptized becoming wrestlers against the devil, an idea we have seen elsewhere (Chrysostom, Ambrose, et al.), but there it is associated with the pre- rather than postbaptismal anointing. However, says Augustine: "The Holy Spirit is signified whether through the water for cleansing and washing, or through the oil for exultation and the inflaming of charity; nor indeed, although the signs are different, does he differ from himself."[53]

As to the presiders of the initiation rites, it is significant that Augustine refers elsewhere to presbyters as ministers of the complete rite. Similarly, according to Canons 32 and 36 of the Third Council of Carthage in 397 C.E., presbyters were forbidden to consecrate chrism, a sure sign that not only were they doing so but also that they were understood to be the ministers of the entire rite.[54] Hence, there is no evidence to support the notion that postbaptismal rites like anointing or handlaying were ever reserved to bishops alone in North Africa. And there is certainly no evidence to suggest the existence of anything other than *one* postbaptismal anointing followed by handlaying, rites integrally connected to baptism itself and associated both with participation in Christ and the gift of the Holy Spirit.

The Reduction to "Sacramental Minimalism" in Augustine's Theology

As noted above, throughout his episcopacy (395–430 C.E.) Augustine found himself in the midst of several controversies threatening the life of the Church in North Africa. Two of these controversies, the

---

[52] *Contra Parmenianum Donatistam*, 4.7, as cited by Mitchell, *Baptismal Anointing*, 82.

[53] DBL, 106.

[54] See Turner, *Sources of Confirmation*, 55–6.

Donatist and the Pelagian, were to have serious and long lasting consequences for sacramental theology, in general, and for the interpretation of Christian initiation, in particular. Western sacramental theology—Roman Catholic *and* Protestant—even today is influenced by the positions of Augustine brought about by these controversies, positions which may be interpreted as bringing about a reduction in the West to a theology of "sacramental minimalism."

The Donatist Controversy. Having its roots in the North African Christian tradition, known to us from the theology of Tertullian and, especially, Cyprian of Carthage, Donatism owes its immediate origins to the aftermath of the Diocletian persecution (311 C.E.). Accusing Caecilian, the newly elected bishop of Carthage, of not having ministered to a group of forty-seven Numidian martyrs imprisoned in Carthage during the persecution, and accusing those who ordained him as being *traditors,* that is, those who had "handed over" the sacred books to the authorities during that persecution, a Bishop Secundus and seventy others elected and ordained a man named Majorinus as the "real" or rival bishop of Carthage. With this event the Donatist Schism (so named for Majorinus' successor Donatus) was born and, in spite of several imperial interventions and local councils in the following years, this schism continued to divide the North African Church until the Arabic conquests of the seventh century, after which we hear very little about North African Christianity in general.[55]

The ecclesiastic-political issues in this schism need not concern us here. Rather, with regard to Christian initiation, the primary issues are theological. That is, following the theology of Cyprian and earlier North African Councils concerning the necessity of rebaptism for heretics and schismatics,[56] the Donatists claimed that they alone were the legitimate church of North Africa and, as such, could alone dispense the true sacraments whose validity and efficacy, in their opinion, depended upon the worthiness and moral character of the

---

[55] On the Donatist controversy and schism in general see W.H.C. Frend, *The Donatist Church: A Movement of Protest in Roman North Africa* (Oxford: Clarendon Press, 1952); W.H.C. Frend, *Saints and Sinners in the Early Church* (Wilmington, Del.: Michael Glazier, 1985) 94–117; W.H.C. Frend, *The Rise of Christianity* (Philadelphia: Fortress Press, 1984); and Geoffrey Willis, *Saint Augustine and the Donatist Controversy* (London: SPCK, 1950) 1–92.

[56] See above, 69–71.

minister. According to them, the real schismatics were the *traditors*, the North African Catholics, who, because they had betrayed Christ, were corrupt and impure and could not, therefore, give either the forgiveness of sins or the Holy Spirit in baptism. Rather, they had become like Judas Iscariot. Hence, it was the North African Catholics, not them, who needed to be rebaptized by them if they were to be saved. W.H.C. Frend summarizes the theology of Donatism, saying:

"The ideas of Donatus and his followers were simple. As God was one, so was his church, and its hallmark was purity. The integrity of the church lay in the integrity of its members, sealed by baptism and working in concord with its bishops. They witnessed to the faith by penance and suffering, and aspired finally to a martyr's death. There was no salvation outside this body of the elect. Other considerations—such as worldwide extent, imperial favor, even communion with apostolic sees . . .—were irrelevant. 'What we look for,' said Petilian . . . 'is the conscience of the giver [of baptism] giving in holiness to cleanse that of the recipient. For he who knowingly receives faith from the faithless receives not faith but guilt.'"[57]

It is in response to Donatism that Augustine developed his interpretation of what constitutes the "valid" administration and the proper minister of baptism. Against the Donatist charge that the Catholic Church in North Africa and elsewhere was a church of traitors and that its ministers, no better than Judas Iscariot himself, were, thus, not able to administer valid sacraments, Augustine argued that:

(1) any baptism that makes use of the proper element of water and the proper words (i.e., the trinitarian baptismal interrogation) is "valid";[58]
(2) any sacrament results from "the word . . . added to the element" and becomes "itself also a kind of visible word" (*Tractates on the Gospel of John* 80.3);[59]
(3) since Christ himself, then, was the true and only minister of baptism, even Judas Iscariot could administer a "valid" sacrament if the proper elements and proper words were used.

[57] Frend, *The Rise of Christianity*, 654.
[58] *Contra litteras Petiliani*, I.6.6. For English translation see NPNF, first series, vol. 4, 515–628.
[59] Ibid., 344.

Jaroslav Pelikan accurately summarizes Augustine's theological approach here, saying:

"The Augustinian theology of grace was . . . obliged . . . to commit itself to the principle that the efficacy of the sacraments, and especially of baptism, was assured 'ex opere operato,' by the sheer performance of the act, rather than 'ex opere operantis,' by the effort of the performer upon the act. . . . This assured the priority of the divine initiative; for it was God, not the bishop or the priest, who did the baptizing, ordaining, and dispensing of sacramental grace."[60]

In developing this position Augustine makes another important distinction that will also come to characterize sacramental theology in the West. Because Christ, and not the minister, was the "origin and root and head" of the baptized, even Donatist (i.e., schismatic) sacraments were to be considered as valid.[61] But it did not necessarily follow for Augustine that these "valid" sacraments were, thereby, "fruitful." The distinction that Augustine makes in this context is between the sacrament or sign itself (*sacramentum*) and its reality or fruitfulness (*res sacramenti*). For those outside the unity of the Church, Christ's baptism does exist but, on account of the sin of schism (which consists of "hatred of the brethren") there is no presence of the fruit of both baptismal regeneration and the forgiveness of sins which is charity or love.[62] Similarly, where there is no charity the Holy Spirit is no longer present.[63] As a result, there can be no proper use or full effect of baptism outside the unity of the one Church. The Donatists, therefore, *did* possess the sacraments of Christ but they possessed them to their condemnation "in the sacrilege of schism."[64] Hence, only by returning to unity with the one Church would baptism ultimately be of benefit to the Donatists themselves. As long as they remained in schism the sacrament would be useless. Geoffrey Willis summarizes Augustine's view of the issue:

---

[60] Jaroslav Pelikan, *The Christian Tradition: A History of the Development of Doctrine*, vol. 1, *The Emergence of the Catholic Tradition (100–600)* (Chicago: University of Chicago Press, 1971) 312–3.

[61] *Contra litteras Petiliania*, I.5.6.

[62] *De Baptismo contra Donatistas*, I.3.4. For English translation see NPNF, first series, vol. 4, 407–514.

[63] Ibid., I.12.19.

[64] Ibid.

"The sacrament itself is not limited to members of the visible Catholic Church, but its use is. Those on whom it is conferred in schism possess it . . . but it is no use to them outside the Church. No grace is available, though the empty shell of the sacrament is possessed. If they remain outside the Church all their lives, they receive nothing. But when they enter the fold of the Church, and are reconciled by the imposition of hands, the latent grace revives, and what was possessed before uselessly, and more probably to the damnation of the recipient, is now crowned with the gift of charity, and begins to fructify the life of the recipient."[65]

One can certainly criticize Augustine on this point. Frend argues, for example, that "a sacrament originating from Christ that failed to benefit its recipient is not possible."[66] Nonetheless, it is important to note that Augustine's primary focus here is on reestablishing the unity of the *one* Church in North Africa and, contrary to the North African theological tradition itself, he is able to recognize the legitimacy of sacraments conferred even among schismatics. Indeed, thanks in large part to Augustine's response to Donatism, as well as to the earlier controversy between Cyprian and Stephen, the Church even today can recognize that the "one baptism for the forgiveness of sins" transcends denominational boundaries.

The Pelagian Controversy. As important and influential for sacramental theology in the West as Augustine's response to the Donatist Controversy was, his response to Pelagianism had equally far-reaching consequences for baptismal theology and practice. Whatever the precise relationship between the British monk Pelagius himself (ca. 400 C.E.) and "Pelagianism," this theological position maintained that human beings, like Adam in the Garden of Eden before the Fall, are born with absolute free will and are able to choose and turn to good as well as evil. In other words, human beings have been created with the possibility of obeying the Law of God perfectly and by so doing come to merit an eternal reward from God. While Adam's sin did bring about the consequences of suffering and death for humanity, the human will itself was unaffected by this sin.[67]

[65] Willis, *Saint Augustine and the Donatist Controversy,* 167.
[66] Frend, *The Rise of Christianity,* 670.
[67] On Pelagianism in general see Pelikan, *The Christian Tradition,* vol. 1, 278–331. On Augustine and infant baptism in general see R. de Latte, "Saint

It was, primarily, in response to the challenges against the widespread practice and long tradition of infant baptism in North Africa by Celestius, a disciple of Pelagius who came to North Africa from Rome after the sack of Rome in 410 C.E., that Augustine develops what has come to be called the theology of "original sin." Contrary to the Pelagian position, Augustine argued that the human will is not free but sick, "curved in upon itself" (incurvatus in se ipsum) and seeks only the gratification of its own self-oriented desires (a condition of concupiscence or lust). Hence, from the moment of birth (if not before), human beings *cannot* choose, will, or do what is good but are in need of the medicine of divine grace in order to choose, will, and do the good. It is this prevenient grace which is necessary in order to heal the will and orient it away from the sinful self to God, who will then continue to grant grace for every good desire and act. Human nature, then, is corrupt, mortally wounded by sin. And if this sin is not cured by the divine physician it becomes the source of all other sin. Without this cure humanity remains a *massa damnata*, a "condemned mass," and those who die unbaptized are not saved, a position that was unacceptable to the later Western Church.

For Augustine the cause of this human sickness leading to condemnation, of course, is the sin of Adam himself, which has been transmitted to all human beings along with suffering and death. Although he refuses to commit himself to any one philosophical position on the precise "moment" when this original sin is transmitted to any particular human being, it is clear that for him it is connected somehow to the process of human reproduction, especially as the sexual act itself is related to sexual "desire." That is, "Augustine clearly taught that original sin and guilt are derived from the act of procreation, 'in virtue of the lustful promptings of his body . . . to serve the purpose of propagation.'"[68]

It is true, of course, that Augustine's theology here is based in part on the fact that rites of exorcism in baptism demonstrated the obvious need for *all* candidates—both adults and infants—to be liberated from

Augustin et le baptême. Étude liturgico-historique du rituel baptismal des enfants chez saint Augustin," *Questions Liturgiques* 57:1 (1976) 41–55.

[68] Carl Volz, *Faith and Practice in the Early Church: Foundations for Contemporary Theology* (Minneapolis: Augsburg Publishing House, 1983) 55.

sin, death, and the devil.[69] If baptism is for the forgiveness of sin, then the fact that infants are baptized (a practice which antedates any theological rationale for it) obviously indicates that they are in need of forgiveness. More than this, however, is it the case that Augustine is trying to be a faithful interpreter of Paul in Romans 5:12, namely: "as sin came into the world through one man and death through sin, . . . so death spread to all because all sinned." But Augustine's text was the then-available *Latin* version of Romans 5:12 ("and so death spread to all *in whom [in quo]* all sinned," rather than *"because* all sinned"). The theological problem, then, was the apparent presence of all people *in* Adam himself. Had he known his Greek better, or at least used a Greek version of Romans 5,[70] his theology of "original sin" undoubtedly would have been different. Rather than focusing on the problem of the presence of the human race *in* Adam, the narrative of Adam and Eve (Genesis 3) would still have functioned, as it did in Origen and among others in the Greek-speaking East, as a fitting model of a fallen humanity, who continues to ratify the "original sin" of Adam by its own sins.

Nevertheless, while it is fashionable today to criticize him for his apparently negative attitudes toward human sexuality, his faulty biblical exegesis, and his pessimism regarding human nature:

". . . it remains a fact of human experience that by nature human beings are driven by self-centered forces. A contemporary author suggests that Augustine's doctrine [of original sin] helps to 'account for the statistical regularity with which [people] who supposedly faced Adam's possibilities always made Adam's choice.'"[71]

Appeal is often made to Augustine's theology to support the practice of infant baptism. But it should be noted that Augustine himself, like Cyprian of Carthage, was a strong defender of the unitive and integral character of the initiation rites as whole, including that of the *communion* of infants. For Augustine, the rites of Christian initiation were not separated. As David Holeton has written:

"Augustine . . . makes the infant the model of the perfect subject for the sacraments. This is in part because the infant images the

---

[69] See MFC 6, 152–3.

[70] On this see Pelikan, *The Christian Tradition,* vol. 1, 299–300.

[71] Volz, *Faith and Practice,* 56.

total helplessness of the human condition. The human creature must come to the Father with the same helpless abandon as the sucking infant does to his mother. . . . There is another dimension to Augustine's use of the infant as the model of the perfect sacramental subject. It is that of the pre-rational, or the non-rational, as the ideal approach to the sacrament. The words with which Jesus reveals the mystery of the eucharist in John 6 are those of infants or the mad. To eat the sacrament is to become a child inwardly. In other words Augustine sees as ideal subjects for the sacraments the two categories of persons we have traditionally excluded: infants and the insane."[72]

Nevertheless, by putting together Augustine's responses to Donatism and Pelagianism one ends up with a baptismal rite and theology which is considerably narrow in its approach in comparison, at least, with the great mystagogues of the West Syrian East and even Ambrose himself. Here, unfortunately, even if his responses to these heretical movements were necessary, we see the beginnings of a minimalistic approach to rite, interpretation, candidate, minister, and Church and a loss of sacramental and liturgical richness in favor of a concern for sacramental validity. While he himself knew a full and rich rite for Christian initiation there is no question but that: "if ever there was a man who held that the solemn paraphernalia of the actual rite was of little importance, but that the sacrament of baptism by water was indispensible for salvation, that man was Augustine."[73] This minimalism in rite, formula, and interpretation will continue to reinforce an unfortunate theology of baptism even today as almost a privatized "minute wash" to rid infants, as soon as possible after birth, of the inherited sin of Adam (not necessarily of Eve) and so to ensure their eternal beatific destiny "in case something should happen." On this issue, at least, Western Christianity not only learned its Augustinian theological foundations well but has been abundantly successful through the centuries in catechizing the faithful. Indeed, although the practice and custom

---

[72] David Holeton, *Infant Communion: Then and Now*, Grove Liturgical Study 27 (Bramcote, Nottingham: Grove Books, 1981) 6.

[73] Frederik van der Meer, *Augustine the Bishop: The Life and Work of a Father of the Church,* trans. Brian Battershaw and G. R. Lamb (London: Sheed and Ward, 1961) 352.

of infant baptism comes long before any theological rationale for it is made, from Augustine on, infant baptism will become seen as *necessary* and *expected,* rather than permitted, in the life of the Church.

CONCLUSION

A homogeneity similar to that of the Christian East in these two centuries, noted in the conclusion of the previous chapter, is present also in the rites of initiation in several distinct churches as they developed within the Christian West. With the notable exception of Rome's unique postbaptismal ceremonies, the overall shape of the rites, as the following chart demonstrates, displays a remarkable degree of commonality:

Ambrose of Milan	Rome	Gaul/Spain	North Africa
PREBAPTISMAL RITES			
Anointing	Anointing	Anointing	Anointing
Renunciation	Renunciation	Renunciation	Renunciation
BAPTISM PROPER			
Baptism	Baptism	Baptism	Baptism
POSTBAPTISMAL RITES			
	White Garment		
Anointing	Anointing	Anointing	Anointing
White Garment			
Pedilavium		*Pedilavium* (?)	*Pedilavium*
Spiritual Seal	Imposition of hands and prayer by bishop		Imposition of hands
	Anointing of forehead by bishop		
Eucharist	Eucharist		Eucharist
		Visit of bishop called "confirmation" or "perfection"	

Similarly, almost all of the interpretive elements noted above for the Christian East,[74] except for the use of the *syntaxis*, are likewise present in the West. In the West, however, prebaptismal rites associated with exorcism and purification—a Romans 6 baptismal interpretation, Easter baptism, and postbaptismal rites associated in some way with the gift of the Holy Spirit—seem not to reflect the same kind of transition that transpired in the Christian East but, rather, further development consistent with what was known in some form already in the pre-Nicene Western sources. This seems to be the case especially for Rome and North Africa.

The major transitions for the West in these centuries are theological and ecclesiastical-hierarchical. That is, Augustine's response to the Donatist and Pelagian controversies, a response I have referred to as a "reduction to sacramental minimalism," focused attention on issues of sacramental validity and on the "need" for the baptism of infants, based on the developing theology of "original sin." The ecclesiastical-hierarchical issues, as we have seen, increasingly centered around defining the precise role of the bishop in the rites of Christian initiation, a role ambiguously referred to as *"confirmare"* or *"perficere"* in relationship to something called *"in confirmatione"* (Spain and Gaul) or associated with the "delivery" of the Holy Spirit in a postbaptismal context (Innocent I).

To whatever *"confirmare," "perficere,"* or *"in confirmatione"* actually refer in these documents, it is important to underscore that the particular ceremonies which will come to be associated with a specific sacramental rite called "confirmation" are those unique postbaptismal rites of Rome. *Only* Rome had an episcopal handlaying rite *and* a second postbaptismal anointing. And in the following centuries, these uniquely Roman postbaptismal episcopal rites will become *the* postbaptismal rites of Western Christianity in general. Increasingly separated from baptism and first communion, and, as we shall see, aided by the interpretation of (Pseudo?) Faustus of Riez, these rites will become a separate "sacrament" altogether. But that, in part, is the subject of chapter 6.

[74] See above, 121–3.

Baptismal Preparation and the Origins of Lent

In the previous two chapters it became quite obvious that there had developed within the fourth- and fifth-century Church a definite preference for celebrating the rites of Christian initiation at Pascha (Easter), with the forty-day preparatory period of "Lent" now coming to serve as the prime time for the final preparation of, depending upon the tradition in question, the elect, *competentes,* or *photizomenoi.* Prior to this period, as we saw in chapter 2 of this study, it is not clear when in the context of the year the rites of initiation were to take place or when or how long the period of preparation for baptism actually was. For the pre-Nicene period, in fact, our only references to the possible length of baptismal preparation are, perhaps, the forty days of the Egyptian tradition, where this period does not seem to be related to Pascha at all, and the three-year catechumenate of the *Apostolic Tradition,* a reference which, as we have also seen, may not be all that reliable for the early third century. But because both Pascha and Lent certainly became closely united with the celebration of the rites of Christian initiation, a relationship underscored and advocated by modern liturgical reform and renewal, it is very important that some attention be given to this relationship as it developed in the early Church. This chapter, then, really an *excursus* into the evolution of a portion of the liturgical year itself, is primarily concerned with the origins of Lent in Christian antiquity. As we shall see, those origins seem to have everything to do with baptismal preparation and only little to do with Pascha specifically.

It was once commonly assumed that this forty-day period of pre-paschal preparation for baptismal candidates, penitents, and the Christian community in general known as Lent (*Quadragesima* or *Tessarakoste,* i.e., "forty") had its origin as a gradual backwards development of the short preparatory and purificatory fast held before the annual celebration of Pascha.[1] According to this standard theory, the

---

[1] See Adolf Adam, *The Liturgical Year: Its History and Meaning after the Reform of the Liturgy* (New York: Pueblo, 1981) 91ff.; Gregory Dix, *The Shape of*

one- or two-day fast before Pascha (as witnessed to by Tertullian in *De ieiunio* 13–14) became extended to include:

(1) the entire week, later called "Great" or "Holy Week," beginning on the preceding Monday;
(2) a three-week period (at least in Rome) including this "Holy Week"; and, finally,
(3) a six-week, forty-day preparation period assimilating those preparing for Easter baptism to the forty-day temptation of Jesus in the desert.

That this pre-paschal period finally became forty days in length in the fourth century has been traditionally explained by an appeal to a shift in world view on the part of the post-Constantinian Christian community. That is, instead of an eschatological orientation to the imminent parousia of Christ little concerned with historical events, sites, and time, the post-Constantinian context of the fourth century reveals a Church whose liturgy has become principally a historical remembrance and commemoration of the *past*; a liturgy increasingly splintered into separate commemorations of historical events in the life of Christ. As the primary and most influential proponent of this theory of fourth-century "historicism," Gregory Dix, explained it:

"The step of identifying the six weeks' fast with the 40 days' fast of our Lord in the wilderness was obviously in keeping with the new historical interest of the liturgy. The actual number of '40 days' of fasting was made up by extending Lent behind the sixth Sunday before Easter in various ways. But the association with our Lord's fast in the wilderness was an idea attached to the season of Lent only after it had come into existence in connection with the preparation of candidates for baptism."[2]

Recent scholarship, however, most notably by Thomas Talley,[3] has necessitated revising previous theories. We can no longer speak of a

_____

the Liturgy (London: Dacre Press, 1945) 347–60; Patrick Regan, "The Three Days and the Forty Days," *Worship* 54 (1980) 2–18; and Pierre Jounel, "The Year," *The Church at Prayer,* vol. IV, ed. A.-G. Martimort (Collegeville: The Liturgical Press, 1986) 65–72.

[2] Dix, *The Shape of the Liturgy,* 354.

[3] Thomas Talley, *The Origins of the Liturgical Year,* 2d ed. (Collegeville: The Liturgical Press, 1986); and Thomas Talley, "The Origin of Lent at Alexan-

single origin for Lent but, rather, of multiple origins for this period, which in the fourth-century post-Nicene context become universally standardized and fixed as the "forty days" that have characterized pre-paschal preparation ever since.

THE PRIMITIVE PRE-PASCHAL FAST

Whenever and however Easter came to be universally celebrated on a Sunday in Christian antiquity, third-century sources indicate that the two-day fast on the Friday and Saturday before the celebration of Pascha was becoming a six-day pre-paschal fast in Alexandria and Syria.[4] Although this extension has often been interpreted as the initial stage in the development of the forty-day Lent (since this week is included in the overall calculation of Lent in later liturgical sources), this six-day preparatory fast is better interpreted as the origin of what would come to be called "Holy" or "Great Week" throughout the churches of the ancient world. Thomas Talley observes that within the later Byzantine tradition Lazarus Saturday and Palm Sunday divide Lent, which precedes them, from the six-day pre-paschal fast of Great Week which follows. These days were known already in fourth-century Jerusalem.[5] Rather than being related specifically to the origins of Lent, therefore, the two-day (or one-week) fast in these third-century sources (with the possible exception of *Apostolic Tradition* 20)[6] seems to have been an independent preparation of the faithful for the imminent celebration of the

---

dria," *Worship: Reforming Tradition* (Washington, D.C.: Pastoral Press, 1990) 87–112.

[4] See Paul F. Bradshaw, "The Origins of Easter," *Two Liturgical Traditions,* vol. 5, *Passover and Easter,* ed. Paul F. Bradshaw and Lawrence A. Hoffman (Notre Dame, Ind.: University of Notre Dame Press, forthcoming).

[5] Talley, *The Origins of the Liturgical Year,* 176–214. See also Talley, "The Origin of Lent at Alexandria," 97–108.

[6] Although, as we have seen, *Apostolic Tradition* 20 refers to a Friday and Saturday (?) fast for those who are to be baptized at the close of a Saturday night vigil, it does not specifically relate either the prebaptismal fast, baptism, or the vigil to Pascha. Hippolytus of Rome himself certainly knew paschal baptism but there is no evidence that the compiler of *Apostolic Tradition,* whoever it may have been, did. On this see Paul F. Bradshaw, *The Search for the Origins of Christian Worship* (New York: Oxford University Press, 1992) 90, 174–8; and Paul F. Bradshaw, "Re-dating the Apostolic Tradition: Some

Pascha itself. Already in the third-century *Didascalia Apostolorum* this fast is related, chronologically, to events in the last week of Jesus' life. In other words, the *Holy Week* fast, properly speaking, is not *Lent* but a pre-paschal fast alone, which overlaps, but should not be confused with, an earlier preparatory period that comes to be known as Lent.

Thanks to the "historicism theory" of Gregory Dix in particular, the development of Holy Week has often been explained as the result of post-Nicene preoccupation with Jerusalem, whose "liturgically minded bishop," Cyril, was fixated on the liturgical commemoration of historical holy events at the very holy places where they once occurred.[7] From Jerusalem as a pilgrimage center, then, these commemorations spread to the rest of the Church and tended to shape the way this week was celebrated elsewhere.

In fact, however, as early as the pre-Nicene *Didascalia Apostolorum*, this week has already been assimilated to events in Jesus' last week. As Robert Taft and John Baldovin have demonstrated for Jerusalem,[8] the situation cannot be explained adequately as a simple interpretive shift from a pre-Nicene eschatological orientation to a fourth-century historical one. "Eschatology" and "history" are not mutually exclusive. As we shall see, even prior to Nicea, the date of Easter, the assimilation of the six-day pre-paschal fast to some chronology of Jesus' final week, and an assimilation of a forty-day fast to the forty-day postbaptismal temptation of Jesus in the desert—although not in relationship to a pre-paschal "Lent"—were already accomplished. Post-Nicene lenten trends were liturgical evolutionary, not revolutionary, trends, and were not suddenly instituted by individual influential figures (like Cyril) in response to the changed situation of the Church in the post-Constantinian world.[9]

Preliminary Steps," *Rule of Prayer, Rule of Faith: Essays in Honor of Aidan Kavanagh, O.S.B.*, ed. John Baldovin and Nathan Mitchell (Collegeville: The Liturgical Press, 1996) 3–17.

[7] Dix, *The Shape of the Liturgy*, 348–53.

[8] Robert Taft, "Historicism Revisited," *Beyond East and West: Problems in Liturgical Understanding* (Washington, D.C.: Pastoral Press, 1984) 15–30; John Baldovin, *The Urban Character of Christian Worship* (Rome: Pont. Institutum Studiorum Orientalium, 1987) 90–3.

[9] See Bradshaw, *The Search for the Origins of Christian Worship*, 65–7.

A THREE-WEEK PRE-PASCHAL PREPARATION

The fifth-century Byzantine historian, Socrates, describes his understanding of the variety of Lenten observances throughout the Christian churches of his day:

"The fasts before Easter will be found to be differently observed among different people. Those at Rome fast three successive weeks before Easter, excepting Saturdays and Sundays. Those in Illyrica and all over Greece and Alexandria observe a fast of six weeks, which they term 'the forty days' fast.' Others commencing their fast from the seventh week before Easter, and fasting three five days only, and that at intervals, yet call that time 'the forty days' fast.' It is indeed surprising to me that thus differing in the number of days, they should both give it one common appellation; but some assign one reason for it, and others another, according to their several fancies."[10]

What is most intriguing about Socrates' statement is his reference to a three-week lenten fast at Rome. Since he corrects himself about Saturdays as non-fasting days in Rome later in this work and since Athanasius (in his Festal Letter of 340 C.E.),[11] Jerome (in a letter to Marcella in 384 C.E.),[12] and Pope Siricius (in a letter to Himerius of Tarragona in 385 C.E.)[13] refer to an established pattern of a forty-day Lent there too, his statement is inaccurate as a fifth-century description. Nevertheless, his reference to "three successive weeks" of fasting appears to be corroborated by later sources of the Roman liturgy. Such evidence includes:

(1) the provision of three *missae pro scrutiniis* (masses for the scrutinies of baptismal candidates) assigned to the third, fourth, and fifth Sundays of Lent in the Gelasian Sacramentary (seventh century); (2) the course reading of the Gospel of John during the last three weeks of Lent (beginning in the *Würzburg Capitulary*, the earliest Roman lectionary [ca. 700 C.E.], on the Friday before the third Sunday in Lent and reaching its conclusion on Good Friday); and (3) the titles *Hebdomada in mediana* (week in the middle) and *Dominica in mediana* (Sunday in the middle), applied, respectively, to the fourth

---

[10] *Historia ecclesiastica* 5.22.
[11] *The Festal Letters of St. Athanasius* (Oxford: n.p., 1854) 100.
[12] *Letter* 24.4 (PL 22.428).
[13] PL 13.1131–47.

week and fifth Sunday of Lent in various *ordines Romani* (ceremonial and rubrical guides) and Roman lectionaries.

In light of all this, Socrates' inaccurate fifth-century description may well indicate the remnant of a well-ingrained three-week lenten period in Rome some time earlier. Such, at least, was the conclusion of Antoine Chavasse,[14] from his analysis of the Johannine readings of the last three weeks on Lent which he was able to reconstruct as an independent set of lections that must once have constituted an original three-week lenten period, including Holy Week.[15] Along similar

[14] See Antoine Chavasse, "La structure du Carême et les lectures des messes quadragésimales dans la liturgie romaine," *La Maison-Dieu* 31 (1952) 76–120; Antoine Chavasse, "La préparation de la Pâque, à Rome, avant le Ve siècle. Jeûne et organisation liturgique," *Memorial J. Chaine* (Lyon: Facultés catholiques, 1950) 61–80; and Antoine Chavasse, "Temps de préparation à la Pâque, d'après quelques livres liturgiques romains," *Rech. de Sc. relig.* 37 (1950) 125–45. For a more detailed summary and discussion of Chavasse's work see my essay, "From Three Weeks to Forty Days: Baptismal Preparation and the Origins of Lent," LWSS, 118–36.

[15] Chavasse noted that the series of Johannine readings during the last three weeks of Lent in early Roman lectionaries and in the Tridentine *Missale Romanum* began with John 4:5-32 on the Friday of Lent III. For some reason, however, it placed John 9:1-38 (Wednesday of Lent IV) and John 11:1-45 (Friday of Lent IV) *before* John 8:46-59 (Sunday of Lent V), and John 10:22-38 (Wednesday of Lent V) with the continuation of John 11 (47-54) on the Friday of Lent V. On this basis he attempted to reconstruct an earlier shape for this Johannine series, which he believed would have corresponded to the three *missae pro scrutiniis* in the Gelasian Sacramentary. According to his reconstruction, John 4:5-32, John 9:1-38, and John 11:1-54 would have been read, respectively, on the third, fourth, and fifth Sundays in Lent in the time of Leo the Great. Even so, at an earlier stage of development this would have constituted a short lectionary series for the Sundays of an original three-week lenten period, including Holy Week. The reason that this series of readings appears in a different sequence in later Roman sources, according to Chavasse, is due to the fact that the baptismal scrutinies along with their readings became shifted to weekdays (ultimately, seven in number) in the later Roman tradition. Thanks to the work of Chavasse, this is precisely the sequence of Sunday Gospel readings assigned to the third, fourth, and fifth Sundays in Lent in series A of the current Roman Lectionary. To these Sundays have been attached the three scrutinies of adult catechumens in the current Roman *Rite of Christian Initiation of Adults*.

lines, Thomas Talley has also concluded that Socrates' reference may reflect an earlier, if not fifth-century, Roman practice.[16]

The possibility of an original three-week Lent, however, is not limited to Rome. On the basis of a detailed structural analysis of the contents of the fifth-century Armenian Lectionary, a lectionary generally understood to reflect fourth-century Jerusalem practice, Mario F. Lages has argued that early Jerusalem practice too knew an original three-week lenten preparation period of catechumens for paschal baptism.[17] Along with these contents—including a canon of lenten readings with concluding psalmody assigned to Wednesday and Friday gatherings at Zion and a list of nineteen catechetical biblical readings assigned to lenten catechesis (which parallel the prebaptismal catecheses of Cyril of Jerusalem)—Lages also pointed to the introductory rubric in the ninth- or tenth-century Armenian rite of baptism and to a pertinent rubric in the fifth-century Georgian Lectionary. The Armenian baptismal rubric reads in part:

"The Canon of Baptism when they make a Christian. Before which it is not right to admit him into the church. But he shall have hands laid on beforehand, *three weeks or more* before the baptism, in time sufficient for him to learn from the Wardapet [instructor] both the faith and the baptism of the church."[18]

And the Georgian Lectionary, while listing the same nineteen catechetical readings as Cyril and the Armenian Lectionary, specifically directs that catechesis is to begin with these readings on the Monday of the fifth week in Lent, that is, exactly *nineteen* days (or approximately three weeks) before paschal baptism.[19]

---

[16] Talley, *The Origins of the Liturgical Year*, 167.

[17] Mario F. Lages, "Étapes de l'evolution de carême à Jérusalem avant le Ve siècle. Essai d'analyse structurale," *Revue des Études Arméniénnes* 6 (1969) 67–102; and Mario F. Lages, "The Hierosolymitain Origin of the Catechetical Rites in the Armenian Liturgy," *Didaskalia* 1 (1967) 233–50. See also Maxwell E. Johnson, "Reconciling Cyril and Egeria on the Catechetical Process in Fourth-Century Jerusalem," *Essays in Early Eastern Initiation*, ed. Paul F. Bradshaw (Bramcote, Nottingham: Grove Books, 1988) 24–6. For the Armenian Lectionary see Athanase Renoux, *Le codex arménien Jérusalem 121*, vol. 2 (Turnhout: Brepols, 1971).

[18] DBL, 60; emphasis added.

[19] Michel Tarschnischvili, *Le grand lectionnaire de l'Église de Jérusalem*, vol. 1 (Louvain: Secrétariat du CorpusSCO, 1959) 68.

That is not all: this early three-week lenten period in Rome and Je-rusalem was customary in other liturgical traditions as well. I have suggested elsewhere that a similar three-week period of final prepa-ration for baptismal candidates is discernible from an analysis of the last three weeks of the forty-day Lent in North Africa, Naples, Con-stantinople, and Spain.[20] For Spain, in particular, this three-week pe-riod appears to be confirmed by the first canon of the Second Council of Braga (572 C.E.), which directs that bishops:

". . . shall teach that catechumens (as the ancient canons command) shall come for the cleansing of exorcism twenty days before baptism, in which twenty days they shall especially be taught the Creed, which is: I believe in God the Father Almighty. . . ."[21]

What Socrates says about the "three successive weeks" of pre-paschal fasting at Rome, therefore, should be seen as the memory of an early Christian practice which was much more universal than Roman in its scope.

On the basis of this discernable pattern in Christian liturgical sources, Lawrence Hoffman has suggested that this practice has its ultimate roots in Judaism.[22] Hoffman notes that, according to rabbinic sources, the feast of Passover itself is preceded by lectionary readings (Exodus 12 or Numbers 19) on the third Sabbath prior to its arrival. These readings stress either preparation for the Passover sacrifice or the necessity of being cleansed from impurity. The Exodus 12 read-ing, he notes further, was cited by Chavasse as an early reading for Good Friday at Rome and the prophetic reading of Ezek 36:25-36 (ac-companying Numbers 19 according to the *Tosefta*) appears on the Wednesday of Lent IV in early Roman lectionaries, that is, two and one-half weeks before Easter. According to Hoffman, therefore, the early three-week Lent—at least in Jerusalem and Rome—was "a Christian application of Judaism's insistence that one count back three weeks from Passover in order to cleanse oneself and prepare for

[20] See Johnson, "From Three Weeks to Forty Days," 191–3.

[21] DBL, 227.

[22] Lawrence A. Hoffman, "The Jewish Lectionary, the Great Sabbath, and the Lenten Calendar: Liturgical Links between Christians and Jews in the First Three Christian Centuries," *Time and Community: In Honor of Thomas Ju-lian Talley,* ed. J. Neil Alexander (Washington, D.C.: Pastoral Press, 1990) 3–20.

the sacrifice of the Paschal lamb."[23] If Hoffman is correct, then, as Talley writes, "this could well suggest that the three-week preparation for Pascha antedates its employment as the framework for baptismal preparation."[24]

The strength and appeal of Hoffman's theory are that it appears to provide a firm rationale for the Christian choice of a three-week period of preparation. The problem, however, is that when we first see whatever evidence there is for this three-week "Lent" (with the exception of Socrates' general reference to fasting) it is already closely associated with the final preparation of catechumens for baptism and not always clearly associated with Easter baptism.

The Armenian baptismal rubric, for example, stresses three weeks of preparation for baptism without specifying when that baptism is to take place. But the early Syrian and Armenian traditions, as we have seen,[25] favored baptism to take place on Epiphany, not Easter, since they understood Christian initiation as the mimesis of the Jordan event interpreted in light of the rebirth imagery of John 3 rather than the paschal imagery of Romans 6. The three-week period of preparation was therefore more probably associated with catechumenal preparation for baptism without having anything to do with Easter.[26] Similarly, thanks again to the work of Talley, it is now common knowledge that prior to the post-Nicene context of the fourth century, the Alexandrian tradition knew neither Easter baptism nor a pre-paschal "Lent" longer than the *one* week of the paschal fast. And, it must be noted, the reference to "three weeks" in the Constantinopolitan liturgy is actually a reference in the *typica* to the enrollment of baptismal candidates exactly three weeks before the celebration of baptism on Lazarus Saturday (the day before Palm Sunday and a full week *before* Easter), a day which in current Byzantine usage still contains the vestige of a baptismal liturgy in its entrance antiphon.[27]

[23] Ibid., 14.

[24] Talley, *The Origins of the Liturgical Year*, 167.

[25] See above, 47–8.

[26] See Gabriele Winkler, *Das armenische Initiationsrituale* (Rome: Pont. Institutum Studiorum Orientalium, 1982) 437–8; and Gabriele Winkler, "The Original Meaning of the Prebaptismal Anointing and Its Implications," LWSS, 58–81.

[27] See Talley, *The Origins of the Liturgical Year*, 189, 203–14.

Because of the primary association of this three-week period with baptismal preparation, the real question, therefore, is whether or not this period must necessarily be connected to Easter and, consequently, to a pre-paschal Lent. Talley has stated that "Pascha was becoming the preferred time for baptism in many parts of the Church" in the third century,[28] but Paul Bradshaw has recently surveyed the evidence for this assertion and comes to a much different conclusion.[29]

According to Bradshaw, the most that can be said about Easter baptism before the fourth century is that there is a *preference* expressed for this practice, a preference *limited* to third-century North Africa (Tertullian) and Rome (the *real* Hippolytus), with its possible celebration on other days by no means excluded. Only in the post-Nicene context of the fourth century does paschal baptism, along with a Romans 6 reinterpretation of baptism as incorporation into the death and resurrection of Christ, become a near universal Christian *ideal.* Even then, however, it does not appear to become the only or dominant custom outside of Rome or north Italy. The letter of Pope Siricius to Himerius of Tarragona (385 C.E.), one of the earliest Roman references to a forty-day Lent, reveals a variety of baptismal occasions in Spain (i.e., Christmas, Epiphany, and the feasts of apostles and martyrs). Evidence from Leo I demonstrates that Epiphany was also a baptismal day in Sicily and that the feasts of martyrs were baptismal occasions elsewhere in Italy. And, similarly, a sermon of Gregory Nazianzus shows that Epiphany baptism was a common practice in Cappadocia. These examples, along with those of Alexandria and Constantinople referred to above, lead Bradshaw to say that "baptism at Easter was never the normative practice in Christian antiquity that many have assumed. The most that can be said is that it was an experiment that survived for less than fifty years."[30]

What, then, may be concluded finally about Socrates' three-weeks and the origins of Lent? As we have seen, it is primarily within the context of final baptismal preparation where references to this three-week period are discerned. But what is most striking is that not all of these sources refer to *Easter* baptism. We seem therefore to have a

[28] Ibid., 167.
[29] Paul F. Bradshaw, "'*Diem baptismo sollemniorem*': Initiation and Easter in Christian Antiquity," LWSS, 137–47.
[30] Ibid., 147.

three-week period of (final) catechetical preparation for baptism that only later gets associated with Easter. It becomes "Lent" simply because Easter gradually becomes the preferred day for Christian initiation. Whenever baptism occurred, it was preceded, as the Armenian baptismal rubric says, by "three weeks or more" of preparation. For those churches (North Africa and Rome) which "preferred" to celebrate initiation at Pascha we may speak of this three-week period as a kind of primitive "Lent." For those which did not have such an early preference, this three-week period was not "Lent" but merely a final catechetical baptismal preparation for whenever baptism itself was to occur. Only when paschal baptism becomes the normative ideal—as Bradshaw says, in the second half of the fourth century—do these variations become blurred, harmonized, and thus brought into universal conformity as part of the newly-developed pre-paschal *Quadragesima* or *Tessarakoste*.

THE FORTY DAYS AS A PRE-PASCHAL SEASON

As already noted, the pre-paschal Lent of forty days, like the universal ideal of paschal baptism itself, also appears to be a fourth-century post-Nicene development. Talley writes:

"the Council of Nicea is something of a watershed for the fast of forty days. Prior to Nicea, no record exists of such a forty-day fast before Easter. Only a few years after the council, however, we encounter it in most of the church as either a well-established custom or one that has become so nearly universal as to impinge on those churches that have not yet adopted it."[31]

From where, then, does this forty-day fast as a pre-paschal preparation period emerge?

Following the initial work of Anton Baumstark and R.-G. Coquin,[32] it is Talley himself who has provided what is rapidly becoming the standard answer to this question by directing scholarly attention to Alexandria. Within this tradition neither Easter baptism nor a pre-paschal

[31] Talley, *The Origins of the Liturgical Year,* 168.
[32] Anton Baumstark, *Comparative Liturgy,* trans. F. L. Cross (London: A. R. Mowbray, 1958) 194; René Georges Coquin, "Une Réforme liturgique du concile de Nicée (325)?" *Comptes Rendus, Académie des Inscriptions et Belles-lettres* (Paris: n.p., 1967) 178–92.

fast of more than one week was customarily known. And, as we saw above in chapter 2, there are references in the sources of this tradition to a *forty-day fast* separate from this one-week pre-paschal fast. Such references, it must be recalled, appear in Origen's *Homilies on Leviticus* 10.2, in the context of remarks concerning the reconciliation of penitent apostates in Peter of Alexandria's *Canonical Epistle* (ca. 305 C.E.), and in the *Canons of Hippolytus* (ca. 336–40 C.E.), the earliest document derived from the so-called *Apostolic Tradition:*

"(Origen): They fast, therefore, who have lost the bridegroom; we having him with us cannot fast. Nor do we say that we relax the restraints of Christian abstinence; for we have the *forty days consecrated to fasting,* we have the fourth and sixth days of the week, on which we fast solemnly."[33]

"(Peter of Alexandria, Canon 1): for they did not come to this of their own will, but were betrayed by the frailty of the flesh; for they show in their bodies the marks of Jesus, and some are now, for the third year, bewailing their fault: it is sufficient, I say, that from the time of their submissive approach, *other forty days* should be enjoined upon them, to keep them in remembrance of these things; *those forty days* during which, though our Lord and Saviour Jesus Christ had fasted, He was yet, after He had been baptized, tempted by the devil. And when they shall have, during these days, exercised themselves much, and constantly fasted, then let them watch in prayer, meditating upon what was spoken by the Lord to him who tempted Him to fall down and worship him: 'Get behind me, Satan; for it is written, Thou shalt worship the Lord thy God, and Him only shalt thou serve.'"[34]

"(*Canons of Hippolytus* 12): during *forty days* they [the catechumens] are to hear the word and if they are worthy they are to be baptized."[35]

"(*Canons of Hippolytus* 20): The fast days which have been fixed are Wednesday, Friday, *and the Forty.* He who adds to this list will receive

[33] English translation from Talley, *The Origins of the Liturgical Year,* 192; emphasis added.

[34] ANF 6, 269; emphasis added.

[35] Paul F. Bradshaw, ed., *The Canons of Hippolytus,* Alcuin/GROW Liturgical Study 50 (Bramcote, Nottingham: Grove Books, 1987) 19; emphasis added.

a reward, and whoever diverges from it, except for illness, constraint, or necessity, transgresses the rule and disobeys God *who fasted on our behalf.*"[36]

While in two of these sources the forty-days of fasting are explicitly related to Jesus' own postbaptismal temptation in the desert, none of them speak of this period in relationship to Pascha and only one of them to baptismal preparation. It would be very difficult, therefore, to interpret these "forty days" as clearly referring to a period connected to a pre-paschal forty-day Lent in Egypt.

Might they, however, be references to a unique and early Alexandrian custom and season? As we have already seen earlier, Talley certainly believes so and, after a detailed analysis of admittedly later Egyptian liturgical sources, concludes that this unique and early Alexandrian forty-day fast soon became a forty-day prebaptismal fast for catechumens begun on the day after Epiphany (January 6), a feast which celebrated the baptism of Jesus. Following the chronology of the Gospel of Mark—the Gospel traditionally associated with the Church of Alexandria—this fasting period concluded forty days later with the solemn celebration of baptism and, in light of Canon 1 of Peter of Alexandria, perhaps with the reconciliation of penitents.

Recall also that in conjunction with baptism, according to Talley, a passage was read from a now lost secret Gospel of Mark (the *Mar Saba Clementine Fragment*),[37] which describes an initiation rite administered by Jesus himself of an unnamed Lazarus-like figure whom Jesus had raised from the dead six days earlier in Bethany. And, it is important to note, the next chapter in Markan sequence (Mark 11) describes Jesus' "Palm Sunday" entrance into Jerusalem. If Talley is correct, the "forty days" of Lent ultimately have an Alexandrian origin. At the same time, this post-Epiphany practice at Alexandria would also explain the Constantinopolitan custom of baptism on Lazarus Saturday as well as the use there of Lazarus Saturday and Palm Sunday to distinguish and separate Lent from Great Week.[38]

---

[36] Ibid., 25; emphasis added.

[37] On this see above, chapter 2, 54–6.

[38] In all fairness it must be noted that Talley's theory is based less on available early Alexandrian evidence and more on a hypothetical reconstruction of early Alexandrian practice discerned from the Markan sequence of Gospel readings for the Saturdays and Sundays of Lent in the later Byzantine lenten

The question remains, however: *How* does this Alexandrian forty-day post-Epiphany baptismal-preparation fast become the pre-paschal Lent? For this there is no clear or easy answer. Coquin thinks that Lent became a universal forty-day pre-paschal period as the result of the Council of Nicea's determination of the calculation to be employed for the annual celebration of Easter throughout the church.[39] The sudden post-Nicene universal emergence of the forty-days of pre-paschal preparation for Easter and for baptism at Easter does suggest that the Nicene settlement included this preference for Easter baptism. This preference was now seemingly followed everywhere except at Alexandria, which, although shifting its traditional forty-day period to a pre-paschal location in order to conform generally to the rest of the church, continued to celebrate baptism itself at the very end of this forty-day period, first on Good Friday, and second, because of the addition of another week of fasting later attached to the beginning of Lent, on the Friday before Holy Week. A vestige of this tradition continues in the Coptic Church today with baptisms not allowed between Palm Sunday and Pentecost.[40]

After Nicea, when the forty days of Lent became attached to pre-paschal preparation throughout the churches of the ancient world, different manners of calculating the actual duration of this season were employed. This resulted in both the differing lengths of Lent and the different fasting practices during Lent within the various churches which caused Socrates to express his surprise that all of them, nonetheless, used the terminology of "forty days" to refer to this period. In Rome, for example, the forty days began on the sixth Sunday before Easter (called *Quadragesima*) and thus, including the traditional pre-paschal two-day fast on Good Friday and Holy Saturday, lasted for a total of forty-two days. But, since Roman practice did not know fasting on Sundays, the total number of fast days was

---

lectionary. In the Byzantine lectionary this Markan sequence is followed until Lazarus Saturday when the reading given is John 11, the "canonical" version, in Talley's opinion, of the account narrated between Mark 10:34 and 10:35 in the *Mar Saba Clementine Fragment*. See Talley, *The Origins of the Liturgical Year*, 194ff.

[39] Coquin, "Une Réforme liturgique du concile de Nicée (325)?" 178–92.

[40] See Paul F. Bradshaw, "Baptismal Practice in the Alexandrian Tradition: Eastern or Western?" LWSS, 82–100.

actually thirty-six. Only much later, with the addition of four fast days beginning on the Wednesday before *Quadragesima* (later called *Ash Wednesday* because of the penitential practices which came to be associated with it), does Roman practice come to know an actual forty-day lenten *fast* before Easter.[41]

Like Rome, Alexandria (as witnessed to by Athanasius' Festal Letters of 330 and 340 C.E.)[42] also originally adopted a six-week lenten period before Easter (including Holy Week). But, with no fasting on either Saturdays or Sundays in this tradition, there was a total of only thirty fast days before the fast of Holy Saturday. As indicated above, a week was added to the beginning of this period, bringing the total to thirty-five days of fasting. Ultimately, even another week was added, resulting in an actual forty-day fast, an eight-week inclusive Lent before Easter.[43]

While other liturgical sources for Jerusalem, Antioch, and Constantinople suggest a six-week Lent with five fast days in each week concluding on the Friday before Lazarus Saturday and Palm Sunday, recall that the Spanish pilgrim Egeria claims that Jerusalem knew a total eight-week pattern—a seven-week Lent and the six-day fast of Great Week—in the late fourth century.[44] Although her statement has often been dismissed as misinformation,[45] as "an experiment that did not last,"[46] or as reflecting the practice of an ascetical community in Jerusalem which began the lenten fast one or two weeks before others did,[47] some comparative evidence has been provided by Frans van de Paverd, who argues in his recent study of John Chrysostom's *Homilies on the Statues* that fourth-century Antioch also knew a similar eight-week lenten pattern.[48]

---

[41] See Regan, "The Three Days and the Forty Days," 11–5.

[42] *The Festal Letters of St. Athanasius,* 21, 100; as cited by Talley, *The Origins of the Liturgical Year,* 169–70.

[43] See Talley, *The Origins of the Liturgical Year,* 219.

[44] *Peregrinatio Egeriae* 46.1–4.

[45] A. A. Stephenson, "The Lenten Catechetical Syllabus in Fourth-Century Jerusalem," *Theological Studies* 15 (1954) 116.

[46] Baldovin, *The Urban Character of Christian Worship,* 92, n. 37.

[47] See Talley, *The Origins of the Liturgical Year,* 174.

[48] Frans van de Paverd, *St. John Chrysostom, The Homilies on the Statues: An Introduction* (Rome: Pont. Institutum Studiorum Orientalium, 1991) xxiii, 210–6, 250–4, 358, 361.

However Lent came to be calculated and organized in these various Christian traditions after Nicea it is clear that this "forty days" was understood eventually as a time for the final preparation of catechumens for Easter baptism, for the preparation of those undergoing public penance for reconciliation on or before Easter (on the morning of Holy Thursday in Roman practice), and for the pre-paschal preparation of the whole Christian community in general. Basing his comments primarily upon the mid-fifth-century lenten sermons of Leo I, Patrick Regan summarizes this focus in the following manner:

"The purpose and character of Lent are entirely derived from the great festival for which it prepares. The Pasch is not only an annual celebration of the passion and passage of Christ, but it is for Christians of the fourth and fifth centuries the yearly reminder of their own incorporation into the paschal event through baptism. Consequently the approach of the Pasch renews in the memory of all the faithful their commitment to live the new life of him who for their sake was crucified, buried, and raised. But it also accuses them of their failure to do so."[49]

Only in the late fifth century and beyond—when infant initiation comes to replace that of adult, thus effectively bringing about the extinction of the catechumenate, and when the system of public penance is replaced by the form of repeatable individual confession and absolution—do the forty days then take on the sole character of preparation of the faithful for the events of Holy Week and the celebration of Easter. Such a focus, extremely penitential and "passion of Jesus" oriented in character and piety with little attention given to its baptismal origins, has tended to shape the interpretation and practice of the "forty days" of Lent until the present day.[50]

[49] Regan, "The Three Days and the Forty Days," 6–7.
[50] Among contemporary Roman Catholics and some Episcopalians, for example, the devotional exercise of the Stations of the Cross is frequently held on the Fridays during Lent. And among Lutherans, in my experience, the lenten tradition of mid-week worship often focuses on the medieval devotion of the so-called Seven Last Words of Jesus from the Cross or includes a partial reading of the Passion narrative each week, often from sources which harmonize the four Gospel accounts. Both practices can tend to turn Lent into a forty-day Passion Sunday or Good Friday.

CONCLUSION

The season of Lent as it developed into a pre-paschal preparation period of "forty days" in length for catechumens, penitents, and Christian faithful within the fourth-century post-Nicene context has multiple and complicated origins. While the development of the six-day pre-paschal fast may have played some role in its initial formation, what evidence there is suggests that this particular fast, although important for the origins of Holy Week, is separate and distinguished from that which came to be understood, properly speaking, as Lent. In other words, the traditional theory that the forty days of Lent merely reflect the historically-oriented backward extension of the six-day pre-paschal fast in an attempt to closely assimilate those preparing for Easter baptism to Jesus' postbaptismal forty-day desert fast is highly questionable, if not clearly wrong. As we have seen, current scholarship argues that such historical assimilation of the forty days to the fast of Jesus was already present before Nicea within, at least, the Alexandrian liturgical tradition, although originally there it had no relationship either to Pascha or, possibly, to baptism at all. But as a fasting period already in place in this tradition it suitably became prebaptismal in orientation because baptismal preparation necessarily included fasting as one of its major components.[51] Then when paschal baptism, interpreted in the light of a Romans 6 baptismal theology, became the normative ideal after Nicea this Alexandrian post-Epiphany pattern could become the pre-paschal lenten pattern. It may be said, therefore, that the sudden emergence of the forty-day lenten season after Nicea represents a harmonizing and standardizing combination of different, primarily initiatory, practices in early, pre-Nicene Christianity. These practices consisted of:

(1) an original forty-day post-Epiphany fast in the Alexandrian tradition, already associated with Jesus' own postbaptismal fast in the desert, which, as a fasting period already in place, became the suitable time for the prebaptismal preparation of catechumens;
(2) the three-week preparation of catechumens for Easter baptism in the Roman and North African traditions; and

---

[51] That those preparing for baptism, as well as the whole community, were expected to fast as part of the immediate preparation for baptism is documented as early as *Didache* 7.4.

(3) the three-week preparation of catechumens for baptism elsewhere either on a different liturgical feast or on no specified occasion whatsoever.

But after Nicea—and probably as the result of Nicea—these practices all became "paschalized" as the pre-Easter lenten *Quadragesima*, although in Alexandria itself this paschalization process, as we have seen, was only partially successful and left the celebration of baptism itself separate from the celebration of Easter.

If current scholarship on Lent, represented primarily by Talley, is correct, the origins of what becomes "Lent" have very little to do with Easter at all. Rather, those origins have to do both with early fasting practices in general and with the final preparation of baptismal candidates for whenever their baptisms might be celebrated. Greater awareness of these origins, therefore, may serve today as a necessary corrective to the orientation, noted above, that frequently still tends to characterize and shape contemporary Christian lenten observance.

Chapter 6

Christian Initiation in the Middle Ages

The further evolution and interpretation of the rites of Christian initiation in the Middle Ages, a period of history normally understood in the West as beginning with the death of Gregory I (604 C.E.) and concluding with the beginnings of the Protestant Reformation (October 31, 1517), is a fascinating story of ritual change, adaptation, and theological adjustment.[1] The period begins with several different liturgical traditions in use throughout the Western Christian world. Here we encounter, for example, the Gallican rites in Gaul (France and Germany); the "Mozarabic" (or "false Arabic") rite in Spain, a rite receiving its name because of the Islamic Moors who governed Spain through much of the medieval period; the Milanese or Ambrosian rite in the Archdiocese of Milan; the Celtic rite (a variation of the Gallican) in the British Isles; and, of course, the Roman rite itself, that particular local rite of the diocese of Rome. While this period begins with all of these distinct Western rites, it will end with the Roman rite itself having become *the* rite of Western Christianity.

Just as it is impossible to understand the liturgical shifts of the fourth and fifth centuries without paying attention to the changed social and political context brought about by the "conversion" of Constantine and its aftermath, so the context of the "Carolingian Reform"—after the emperor Charlemagne—of the ninth century is equally important for understanding liturgical change in the medieval West. For, it is with Charlemagne himself that *the* liturgy of Rome was to become normative and paradigmatic for Western Christianity in general.

---

[1] For good summaries of the history and theologies of the Church throughout the Middle Ages see Richard W. Southern, *Western Society and the Church in the Middle Ages* (Harmondsworth, Middlesex: Penguin Books, 1970); and Jaroslav Pelikan, *The Christian Tradition: A History of the Development of Doctrine*, vol. 3, *The Growth of Medieval Theology (600–1300)* (Chicago: University of Chicago Press, 1978).

In his important book on the various theologies of the Eucharist throughout the history of the Church, Gary Macy describes this period in the following manner:

"The year 800 marks a turning point in the history of western Europe. First of all, for the first time since the Roman empire had come under attack in the fifth century, a kind of unity and peace had been enforced on central Europe by the powerful warlord and leader of the Franks, Charles the Great (or in French, Charlemagne). Secondly, in a dramatic move, the west officially and formally broke diplomatic ties with the east when Pope Gregory III crowned a reluctant and astounded Charlemagne emperor on Christmas Day, 800. Charlemagne was not just crowned emperor in the west, but the true Roman emperor, successor to Julius Caesar and Caesar Augustus. Needless to say, this did not go down well in Constantinople, but by this time, there was little empress Irene could do. The west turned traitor to the old empire and began to chart an independent course. . . . Charlemagne was chosen by the papacy to restore order and Christianity to western Europe. Even before his coronation, Charles had set about the reformation of his empire with the same vigor and resourcefulness that he once used to smash his enemies. One of Charlemagne's first orders of business was the preaching and teaching of Christianity to his people. For this purpose, he imported to his court the best scholars to be had and even borrowed the pope's own mass book so that copies could be made and sent out to all the bishops. To an illiterate people the liturgy was extremely important, as here the common folk could see the central mysteries of Christianity acted out in a kind of pantomime."[2]

Charlemagne found little resistance to such an attempt at liturgical or ecclesiastical uniformity throughout the empire, even if absolute liturgical uniformity was never really attained in the West. Nevertheless, it is important to note that this attempt was imperial and *not* the result of the papacy trying to impose Roman usage universally on the West. No such papal involvement, in fact, was really needed. Rather, it was quite natural in the West for pilgrims to go to Rome, visit the holy places, attend papal liturgies in the great Roman basilicas, and to begin copying at home what they had seen and experienced there. In

[2] Gary Macy, *The Banquet's Wisdom: A Short History of the Theologies of the Lord's Supper* (New York: Paulist Press, 1992) 68–9.

other words, western Europe was quite favorably disposed toward Rome and its liturgy in general even before Charlemagne sought to make Roman practice normative for all. As James White has written:

"The liturgical role of Rome was far from deliberate. Because of the prestige accorded the holy city as the resting place of the martyrs, Roman ways of worship were widely imitated even though Rome rarely sought to promote them outside of nearby regions of Italy. . . . *Romanitas* or the imitation of Rome as the most impressive model for liturgy became a common western practice. . . . But for the most part, Rome took a hands off approach. Its influence was largely from respect not from coercion. Charlemagne tried to use liturgy as a means of unifying his empire in the ninth century but with little cooperation from Rome. Gregory VII interfered in the worship of the Spanish churches in the eleventh century by trying to force relinquishment of the Mozarabic rite in favor of the Roman rite but with only partial success. . . . Liturgical centralization was impossible in any case before the invention of the printing press. As late as 1549, Cranmer noted England still had various uses: 'some following Salisbury use, some Hereford use, some of the use of Bangor, some of York, and some of Lincoln.'"[3]

Because of this wide-spread influence and imitation of Roman liturgical practice, this chapter, unlike the previous ones, begins with the Roman rite itself as that rite is known from the available documents. Only then can we see most clearly the distinctive character of the other rites celebrated in the various churches of the medieval West and how the eventual adoption and adaptation of the Roman rite brought about some serious changes and consequences even for Rome itself.

ROME

Between the so-called *Apostolic Tradition*, ascribed to Hippolytus of Rome in the early third century, and the next sources for the Roman rites of initiation there is a considerable time gap of several centuries. In fact, after the *Apostolic Tradition*, if that document is indeed Roman, our first liturgical document witnessing to initiation rites at

---

[3] James F. White, *A Brief History of Christian Worship* (Nashville: Abingdon Press, 1993) 78–9.

Rome is the so-called Leonine or Verona Sacramentary. As we have seen already, this collection or *libellus* (i.e., "booklet") of prayers and various liturgical formulas to be used by a presbyter for the celebration of Mass contains a set of prayers related to Christian initiation on the feast of Pentecost. Unfortunately, other than being the last known document to refer to the cup of milk and honey in the giving of first communion and showing that initiation obviously occurred also on Pentecost in Rome, this set of Mass prayers really tells us nothing about the rites of Christian initiation themselves.

The basic available documents for understanding and interpreting the Roman rites of initiation in the Middle Ages are even later. They are the Gelasian Sacramentary [4] and *Ordo Romanus XI*,[5] two documents which both witness to the ritual structure of Roman initiatory practice in the seventh and eighth centuries. A sacramentary, as we have seen before, is a liturgical book for the use of the presider at several liturgical rites, including, of course, the Eucharist and consists of the appropriate presidential prayers for the celebration of those rites. An *ordo*, as we have also seen, is a rubrical guide to the ceremonies to be performed in those various sacramental rites. These *ordines* were needed especially in those areas outside of Rome, such as Gaul, when, with Charlemagne and after, the Roman Liturgy itself became imposed, copied, and/or imitated.

The Gelasian Sacramentary and Ordo Romanus XI

In broad outline, at least, the initiation rites in the Gelasian Sacramentary and *Ordo Romanus XI* both confirm the overall structure of those rites as they have been presented to us earlier from the so-called *Apostolic Tradition,* the *Canones ad Gallos,* the letter of Innocent I to Decentius, and the witness of John the Deacon. Nevertheless, these documents also witness to several changes that had taken place during the intervening years. Catechumens (now primarily infants), for example, were both enrolled in the catechumenate and "elected" for

---

[4] The critical edition is that of Leo Cunibert Mohlberg, ed., *Liber sacramentorum romanae aeclesiae ordinis anni circuli* (Rome: Herder, 1960); English translation cited below is from MFC 6, 92–107.

[5] The critical edition of the *Ordines Romani* is that of Michel Andrieu, *Les Ordines Romani du Haut Moyen Age,* 6 vols. (Louvain: Spicilegium Sacrum Lovaniense Administration, 1956–65). *Ordo XI* appears in vol. 2, 327–36. English translation below is from DBL, 196–204.

baptism not at the beginning of Lent but on Monday in the third week of Lent, with rites that included the blessing and giving of salt as well as the signing of the elect with the cross during a lengthy and solemn exorcism. Such a rite also constituted the first of several scrutinies. In fact, while the Gelasian Sacramentary does witness to the traditional Roman practice of three scrutinies during Lent in its mass texts for the third, fourth, and fifth Sundays in Lent, both the Gelasian Sacramentary and *Ordo XI* clearly indicate that, by this time, the scrutinies themselves had shifted to weekdays, had become essentially exorcisms rather than occasions for real catechesis or examination of the elect, and had grown to seven in number. *Ordo XI* provides justification for the number seven, saying:

"It is to be so ordered that from the first scrutiny which takes place in the third week of Lent to the vigil of the Pascha on Holy Saturday there shall be seven scrutinies, corresponding to the seven gifts of the Holy Spirit, so that when the sevenfold number is completed there may be given to them the sevenfold grace of the Spirit."[6]

Apart from the overall exorcistic orientation of all seven of these scrutinies, the first, third, and seventh included other important elements as well the exorcisms. The first, as we have just seen, was combined with the rites for enrollment in the catechumenate and election. The third, taking place on Monday of the sixth week of Lent, included the solemn and lengthy delivery *(traditio)* of the Gospels, with short passages read from each one and a brief catechetical explanation of each one given, the *traditio* of the Nicene Creed (in both Greek and Latin), and the *traditio* of the Our Father. While the rite for the *traditio* of the Gospels is called "The Explanation of the Four Gospels to the Elect at the Opening of the Ears," neither of these documents indicates clearly whether such an *apertio* ("opening") any longer took place at this point. The seventh and final scrutiny in these documents is made up of several catechumenal and prebaptismal rites and took place on Holy Saturday morning at 9:00. Following a final exorcism, an *apertio* rite was performed on the ears and nostrils of the elect with spittle, the elect were anointed on the breast and between the shoulder blades with exorcised oil, Satan was renounced in a three-fold question and answer format, the Creed was returned (the *redditio*

[6] DBL, 202.

symboli), actually recited by the bishop while he imposed hands on the heads of the elect, and the elect were dismissed until the time of the Easter Vigil.

The baptismal and postbaptismal rites themselves took place, of course, during the Easter Vigil. After the twelve Old Testament vigil readings with their appropriate canticles and concluding prayers were completed, the baptismal font and waters were blessed with a lengthy prayer of consecration, including, according to *Ordo XI*, a pouring of chrism into the waters where it was mixed and stirred by the bishop and then sprinkled over the assembly. This pouring and mixing of chrism with the baptismal waters was done, undoubtedly, to accompany and highlight the following words from the consecration prayer: "May the power of your Holy Spirit descend into every part of the water of this font and make fruitful the whole substance of the water of regeneration."[7] Next, baptism itself was administered according to a question and answer format related to the three traditional credal questions:

> Do you believe in God the Father almighty?

Response: I believe.

> And do you believe in Jesus Christ his only Son our Lord, who was born and suffered?

Response: I believe.

> And do you believe in the Holy Spirit, the holy church, the remission of sins, the resurrection of the flesh?

Response: I believe.

> *Then singly dip [each infant] three times in the water.*[8]

While Roman liturgical documents from the mid ninth century on will come to include both the complete Apostles' Creed,[9] either in de-

---

[7] MFC 6, 105.

[8] Ibid., 106.

[9] On the provenance and development of this creed see John Norman Davidson Kelly, *Early Christian Creeds*, 3d ed. (New York: D. McKay Co., 1972) 398–434.

claratory (i.e., "I believe . . .") or question and answer form, and an indicative baptismal formula (i.e., "I baptize you in the name of the Father, and of the Son, and of the Holy Spirit. Amen")[10] to accompany the immersion, submersion, or pouring, these influential documents display fidelity to the earlier Roman pattern in which the credal questions and answers themselves constituted the baptismal "formula."

The postbaptismal rites of the Gelasian Sacramentary and *Ordo XI* are also consistent with what we have seen structurally already in earlier Roman documents. Here, however, we finally have clear prayer texts and formulas to accompany what prior to these documents have been only allusions. According to the Gelasian Sacramentary, these rites were as follows:

When an infant has emerged from the font [the third time] the presbyter signs him [her] on the head with chrism, with these words:

Almighty God, Father of our Lord Jesus Christ, who has regenerated you by water and the Holy Spirit [see John 3:5] and has given you remission of all your sins, he it is who anoints you with the chrism of salvation for eternal life in Christ Jesus our Lord.

[The sponsor] responds: Amen.

Next the sevenfold gift is given to them by the bishop. To seal [ad consignandum] *them he imposes his hand on them with these words:*

Almighty God, Father of our Lord Jesus Christ, who has regenerated your servants by water and the Holy Spirit [see John 3:5] and has given them the remission of all sins: Lord, send upon them your Holy Spirit, the Paraclete, and give them the spirit of wisdom and understanding, the spirit of counsel and might, the spirit of knowledge

---

[10] As far as I can tell the first use of this formula in a "Roman-type" book occurs in the supplement added to the sacramentary sent to Charlemagne by Pope Hadrian I, a "Gregorian" sacramentary called the *Hadrianum*. Because this was an incomplete Roman Mass book, it was necessary for a supplement to be added in order that it might be more useful for Charlemagne's attempt at liturgical unification. The supplement, including the rites of initiation, was added by Benedict of Aniane, one of Charlemagne's liturgical advisors. See Jean Deshusses, ed., *Le Sacramentaire Grégorien*, Spicilegium Friburgense 16 (Fribourg: Éditions universitaires, 1971) 378.

and faithful devotion, and fill them with the spirit of fear of God [see Isa 11:2], in the name of our Lord Jesus Christ, with whom you live and reign always God with the Holy Spirit throughout every age of ages. Amen.

Then he signs them on the forehead with chrism, saying:

> The sign of Christ for eternal life.

Response: Amen.

> Peace be with you:

Response: And with you.[11]

To these rites *Ordo XI* adds some interesting rubrical directions and explanations. For example, between the first postbaptismal anointing and the rites of handlaying and anointing administered by the bishop, *Ordo XI* directs that the infants are to be carried to the "pontiff" (i.e., bishop), seated on his throne, who "gives to each a stole [*stola*] and overgarment [*casula*] and chrismal cloth and ten coins, and they are robed."[12] This chrismal cloth, of course, was the band or veil of linen worn on the head of the newly baptized, already referred to above in the letter of John the Deacon to Senarius, and the stole and overgarment are probably references to the white baptismal garments in which the newly baptized were clothed, with stole in this particular case simply meaning an undergarment. Nevertheless, the use of *stola* and *casula* does suggest some association to the rite of presbyteral ordination, especially since newly ordained presbyters would themselves be invested with a stole and chasuble. Hence, it would be hard not to see some kind of relationship being established here with the universal priesthood of the baptized.[13] The significance of the giving of ten coins to the newly baptized by the pontiff, however, is not clear. Possibly, if the pontiff in question is intended to be the pope himself, it refers to a custom associated with papal liturgy exclusively.

---

[11] Translation is adapted from MFC 6, 106.

[12] Translation is adapted from DBL, 203.

[13] On this see the suggestive comments of Aidan Kavanagh, "Unfinished and Unbegun Revisited: The Rite of Christian Initiation of Adults," LWSS, 259–73, esp. 267–73.

With regard to the bishop's handlaying and prayer, *Ordo XI* explicitly refers to this as the bishop *"confirming* them with an invocation of the sevenfold grace of the Holy Spirit,"[14] and draws special attention to the bishop's anointing by directing that "Great care must be taken that this is not neglected, because it is at this point that every baptism is confirmed and justification made for the name of Christianity."[15] Since *ordines* like this, it must be recalled, were designed especially for those areas outside of Rome where the Roman rite itself was being introduced, such an emphasis here is obviously intended to underscore what would have been a new, unclear, and, hence, frequently *neglected* element as that rite was coming to be adopted. Indeed, rubrics and directives like this are not normally needed unless something desired, in fact, is not taking place. As we shall see, such directives about "confirmation" abound in the medieval West.

The conclusion of the rites of initiation in both of these documents is, of course the reception of first communion at the Easter Vigil Eucharist. As *Ordo XI* makes perfectly clear, first communion is still being given to infants, who, by now, have certainly become the regular candidates for Christian initiation in general: "After this they go in to Mass and all the infants receive communion. Care is to be taken lest after they have been baptized they receive any food or suckling before they communicate."[16] And, in reference to the practice of post-baptismal mystagogy, all that remains in these documents is the following directive: "Afterwards let them come to Mass every day for the whole week of the Pascha and let their parents make oblations for them."[17] Yet, we do know from elsewhere that the earlier process of mystagogy also continued, at least in theory, with the attendance of the newly baptized at daily Vespers celebrated in the various Roman basilicas throughout Easter week.[18]

Subsequent Developments in the Roman Rite

The rites of initiation in the Gelasian Sacramentary and *Ordo XI* already display some sign of shortening and compression. Especially is

[14] DBL, 204; emphasis added.
[15] Ibid.; emphasis added.
[16] Ibid.
[17] Ibid.
[18] See John Leonard's 1990 Notre Dame doctoral dissertation on *Stational Vespers* in the Roman churches during the early medieval period.

this the case in the limitation of the entire catechumenal process of enrollment, election, and the (now seven) scrutinies to the final three weeks of Lent. Such a compression of the catechumenate was brought about, undoubtedly, by the growing dominance of infant baptism itself in the Roman church. Nevertheless, as Michel Dujarier has written:

". . . we must stress that there was a kind of 'catechumenate' for infants. It is interesting to note that, even for babies, the celebration of baptism was not limited to one single liturgical ceremony. The practice of seven scrutinies on the weekdays of Lent developed when there were many infants among the candidates. The testimony of Caesar of Arles in the sixth century is irrefutable: addressing himself to mothers bringing their babies to the scrutinies, he urged them not to miss these celebrations. This custom was undoubtedly a vestige of the tradition of baptizing infants at the same time as adults. . . . This custom also had the great advantage of having the parents of these infants participate in the preparation for baptism. Since the parents 'answered' for their children, it was normal that they make the catechetical and liturgical journey leading to baptism."[19]

As the Roman rites of initiation continued to develop throughout the medieval period, however, a further compression of the rites was brought about with the entire rite itself, including what had once been the catechumenate, becoming limited precisely to "one single liturgical ceremony." Signs of this eventual development are present already in another section of the Gelasian Sacramentary itself. In a section recognized to contain several "Gallican" additions to the Roman rite there is included a separate order for the initiation of a "sick catechumen."[20] In this particular rite, following a series of special prayers for restoration to health, the catechumenal ceremonies of the *traditio* of the Creed and Lord's Prayer, together with all of the rites associated with the seventh scrutiny on Holy Saturday morning above, formed merely an extended introduction to the rite of baptism itself. After an abbreviated blessing of the font and waters, baptism and the postbaptismal anointing were administered in the same way as we have seen already. But in *this* rite

[19] Michel Dujarier, *A History of the Catechumenate: The First Six Centuries* (New York: Sadlier, 1959) 133.
[20] See DBL, 193–6.

the postbaptismal anointing was followed immediately by the reception of first communion either at a special baptismal Mass or from the reserved Eucharist. The postbaptismal rites of handlaying and anointing associated with the bishop, therefore, were added only *after* first communion had already been given! Although the document is unclear, the assumption here, presumably, was that if the sick catechumen survived, then, at some point, the bishop would "complete" the neophyte's initiation by supplying what had been omitted, namely, his handlaying prayer and second anointing.

As we shall see further below, not only does this ritual sequence, with the episcopal rites added *after* first communion, seem to be one of the ways that the Roman rite itself came to be adopted in Gaul, but this pattern will also become highly influential in the further development of the rites for *infant* baptism throughout the West. As Mark Searle has noted, so frequently was this Gelasian rite of initiation for the dying used for infants throughout the Middle Ages, in fact, "that it eventually came to serve as the basis for the rite of infant baptism in the Roman Ritual of 1614,"[21] the standard and official ritual used by Roman Catholic priests from that time through the early twentieth century.

With regard to further evolution of the postbaptismal rites in the Roman tradition during the course of the Middle Ages, it is important to note the slight changes that also occur here. While the overall structure of these rites will remain, essentially, the same (that is, the bishop's handlaying prayer for the seven-fold gift of the Holy Spirit and the subsequent anointing on the candidate's forehead with chrism), medieval liturgical books for the specific use of bishops called pontificals demonstrate some shifts both in ritual practice and in accompanying formulas. According to these documents, the actual imposition of hands by the bishop during the prayer for the seven-fold Spirit, for example, appears to move from a literal imposition of the hand (Gelasian Sacramentary), to a raising of the hand collectively over the newly baptized, to an individual imposition of both hands *before* the prayer is offered, to, finally, a collective imposition of both hands either before or during the prayer.[22]

[21] Mark Searle, "Infant Baptism Reconsidered," LWSS, 369.
[22] On this see Gerard Austin, *Anointing with the Spirit* (New York: Pueblo, 1985) 20–3.

Similarly, while both the Gelasian Sacramentary and *Ordo XI* state that the formula for the bishop's anointing was simply, "the sign of Christ for eternal life. . . . Peace be with you," the earliest of the pontificals, the tenth-century Romano-Germanic Pontifical, so named because of its mixed origins, indicates that the formula had become "I *confirm* and sign you in the name of the Father, and of the Son, and of the Holy Spirit."[23] Two centuries later, in what is called the *Roman Pontifical of the Twelfth Century,* the formula has further changed to "I sign you with the sign of the cross and I confirm you with the chrism of salvation. In the name of the Father and of the Son and of the Holy Spirit. . . . Peace be with you."[24] Finally, the thirteenth-century *Pontifical of William Durandus,* bishop of Mende in southern France, while repeating the anointing formula of the *Roman Pontifical of the Twelfth Century,* adds that a light blow *(alapa)* on the cheek is to be given to the candidate by the bishop during the words "Peace be with you." In other words, the kiss or sign of peace becomes the "pat of peace." This *Pontifical of William Durandus,* of course, was to become the primary model for all subsequent Roman pontificals until the official and standard edition was published in 1596. Hence, the ritual for "confirmation" in the Roman liturgical tradition included a collective imposition of hands by the bishop at the beginning of the prayer for the sevenfold gift, the anointing with chrism on the forehead, accompanied by the formula "I sign you with the sign of the cross and I confirm you with the chrism of salvation," and the *alapa* during the words, "Peace be with you." This, in fact, was the overall ritual of confirmation experienced by countless Roman Catholics from the thirteenth century up until the 1971 reform of the rite itself.

What must not be forgotten, however, is that the rites of initiation as they are presented in these documents, with the exception of the Gelasian rite for a "sick catechumen," were still complete, unitive, and integral rites in Rome. That is, whether the candidate for initiation was an infant (more often) or an adult (increasingly less so), all of the rites of baptism, anointing, "confirmation," and first communion were celebrated together. In the words of J.D.C. Fisher:

---

[23] The text is cited from Austin, *Anointing with the Spirit,* 21; emphasis added. On the pontificals in general see Cyrille Vogel, *Medieval Liturgy: An Introduction to the Sources,* rev. and trans. William G. Storey and Niels Krogh Rasmussen (Washington, D.C.: Pastoral Press, 1986) 225–56.

[24] The translation is adapted from Austin, *Anointing with the Spirit,* 21.

"From the 8th to the 12th centuries the Roman rite of initiation underwent little change; most of the ceremonies of the Gel. and Ordo XI have been preserved, the pattern of the rite is unchanged, and its integrity unimpaired, baptism, confirmation and first communion still being, as in primitive times, three parts of one coherent whole."[25]

In the following centuries, as we shall see, this was to change significantly both in ritual celebration and theological interpretation. But before these changes can be considered in detail, it is necessary to look briefly at the rites of Christian initiation elsewhere in the medieval West.

THE WESTERN MEDIEVAL RITES OUTSIDE OF ROME

The rites of Christian initiation during the early Middle Ages in Spain, North Italy (Milan), and Gaul reveal a ritual pattern and theological interpretation rather distinct from that at Rome for the same period.[26] While in chapter 4 the relevant decrees of various local late-fourth- and early-fifth-century Spanish and Gallican councils were already noted, the *liturgical* evidence for the initiation rites in these traditions becomes available only in the extant documents remaining from the early medieval period. These are briefly discussed and analyzed in what follows.

Spain

A problem with interpreting the rites of Christian initiation in Spain in the Middle Ages is that we do not know much about them before a certain amount of Roman influence is already present and some liturgical revision in relationship to Rome is under way. Nevertheless, what we do see in the extant documentary evidence is enough to suggest that they were different from those at Rome in some significant ways.[27]

While little evidence remains of an actual catechumenate in the Spanish sources, Isidore of Seville (+ 636 C.E.) in his *De Ecclesiasticis*

---

[25] John Douglas Close Fisher, *Christian Initiation: Baptism in the Medieval West* (London: SPCK, 1965) 27.

[26] Excellent studies of these various rites appear in ibid., and Leonel L. Mitchell, *Baptismal Anointing* (London: SPCK, 1966).

[27] On the Spanish or "Mozarabic" rites, in general, see T. C. Akeley, *Christian Initiation in Spain, c. 300–1100* (London: Darton, Longman & Todd, 1967).

Officiis[28] makes the customary and traditional distinctions between catechumens and *competentes* and refers to traditional ceremonies such as exorcism and the giving of salt at the beginning of the catechumenal process. Similarly, both Hildephonse (or Ildefonse) of Toledo (+ 669 C.E.) in his *De Cognitione Baptismi*[29] and the eleventh-century *Liber Ordinum* (a Spanish pontifical reflecting a much compressed ritual order)[30] refer to rites of exorcism, scrutinies, and to the *effeta* or *apertio* (including, as well as the ears, the signing of the mouth, rather than the nose, with oil). From Hildephonse we also learn that, unlike Rome, the day for the *redditio symboli* was on Holy or Maundy Thursday; from the *Liber Ordinum* we learn that the *traditio symboli*, as in Ambrose of Milan, took place on Palm Sunday.

Concerning the rite of the *effeta* or *apertio*, the overall context is exorcistic. Nevertheless, in the *Liber Ordinum* the anointing formula for this *effeta* refers directly to the Holy Spirit: "Effeta, effeta, with the Holy Spirit unto the odor of sweetness, effeta. He has done all things well: he makes the deaf to hear and the dumb to speak."[31] It is also interesting to note that in the blessing of the font the *Liber Ordinum* contains no reference whatsoever to the death and resurrection of Christ. Rather, the overall emphasis is on the restoration of Adam's innocence in paradise and the new birth that baptism brings:

"Restore the innocence which Adam lost in paradise. . . . May they receive the likeness of God, which once was lost by malice of the serpent: may the iniquities which follow upon their disobedience be carried away in this pure stream. May they rise up unto rest: may they be brought forward unto pardon: that being renewed in the mystic waters they may know themselves to be redeemed and reborn."[32]

Both the reference to the Holy Spirit in a prebaptismal context and the strong focus on baptism as new birth suggest here some parallels

---

[28] PL, 83. For an English translation of the relevant materials see DBL, 109–11.

[29] PL, 96. For an English translation of the relevant materials see DBL, 111–3.

[30] M. Férotin, ed., *Monumenta Ecclesiae Liturgica*, vol. 5 (Paris: Firmin Didot, 1904). For an English translation of the relevant materials see DBL, 115–26.

[31] Translation adapted from DBL, 118.

[32] Translation adapted from ibid., 119–20.

with or influence of the early Syrian tradition. Indeed, there is a strong pneumatic focus and emphasis on Jesus' own baptism by John throughout the baptismal descriptions of both Hildephonse and the *Liber Ordinum*.

In terms of the administration of baptism itself the Spanish sources indicate a peculiarity not known in other liturgical traditions of East or West. After the customary three credal questions and answers, Hildephonse indicates that baptism was administered by a *single* rather than three-fold sprinkling or immersion accompanied by the trinitarian formula. Such a unique ritual practice Hildephonse defends by saying:

"That he is once immersed, he is sprinkled in the name of the one Deity. But if he were immersed three times, the number of the three days of the Lord's burial is revealed. And therefore within the limits of our faith differing customs are not opposed to one another. But because the heretics by this number of immersions are accustomed to rend the unity of the Godhead, it is by God's guidance that the Church of God observes the practice of one sprinkling only."[33]

The "heretics" to whom Hildephonse refers here are the descendants of the Arians, whose influence in Spain continued for some time there throughout the early medieval period. At the same time, Hildephonse is referring undoubtedly to a decision of the Fourth Council of Toledo in 633 C.E., which justified the continuation of this practice of a single immersion by direct appeal to the advice of Pope Gregory I some years earlier. As Canon 6 of this council directs, Gregory himself had advised the Spanish Church *not* to change its own custom, even if it meant that Spanish sacramental practice thereby would remain distinct from that of Rome:

"Concerning the sacrament of baptism, some priests in Spain baptize candidates with three immersions and some with one: therefore some people suppose a state of schism to exist and the unity of the faith to be broken for while differing . . . customs prevail, some people maintain that others are not baptized. We are informed by precepts of the Apostolic See what we ought to do in this diversity, following not our own but our fathers' institution. Gregory of blessed memory,

---

[33] Translation adapted from ibid., 115.

Bishop of the Roman Church . . . when the most holy bishop Leander asked him what should be done about this diversity in Spain, replied . . . in these terms: '. . . differing customs within the one faith of the Church can do no harm. We ourselves immerse three times and signify thereby the three days in the tomb, so that when the child is taken from the water for the third time the resurrection after three days is expressed. . . . No difficulty can be raised if a candidate were immersed in the water but once, since in the three persons [of the Trinity] there is but one substance; no objection can be raised, whether a child is immersed three times or once, since in three immersions the Trinity of persons is indicated and in one immersion the Unity of the Godhead. But if until now the heretics have been baptizing by triple immersion, I do not think that you should do the same, lest in counting the immersions they divide the Godhead, and lest while they continue to do what they were doing, they may boast that they have overcome your own practice. . . .' And therefore let us observe single immersion."[34]

Whether this *single* immersion was an innovation in Spanish liturgical practice brought about by the continued influence of Arianism or was an earlier and traditional Spanish custom, now needing to be defended in the context of widespread Arian influence, is not known.[35] But in either case this Spanish peculiarity certainly underscores not only the diversity of initiation rites in the Western Middle Ages but an earlier tolerance of liturgical diversity in the West on the part of Rome itself.

In distinction to the Roman rite as well, all three of the Spanish documents noted above refer to only *one* postbaptismal anointing with chrism followed by an imposition of the hand with prayer. But here there is no consistency in the way that these rites are interpreted. Both Isidore and Hildephonse indicate that the postbaptismal anointing is priestly and royal, after Christ as both priest and king,

---

[34] Translation adapted from ibid., 224.

[35] My graduate student, the Rev. James Lodwick, is writing his Notre Dame doctoral dissertation on the rites of Christian initiation in Spain and has begun to suggest that the single immersion documented in these sources is, in fact, an earlier and traditional Spanish custom testifying to the diversity of early baptismal custom rather than a deliberate anti-Arian practice. Hopefully, his completed dissertation will shed clear light on this controversial issue.

and that it provides justification for the name of Christian (i.e., the "anointed one"). But while Isidore, referring to Acts 8 and 19, apparently understands the following handlaying rite as related to bishops "giving" the Holy Spirit, Hildephonse, referring to Mark 10:13 (Jesus' blessing of the children), calls this imposition of the hand a "blessing," makes no reference to bishops, and refers to the postbaptismal anointing itself as the "unction of the Spirit."[36] In this postbaptismal location, the *Liber Ordinum* has a lengthy prayer unparalleled anywhere for the conferring of the Holy Spirit by the imposition of the hand of the "priest," and it is to the chrism, *already* administered, that the prayer repeatedly refers:

"O God, you, who in this sacrament wherein people are reborn, send your Holy Spirit upon water, in such fashion that the Creator commands his creature and by its office cleanses those who are washed thereby, whom you would perfect *[confirmaret]* with your bountiful gift; you, who by water would take away the stain of sin and by your own self would complete the grace of the sacrament, and therefore have commanded that the unction of chrism shall follow the administration of baptism: we therefore pray and beseech you, O Lord, following your commandments as we are able, to pour your Holy Spirit upon these your servants. Amen. The spirit of wisdom and understanding. Amen. The spirit of counsel and might. Amen. The spirit of knowledge and godliness. Amen. Fill them, both men and women, with the spirit of your fear [Isa 11:2, 3], you who inspire people to follow your saving commandment and breathe upon them a heavenly gift. And so grant that being strengthened in the name of the Trinity, they may by this chrism be accounted worthy to become Christs, and by the power of Christ to become Christians."[37]

This prayer is followed immediately by the placing of the veil or chrismal cloth on the head of the newly baptized and then by first communion either during the Mass, or, given the late date of the *Liber Ordinum,* from the reserved Eucharist.

The text of the above prayer from the *Liber Ordinum* is certainly late enough to have been highly influenced by Roman practice. Similarly, scholars note that by appealing to Acts 8 and 19, as well as to bishops,

---

[36] DBL, 115.
[37] Translation adapted from ibid., 121–2.

Isidore himself, in his description of the imposition rite, is obviously making reference to the famous Letter of Innocent I to Decentius of Gubbio, if not directly quoting it. Nevertheless, in all three of the above documents there remains only *one* postbaptismal anointing and a handlaying rite with no indication whatsoever that these post-baptismal rites are somehow reserved to the bishop alone. The double anointing first by the presbyter and then by the bishop, present in the Roman rite, is nowhere to be found here. Perhaps the handlaying prayer itself, then, is nothing more than a concluding prayer of bless-ing underscoring the benefits of both baptism and chrismation, which, via Roman influence in, at least, the *Liber Ordinum,* has become associ-ated more closely with the Holy Spirit. But it must be emphasized that in none of these sources is there indicated or implied any kind of shift of place from baptistery to episcopal rites in the assembly or any reference at all to an episcopal act separate from baptism itself. The rites as they are presented are complete in themselves; whoever presided at them, whether bishop or presbyter (priest), presided at the entire rite, including the postbaptismal anointing and handlaying.[38] An equivalent to the Roman postbaptismal rites associated with the bishop alone, therefore, simply does not appear in the Spanish sources. The only logical conclusion can be that the Church in Spain considered the rites as they are presented here to be the full rites of Christian initiation in water and the Holy Spirit.

North Italy: Milan

As with the *Liber Ordinum* for the Spanish rites, so also the extant documents for the "Ambrosian" or "Milanese" rite are several cen-turies later than the fourth-century witness of Ambrose of Milan in his *De Sacramentis* and *De Mysteriis.* Here, in particular, we have the tenth-century *Ambrosian Manual,*[39] a ritual for use at the cathedral at Milan, and the twelfth-century *Ordo of Beroldus,*[40] a guide to the litur-gical ceremonies for the archbishop at the same cathedral, compiled

[38] See Akeley, *Christian Initiation in Spain,* 178ff. and 192–3.

[39] Marcus Magistretti, ed., *Monumenta veteris liturgiae Ambrosianae,* vol. 3 (Milan: Ulricum Hoepli, 1904). An English translation of the relevant sections appears in DBL, 133–47.

[40] Marcus Magistretti, ed., *Beroldus, sive, Ecclesiae Ambrosianae Mediolanensis Kalendarium et Ordines, Saec. XII* (Milan: J. Giovanola, 1894). An English trans-lation of the relevant sections appears in DBL, 147–52.

by one of that cathedral's officials. Compared with the Spanish sources, however, it is harder to detect much Roman influence here.

Some remnants of an earlier catechumenal process appear in these texts. While the *Ambrosian Manual* witnesses to an enrollment or election of *competentes* at the beginning of Lent and to at least one scrutiny on the second Saturday in Lent, the *Ordo of Beroldus* makes reference to three scrutinies during Lent and to enrollment itself taking place on the fourth Saturday of Lent, an obvious compression of an earlier process. And, along with the customary catechetical ceremonies of the giving of salt and frequent exorcisms throughout the period of final catechetical preparation, the *Manual* also includes an exorcism of ashes scattered on sackcloth on the second Saturday of Lent. Similarly, these documents both testify to a *traditio symboli* on the day before Palm Sunday. Neither, however, indicates whether or not a *redditio symboli*, other than the credal interrogations in the context of the rite of baptism itself, occurred at some specific time as well.

As in Ambrose himself a rite of *apertio* or *effeta* ("opening") on the ears and nostrils, now with spittle, occurs following the renunciation of Satan, a ceremony taking place on the fourth Saturday in Lent. This is followed in the *Manual* and the *Ordo of Beroldus* by an anointing of the *competentes'* shoulders and breast. While the context here is surely exorcistic, the prayer in the *Manual* for the "exorcism" of this oil asks: "that to all who are anointed with it it may be unto the adoption of the children of God through the Holy Spirit." And the formula used for this anointing is not exorcistic at all, but simply: "I anoint you with the oil of salvation in Christ Jesus our Lord unto eternal life."[41] Here again, as in Spain, may be some kind of remnant of an earlier non-exorcistic interpretation of the prebaptismal anointing.

With regard to the administration of baptism itself in these documents, after chrism was poured into the baptismal water and mixed with it, the three credal questions were asked and the candidate was then immersed three times according to the formula "I baptize you . . . ." Immediately after this, the neophytes were anointed with chrism, which accompanied the making of the sign of the cross on their foreheads! This anointing was administered with the formula known already by Ambrose himself and present in the medieval Roman documents as well, namely: "Almighty God the Father of our

[41] Translation adapted from DBL, 142–3.

Lord Jesus Christ, who has regenerated you by water and the Holy Spirit, and has given you the forgiveness of all your sins, himself anoints you with the chrism of salvation, in Christ Jesus our Lord."[42] Following this anointing the *pedilavium* took place, a concluding prayer was offered, and first communion was given.

Again, as in Spain, it is important to note that the whole rite as presented in these Ambrosian texts was, apparently, a *complete* rite of Christian initiation. Again, as well, there is absolutely no reference to any separate postbaptismal rites like handlaying or second anointing reserved to the bishop. In relationship to the earlier witness of Ambrose himself, one might certainly ask about the presence of what he called the spiritual seal, that rite he described in relationship to the sevenfold gift of the Holy Spirit taking place after the *pedilavium* and before the reception of first communion.[43] Indeed, while both the *Manual* and the *Ordo of Beroldus* are late enough to have been influenced by the Roman practice of those episcopal postbaptismal rites, and while the *Ordo of Beroldus* itself is a rubrical guide not only for presbyters but for the archbishop himself (!), they display absolutely no sign of that practice or influence. Instead, these documents contain simple concluding prayers to end the entire rite, prayers of thanksgiving which make no reference to any additional rites at all. Two such prayers are provided in the *Manual:*

"Let us who have performed and completed the sacraments of divine baptism give unwearied thanks to the Lord of heaven and earth, to God the Father Almighty; and let us humbly ask him that he may grant us and all his household to be partakers of the glorious resurrection of our Lord Jesus Christ. By the favor of the same our Lord Jesus Christ his Son, who lives and reigns with him, God in the unity of the Holy Spirit, now and forever. Amen."[44]

"Almighty, everlasting God, who has regenerated your servant N. by water and the Holy Spirit, and who has given him forgiveness of all his sins, grant him an abiding wisdom to acknowledge the truth of your divinity. Through our Lord. . . ."[45]

---

[42] Translation adapted from ibid., 147. See also 152.
[43] See above, chapter 4, 137–40.
[44] Translation adapted from DBL, 142.
[45] Translation adapted from ibid., 147.

Whatever Ambrose's "Spiritual Seal" may have been in the context of late-fourth century Milan, the later documents of the Ambrosian rite contain no remnant of it.

Gaul

The overall importance of what is called the Gallican tradition in relation to the further development of the rites of Christian initiation in the medieval West cannot be overemphasized. We have already seen above in chapter 4, for example, that it is primarily from various local fifth-century councils in southern Gaul and from the famous Pentecost sermon attributed to Faustus of Riez that the terminology of "confirmation" itself begins to enter into the practice and theology of Christian initiation in the West, with special reference to post-baptismal acts associated with the ministry of bishops. Equally important, however, are the extant medieval liturgical documents from north Gaul, namely, the *Missale Gallicanum Vetus* (Old Gallican Missal),[46] the *Missale Gothicum* (Gothic Missal),[47] and the Bobbio Missal,[48] all of which are eighth-century documents. Supporting evidence for the rites presented in those texts appears also in the Stowe Missal,[49] a liturgical text of Irish provenance and a source for liturgy in the British Isles, also dated in the late eighth century. While a detailed examination of these important sources is beyond the scope of this study, it is important to note in general that the *liturgical* evidence they supply is more akin to what we have seen in Spain and Milan than it is either to Rome or to the practices described in the Gallican councils and the sermon attributed to Faustus.

Concerning remnants of an earlier catechumenate, general similarities with what we have seen elsewhere in the Spanish and Ambrosian

[46] Leo Cunibert Mohlberg, ed., *Missale Gallicanum Vetus*, Rerum Ecclesiasticorum Documenta 3 (Rome: Herder, 1958). No English translation of this text is available.

[47] Leo Cunibert Mohlberg, ed., *Missale Gothicum*, Rerum Ecclesiasticorum Documenta 5 (Rome: Herder 1961). An English translation of the relevant texts appears in DBL, 159–64.

[48] E. A. Lowe, ed., *The Bobbio Missal*, Henry Bradshaw Society 58 (London: Harrison and Sons, 1917–24). An English translation of the relevant texts appears in DBL, 204–13.

[49] George F. Warner, ed., *The Stowe Missal*, Henry Bradshaw Society 32 (London: Harrison and Sons, 1906–15). An English translation of the relevant texts appears in DBL, 213–21.

rites with exorcisms, the giving of salt, an *apertio* or *effeta*, an opening of the Gospels (as in the Gelasian Sacramentary), and the *traditio symboli* on Palm Sunday occur also here. More importantly, Gabriele Winkler has drawn attention to the fact that the rites described in these Gallican documents have a strong pneumatic orientation throughout, much as we saw in the early Syrian tradition.[50] According to Winkler, such "Syrian" elements include, first of all, an expressed giving of the Holy Spirit *before* baptism in the Bobbio Missal, where, within a rite called an "Order for Making a Christian," the presider breathes into the mouth of the candidate and says: "N., receive the Holy Spirit, may you guard him in your heart."[51] Second, the prebaptismal anointing, again in the Bobbio Missal, at least, is related to the anointing of David by Samuel, reminiscent of the earlier Syrian emphasis on the prebaptismal messianic anointing of the head. Third, Winkler notes that throughout all of these documents the primary and overall theology of baptism comes more from the new birth focus of John 3 than from the emphasis on baptismal participation in the death and burial of Christ in Romans 6, a text referred to rarely and then only in the *Missale Gallicanum Vetus*. And, finally, allusion to the Jordan is made in the prayers for the blessing of the font in all of these documents. If then, it is possible that earlier Eastern or Syrian traits are present in the Spanish and Ambrosian rites, it becomes quite probable that this is the case here.

After baptism itself, administered here with an indicative formula following the customary credal questions and answers, the postbaptismal rites included, with some variation of order in the documents, a single anointing with a formula much like that used in the Ambrosian and Roman rites, (also called "the garment of immortality" in the *Missale Gothicum*),[52] a vesting in a baptismal garment, the *pedilavium,* a concluding prayer, and the reception of first communion. According to Winkler, the presence of the *pedilavium* here, as well as in the Ambrosian rite, is another sign of early Syrian influence in these texts. And, as we have seen already in Spain and Milan, it is important to emphasize that these documents contain only one post-

---

[50] Gabriele Winkler, "Confirmation or Chrismation? A Study in Comparative Liturgy," LWSS, 202–18.

[51] Translation is adapted from DBL, 209.

[52] See ibid., 162.

baptismal anointing and make no reference to any episcopal imposition of hand(s) or second anointing.

Based undoubtedly on seeing the structure of the so-called *Apostolic Tradition* as the earliest and normative pattern for Christian initiation in the West, scholars have often assumed that an episcopal imposition of hands and/or second anointing were originally included in the Spanish, Ambrosian, and Gallican rites as well. Somewhere along the way, then, perhaps related to the difficulty of bishops being able to be present for all baptisms, these episcopal rites disappeared from the non-Roman West only to be restored later when the Roman rite itself became adopted and adapted. Such seems to be the implication of the work of J.D.C. Fisher[53] and E. M. Finnegan.[54]

More recent scholarship, however, has argued convincingly in a different direction altogether. Winkler, for example, concludes that:

". . . one must seriously doubt whether the initiation rites represented by these documents ever included any postbaptismal rite other than the one anointing, performed either by a bishop or a presbyter. There probably never was a separate laying on of the hand combined with a second anointing reserved to the bishop. . . . I believe that these liturgical formularies reflect an archaic shape of initiation rites where either the bishop or the presbyter could confer baptism, including the postbaptismal anointing. . . . Evidence from Spain dating from the fourth to the seventh centuries tends to corroborate this hypothesis."[55]

Independent of Winkler, and without reference to the possibility of early Syrian influence, Joseph Levesque has come to similar conclusions on the shape and meaning of the Gallican rites themselves. Based on a careful and highly detailed analysis of the postbaptismal rites in these extant Gallican texts, Levesque writes:

"The primary sacramentary texts, especially the Gothicum, have repeated references to Scriptural themes such as the forgiveness of sins,

---

[53] See Fisher, *Christian Initiation*, 53ff.

[54] E. M. Finnegan, "The Origins of Confirmation in the Western Church: A Liturgical-dogmatic Study of the Development of the Separate Sacrament of Confirmation in the Western Church Prior to the Fourteenth Century," Ph.D. dissertation (Trier, 1970).

[55] Winkler, "Confirmation or Chrismation?" 207–8.

rebirth *ex aqua et spiritu* [through water spirit], regeneration, the 'Old Man vs. New Man,' and the 'Spirit of Adoption.' Along with references indicating the fullness of grace and the sevenfold gift of the Spirit these themes blend and pervade all the baptismal and postbaptismal texts and convince one that the ceremony is a complete unit. This author believes that 'theologically' the rites celebrated were adequate and complete as a celebration of full Christian Initiation."[56]

The Shape of Christian Initiation in the Non-Roman Medieval West
The above brief survey of the extant liturgical documents for the rites of Christian initiation in Spain, Milan, and Gaul during the early Middle Ages demonstrates that, outside of Rome, the overall shape of Christian initiation in the West was much closer to that of the West Syrian East in the fourth and fifth centuries than to what we know to have been the case in the Roman tradition itself. That is, with special regard to postbaptismal ceremonies, these Spanish, Ambrosian, and Gallican rites appear to reflect a non-Roman Western liturgical tradition which did not know any more than one postbaptismal anointing and no postbaptismal rites reserved exclusively to bishops. While a postbaptismal imposition of the hand(s) rite in relationship to the gift of the Holy Spirit does appear in the Spanish sources (e.g., the *Liber Ordinum*) and the *pedilavium* appears in both the Ambrosian (the *Ambrosian Manual* and the *Ordo of Beroldus*) and Gallican texts, neither of these rites are episcopal acts but are administered by whomever it was—bishop or presbyter—who presided at the rites of initiation as a whole. The *only* episcopal requirement, as is known from the earlier local Western councils, was that the chrism to be used for the postbaptismal anointing be consecrated by and obtained from the local diocesan bishop. Such a requirement, of course, was also the norm throughout the Christian East, which by means of the chrism itself underscored the presidential role of the bishop in Christian initiation even if he was not physically present.

Finally, it must be underscored here that whatever is meant in the canons and decrees of the various local Spanish and Gallican councils in their references to bishops "perfecting" or "confirming" after bap-

[56] Joseph Levesque, "The Theology of the Postbaptismal Rites in the Seventh and Eighth Century Gallican Church," LWSS, 201.

tism, the extant *liturgical* documents from these traditions provide no corroborating evidence at all and do not use the terminology of "confirmation." Such a lack of liturgical evidence would certainly underscore the argument that whatever ritual actions a bishop may have performed as a part of his "confirmation" of baptism administered by another, an imposition of hand(s) rite and/or anointing with chrism were done only in exceptional situations (e.g., baptism by a lay person or deacon, or the failure of a presbyter to obtain chrism blessed by a bishop). Nevertheless, if this, indeed, is the case, as the evolution of the rites continues in the Middle Ages and the Roman rite itself becomes theoretically adopted in all of western Europe, it is this exception that will become the rule.

THE FURTHER DEVELOPMENT OF CHRISTIAN INITIATION IN THE MEDIEVAL WEST

Ever since the appearance of an important article in 1947 by J. G. Davies,[57] it has been customary for liturgical scholars to refer to what happened in the medieval evolution of the rites of Christian initiation as a process of "disintegration," "dissolution," and "separation." That is, the unitive rites of initiation we have seen in previous chapters, in Rome through the twelfth century, and in the non-Roman rites of the West now become broken up into completely separate rites. For this process the classic study of J.D.C. Fisher, *Christian Initiation: Baptism in the Medieval West*,[58] remains a most helpful and indispensable guide. Fisher speaks of four developments related to this disintegration or separation:

(1) the separation of confirmation from baptism;

(2) the separation of communion reception from Christian initiation;

(3) the separation of initiation from Easter/Pentecost; and

(4) the fragmentation of the unitive rite of initiation into three distinct sacraments separated further by increasingly larger intervals of time.

[57] J. G. Davies, "The Disintegration of the Christian Initiation Rite," *Theology* 50 (1947) 407–12.
[58] Fisher, *Christian Initiation*. See also Nathan Mitchell, "Dissolution of the Rite of Christian Initiation," *Made, Not Born* (Notre Dame: University of Notre Dame Press, 1976) 50–82.

While accepting Fisher's overall approach, scholars today would want to nuance it somewhat. If, for example, a distinct liturgical tradition did not know of rites equivalent to those episcopal acts coming to constitute "confirmation" in the Roman Rite, it would be hard to speak of a disintegration or dissolution of confirmation *from* baptism within that particular tradition. Rather, something like Roman confirmation would have to be seen as an "addition" to those rites, becoming adopted only when the Roman rite itself was adopted. Or, along similar lines, in light of our previous chapter on the development of preferred baptismal days and the season(s) of baptismal preparation in early Christianity, it would be quite difficult to speak of Christian initiation being separated from Easter/Pentecost in those liturgical rites which already knew a tradition of baptismal days and seasons either apart from or in addition to Easter/Pentecost. Hence, given the *preference* for initiation at Easter/Pentecost in the early North African and Roman Rites alone, any claim of separation or disintegration would have to be limited to those traditions. But even here, the North African tradition, as far back as the middle of the third century, certainly did not limit Christian initiation to Easter/Pentecost. Tertullian had said that any time and any day were suitable days. With regard to infant initiation, at least, it should be recalled that Cyprian of Carthage reports that one need not wait even eight days before their baptism.[59] And, for that matter, even Innocent I at the beginning of the fifth century can boast, with some exaggeration, that every day in Rome "the divine sacrifice or the office of baptism" took place.[60]

Nevertheless, Fisher's categories of the separation of confirmation from baptism, the separation of first communion from initiation, and the further separation of all the initiation rites into separate and distinct sacramental moments still provide a helpful guide in organizing and analyzing the further development of initiation in the medieval West. And, at the same time, the increasing normativity of infant baptism in this period does certainly suggest a separation of initiation, if not from Easter/Pentecost exclusively, at least from the Sundays, feasts, and seasons of the liturgical year in general. For our

[59] See above, 67–8.
[60] As cited in Paul Bradshaw, "'Diem baptismo sollemniorem': Initiation and Easter in Christian Antiquity," LWSS, 145.

purposes here, however, these categories can be treated under two general headings: (1) the emergence of "confirmation" and its "separation" from baptism, and (2) the dominance of infant baptism and its consequences.

The Emergence of "Confirmation" and Its "Separation" from Baptism

A number of factors in the West will contribute to the development of confirmation and to its eventual separation from baptism. The fact that from early on the rites of Christian initiation involved the whole Church and, hence, all the orders of ministers—bishops, presbyters, and deacons—meant that if initiation was sought when all the orders were not represented, various possibilities were open for the celebration of the rites: (1) the rites could be deferred until all of the various orders were present; (2) one minister (i.e., the presbyter) could take the part of another (i.e., the bishop); or (3) the parts of the rite normally performed by the absent minister (i.e., the bishop) could be omitted until he was able to be present. The great increase in numbers of Christians after the Peace of the Church under Constantine, and the increasing size of dioceses in most parts of the world thereafter, made it impossible for bishops to be present at all celebrations of Christian initiation. One solution would have been to reduce the size of dioceses, but this was not done. Another solution, apparently followed at Rome for several centuries, was to have assistant bishops preside at the full rites of initiation in the titular churches of the city. And still another solution, apparently followed almost everywhere in both East and West *except* at Rome, was to have presbyters preside at the entire rite, in which, given the expectation that chrism would both be consecrated by and obtained from the local bishop, the bishop's presidential role over initiation was still signified, if only in a vicarious manner.

While in Rome itself the decision to make use of other bishops for the celebration of the entire rite was eminently practical and workable, problems soon developed in relationship to the adoption of the Roman rite elsewhere.[61] Already in the early fifth century, as we have

---

[61] For this section, see especially Austin, *Anointing with the Spirit*, 14–20; Aidan Kavanagh, *Confirmation: Origins and Reform* (New York: Pueblo, 1988) 65–71; Frank Quinn, "Confirmation Reconsidered: Rite and Meaning," LWSS, 219–37; and Mitchell, "Dissolution of the Rite of Christian Initiation," 50–82.

seen, Innocent I strongly advocated to Decentius in Gubbio that within the postbaptismal rites, whether the bishop was present or not, presbyters could anoint only the top of the head of the newly baptized with chrism. It is, Innocent stated boldly, the prerogative of bishops alone, when "delivering the Holy Spirit," to anoint and sign the forehead. As the Roman rite, especially the bishop's postbaptismal ceremonies of handlaying and anointing, was adopted throughout western Europe, thanks to Charlemagne's program of liturgical, ecclesiastical, and political uniformity, it encountered primarily in Gaul the terminology of "confirmation" used already, as we have also seen, in various local councils to refer to the bishop's postbaptismal involvement in Christian initiation.

It is not altogether clear, however, which of the Roman postbaptismal rites to be performed by the bishop—whether the handlaying with prayer for the sevenfold gift of the Holy Spirit or the subsequent anointing—comprised this newly developing "confirmation" rite in the early Middle Ages. In the texts of the Gelasian Sacramentary for the regular celebration of Christian initiation at Rome, as we have seen, the rubrics draw attention to the bishop's handlaying and prayer, saying, "*Next the sevenfold gift is given to them by the bishop. To seal [ad consignandum] them he imposes his hand with these words: Almighty God, Father of our Lord Jesus Christ. . . .*" But *Ordo XI*, of definite Gallican provenance, explicitly refers to this as the bishop "*confirming . . .* with an invocation of the sevenfold grace of the Holy Spirit," and, as we have also seen, this ordo draws special attention to the bishop's anointing by directing that "*great care must be taken that this is not neglected, because it is at this point that every baptism is confirmed and justification made for the name of Christianity.*" For that matter, even Innocent I was not completely clear as to which of the postbaptismal rites reserved to the bishop he considered to constitute the "delivery of the Holy Spirit," only that the anointing on the forehead with chrism was the bishop's perogative in the administration of those rites. Similarly, it is quite clear that the rite Faustus of Riez described in his homily is an episcopal rite of "handlaying" with no reference to a subsequent anointing at all. And yet, when Thomas Aquinas treats confirmation in his *Summa Theologiae*, there is no question but that the rite which constitutes confirmation has now become the episcopal anointing with chrism together with its accompanying formula. Reflecting the theological legacy of Augustine of Hippo's own focus on what constituted a valid sacrament, Thomas expresses the further development of medieval scholasticism in treating sacraments according to their "matter" and "form" when he defends chrism as the proper sacramental matter for this sacrament and the formula of *Roman Pontifical of the Twelfth Century*, namely, "I sign you with the sign of the cross and I confirm you with the chrism of salvation. In the name of the Father and of the Son and of the Holy Spirit," as its proper form.[62]

The most confusing interpretation of both the rite of confirmation and its interpretation comes from Pope Innocent III (1198–1216) when he says that:

". . . the imposition of the hand is represented by the chrismation of the forehead. It is called 'confirmation' by another name, because through it the Holy Spirit is given for growth and strength. For this reason, although a simple priest or presbyter may produce other oils, only the high priest, that is the bishop, ought to confer this one, because it is told concerning the apostles alone, whose successors are the bishops, that they gave the Holy Spirit through the imposition of the hand, as a reading of the Acts of the Apostles shows."[63]

For Innocent III, in a strange twist of logic that continues to shape the interpretation of confirmation today,[64] it is now the bishop's *anointing* that represents the apostolic imposition of hands. Why, it might surely be asked, would it not be the bishop's handlaying and prayer for the sevenfold Holy Spirit itself that would best *represent* or signify this apostolic practice? Something has definitely changed.

In light of these differing emphases and interpretations, it is quite obvious that in Gaul especially attention was increasingly focused not on the bishop's handlaying and prayer but on the anointing. So strong was this focus, in fact, that eventually the very formulas used

---

[62] See *Summa Theologiae*, q. 72, in J. J. Cunningham, ed., *St. Thomas Aquinas: Summa Theologiae*, vol. 57, *Baptism and Confirmation* (3a. 33–72) (Washington, D.C.: Pastoral Press, 1975) 187–227. Nathan Mitchell has demonstrated in "Dissolution," 61–4, that the particular rite of confirmation that Thomas knew was, most likely, the Roman Pontifical of the Twelfth Century.

[63] Text is cited from Paul Turner, *Sources of Confirmation: From the Fathers through the Reformers* (Collegeville: The Liturgical Press, 1993) 81; emphasis added.

[64] See below, 357.

for this anointing in the Roman pontificals came to employ the term "confirmation" (e.g., "I sign you . . . and I *confirm* you . . ."). What is most peculiar about this, however, is that while within the Roman rite itself the specific emphasis on the sevenfold gift of the Holy Spirit always occurred within the handlaying prayer and *never* in connection with the anointing, it is the bishop's anointing with chrism with its trinitarian formula that became the special sacrament of the gift of the Holy Spirit. Frank Quinn writes of this change in emphasis, saying:

"Confirmation continues to refer to episcopal handlaying in the Roman *ordines* and pontificals; but it is also identified with chrismation, even entering into the formula of administration. When western rites outside of Rome accept the peculiar second postbaptismal anointing into their baptismal structure, confirmation terminology with reference to consignation becomes general in western Europe. Most likely, chrismation seemed more important, or at least more concrete, than did handlaying and prayer."[65]

This unique Roman postbaptismal rite, of course, is not the only rite that experienced this kind of shift in emphasis and interpretation within this same medieval time period. As Quinn himself notes further: "Similar ritual shifts occurred in the ordination rites when, in the Middle Ages, the *traditio instrumentorum* [i.e., the giving of the chalice and paten after an anointing of the ordinand's hands] was emphasized over the more ancient *handlaying with prayer for the Spirit*."[66] Interestingly enough, it was precisely in the synthesis of the Roman and Gallican rites for ordination that this transition took place and, significantly, for Aquinas himself it would be this rite of the *traditio instrumentorum* together with its formula that he would identify as constituting the "matter" and "form" of the sacrament of orders.[67] As with the rite of presbyteral ordination, then, it can be

---

[65] Quinn, "Confirmation Reconsidered," 230.

[66] Ibid., 230, n. 33; emphasis added. See also Mitchell, "Dissolution," 71.

[67] Thomas Aquinas, *Summa Theologiae*, Supplement, q. 37. On the development of ordination rites in general see Harry Boone Porter, *The Ordination Prayers of the Ancient Western Churches* (London: SPCK, 1967); and Paul Bradshaw, *Ordination Rites of the Ancient Churches of East and West* (New York: Pueblo, 1990).

said that the postbaptismal rites of Christian initiation at Rome, associated explicitly with the ministry of bishops, passed from Rome to the rest of western Europe, where they were adopted, adapted, and changed. From there, at the risk of oversimplifying a complex process, through the development of various liturgical documents (e.g., *ordines* and pontificals) ultimately accepted in Rome, those same postbaptismal rites would return to Rome as constituting now a specific *sacrament* of the Holy Spirit, reserved, except in special cases, to the ministry of bishops alone.

When the Roman postbaptismal rites of episcopal handlaying with prayer and anointing were adopted elsewhere in the Middle Ages it was often the case that these rites, as in the Gelasian order for a "sick catechumen," did not occur in their traditional *Roman* position between baptism and first communion but were added at some point *after* both baptism and first communion had already been administered. In other words, it is not so much the case that "confirmation" gets *separated* from baptism outside of Rome but that the Roman postbaptismal rites, which came to be interpreted as confirmation, became an *addition* to the rites of Christian initiation elsewhere. Alcuin of York (735–804 C.E.), one of Charlemagne's principal liturgical advisors, in fact, gives such a direction for the celebration of the rites of initiation, saying that "if the bishop is there it is necessary that they be confirmed with chrism at once, and afterwards that they receive communion. If the bishop is absent, they may receive communion from the presbyter. . . ."[68] This direction, through Benedict of Aniane's supplement to the Roman papal sacramentary sent by Pope Hadrian I to Charlemagne (called the *Gregorian Hadrianum*), would soon become the normal practice in the non-Roman West. While it is clear that Alcuin himself was attempting to respect the very structure of the Roman rite he had received, the fact that he permits and even directs this alternative ritual pattern leads J.D.C. Fisher to say that:

"The most notable feature of Alcuin's rite is the presence of the episcopal hand-laying after the communion of the baptized. Alcuin himself offers no explanation of this unusual practice, nor does he say how many churches followed the use which he has outlined in brief. It may be that the Churches which used Alcuin's rite, having been accustomed

---

[68] Turner, *Sources of Confirmation,* 17.

to an initiation which lacked episcopal handlaying and anointing, when ordered by Charlemagne to conform to the Roman use, added the missing episcopal acts at the very end rather than break the unity of what had been to them a single and complete unity."[69]

Whatever Alcuin himself may have intended, however, there is no question but that these episcopal postbaptismal rites were often delayed outside of Rome and because of this the interval between baptism and confirmation grew longer due, in part, to the rarity of episcopal visits to parishes throughout the vast dioceses of western Europe. As Aidan Kavanagh notes:

"This evolution, accomplished by the gradual adoption of Roman elements into Gallican liturgies over a span of some three centuries, forced out older Gallican practices of 'confirmation' and placed their Roman successor more and more subsequent to baptism itself—separated first by the baptismal eucharist, then by Easter week, and finally by the time it took for a circuit-riding Gallic bishop to make his rural rounds."[70]

It is such a shift that will give rise to theological speculation and interpretation in defense of this new practice. Either as separated from baptism and first communion, or as an addition to baptism and first communion outside of Rome, confirmation will become a rite and sacrament in search of a theological meaning and interpretation, a meaning and interpretation increasingly supplied by scholastic theology. When these Roman postbaptismal rites, associated with the gift of the Holy Spirit, remain connected intimately to baptism and first communion there is no question but they continue to serve both as the ritualizing or sacramentalizing of that gift of the Spirit *in* baptism and the means by which those newly baptized "in water *and* the Holy Spirit" are welcomed into the Eucharistic assembly. The problems arise when this Roman "rite of the Holy Spirit" is *not* connected to baptism at all but added later as a separate and self-contained rite.

Since no one could (or would) deny that baptism itself "gave" the Holy Spirit, medieval theologians struggled to find the appropriate language to distinguish and clarify the meaning of what was now

[69] Fisher, *Baptism in the Medieval West*, 61.
[70] Kavanagh, *Confirmation*, 68.

seen as "two" gifts of the Holy Spirit in Christian initiation. Alcuin himself, for example, suggested that the special gift of the Spirit in confirmation was so that the candidate might be "strengthened by the Holy Spirit in order to preach to others."[71] Rabanus Maurus (784–856 C.E.), Alcuin's own student who was to become the archbishop of Mainz, argued that while the first postbaptismal anointing by the presbyter was for the Holy Spirit's salvific "habitation" or "indwelling" of the soul of the newly baptized, the purpose of the episcopal anointing in confirmation was for "the sevenfold grace of the same Holy Spirit . . . to come upon people with all fullness of sanctity and knowledge and power."[72] Others were to make similar distinctions. Peter the Lombard (ca. 1100–60 C.E.), the great "Father of Scholasticism," who was the first ever to enumerate seven distinct sacraments in the life of the Church, writes that "the power of this sacrament is the gift of the Holy Spirit for strength, who was given in baptism for forgiveness."[73] And, among others, Nicholas of Clairvaux (1145–51 C.E.) says in a homily that: "in baptism the Spirit is given for grace, here it is given for struggle. There we are cleaned from iniquity, here we are fortified with virtues."[74]

If the theological distinctions made by these scholastic theologians sound reminiscent of the words of the famous fifth-century Pentecost homily attributed to Faustus of Riez, they do so with good reason. For, it is within this same time period of the Carolingian reform that Faustus' homily reappears. Now, however, his words about *confirmation* providing "an increase for grace" and a "strengthening" for battle are attributed to a fictitious pope named Melchiades and are cited as such in a collection of forged papal documents known as the *False Decretals*. In the Middle Ages, however, these decretals were recognized as authentic and from them Faustus' words would pass into what is known as the *Decretum* of Gratian, a twelfth-century legal document, which was to serve as the foundation for canon law in the medieval period. From there Peter the Lombard incorporated Faustus' interpretation of confirmation into his famous *Sentences*. And it was Lombard's *Sentences* that would serve as the basic introductory

---

[71] Fisher, *Baptism in the Medieval West*, 61.
[72] Text is cited from Turner, *Sources of Confirmation*, 36.
[73] Text is cited from ibid., 40.
[74] Text is cited from ibid., 40.

text book for the study of theology throughout the Middle Ages. Not surprisingly, then, it is on the basis of Lombard's *Sentences* that Thomas Aquinas can write in his own important and highly influential *Summa Theologiae* that:

". . . people also receive a spiritual life through baptism, which is spiritual regeneration. But in confirmation people receive as it were a certain mature age of spiritual life. For this reason, Pope Melchiades says, 'The Holy Spirit who descends upon the waters of baptism in a salvific falling bestows on the font a fullness toward innocence. In confirmation it presents an increase for grace. In baptism we are reborn for life. After baptism we are strengthened.' And therefore it is clear that confirmation is a special sacrament."[75]

Although Thomas himself nowhere correlates this "mature age of spiritual life" with the chronological age of recipients (the soul, after all, is immortal), his interpretation will come to be highly influential later in support of the practice of reserving the administration of confirmation to a particular age. In Thomas himself, however, as Austin notes, "maturity is described as a preparation for a spiritual battle outside one's self." He continues:

"For Aquinas, confirmation, like baptism and holy orders, imprints a character, which is a 'certain kind of participation in the priesthood of Christ.' . . . In his treatment of the sacraments in general, Aquinas likens the character of confirmation to that of baptism, by which one is given the power to receive all the other sacraments. Later on, in dealing specifically with the character of confirmation, he differentiates the two characters: 'Through the sacrament of confirmation a man is given spiritual power for activity that is different from that for which power is given in baptism. For in baptism power is received for performing those things which pertain to one's own salvation in so far as one lives for oneself. In confirmation a person receives power for engaging in the spiritual battle against the enemies of faith.'"[76]

What happens theologically, then, is that in the medieval West the images associated previously with the prebaptismal anointing in

[75] Text is cited from Turner, *Sources of Confirmation*, 41–2.
[76] Austin, *Anointing with the Spirit*, 27.

some traditions (e.g., combat and struggle against Satan) now become attached to confirmation itself as a rite of spiritual maturity, growth, and combat. In such a context, the *alapa* or "pat of peace," noted above in the *Pontifical of William Durandus,* would itself come to be interpreted as a sign of the struggles and sufferings the confirmed would now endure as "soldiers of Christ" in the world.

Confirmation, therefore, emerges in the West as a distinct rite, separate from baptism itself, as a special sacrament of the Holy Spirit for an increase of grace, strength to live and fight the battles of the Christian life, and as a sacrament of "maturity." This development, as we have seen, appears to reflect a synthesis of the specifically *Roman* episcopal postbaptismal rites of handlaying with prayer and anointing with the Spanish-Gallican practices of episcopal oversight and supervision of baptism, a practice already called "confirmation" there.

It would be incorrect to conclude, however, that either the rite itself or its theological interpretations would immediately be accepted by clergy and/or faithful alike throughout the Church in Europe. The exact opposite, in fact, was more likely to be the case as the western Middle Ages abound with repeated attempts on the part of bishops, diocesan, and general councils to impress upon people the necessity of confirmation. J.D.C. Fisher gives several examples of these attempts in England, Belgium, and Germany, writing:

"Some thirteenth-century councils in England found it necessary to set an age limit by which children must have been confirmed, and to threaten parents with dire penalties if they failed to see that it was done. Thus the *Constitutions* of Richard Poore (c. 1217), after ordering the clergy frequently to warn their people to have their children confirmed, declared that, if through parental negligence a child was not confirmed by the age of five, his father and mother should be denied entry into the church until the omission had been made good; and a similar penalty was imposed upon clergy who were negligent in this matter. The Council of Worcester (1240) threatened parents with the same punishment if their children were not confirmed by the age of one, but out of regard for the practical difficulties modified this by adding the words, 'provided they had access to a bishop, or it was well known that he was passing through the vicinity.' Richard of Chicester (1246) ordered parents to present their children for confirmation by the age of one; if they failed to do so they were to be punished. . . . At the Council of Exeter (1287) parents were ordered to have their children confirmed by the age of three . . . : if they were negligent in this, they were to fast every Friday on bread and water until their children were confirmed. . . . The Statutes of John of Liège (1287) ordered confirmation to be received at the age of seven or under. . . . The Council of Cologne seven years previously in almost exactly the same terms had fixed the age as seven years or older. This is an early instance of the rule which was to become common in the sixteenth century. . . . The apparent contradiction . . . can be explained on the reasonable assumption that, where diocesan regulations required that confirmation be received by the age of seven, most parents in practice waited until their children had already reached that age before they presented them, so that it became common for confirmation candidates to be at least seven years old and frequently older still . . . and the Council of Lambeth, held under archbishop Peckham in 1281, found that a very large number of people had grown old in evil ways without having received the grace of confirmation. To obviate this 'damnable negligence' a new sanction was imposed that nobody should be admitted to the sacrament of the Lord's body and blood, save when in danger of death, unless he had been confirmed, or had been reasonably prevented from receiving confirmation."[77]

Such frequent legislation regarding confirmation certainly indicates, in the words of Gerard Austin, that confirmation became the "neglected sacrament" in the medieval Western Church.[78] Equally important is that this legislation also demonstrates that a concern for the "age" at which confirmation is to be administered has its origins in these various conciliar attempts to set not a *minimal* age for its reception but a *maximal* age (varying from age one, three, seven, or even ten) *by* which confirmation was to have *been* received already! In other words, what will become the minimal "canonical age" of seven for the reception of confirmation in the Roman Church, the so-called "age of reason" or "discretion," became such on account of clerical and parental negligence and delay! And while the type of ritual process envisioned by the Roman books, with confirmation by the bishop following baptism immediately, remained the ideal, the delay of several years be-

[77] Fisher, *Baptism in the Medieval West,* 122–4.
[78] Austin, *Anointing with the Spirit,* 20.

tween baptism and confirmation would find theological support in the understanding that confirmation provides an increase of grace, gives power to do spiritual battle, and is the sacrament of "maturity." With this the door is thrown wide open for the popular understanding that confirmation is the special sacrament for adolescents!

The Dominance of Infant Baptism and Its Consequences

If, due to its ambiguous origins, unconvincing theology, and parental and clerical apathy, confirmation was the "neglected sacrament" of the Middle Ages, the importance and necessity of baptism was not seriously questioned. Even so, the rite and sacrament of baptism itself was to undergo serious and far reaching changes in this period as well, with both liturgical and theological consequences.

Both John the Deacon and the Gelasian Sacramentary, as we have seen, witness to the fact that infants were fully initiated along with adults according to the traditional Roman ritual pattern of Christian initiation from enrollment in the catechumenate during Lent through the rites of baptism, "confirmation," and first communion at the Easter Vigil. But the increasing influence of the Augustinian doctrine of original sin would create the demand that infants be baptized "as soon as possible" (*quamprimum*) after birth. While scholastic theology itself was uncomfortable with the harsh conclusions of Augustine on the eternal damnation of the unbaptized and developed the theological construct of "limbo" to soften the blow,[79] *quamprimum* baptism in the West, based on original sin, was here to stay. Hence, whatever the actual practice may have been historically, the ancient North African–Roman ideal of baptism at Easter/Pentecost, although still present in the liturgical texts and legal canons, gave way to the general consensus that children must be baptized, at least, within a week of birth.

The great irony in this is that, in the context of the Pelagian controversy, Augustine himself had developed his theology of original sin largely based on the already existing practice of infant baptism within the North African Church of the fourth and fifth centuries. But, as Mark Searle notes:

"In the ninth century Walafrid Strabo reversed Augustine's argument: 'Since all who are not delivered by God's grace will perish in

---

[79] Cf. Aquinas, *Summa Theologiae*, Supplement, q. 69.

original sin, including those who have not added to it by their own personal sin, it is necessary to baptize infants.' Thereafter the practice of infant baptism will be justified on the basis of the doctrine of original sin, not vice versa. . . ."[80]

Similar theological rationales and diocesan regulations for the *quamprimum* baptism of infants occur throughout the Middle Ages. A twelfth-century anonymous source from France says, for example, that:

"The canons order that baptism be celebrated only on Holy Saturday or on Pentecost, except in case of necessity. But this precept has adults in view. In the early Church adults who were sick could say so, and then they were baptized. Moreover, the fact that many were baptized at the same time augmented the glory of the Christian name. But all this does not apply to little children, for who is more ill than an infant who cannot make it known that it is ill? The baptism of children should therefore not be put off, for they may die of the least ailment."[81]

From Italy, the fourteenth-century *Constitutions of Padua* required baptism within eight days after birth and various other diocesan synods throughout Europe ordered that baptism be administered "without delay," some even attempting to require that it take place within twenty-four hours of birth.[82] Others stated that "whoever departs this life unbaptized will not only be deprived of the kingdom of God, but will for his original sin suffer eternal punishment." The famous Bernard of Clairvaux (+ 1153) said that as long as "the grace of baptism is denied to them, the life of Christ is unattainable by the infant children of Christians, and the way of salvation is closed to them."[83] As late as 1442, the Council of Florence decreed:

"Concerning children: because of the danger of death, which occurs frequently enough, since nothing else can be done for them except to

---

[80] Searle, "Infant Baptism Reconsidered," 375.

[81] Cited by Robert Cabié, "Christian Initiation," *The Sacraments,* vol. 3 of *The Church at Prayer: A New Edition,* ed. A. G. Martimort et al. (Collegeville: The Liturgical Press, 1988) 71.

[82] See Fisher, *Baptism in the Medieval West,* 111ff.

[83] Ibid., 112.

baptize them, whereby they are snatched from the power of the devil and adopted as children of God, the Council admonishes that holy baptism is not to be delayed for 40 or 80 days or for some other period of time, as some are wont to do [i.e., the Christian East!], but they should be baptized as soon as conveniently possible [*quamprimum commode fieri potest*]. Therefore, in imminent danger of death, let them be baptized in the form of the Church even by a layman or woman, if no priest is at hand, quickly and without delay."[84]

But perhaps one of the best examples of *quamprimum* baptism in the medieval West is that of Martin Luther himself in 1483. Born on November 10, 1483, Luther was baptized on the very next day, November 11, the feast of St. Martin of Tours.

Two major but related consequences arise from this medieval shift to the *quamprimum* baptism of infants based on the Augustinian theology of original sin: the traditional catechumenate disappears and infant initiation becomes infant baptism exclusively.

The disappearance of the catechumenate. In the early Middle Ages there had been occasional attempts by Church leaders such as Boniface, the eighth-century "Apostle of Germany," and Alcuin of Tours to restore some kind of minimal adult catechumenate (two months or forty days, respectively) in the conversion of the "barbarian" tribes of the north. Alcuin himself had attempted such a catechumenate in the wake of Charlemagne's own imperial programs of mass baptisms and "evangelism" by force or violence.[85] But *quamprimum* baptism sounds the death knell for the catechumenal process in relationship to baptism as a whole, even the experience of minimal parental preparation that would have indirectly accompanied the process throughout the lenten scrutinies as they appeared in the Gelasian Sacramentary and *Ordo Romanus XI*.

Connected with the earlier known practice of the "emergency initiation" of sick catechumens, who, if they survived would later be expected to have their baptisms "confirmed" or "perfected" by the bishop, as some earlier Western local councils seem to indicate (e.g.,

[84] Cited by Searle, "Infant Baptism Reconsidered," 369–70.

[85] On these attempts see Peter Cramer, *Baptism and Change in the Early Middle Ages c. 200–c. 1150*, Cambridge Studies in Medieval Life & Thought, Fourth Series, vol. 20 (Cambridge: Cambridge University Press, 1993) 185ff.

Elvira), the *quamprimum* baptism of infants essentially becomes itself, in the words of Mark Searle, "a form of clinical baptism," that is, a "rite for the dying."[86] Certainly the above noted legislation directing baptism "without delay" points strongly in that direction. As such, combined with the high infant mortality rate in the Middle Ages, a period of time in which total life expectancy would be somewhere around the age of forty, the rites themselves would have to be telescoped or compressed into a very short period of time and would certainly have to be performed at a time when all the orders of the Church could not be represented.

This, of course, is exactly what happened with the rites for infant baptism. What had been the catechumenate is increasingly reduced and compressed into a *single* ceremony, now taking place as a preparatory rite either at the door of the church or in close proximity to the baptismal font. In the first printed edition of the *Roman Ritual* (1487), for example, this is precisely what we see to have taken place. Before baptism itself the infant is ritually made a catechumen with the traditional ceremonies of the giving of salt, signings with the cross, and a series of exorcisms at the church door, followed at the font by the recitation *(traditio)* of the Our Father and Apostles' Creed, the *apertio* or *effeta,* the threefold renunciation of Satan, and an anointing of the candidate's breast and back. Any catechesis itself, now limited to the parents' teaching of their child the Apostles' Creed, the Our Father, and the Hail Mary, would occur, necessarily of course, after baptism as the child grew.[87]

Several factors contributed to this change of emphasis. Among them would certainly be the development and increasing postponement of confirmation itself to the "catechetical" age of seven or above. At the same time, the increasing tendency of scholastic theology to narrow the treatment of sacramental theology to the categories of "matter" and "form" made the other ceremonies associated with the rite of lesser importance. Thomas Aquinas himself, for example, reflects this increasing sacramental minimalism, saying:

"In baptism certain things are done which are *necessary* for the sacrament and certain others which pertain to the *solemnity* of the sacra-

---

[86] Searle, "Infant Baptism Reconsidered," 369.
[87] See Fisher, *Baptism in the Medieval West,* 115–7.

ment. *Necessary* for the sacrament are the form which designates the principal cause of the sacrament, the minister who is the instrumental cause, and the use of the matter, viz. washing with water which designates the principal effect of the sacrament. The other things which the Church observes in the baptismal rite all pertain to the solemnity of the sacrament. Three reasons can be given for the use of these things in sacramental administration. First of all, to arouse the devotion of the faithful and reverence for the sacrament. . . . Secondly, to instruct the faithful. . . . Thirdly, because the devil's power to impede the effect of the sacrament is held in check through the prayers, blessings and the like."[88]

Contributing further to an increasingly minimalistic approach was also the change beginning in the manner and mode of administering baptism itself during this period. While liturgical documents still indicated a preference for immersion or submersion, and baptismal fonts generally remained large enough to accommodate easily the immersion or submersion of infants, there does develop, in France primarily, a marked preference for pouring or sprinkling the water on the candidate during the baptismal formula. Although, as we have seen, this practice of "affusion" is also a very ancient practice in the history of initiation (see the *Didache*), by the end of the Middle Ages it had tended to replace immersion and submersion as the common and regular practice. Such a change in practice will contribute even further in the following centuries to the building of smaller fonts with minimal amounts of water.[89]

By far, however, the most significant factor in this shift of emphasis, undoubtedly, was the separation of first communion from Christian initiation altogether. As we have seen repeatedly throughout this

[88] *Summa Theologiae* III, a. 66, 10.4; emphasis added.

[89] Hughes Oliphant Old, *The Shaping of the Reformed Baptismal Rite in the Sixteenth Century* (Grand Rapids, Mich.: Eerdmans, 1992) 264–72. On the changes in the architecture of baptismal fonts see S. Anita Stauffer, *On Baptismal Fonts: Ancient and Modern,* Alcuin GROW Liturgical Study 29–30 (Bramcomte, Nottingham: Grove Books, 1994); and *Re-examining Baptismal Fonts: Baptismal Space for the Contemporary Church,* dir. Mitch Groethe, prod. Fredric Petters, 36 min., The Liturgical Press, 1991, videocassette. The classic study of baptismal fonts is John Gordon Davies, *The Architectural Setting of Baptism* (London: Barrie and Rockliff, 1962).

study, from the various practices of Christian initiation in the early churches before the Council of Nicea, through the fourth and fifth centuries, and all the way through and including the early medieval documents themselves, *all* newly baptized Christians—both infants and adults—regularly completed their baptism into Christ by the immediate reception of first communion either at the baptismal Eucharist or from the reserved Eucharist. Recall here that *Ordo XI* specified clearly that: "after [the rites of baptism and confirmation] they go in to Mass and all the infants receive communion. Care is to be taken lest after they have been baptized they receive any food or suckling before they communicate." And, as we saw above in Alcuin's directions concerning the Gallican adaptation of the Roman rite, the following statement appears: "if the bishop is there it is necessary that they be confirmed with chrism at once, and afterwards that they receive communion. If the bishop is absent, they may receive communion from the presbyter." Such, as we have also seen, remained the common pattern through the twelfth century, at least at Rome. How communion was actually distributed to baptized infants varied from place to place. With some concern developing from the eleventh-century on about children's ability to swallow and consume the eucharistic host, communion under the one element of wine from the chalice, administered by either a finger dipped in the chalice or by a "leaf" or spoon came to be the regular practice.[90] Balthasar Fischer, in fact, sees the modern custom of giving silver spoons for baptismal or baby gifts as remnants of this older communion practice.[91]

Nevertheless, by the thirteenth century, in general, the practice of infant communion at baptism was rapidly disappearing in the West. And the Fourth Lateran Council (1215), along with defining the doctrine of "transubstantiation," regarding the change of the bread and wine into Christ's body and blood in the Eucharist, also directed: (1) that the reception of communion was not obligatory for those younger than the "age of discretion," that is, age seven; (2) that "first confession" was required of those who, having reached this age, presented themselves for first communion; and (3) that confession and the reception of communion were required, at least once a year at

---

[90] On this see Fisher, *Baptism in the Medieval West,* 101–8.

[91] Cited in David Holeton, *Infant Communion: Then and Now,* Grove Liturgical Study 27 (Bramcote, Nottingham: Grove Books, 1981) 8.

Easter, of all who had reached this age,[92] a requirement still referred to today as one's "Easter duty." On the implications of both the separation of confirmation from baptism and this separation of communion from initiation, J.D.C. Fisher summarizes, saying:

"For over a thousand years the Church in the West gave confirmation to children at any age at their initiation. . . . But when because of practical difficulties and other causes, . . . it came about that the majority of candidates for confirmation were not infants but adolescents, the Church in the West began to say, 'Infants are not now presented for confirmation: therefore infants do not need confirmation; the Church normally gives confirmation to adolescents: therefore the grace conveyed by confirmation must be the spiritual strength particularly needed by those entering adolescence.' Similarly for a thousand years the Western Church saw nothing objectionable in giving communion to newly baptized infants. But when in the 12th and 13th centuries the doctrine of transubstantiation was established, making the Church unwilling to tolerate any longer those accidents which were bound to occur sometimes in the communicating of infants, the communion of infants came to an end, though not at the same time in all Churches. Then after infants had in fact ceased to receive communion, the Church began to say, 'Infants are not allowed to receive communion; the Church cannot be supposed to have excluded them from communion without good cause; therefore infants have no need of sacramental communion, and the grace which they receive in baptism must be supposed to suffice until they are of an age to commit actual sin.'"[93]

It must be noted, however, that it is not so much the *doctrine* of transubstantiation that led to the decline of infant communion. More important reasons were the changes occurring in communion practices themselves prior to the promulgation of this thirteenth-century doctrine. Such changes included the lack of frequent communion participation on the part of the laity in general, the growing clericalization of the Eucharist due, in part, to developments in the theology of priestly ordination, a growing and increasing scrupulosity about the eucharistic elements themselves (e.g., "may lay persons receive communion in the hand or only in the mouth from the consecrated

[92] See Fisher, *Baptism in the Medieval West*, 105.
[93] Ibid., 139.

hands of a priest?"), and, especially, the withdrawal of the cup from the laity, and the concomitant development of a eucharistic piety centered almost exclusively on devotion to the host. When the cup was withdrawn from the laity, previous practices of communing infants even from the chalice alone naturally disappeared as well.[94] Nevertheless, as David Holeton has written:

"To suggest that the practice began to disappear with the proclamation of transubstantiation and the withdrawal of the chalice from the laity is to miss the principal point. A Christian society that has degenerated to such a state that it becomes necessary to legislate that Christians need receive the eucharist once a year is fertile for most everything to take place in the context of baptism and the eucharist. The whole vision of what the eucharist was, and what its relationship was to the community, had so changed that the process could take place unresisted, except in those places where tradition was being asserted for political rather than theological reasons."[95]

Infant initiation becomes infant baptism. Closely related to the first consequence of the medieval Western shift to the *quamprimum* baptism of infants, the second consequence, in light of the same significant factors summarized above, became inevitable. Ultimately separated from both confirmation and first communion by (seven or more) years, and, thanks to Lateran IV, by the addition of yet another sacramental rite *before* first communion, the earlier process of infant *initiation* became infant *baptism* alone, a reduced and compressed rite more often than not celebrated in private rather than as part of the public liturgical life of the Church. What the earlier churches of both

[94] For further discussion of changes in communion practices, in addition to Fisher, *Baptism in the Medieval West*, 101–8, see especially Nathan Mitchell, *Cult and Controversy: The Worship of the Eucharist Outside Mass* (New York: Pueblo, 1982), Ruth Meyers, "Infant Communion," *Children at the Table: A Collection of Essays on Children and the Eucharist*, ed. Ruth Meyers (New York: Church Hymnal Corp., 1995) 146–64, and E. Brand, "Baptism and Communion of Infants: A Lutheran View," LWSS, 350–64.

[95] David Holeton, "The Communion of Infants and Young Children: A Sacrament of Community," *And Do Not Hinder Them: An Ecumenical Plea for the Admission of Children to the Eucharist*, ed. Geiko Muller-Fahrenholz, Faith and Order Paper 109 (Geneva: World Council of Churches, 1982) 63.

East and West kept together in a unitive and integral rite, the Western Middle Ages, to paraphrase the marriage rite, "rent asunder" into four separate and distinct sacraments:

(1) baptism in infancy with the postbaptismal anointing with chrism given by a presbyter (priest);

(2) first confession at age seven in preparation for first communion;

(3) first communion;

(4) confirmation by a bishop at age seven (or later), either before or after first communion, depending upon the availability of the bishop and the responsibility of parents and parish clergy.

In such a way, infant baptism was to become little more than a solemn "operation on the child,"[96] a solemn exorcism designed to rid the child from his/her inherited original sin, or, given its close association to birth, a "naming ceremony" for the child ("christening"). With regard to this, Mark Searle is certainly correct when he notes that:

"What is not always recognized is that with this unwitting change of policy, the Western Church gave up trying to initiate infants. Once infant baptism is recognized as a form of clinical baptism—an emergency measure—it has to be acknowledged that, with the move to defer confirmation and first Communion, *Christian initiation was in fact deferred until the child was old enough to be catechized.* Instead of initiating infants, as had been the universal policy of the first millennium or more, the Church now put them on hold—baptizing them as a precautionary measure—until they came of age. . . . The net result is that, beginning in the late thirteenth century and universally from the sixteenth, the Roman Catholic Church has really only initiated 'adults,' even though it continued to baptize the newborn as a precautionary measure within a few hours or days of birth."[97]

Such is the legacy for the rites of Christian initiation and their interpretation that the medieval period in the West left to the following centuries.

---

[96] Cramer, *Baptism and Change in the Early Middle Ages,* 137.
[97] Searle, "Infant Baptism Reconsidered," 370–1; emphasis added.

CONCLUSION: THE ALTERNATIVE PATTERN
OF THE CHRISTIAN EAST

The process of ritual and theological disintegration, dissolution, or separation summarized in this chapter, of course, is a *uniquely* Western Christian phenomenon. That the evolution of Christian initiation *could* have gone in a different direction altogether is demonstrated by the rites of the Eastern Christian churches. While infant baptism became and remained common throughout the entire Christian world, the various liturgical rites of initiation in the Christian East never experienced the separation of "confirmation" from baptism, the separation of communion from initiation, or the splitting up of the rites of Christian initiation into separately occurring sacramental events. Rather, the earlier integral and unitive pattern, seen already in the great Eastern mystagogues of the fourth and fifth centuries, continued through the centuries—as still today—to constitute the ritual process of Christian initiation in its entirety.

It is beyond the scope of this study to analyze each of the seven distinct living rites of the Christian East, both Orthodox and Eastern Catholic, i.e., the Byzantine, Armenian, Coptic, Ethiopic, East Syrian (Syro-Malabar and Assyro-Chaldean), West Syrian or Antiochene, and Maronite (Lebanese). For our purposes here, however, since enough similarity exists between them in the ritual pattern for and theological interpretation of Christian initiation, such detailed study and analysis is not all that necessary. A brief look only at the Byzantine rite, then, the dominant, largest, and most influential liturgical tradition in the Christian East, as it achieves its final form in the Middle Ages will have to suffice here.[98]

---

[98] On the Byzantine rite for baptism see especially Alexander Schmemann, *Of Water and the Spirit: A Liturgical Study of Baptism* (Crestwood, N.Y.: St. Vladimir's Seminary Press, 1974); and M. Arranz, "Les Sacrements de l'ancien Euchologe constantinopolitain," (9 articles): 1, *Orientalia Christiana Periodica* [hereafter OCP] 48 (1982) 284–335; 2, OCP 49 (1983) 42–90; 3, OCP 49 (1983) 284–302; 4, OCP 50 (1984) 43–64; 5, OCP 50 (1984) 372–97; 6, OCP 51 (1985) 60–86; 7, OCP 52 (1986) 145–78; 8, OCP 53 (1987) 59–106; and 9, OCP 55 (1989) 33–62; and M. Arranz., "Evolution des rites d'incorporation et de réadmission dans l'église selon l'Euchologe byzantin," *Gestes et paroles dans les diverses familles liturgiques*, ed. A. Pistoia and A. Triacca (Rome: Centro liturgico vincenziano, 1978) 31–75. For overall introductions to the Byzantine liturgical tradition see Robert Taft, *The Byzantine Rite: A Short History*

Within the *Barberini Euchologion*,[99] the earliest extant document for the Byzantine rite in the medieval period, along with indications of an adult catechumenate with instructions, the renunciation of Satan, the profession of the Nicene Creed, and a syntaxis all leading to Easter baptism, two prayers are included with specific relationship to the initiation of infants: (1) a prayer for the sealing of the infant with the cross on the forehead, breast, and mouth on the eighth day after birth, when the infant was named, and (2) a prayer associated with the presentation of the infant to the Church on the fortieth day after birth. These prayers are followed in the *Barberini Euchologion* with additional prayers for the making of a catechumen, three prebaptismal exorcisms, renunciation, profession, *syntaxis*, and the order of baptism itself. What is most intriguing about these specific prayers for infants on the eighth and fortieth days after birth is that, unlike in the medieval West, infants were obviously not baptized *quamprimum*. Rather, some vestige of the overall catechumenal process remained in effect as it still does in some of the Byzantine churches today.

Within the rites of initiation themselves, the prebaptismal anointing remained a full body anointing with the "oil of gladness," baptism was (and is) administered by full submersion with the same passive formula (i.e., "Such a one [or N.], the servant of God is baptized in the name...") so vigorously defended by both Chrysostom and Theodore centuries before, and immediately after baptism, following a prayer for the gift of the Holy Spirit, the newly baptized are anointed with chrism in the form of the cross on the forehead, eyes, nostrils, mouth, and ears as the priest says, "the seal of the gift of the Holy Spirit." In the *Barberini Euchologion* this is followed by the Divine (eucharistic) Liturgy, although today first communion—including still the communing of infants (!)—is usually given from the reserved Eucharist.

As in the churches of the non-Roman West in the early middle ages, the Eastern rites knew—and still know—of only *one* postbaptismal anointing or chrismation, administered by bishops or presbyters

(Collegeville: The Liturgical Press, 1992); and Hans-Joachim Schulz, *The Byzantine Liturgy* (Collegeville: The Liturgical Press, 1986).

[99] See the new critical edition of this document, edited by Stefano Parenti and Elena Velkovska, *L'Eucologio Barberini gr. 336*, Bibliotheca "Ephemerides liturgicae," Subsidia 80 (Rome: CLV, 1995). An English translation of the relevant sections appears in DBL, 69–82.

using chrism that was consecrated by the bishop (today by the patriarch alone). Whether that chrismation included only the five signings of the Byzantine rite, the nine of the Armenian (the five of the Byzantine plus the hands, the heart, the backbone, and the feet),[100] the thirty-six (!) of the Coptic rite,[101] or did not even enter the East Syrian liturgical tradition until the seventh century, the churches of the Christian East are unanimous in their interpretation of this anointing as associated with the gift of the Holy Spirit, an association first made, it should be recalled, in the mystagogical catecheses of Cyril of Jerusalem in the late fourth century.

As the "seal of the Holy Spirit," this postbaptismal chrismation has remained intimately connected to baptism itself in the Christian East and, as such, should never simply be equated with Western "confirmation." If anything, this *single* anointing in the Eastern rites corresponds to the *first* postbaptismal anointing of the Roman rite and not to the second anointing administered traditionally in the Roman rite by the bishop alone (or by his delegate). In fact, the churches of the Christian East only came to call this postbaptismal anointing "the *sacrament* of chrismation" because of encounters with the West and the influence of Western scholastic theology. In the words of Thomas Hopko:

"The practice of counting the sacraments was adopted in the Orthodox Church from the Roman Catholics. It is not an ancient practice of the Church and, in many ways, it tends to be misleading since it appears that there are just seven specific rites which are 'sacraments' and that all other aspects of the life of the Church are essentially different from these traditional actions. The more ancient and traditional practice of the Orthodox Church is to consider everything which is in and of the Church as sacramental or mystical."[102]

While it is true that chrismation is used apart from baptism in the eastern churches—like confirmation in the Roman rite as well—to receive into their membership persons baptized within other Christian traditions, its close and inseparable connection with baptism has never been lost. As Paul Turner summarizes:

[100] DBL, 65–6

[101] See ibid., 96.

[102] Cited by Dennis Smolarski, *Sacred Mysteries: Sacramental Principles and Liturgical Practice* (New York: Paulist Press, 1995) 1.

"In the east, chrismation is offered to adults, children, and infants alike. When adults are baptized and chrismated, they symbolize their conversion and commitment to Christ. When children are baptized and chrismated, they enter the mystery of Christ which will continue to unfold throughout their lives. Chrismation is not so much the second mystery, as it is the very fulfillment of baptism. While baptism incorporates us into Christ's new risen existence, chrismation makes us partakers of his Spirit, the very source of this new life and of total illumination."[103]

By keeping baptism, the postbaptismal rites associated with the Holy Spirit, and the reception of first communion together within a single, unitive, and integrated process of Christian initiation, including the retention of some elements of the prebaptismal catechumenate even for infants, the Christian East was thus able to avoid the problems associated with "confirmation" as a separate sacrament of strength and maturity for those at the "age of discretion" in the West. With the retention of such an integral pattern, catechesis itself becomes, essentially, "mystagogy" rather than preliminary instruction and preparation for the reception of sacraments. That is, through life-long postbaptismal catechesis the baptized, chrismated, and communed are continually formed to live out the "mysteries" which they have already received and in which they were sealed from the beginning. In such a way the churches of the Christian East continued to *initiate* infants rather than simply *baptize* them and "put them on hold" until later.

While, as noted above, the medieval West itself could have gone in this direction as well, such was not to be the case until the modern period of liturgical reform and renewal itself. For, as we shall see below in chapter 8, the modern reforms of the rites of Christian initiation throughout several Western churches across denominational lines—in texts, in the overall ritual pattern, and in theological interpretation—are largely indebted to a recovery of what has been the regular practice of the churches of the East for several centuries. Before we can analyze this development, however, it is necessary to look at the influence of the medieval West on the churches of the sixteenth-century Protestant and Catholic Reformations.

---

[103] Paul Turner, *Confirmation: The Baby in Solomon's Court* (New York: Paulist Press, 1993) 34.

Chapter 7

Christian Initiation in the Protestant and Catholic Reforms of the Sixteenth Century

The pattern of Christian initiation in its disordered and separated sequence, as it had come to be celebrated and interpreted throughout the medieval West, would be inherited by and highly influential within those churches which owe their immediate origins to the sixteenth-century Protestant and Catholic Reformations.[1] Singled out for particular treatment in this chapter are the most influential of the Protestant Reformers: Martin Luther (1483–1546), Ulrich Zwingli (1484–1531), Martin Bucer (1491–1551), John Calvin (1509–64), and Thomas Cranmer (1489–1556), as well as the Roman Catholic liturgical reforms and related theological interpretations coming out of the Council of Trent (1545–63).

The particular theological, political, cultural, and historical factors which contributed to bring about the sixteenth-century Reformation in the first place are several, well described elsewhere,[2] and, thus, beyond the limited scope of this study. Nevertheless, it is important to

---

[1] Detailed analyses and ritual texts appear in J.D.C. Fisher, *Christian Initiation: The Reformation Period* (London: Society for Promoting Christian Knowledge, 1970); and Hughes Oliphant Old, *The Shaping of the Reformed Baptismal Rite in the Sixteenth Century* (Grand Rapids, Mich.: Eerdmans, 1992). See also James F. White, *Protestant Worship: Traditions in Transition* (Louisville: Westminster/John Knox Press, 1989). This chapter is highly dependent upon these excellent and significant studies.

[2] Very good standard studies of this period, if now somewhat dated, include Roland Bainton, *The Reformation of the Sixteenth Century* (Boston: Beacon Press, 1952); and Owen Chadwick, *The Reformation,* Pelican History of the Church, vol. 3 (Harmondsworth: Penguin, 1968). For an excellent treatment of the theological and doctrinal issues in the Reformation see Jaroslav Pelikan, *The Christian Tradition: A History of the Development of Doctrine,* vol. 4, *Reformation of Church and Dogma (1300–1700)* (Chicago: University of Chicago Press, 1983).

note generally that both ecclesial and social life in the late or high Middle Ages were ripe for some kind of far-reaching reform and renewal, one that would reach down to the very roots of Western society and culture. As Herman Wegman notes:

". . . people were deeply disappointed in both church and state. The call for reform was widespread, especially for reform of the church. In making such a call people looked to the past. The early church was the ideal from which the church had now strayed, so far that nothing seemed to remain from that early period. Holiness, purity, poverty, zealous faith had all disappeared, or so it was thought. The humanists with their growing historical insight had a distaste for what we now call 'the Middle Ages.' They saw it as a barbaric time of bad Latin and impossible metaphysics. Especially the clergy and the pope were responsible for these ills. At the Councils of Constance and Basel this dissatisfaction and a certain kind of antipapalism had already appeared, but now this tendency was becoming much more evident. Certain forms of anticlericalism were to be found not only in the scholarly circles but also among the faithful. Savanarola brought the city of Florence into revolt against the pope and his 'clique,' i.e., the Curia, which consisted mostly of the pope's relatives. The people began to criticize just like the learned. The development of printing brought books onto the market and many people learned to read them. Once people began to pore over the works of someone like Erasmus, it was not long before they too became reform-minded. The church, which had for many years looked upon learning and scholarship as its monopoly, now lost claim and became the object of a bitter critique carried on by learning, once the church's handmaid."[3]

Nationalism, the increasing loss of ecclesiastical and/or papal control of western Europe, the biting critiques of humanist scholars and others, and the so-called "Gutenburg Revolution," i.e., the discovery of the printing press, and with it the possibility of mass-produced pamphlets and books, all contributed in bringing about the sixteenth-century Reformation. In such a changed historical context, the rites of Christian initiation inherited from the Middle Ages will themselves become either drastically reformed and reshaped, according to vari-

[3] Herman Wegman, *Christian Worship in East and West: A Study Guide to Liturgical History* (Collegeville: The Liturgical Press, 1985) 298.

ous theological perspectives, or, as in the case of the Roman Catholic Church, defended strongly at all costs against the attacks of the Protestant Reformers. Nevertheless, as we shall see in what follows, very little actually changed with regard to the overall pattern of Christian initiation itself.

CHRISTIAN INITIATION ON THE EVE OF THE PROTESTANT REFORMATION

As we saw in the previous chapter, the rites of Christian initiation in the medieval West had evolved into a sequence of *four* distinct sacraments administered separately at intervals according to the age of the candidates. Similarly, as we also saw, infant baptism itself had increasingly become little more than an operation performed upon the infant, a solemn exorcism and "naming" ceremony. Indeed, thanks to Peter the Lombard and to scholastic theology after him, baptism had become but the first of *seven* distinct sacraments in the Western Church. The Council of Florence (1438–45) in its *Decree for the Armenians,* a short-lived attempt at reconciling the churches of the Latin West with the Greek-speaking East, had codified these seven sacraments of the Church in the following manner:

"There are seven sacraments of the New Law, *viz.* baptism, confirmation, the eucharist, penance, extreme unction, orders, and marriage. These are quite different from the sacraments of the Old Law, which did not cause grace, but foreshadowed the grace that was to be bestowed solely through the passion of Christ. Our sacraments, however, not only contain grace, but also confer it on those who receive them worthily. The first five have been ordained for the spiritual perfection of every individual in himself, the last two for the government and increase of the whole Church. Through baptism we are spiritually reborn; through confirmation we grow in grace and are strengthened in faith. Having been regenerated and strengthened, we are sustained by the divine food of the eucharist. But if we become sick in soul through sin, we are healed spiritually through penance, and healed spiritually as well as physically, in proportion as it benefits the soul, through extreme unction. Through orders the Church is governed and grows spiritually, while through marriage it grows physically. . . . Three elements are involved in the full administration of all these sacraments, *viz.* things as the matter, words as the form, and the person of the minister performing the sacrament with the intention of doing what the Church does. If any one of these is lacking, the sacrament is not effected. There are three of the sacraments, baptism, confirmation, and orders, which imprint on the soul an indelible character, i.e., a kind of spiritual seal distinct from the others. They are not, therefore, to be received more than once by the same individual. The rest, however, do not imprint a character and may be performed more than once."[4]

While this particular decree did not treat the question of the "institution" of the sacraments in its reference to the necessary elements in sacramental administration (i.e., matter, form, and intention), it is well known that from the time of Thomas Aquinas on the divine or dominical institution of each individual sacrament was often added as a fourth necessary element as well. Indeed, this question of dominical authority and institution in relationship to individual sacraments is what would lead all of the Protestant Reformers, in large part, to a radical critique and revision of the medieval sacramental system in general.

Although confirmation had become the great "neglected sacrament" of the Middle Ages and, since Lateran IV (1215), first communion had been tied increasingly to first confession at about age seven, baptism itself was anything but neglected. In his recent study of the baptismal rites of the Protestant Reformers, Hughes Oliphant Old notes that the rite of baptism in the late Middle Ages:

". . . was still essentially faithful to much that was clearly Christ's institution. It was still the sacrament of the washing away of sins and entrance into the kingdom of God. Baptism was celebrated within a few days of birth, and consequently it did stand at the beginning of the Christian life. Baptism usually coincided with the first time the child came to church. Baptism clearly marked the beginning of the Christian life. In spite of the influence of Nominalism it still preserved an amazing objectivity. Maintaining the Latin language had helped in preserving the objectivity of what was done. In spite of the heavy overlay of supplementary rites, the words of Christ were still in place. In spite of the Pelagian tendencies of much late medieval

[4] Text cited from John H. Leith, ed., *Creeds of the Churches: A Reader in Christian Doctrine, from the Bible to the Present*, 3d ed. (Atlanta: John Knox Press, 1982) 60–1.

scholasticism, there was much in the rite which did speak of God's free grace. The sacrament was available to every child in Christendom. No one was denied baptism regardless of social class, education, the legitimacy of one's birth, or the moral standing of one's parents. Baptism was free to all. What could speak more clearly of the grace of God?"[5]

Nevertheless, this "heavy overlay of supplementary rites" did have several consequences for how the rite was celebrated and interpreted. As we saw in the previous chapter, the ceremonies formerly associated with the catechumenal process throughout Lent with its frequent instructions and scrutinies had now become shortened and compressed into a *single* ceremony held at the church door. What may have been necessary for reasons of propriety in an earlier period when adult men and women were the candidates for initiation was still reflected in the rite by the inclusion of different prayers for male and female infants. And, since many of these ceremonies had become exorcistic in content over the years, it is not surprising that within the late medieval prebaptismal rites there remained what Old calls a "preponderence of exorcism": e.g., exsufflations (blowing in the face of the child), the exorcism and giving of salt, further and frequent exorcisms of the candidates themselves, and the *apertio* or *effeta*, all taking place at the church door, and, upon arrival at the font, often a further exorcism of the baptismal water itself, if it had not been blessed already on a previous occasion.[6] Given this, it is also no wonder that baptism in the late Middle Ages was often understood by people, who frequently imagined their own world to be filled with demons and evil spirits, as a rite designed to "chase the devil out" from someone.[7]

While late medieval Latin rituals varied in detail from diocese to diocese and from region to region, and would continue to do so until 1614 and long after, in all of them a recently born infant was made a catechumen, elected to baptism, and baptized all within a single ceremony and in a matter of a very few minutes. It is also important to note that the baptismal rite itself had been adapted to infants as the primary candidates in other ways. For example, the use of the Gospel

[5] Old, *The Shaping of the Reformed Baptismal Rite*, 30–1.
[6] Ibid., 10–6.
[7] Ibid., 16.

texts of Matthew 19:13-15 and Mark 10:13-16, the accounts of Jesus blessing little children, to which appeal had been made in defense of infant baptism since the time of Tertullian,[8] had now been incorporated into the rites themselves as "proof texts" for the practice. Furthermore, such an inclusion of texts like these might also underscore the privatized and rather independent nature of infant baptism itself in this period. That is, within the public celebration of Christian initiation during the Eucharistic liturgy on Sundays or principal feasts like Easter and Pentecost, the biblical readings would naturally be those assigned in the lectionary. The rites themselves would simply take place within that overall liturgical context. But by the inclusion of particular biblical readings the rite has become now a self-contained unit with no necessary correlation to the public liturgical life of the Church at all.

It is also important to note that any kind of real catechesis in relationship to Christian initiation had by this time clearly ceased in any active or conscious manner. An important rubric following baptism in the *Sarum Rite,* a rite which would influence the Reformation in England, directs that:

"If a bishop is present he [i.e., the newly baptized] must be immediately confirmed and next communicated, if his age require it. . . . If he be an infant let the father and mother be enjoined to preserve their child from fire and water and all other dangers until the age of seven years: and if they do it not, the godfathers and godmothers are held responsible. Likewise the godmothers should be enjoined to teach the infant the *Our Father,* and *Hail Mary,* and *I believe in God,* or cause them to be taught them . . . and that the infant be confirmed as soon as the bishop comes within a distance of seven miles."[9]

Such rubrics are widespread in the late medieval Latin rituals and it appears to be the case that catechesis itself, now only *postbaptismal* catechesis, of course, had thus become limited to the memorization of these three texts: the Our Father, the Hail Mary, and the Apostles' Creed. For those who could read (and afford) books, various devotional booklets, often highly penitential in nature, *Books of Hours,* containing the *Little Office of the Blessed Virgin Mary* and/or the *Office of*

[8] See above, chapter 2, 65–6.
[9] DBL, 247–8.

the Dead, other select Psalms, and other tracts or treatises on the ceremonies of the Mass (the *expositiones missae*), for example, would have provided some further instruction. But for the ordinary Christian any kind of organized catechetical formation appears to have been severely lacking.

On the eve of the Reformation, then, baptism itself had become: a rite administered almost exclusively to infants as a precautionary step, i.e., a rite for the dying, designed to rescue the candidate from the power of original sin and death; a rite filled with exorcisms designed to snatch the infant away from the grasp of Satan; a self-contained rite with no necessary relationship to the public liturgical life of the Church; a rite in which catechesis proper had been replaced by the exorcisms themselves; a rite leading to a process of catechetical formation which was limited to the memorization of a few texts; and a rite increasingly narrowed by scholastic theology to the categories of matter, form, intention, and dominical institution. Such is the rite and its interpretation inherited by both Protestants and Roman Catholics in the sixteenth century. How the Protestant and Catholic Reformation responded to this rite is the subject to which we now turn.

CHRISTIAN INITIATION
IN THE PROTESTANT REFORMATION

The Protestant Reformers of the sixteenth century, according to J.D.C. Fisher:

". . . criticized the medieval rite of baptism on five main counts. (1) Since it could be shown from Scripture that by divine appointment baptism must be administered with water in the name of the Trinity, nothing else was essential to the rite; the blessing of the font and the use of oil, candles, salt and spittle being therefore unnecessary additions introduced by men. (2) These additions gave rise to superstition. (3) The prevalent custom of baptizing children at any time in an almost empty church detracted from the honour due to a holy sacrament, and obscured the ecclesial element in baptism. (4) Not enough care was given to choose suitable godparents. (5) The service was not meaningful because it was in Latin."[10]

[10] J.D.C. Fisher, "Lutheran, Anglican, and Reformed Rites," *The Study of Liturgy*, rev. ed., ed. C. Jones, G. Wainwright, E. Yarnold, and P. Bradshaw (London: SPCK; New York: Oxford University Press, 1992) 155.

While Fisher is certainly correct in his overall list of sixteenth-century Protestant critiques of the late medieval baptismal rite, it is important to note that the ultimate origin of these critiques is to be found in the first detailed attack against the medieval sacramental system in general, namely, Martin Luther's 1520 treatise called *The Babylonian Captivity of the Church*. In this polemical and lengthy treatise, where Luther—Augustinian friar, biblical scholar, and university professor—claimed that just as the Jews had been captive in Babylon in the sixth-century B.C.E. so the true meaning of the sacraments and Christian freedom itself had been held captive by Rome, he built the foundation for almost all subsequent Protestant sacramental theology. Inheriting the traditional medieval scholastic definition of the necessary elements (e.g., matter, form, minister, and dominical institution) which constituted a sacrament, Luther wrote:

"To begin with, I must deny that there are seven sacraments, and for the present maintain that there are but three: baptism, penance, and the bread. All three have been subjected to a miserable captivity by the Roman curia, and the church has been robbed of all her liberty. Yet, if I were to speak according to the usage of the Scriptures, I should have only one single sacrament [Christ, 1 Tim 3:16], but with three sacramental signs, of which I shall treat more fully at the proper time."[11]

But later in this same treatise he backed away from penance as a specific "sacrament," saying:

". . . it has seemed proper to restrict the name of sacrament to those promises which have signs attached to them. The remainder, not being bound to signs, are bare promises. Hence, there are, strictly speaking, but two sacraments in the church of God—baptism and the bread. For only in these two do we find both the divinely instituted sign and the promise of forgiveness of sins."[12]

James F. White is absolutely correct in pointing out that in his limiting of the Church's genuine sacraments to baptism and Eucharist alone, Luther "brings to a logical conclusion one possible development of the late-medieval concept of the number of sacraments."[13]

[11] Martin Luther, *The Babylonian Captivity of the Church*, LW 36, 18.
[12] Ibid., 127.
[13] White, *Protestant Worship*, 38.

That is, if sacraments themselves are defined according to what scholastic theology considered to be the necessary elements, then, based on the command and institution of Christ, as that command is recorded in the New Testament, the reduction from seven to two "dominical sacraments" is perfectly logical.

To be completely fair, however, Luther's approach to the sacraments is not based simply on those scholastic categories of matter, form, intention, and dominical institution. Rather, instead of focusing exclusively on what scholasticism considered to be the "form" of the sacraments, i.e., the "formulas" recited in their administration, Luther considered the dominical "words of institution" to be the very key and central element in the sacraments, the very "promise" of God to do what the "formulas" in the sacraments proclaim that God does. And, since it is faith alone for Luther which justifies and saves, that saving faith is trust not in the sacramental *rite* itself but in the divine promise proclaimed in and by the sacrament. Hence, as White says: "Luther's theology of salvation shapes his theology of the sacraments. Since salvation is a divine gift, not a human work, the sacraments are subject to the same order of salvation. They are signs and promises of what God does for humans and, like redemption, can only be received in faith."[14]

Luther's reduction from seven to two sacraments, based, biblically, on the command of Christ ("Go . . . baptize," and "Do this in memory of me") and the promise of Christ ("The one who believes and is baptized shall be saved," and "This is my Body. . . . Blood, given and shed for you for the forgiveness of sins") was inherited in some way by all of the Protestant Reformers. Although the Lutheran tradition itself never has come to a consensus on the precise number of genuine "sacraments" in the Church (with penance [called "absolution"], ordination, and even prayer itself appearing in some lists),[15] other traditions developing out of the Protestant Reformation tended to limit the sacraments, or dominical "ordinances," as some came to call them, to baptism and Eucharist ("Lord's Supper") alone. Awareness of this overall reduction and limitation in sacramental

---

[14] Ibid.

[15] See the *Apology of the Augsburg Confession* and *The Smalcald Articles* in Theodore Tappert et al., trans. and ed., *The Book of Concord* (Philadelphia: Muhlenberg Press, 1959) 211ff. and 310.

theology is essential in coming to understand the particular approaches of the various Reformers to the rites and interpretation of Christian initiation.

Baptism Among the Protestant Reformers

Martin Luther. The Lutheran Reformation, as it is often called, was a "conservative" movement, both theologically and liturgically, valuing highly and retaining much of the Western Latin liturgical tradition in its own reforms of the sacramental rites of the Church. This is especially the case with the rite of baptism as it had come to be in the late Middle Ages. And the reason for this, of course, was the theology of Martin Luther himself.

Luther was, above everything else, a theologian of baptism. His own theology and, one might say, his "spirituality," were baptismal to the core. Baptism, as he wrote in his 1519 treatise, *The Holy and Blessed Sacrament of Baptism,* is nothing other than a rehearsal for death itself and, as a consequence, Christian life is to be a daily death to sin and resurrection to life, a remembering of and living out of baptism which will come to its ultimate fulfillment only in the final death when the old self—the old Adam—dies completely in order to be raised up to live with God forever.[16] Indeed, "the life of a Christian, from baptism to the grave, is nothing else than the beginning of a blessed death. For at the Last Day God will make him altogether new."[17] And, in his *Small Catechism* in 1529, in answer to the question, "What does such baptism with water signify?" he stated: "It signifies that the old Adam in us, together with all sins and evil lusts, should be drowned by daily sorrow and repentance and be put to death, and that the new man should come forth daily and rise up, cleansed and righteous, to live forever in God's presence."[18]

Since Luther's theology of the sacraments is closely related to his central emphasis on "justification by faith alone rather than works," and since he *strongly* affirmed infant baptism at the same time, some have seen a logical inconsistency in his approach.[19] For, if it is *faith* in the divine Word and promise which saves, then the only logical con-

---

[16] Martin Luther, *The Holy and Blessed Sacrament of Baptism,* LW 35, 29–43.
[17] Ibid., 31.
[18] Tappert, *The Book of Concord,* 349.
[19] See Fisher, *Christian Initiation,* 5.

clusion would appear to be that infant baptism itself should be omitted in favor of "believer's baptism" alone, that is, that baptism should be only for those who can demonstrate that they have that necessary trusting faith needed for salvation.

It is true, of course, that Luther did defend infant baptism on the basis of the traditional practice of the Church, on the "vicarious faith" of the Church, and on the fact that Christ himself received children and blessed them (see Mark 10:13-16). At the same, Luther was also willing to admit some sense in which infants do have faith, an insight, by the way, often confirmed in our own day by social scientists and religious educators. For Luther, in particular, faith is not only cognitive or rational but unrational and prerational as well. That is, in the Pauline New Testament sense of the word, faith is not intellectual acceptance of or assent to propositional, dogmatic revelation, but trust of Another. And such trust develops only in relationship, only in an environment, in a community of trust such as the family or Church. James Fowler, for example, writes that:

"We are endowed at birth with nascent capacities for faith. How these capacities are activated and grow depends to a large extent on how we are welcomed into the world and what kinds of environments we grow in. Faith is interactive and social; it requires community, language, ritual, and nurture. Faith is also shaped by initiatives from beyond us and other people, initiatives of spirit and grace. How these latter initiatives are recognized and imaged, or unperceived and ignored, powerfully affects the shape of faith in our lives."[20]

Luther's speculations seem to point in a similar direction.

Nevertheless, neither the tradition of the Church, the "vicarious faith" of the Church, Jesus' reception and blessing of children, nor the possibility of infant faith, however such "faith" may be understood, constitute the full explanation of why Luther retained the baptism of infants. Rather, that explanation is to be found in Luther's theology of justification itself. "Justification by faith alone" is but the shorthand or popularized version of what is more properly stated as "justification by grace alone, on account of Christ alone, received

[20] J. Fowler, as cited by Ruth Meyers, ed., *Children at the Table: The Communion of All the Baptized in Anglicanism Today* (New York: Church Hymnal Corp., 1995) 160.

through faith alone." All three elements are necessary and the reference to one of these three, for Lutherans, automatically implies the other two. In other words, God's gracious act of salvation in Christ, in classic Augustinian fashion, always comes first as God's own act of justifying the sinner in which the human person is declared righteous before God by the very word and promise of God, a promise made effective on the basis of the life, death, and resurrection of Jesus Christ. This word and promise is received *through* faith and trusted and believed *by* faith. But faith merely appropriates or receives what God has already done and promises to do in Christ. As such, faith itself—like salvation—is not a human work at all but is entirely dependent upon the external Word and promise of God.

How, then, does one receive this faith? The answer, of course, is through the work of the Holy Spirit in the Church. As Luther wrote in the explanation of the third article of the Apostles' Creed provided in his *Small Catechism*:

"I believe that by my own reason or strength I cannot believe in Jesus Christ, my Lord, or come to him. But the Holy Spirit has called me through the Gospel, enlightened me with his gifts, and sanctified and preserved me in true faith, just as he calls, gathers, enlightens, and sanctifies the whole Christian church on earth and preserves it in union with Jesus Christ in the one true faith. In this Christian church he daily and abundantly forgives all my sins, and the sins of all believers, and on the last day he will raise me and all the dead and will grant eternal life to me and to all who believe in Christ. This is most certainly true."[21]

Similarly, the *Augsburg Confession* of 1530, the primary Lutheran confessional document, summarizes Luther's theology by saying:

"To obtain such faith God instituted the office of the ministry, that is, provided the Gospel and the sacraments. Through these, as through means, God gives the Holy Spirit, who works faith, where and when God pleases, in those who hear the Gospel. And the Gospel teaches that we have a gracious God, not by our own merits but by the merit of Christ. . . ."[22]

[21] Tappert, *The Book of Concord,* 345.
[22] Ibid., 31.

Thus, faith is precisely a gift of God, the ability to believe is a gift of the Holy Spirit who operates within the proclamation of the Word and administration of the sacraments in order to proclaim continually God's justifying act in Christ and so make people into believers.

There is, then, no logical inconsistency in Luther's approach.[23] The "faith" which receives and trusts the promise given in baptism is worked by the same Holy Spirit who is operative in and bound inseparably to that sacrament. In other words, baptism itself *is* the way in which God's salvific message of justification is proclaimed. Faith, which is worked by the Holy Spirit precisely *in* this sacrament, is nothing other than trust in what this sacrament declares to be true, that is, "forgiveness of sins," deliverance "from death and the devil," and the granting of "eternal salvation."[24] That is the "word" and promise of baptism which is to be believed. So important is this sacramental objectivity of baptism that Luther can say in his *Large Catechism* that:

". . . when the Word accompanies the water, Baptism is valid, even though faith be lacking. For my faith does not constitute baptism but receives it. Baptism does not become invalid even if it is wrongly received or used, for it is bound not to our faith but to the Word."[25]

That is, baptism is the Word proclaimed, a Word embodied or incarnated in the water.

Far from trying to find a suitable reason for the retention of infant baptism, then, the baptism of infants becomes for Luther a most fitting paradigm of God's gracious justifying act altogether. Not only is an infant a model of complete dependency and trust, but precisely as one who can claim no works, merits, or personal decisions, an infant witnesses to Luther's theological understanding that salvation is entirely God's act alone. That is, infant baptism testifies to the reality that faith and repentance are not prerequisites *for* baptism but, rather, life-long consequences *of* baptism. And, that such life-long development of trusting faith in the baptismal promises of God was something Luther considered as necessary is certainly demonstrated by

[23] See the very helpful essay by Bryan D. Spinks, "Luther's Timely Theology of Unilateral Baptism," *Lutheran Quarterly* 9 (spring 1995) 23–45.

[24] *Small Catechism*, in Tappert, *The Book of Concord*, 348–9.

[25] Ibid., 443; emphasis added.

the fact that he becomes the "father" of the catechism, producing his *Small Catechism* for the instruction of children by their parents and his *Large Catechism* for the instruction of adults (and, undoubtedly, parish clergy). Since such catechesis, necessarily, becomes entirely postbaptismal it is hard not to see parallels with the earlier tradition of mystagogy. That is, the full explanation and meaning of baptism are given only *after* the event itself. While this is always inevitable in the case of infants, Luther's overall focus on the objective, external, and gift nature of baptism as God's prior justifying act of grace coming before any sort of human response to the gift of salvation does suggest that, even in the case of adults, sacramental "preparation" is much less important than postbaptismal "mystagogical" catechesis in the meaning and life-long implications of what the reception of this baptismal gift entails.

In spite of Luther's severe criticisms of the medieval sacramental system in general, he was not very critical of the late medieval baptismal rite that he had known and used. In *The Babylonian Captivity*, in fact, he says of baptism in this time period:

"Blessed be God and the Father of our Lord Jesus Christ, who according to the riches of his mercy [Eph 1:3, 7] has preserved in his church *this sacrament at least, untouched and untainted by the ordinances of men,* and has made it free to all nations and classes of mankind, and has not permitted it to be oppressed by the filthy and godless monsters of greed and superstition. For he desired that by it little children, who were incapable of greed and superstition, might be initiated and sanctified in the simple faith of his Word; even today baptism has its chief meaning for them."[26]

Luther was highly critical in regard to his understanding that the very gift and promise of baptism was not being clearly proclaimed or taught in the Church of his day. In part this was due to the failure of catechesis, a failure his own *Catechisms* attempted to remedy, and in part it was due to the fact that the rite itself was administered in Latin ("those present cannot understand a word of what is said and done"),[27] a fact that his own baptismal reforms in German sought to address.

[26] LW 36, 57; emphasis added.
[27] Martin Luther, *The Order of Baptism, 1523*, LW 51, 101.

In 1523 Luther prepared a *Taufbüchlein* ("little baptism book") for use in the church at Wittenberg. Based on the *Latin Magdeburg Rite* of 1497, this rite, although composed entirely in German, was but a minor simplification of that rite itself. Hence, Luther retained the customary prebaptismal ceremonies of exsufflation, the giving of salt, exorcisms with signings of the cross (though reduced in number), the *effeta* with the use of spittle, the three-fold renunciation of Satan and profession of faith, and anointing. Similarly, baptism with the trinitarian formula, the postbaptismal anointing with its traditional prayer, the giving of the white garment, and the presentation of the lighted candle were all retained as well. In a very real sense, this first *Taufbüchlein* was simply the late medieval Latin baptismal rite in German translation and, except for the use of German, anyone presenting their child for baptism according to this rite would have experienced little that was different from the previous rites which had been in use. Indeed, there is not even any mention that this rite should be done in the context of public worship.

There are, however, at least two significant changes that did occur within this "new" rite. First, between the giving of the salt and the series of prebaptismal exorcisms, Luther inserted a prayer of his own composition called the *Sindflutgebet* or Flood Prayer. While based on other traditional texts and classic baptismal imagery, most notably those associated with the biblical readings and prayers for the blessing of the baptismal font in Easter Vigil liturgies, this prayer, in the words of Herman Wegman, "is worded so that [Luther's] theology of justification would be expressed."[28] This prayer reads:

"Almighty eternal God, who according to thy righteous judgment didst condemn the unbelieving world through the flood and in thy great mercy didst preserve believing Noah and his family, and who didst drown hardhearted Pharaoh with all his host in the Red Sea and didst lead thy people Israel through the same on dry ground, thereby prefiguring this bath of thy baptism, and who through the baptism of thy dear Child, our Lord Jesus Christ, hast consecrated and set apart the Jordan and all water as a salutary flood and a rich and full washing away of sins: We pray through the same thy boundless mercy that thou wilt graciously behold this N. and bless him

---

[28] Wegman, *Christian Worship in East and West*, 308.

with true faith in the spirit so that by means of this saving flood all that has been born in him from Adam and which he himself has added thereto may be drowned in him and engulfed, and that he may be sundered from the number of the unbelieving, preserved dry and secure in the holy ark of Christendom, serve thy name at all times fervent in spirit and joyful in hope, so that with all believers he may be made worthy to attain eternal life according to thy promise; through Jesus Christ our Lord. Amen."[29]

The second change is not clearly noticeable from the texts of this rite but is probably the more significant of the two. According to the rubric attached to the baptismal formula in this 1523 rite, the one baptizing is directed to "take the child and dip him in the font and say: And I baptize thee in the name. . . ."[30] By itself this rubric is not all that unusual and, in fact, is quite consistent with what is directed in other late medieval baptismal rituals. What is new, however, is the seriousness with which Luther took it. While, as we have seen, various modes of baptismal administration had been practiced (submersion, immersion, and affusion) since the days of the early Church, the preferred traditional modes were either submersion or immersion and Luther himself was adamant that baptism be administered by submersion, a literal three-fold dipping of the naked infant in the font. As early as 1519 he wrote in defense of this practice: "For baptism, as we shall hear, signifies that the old man and the sinful birth of flesh and blood are to be wholly drowned by the grace of God. We should therefore do justice to its meaning and make baptism a true and complete sign of the thing it signifies."[31]

In 1526 Luther produced a second *Taufbüchlein*, a more abbreviated version of his 1523 rite. His reason for doing so was related to a growing concern among his early followers that several of the "human ceremonies" which had been added to the baptismal rite over the centuries had come to cloud over what was considered to be essential in the sacrament, that is, the baptismal washing with the trinitarian formula itself. In this 1526 rite, then, Luther reduced the exorcisms further and omitted the exsufflation, the giving of salt, the *effeta*, the pre- and postbaptismal anointings, and the presentation of

[29] Luther, *The Order of Baptism, 1523*, 97.
[30] Ibid., 100.
[31] Martin Luther, *The Holy and Blessed Sacrament of Baptism*, LW 35, 29.

the lighted baptismal candle. While these ceremonies all disappeared, Luther did retain the prayer traditionally associated with the post-baptismal anointing. But he changed its emphasis away from anointing and had it accompany the giving of the baptismal garment: "The almighty God and Father of our Lord Jesus Christ, who hath regenerated thee through water and the Holy Ghost and hath forgiven thee all thy sin, strengthen thee with his grace to life everlasting. Amen. Peace be with thee. *Answer.* Amen."[32]

Lutheran baptismal rites throughout the sixteenth century, within the various German *Church Orders* and worship books among Lutherans elsewhere, tended to follow either Luther's 1523 or 1526 rites. Generally speaking, however, it was the 1526 *Taufbüchlein* that became the more standard model and would continue to have the most influence on subsequent Lutheran baptismal practice throughout the centuries. Gradually, even the exorcisms, Flood Prayer, and the postbaptismal clothing retained by Luther in his 1526 rite would also become omitted, as would Luther's strong insistence on baptismal dipping as a "true and complete sign of the thing it signifies." Baptismal submersion did not get off the ground among the churches of the Reformation.[33] But the traditional postbaptismal anointing prayer, associated with the garment in 1526, would continue among Lutheran baptismal rites, becoming associated finally with an imposition of the hand in blessing at the conclusion of the rite.

Ulrich Zwingli. If Luther and the subsequent Lutheran tradition represent a rather conservative approach to the Western liturgical tradition, as well as retaining an objective understanding of the sacraments, Ulrich Zwingli, the Reformer and parish priest of the Great Minster in Zurich, Switzerland, from 1523 until his death in battle in 1531, represents another side and another approach altogether.[34] According to Zwingli, "the external baptism of water cannot effect spiritual cleansing." Therefore, as he continues:

"Water baptism is nothing but an external ceremony, that is, an outward sign that we are incorporated and engrafted into the Lord Jesus Christ and pledged to live to him and to follow him. And as in Jesus

---

[32] Martin Luther, *The Order of Baptism Newly Revised, 1526,* LW 51, 109.

[33] On this see Old, *The Shaping of the Reformed Baptismal Rite,* 273ff.

[34] On Zwingli in general see White, *Protestant Worship,* 59–63.

Christ neither circumcision nor uncircumcision avails anything, but a new creature, the living of a new life (Galatians 6), so it is not baptism which saves us, but a new life. . . . Baptism cannot save or purify. . . . For though the whole world were arrayed against it, it is clear and indisputable that no external element or action can purify the soul."[35]

Furthermore, sacraments, for Zwingli, did not convey the grace that they signify "for by that argumentation restriction would have been placed on the liberty of the divine Spirit, who distributes to every one as he will, that is, to whom and when and where he will."[36] What was important for him, then, was not the exterior sacramental sign or rite but the interior baptism of the Holy Spirit, a "baptism" which was possessed by all who had faith in Christ regardless of whether they had received water baptism or not. "No one is saved except by faith," he wrote, "and faith is not born except by the teaching of the Holy Spirit." Similarly, Zwingli asked, "Why does he need baptism who has already been assured by faith in Christ that his sins are done away?"[37]

While such an overall approach to the sacraments would suggest strongly that Zwingli would be against infant baptism in favor of believers' baptism only as "an outward sign that we are incorporated and engrafted into the Lord Jesus Christ and pledged to live to him and to follow him," he actually defended it by a number of arguments. First, he claimed that the children of Christians are no less children of God than their parents are, and, since they are God's children baptism should not be refused to them. Hence, birth to Christian parents within the "covenant" community, for Zwingli, seemed to convey membership in that community automatically. That is, birth to Christian parents already constituted their divine "election" to salvation and so their baptism was simply an external sign of what was true for them already. Second, as a sign of membership in the covenant community, infant baptism had its parallel with circumcision among the Jews. Just as circumcision was given to Jewish children (at least to males), so should baptism be given to the children of Christians. He wrote:

[35] Ulrich Zwingli, *Of Baptism* (1525), LCC, XXIV, as cited in James F. White, *Documents of Christian Worship: Descriptive and Interpretive Sources* (Louisville: Westminster/John Knox Press, 1992) 171.

[36] Cited in Fisher, *Christian Initiation*, 129.

[37] Ibid.

". . . note that God calls it [circumcision] a contract or covenant. . . . Similarly, baptism in the New Testament is a covenant sign. It does not justify the one who is baptized, nor does it confirm his faith, for it is not possible for an external thing to confirm faith. For faith does not proceed from external things. . . . Hence . . . with this external sign you are to *dedicate* and *pledge* them to the name of the Father, the Son, and the Holy Ghost, and to teach them to observe all the things I have committed to you. . . . All that I am now claiming is this: I have proved that baptism is an initiatory sign, and that those who receive it are *dedicated and pledged* to the Lord God. . . . Baptism is simply a *mark* or *pledge* by which those who receive it are dedicated to God."[38]

Finally, while the practice of infant baptism is not commanded explicitly in Scripture, Jesus' own act of "blessing children" (Mark 10:13-16) served for Zwingli as an authoritative biblical model for continuing the practice. However, as J.D.C. Fisher notes, "while Zwingli's argument may succeed in showing that infants are eligible for baptism, it hardly proves that they need it."[39]

Like Luther, Zwingli also was responsible for two baptismal rites. The first, published in 1523 and composed by Leo Jud, Zwingli's colleague in Zurich, was called "A short and public form for the tender in faith for the baptism of children." This rite was essentially an adaptation of Luther's first *Taufbüchlein* of the same year. In addition to containing many of the traditional medieval ceremonies (exorcism, salt, pre- and postbaptismal anointings, garment, but no candle), it also included, of course, Luther's own Flood Prayer. One of the major differences was that this Zurich rite was designed explicitly for use in the public worship of the church.

In 1525 Zwingli himself undertook a drastic revision of this rite and produced a new one called "the form of baptism which is now used at Zurich, and all the additions, which have no foundation in the word of God, have been removed."[40] Along with the deletion of those ceremonies we might expect to be removed, this latter rite significantly contained neither a renunciation of Satan nor a profession of faith. Other than a revised version of Luther's Flood Prayer and

[38] Zwingli, *Of Baptism* (1525), LCC, XXIV, as cited in White, *Documents of Christian Worship*, 170–1; emphasis added.

[39] Fisher, *Christian Initiation*, 130.

[40] Ibid., 129–31.

the retention of the white garment, the baptismal rite itself was reduced to the use of water (like Luther, Zwingli *did* prefer submersion as the mode), the trinitarian formula, and the "proof text" for infant baptism from Mark 10:13-16. Any questions in this rite are directed explicitly to the sponsors (i.e., "Will ye that this child be baptized?" and "Name this child").

Zwingli's revision of Luther's Flood Prayer makes it clear that this 1525 rite distinctly reflects his own theology of baptism as little more than an external sign of "dedication" and "pledging" of the infant to future faith. While Luther's own prayer refers to baptism *itself* as "a salutary flood and a rich and full washing away of sins" and asks that "by means of this saving flood all that has been born in him from Adam and which he himself has added thereto may be drowned in him and engulfed," Zwingli's revision asked only:

". . . that thou wouldest graciously look upon this thy servant, N., and kindle the light of faith in his heart whereby he may be incorporate into thy Son, and with him be buried in death and raised again to newness of life; that so, following him daily, he may joyfully bear his cross, and hold fast to his with true faith, firm hope, and fervent charity."[41]

That is, the occasion of baptism appears to provide but the context for the assembled congregation to intercede for the candidate that on the basis of future faith he or she may ultimately be "incorporate . . . buried . . . raised" and come to "follow" Christ.

Martin Bucer. At the same time that Zwingli was turning infant baptism into a "rite of infant dedication" and reception into the congregation, the influential Martin Bucer (1491–1551), a former Dominican priest, who was to influence the overall shape and interpretation of the rites of Christian initiation among Lutherans, Reformed, and Anglicans, was busy in Strassburg with his own similar revisions of the late medieval rite of baptism.[42] According to Bucer:

"Our principal reformation is with baptism, since we by the Word teach that the exterior baptism is to be held as a sign of the proper

---

[41] Ibid., 130.
[42] See Old, *The Shaping of the Reformed Baptismal Rite,* 51–62.

baptism of Christ, that is, of the interior cleansing, rebirth and renewal . . . and that the washing away of sins and the renewal of the Spirit of all should only be attributed to Christ, who by his Spirit makes the elect pure, believing and blessed."[43]

Among Bucer's concerns for the reform of baptism, shared by almost all of the sixteenth-century Protestant Reformers, was that baptism should be administered in public, within the Sunday worship of the local congregation. Private and/or "emergency" baptisms, although continued among Lutherans, were discouraged and tended to be omitted entirely within the Reformed tradition in general. Together with this Bucer strongly emphasized the role of godparents and sponsors in undertaking an obligation to guarantee that the one to be baptized would not only be raised in the Christian faith but provided with extensive catechetical instruction. Through Bucer's leadership such an emphasis on the godparents appeared at Strassburg within the baptismal rites themselves and, from there, into Reformation baptismal rites in general. After an "exhortation" or "instruction" on the meaning and implications of baptism, the rite in use at Strassburg from 1525 through 1530 included a brief introduction and explanation of baptism as an "outward sign" to be fulfilled "internally," the public recitation of the Our Father and Apostles' Creed, a prayer for the Holy Spirit to "seal" and "confirm" the heart of the candidate so that "thy inward renewal and the regeneration of the Spirit may truly be signified by this our baptism," and the reading of Mark 10:13-16 with a brief admonition and an address to the sponsors in the following manner: "You godparents and you brothers and sisters shall each of you teach this child Christian order, discipline and fear of God, each of you, as God gives him grace. *Answer:* We will."[44] After this promise the rite itself concluded with the naming of the child and the administration of baptism (by "pouring") with the trinitarian formula. All other ceremonies such as anointing, baptismal garment, and candle were omitted as "human inventions without warrant in God's word."[45]

[43] Martin Bucer, *Grund und Ursach,* as cited by Wegman, *Christian Worship in East and West,* 309.

[44] Text cited in Fisher, *Christian Initiation,* 37.

[45] Ibid., 34.

In *The Strasbourg Order of Baptism after 1537* this focus on the covenantal responsibilities of parents and godparents was stronger still. The introduction to the recitation of the Apostles' Creed contained the following invitation: "So now confess with me our holy Christian faith and thus arouse yourselves that you may grow valiant in the same and faithfully bring this infant *(these children)* up to share this faith." Immediately after the Apostles' Creed the minister continued, saying:

"Now let us baptize this child *(these children)* into the fellowship of this faith. Know and recognize him *(them)*, all of you, as (a) member(s) of Christ, our Lord, and your own fellow member(s), and let each one of you see, so far as he may ever be enabled thereto by the Lord, that this infant *(these infants)* may be brought up in the Lord, that we all through my ministry which I shall perform here on behalf of the whole community of the church may incorporate him *(them)* now in the Lord by holy baptism. You, however, who have been specially invited and named as godparents, must show particular diligence and, so far as your other godly obligations allow you, prove yourselves spiritual fathers and mothers to him *(them)*. May our dear Lord Jesus grant that you and we may all faithfully perform this. Amen."[46]

By placing these postbaptismal responsibilities and obligations on the part of godparents, parents, and the whole Christian community within a *prebaptismal* context a significant shift has occurred with regard to the rite of baptism in Western Christianity in general. While, as we have seen, the late medieval rites of baptism tended to include some kind of reference or admonition to subsequent catechesis either during or *at the conclusion of the rite* in preparation for confirmation later (see the *Sarum Rite* above), and while Luther's own *Catechisms* (although not his rites) certainly underscored that baptism was to be followed by catechesis, the placing of explicit responsibilities and obligations *before* baptism has vast theological implications. In a recent and compelling article, Anglican liturgist Bryan Spinks has drawn attention to the contrast between what he calls "Luther's unilateral approach to baptism" and the "bilateral covenant" which, from Zwingli and Bucer on, characterized the approach of some within the Reformed tradition.[47] In distinction to Luther's under-

---

[46] Ibid., 41.
[47] Spinks, "Luther's Timely Theology of Unilateral Baptism," 23–45.

standing of baptism as the objective, salvific, and effective sacramental act of God here and now through water and the Holy Spirit, which can only be *received* by human beings in faith, but is *not* given as a consequence of that faith, the theology of Zwingli and Bucer tended to emphasize the necessity of promises, duties, and obligations on the part of parents, sponsors, and the community as the very condition *for* the giving of baptism. In other words, if Luther's approach to baptism was unilateral and unconditional, the approach of Zwingli and Bucer appeared to make baptism conditional and bilateral, dependent not only on the promise of God but on the prior faith-response of parents and godparents. In both of Luther's rites, as in the late medieval rites themselves, the gift of baptism was administered without any strings attached or any particular response, apart from the renunciation of Satan and profession of faith, demanded on the part of anyone. Even his catechesis, as we have seen, was directed toward understanding the meaning of the baptismal gift already received. With Zwingli and Bucer, however, baptism becomes primarily a "pledge" or "oath" that the infant, who by birth to Christian parents is already part of God's elect and now solemnly dedicated, will be brought up in the Christian faith and so one day make his or her own faith response. In spite of the fact that their rites invoked the Holy Spirit explicitly, that the Holy Spirit might be connected in some objective manner with the water of baptism itself as God's gracious act of justifying the sinner was not part of their overall approach. Instead, the external rite itself only signified what was to take place by that Spirit internally.

John Calvin. In contrast to Zwingli and Bucer, John Calvin, the great Reformer of Geneva, Switzerland, often called the first systematic theologian of the Protestant Reformation due to his multivolume *Institutes of the Christian Religion* (originally published in 1536 with the final version appearing in 1559), had a much higher appreciation for the sacraments as vehicles of God's grace and mercy for human beings. James White summarizes Calvin's overall understanding of Church and sacraments, saying:

"Calvin's understanding of people is central to his whole approach to worship, and it is best to begin with this aspect of his thought and its consequences. No one had a dimmer view of the prospect of humanity left to itself than Calvin, a view summed up in his view that 'no part [of man] is immune from sin and all that proceeds from him is to

249

be imputed to sin.' Not only is humanity perverse but also ignorant of its own good. Such perversity and stupidity can be overcome only by God's grace, and God out of mercy has chosen to liberate a select number from the limitations of their humanity. God has gathered all the chosen in the church, where they might be instructed, disciplined, and joined together in praising their Redeemer for gratuitous mercy in choosing them. . . . But the mercy of God does not end there. The Creator, knowing even better than humans their capacity, 'so tempers himself to our capacity,' providing for the elect visible means to help them know God's mercies. The institution of sacraments provided those visible signs of God's love whereby God 'imparts spiritual things under visible ones.' There is a world of difference between Calvin's concept of the importance of signs, for humans to experience God's self giving, and Zwingli's dualism between nature and spirit. Calvin had recovered the biblical mentality that God uses material things to give us spiritual things. . . . Calvin saw the necessity of the church as the visible embodiment of God's will to save the elect. . . . The church was essential to salvation, and baptism was the entrance to the church."[48]

According to Calvin, a sacrament may be defined as a "testimony of divine grace toward us, confirmed by an outward sign, with mutual attestation of our piety toward God."[49] Contrary to Zwingli, who argued that the sacraments are, primarily, signs of the Church's "pledge" toward God, Calvin focused on their God-to-us direction. He continued:

"It is therefore certain that the Lord offers us mercy and the pledge of his grace both in his Sacred Word and in his sacraments. But it is understood only by those who take the Word and sacraments with sure faith, just as Christ is offered and held forth by the Father to all unto salvation, yet not all acknowledge and receive him."[50]

Indeed, based on the sacramental vocabulary of Augustine, the sacraments for Calvin were "visible Words," visible testimonies, or

---

[48] White, *Protestant Worship*, 64.
[49] Calvin, *Institutes of the Christian Religion*, 4.14.1, LCC, XXI, as cited in White, *Documents of Christian Worship*, 132.
[50] Ibid., 133.

demonstrations of what God did and does for human salvation. As such, the sacrament of baptism itself "testifies" to God's forgiveness of sins, the mortification of the flesh and new life in Christ, and our union with the fellowship of Christ in the Church.[51] But does baptism really grant this to anyone objectively for Calvin or does it simply provide a sign to confirm what God grants already irrespective of the sacraments?

The answer to that question is difficult to determine. On the one hand, Calvin could and did say that a sacrament *is* an action done by God *for* people, "an outward sign by which *the Lord* seals on our consciences the promises of his good will toward us in order to sustain the weakness of our faith."[52] Similarly, given his high view of the visible Church, it is significant that he says that "baptism is the sign of the initiation by which we are received into the society of the church, in order that, engrafted into Christ, we may be reckoned among God's children."[53] As an act done by God in the Church, then, Calvin witnessed to a potentially high sacramental theology and a high ecclesiology, neither of which tended to have had a lasting influence within the various expressions of "Calvinism" until the present day.

On the other hand, when confronted with the question of the relationship between the reception of baptism and salvation, it seems that for Calvin, like Zwingli, baptism itself was only a sign or "testimony" of what is already true on the basis of God's word and promise themselves! That is, with regard to infant baptism specifically, Calvin could write that:

"The children of believers are baptized *not* in order that they who were previously strangers to the church may then for the first time become children of God, but rather that, because by the blessing of the promise *they already belonged to the body of Christ,* they are received into the church with this *solemn sign.*"[54]

In reversal of the classic adage of Tertullian, Calvin, like Zwingli, appears to have thought that "Christians are born," and "not made"

---

[51] See ibid., 172–3.
[52] Ibid., 132; emphasis added.
[53] Ibid., 171.
[54] Ibid., 172; emphasis added.

such through the rites of baptism. Similarly, nothing like "emergency baptism" would be considered necessary or even worthwhile. While it is true that for Calvin the sacraments were effective as concrete "signs" of God's grace and mercy, the key word in his sacramental theology appears to be "testimony." Baptism may be one of the two God-given sacramental signs by which God "tempers himself to our capacity" on account of our human need for such physical and earthly signs. But, as a sign, testimony, or "visible word," baptism does not necessarily convey what it signifies as much as it provides a *"mirror of spiritual blessings."*[55] According to Calvin, the sacraments were instituted and given to people "to direct and almost lead [them] by the hand to Christ, or rather, as images, to represent him and show him forth to be known." In other words, as a "visible word," baptism provides, as it were, one "picture" or "image" of God's salvation. The Lord's Supper provides another. But just as one can respond to the gift of salvation in the words of Scripture or preaching with either faith or disbelief, so can one respond to the gift of salvation depicted and visibly illustrated in the sacraments with either faith or disbelief. Regarding this, Calvin could not have been more clear. He wrote:

"Let it be regarded as a settled principle that the sacraments have the same office as the Word of God: to offer and set forth Christ to us, and in him the treasures of heavenly grace. . . . *They do not bestow any grace of themselves,* but announce and tell us, and (as they are guarantees and tokens) ratify among us, those things given us by divine bounty."[56]

With such an emphasis on the sacraments as "visible words," it is no wonder, inheriting from Zwingli and Bucer the tradition of baptism being administered within the public worship of the church, that Calvin would underscore this public administration as a way to re-awaken or cause faith in those who witnessed it. Such public administration served for Calvin as an invitation to the members of the assembled community to recall their own baptism and the fact that they themselves had been washed clean of all guilt and sin in the blood of Christ.

The overall ambiguity of Calvin's sacramental theology appeared also in his Genevan baptismal rite, contained in *The Form of Prayers*

[55] Ibid., 133; emphasis added.
[56] Ibid., 133–4.

and Ecclesiastical Chants with the Manner of Administering the Sacra-
ments and Solemnizing Marriage, according to the Custom of the Ancient
Church, 1542.[57] Just as Luther's 1523 and 1526 baptismal rites would
be influential in subsequent Lutheran liturgical development, so this
Form of Prayers would set the standard for Reformed worship in general with Geneva itself becoming the center and model of Reformed
worship throughout the world. Since Calvin had been in Strassburg
with Martin Bucer from 1538 until 1540, Bucer's own theology and
rites were bound to have had some influence on his own liturgical reforms. Among these influences, undoubtedly, was Calvin's insistence
on the public nature of baptism, as noted above, and the overall reduction of the rite to pouring water with the formula alone, the other
traditional ceremonies omitted as "not of God's ordinance." Part of
Bucer's influence as well was the strong emphasis on subsequent
catechesis within the rite which the parents of the candidate
promised to fulfill. At the conclusion of an extended exhortation on
baptism and a prayer of invocation with the Our Father, highly didactic in tone, these parental responsibilities were underscored in a
prebaptismal context as follows:

"Since it is a matter of receiving this infant into the company of the
Christian church, do you promise, when he comes to the age of discretion, to instruct him in the doctrine which is received among the
people of God, as it is briefly summarized in the confession of faith
which we all have . . . ? I believe in God the Father, etc. . . . You
promise then to take trouble to instruct him in all this doctrine, and
generally in all that is contained in the holy scripture of the Old and
New Testament, to the end that he may receive it as the sure word of
God, coming from heaven. Also you will exhort him to live according
to the rule which our Lord has set forth for us in the law, which
briefly consists in these two points, that we love God with all our
mind, our heart and strength, and our neighbour as ourselves. Likewise, according to the exhortations which he has given by his prophets and apostles, that renouncing himself and his own desires, he
may devote himself and consecrate himself to glorify the name of
God and of Jesus Christ and to edify his neighbours."[58]

[57] Fisher, *Christian Initiation*, 112–7.
[58] Ibid., 116.

Within the baptismal exhortation itself it is also stated clearly that the gifts of God (i.e., regeneration of the Holy Spirit and the forgiveness of sins):

". . . are *conferred* on us, when it pleases him [God] to incorporate us in his church by baptism. For in this sacrament he testifies to us the remission of our sins. And for this cause he has appointed the sign of water, to signify to us that, as by this element the bodily defilements are cleansed, so he wishes to wash and purify our souls, so that no more may there appear any stain in them. . . . Thus we receive twofold grace and benefit from our God in baptism, provided that we do not destroy the force of this sacrament by our ingratitude. That is, we have in it sure testimony that God wishes to be a merciful Father to us, not imputing to us all our faults and offenses: secondly that he will assist us by His Holy Spirit."[59]

But at the same time, the baptism which is received by the infant candidate is little other than the Christian replacement for Jewish circumcision as a sign of the covenant with God, and, as the prayer of invocation makes clear, infants are baptized into *future* repentance and faith, a repentance and faith dependent on subsequent catechesis:

"Lord God, Father eternal and almighty, since it has pleased thee by thine infinite mercy to promise us that thou wilt be our God and the God of our children, we pray thee that it may please thee to confirm this grace in this present infant, born of a father and mother whom thou hast called into thy church, and, as he is *offered* and *consecrated* to thee by us, that thou wouldest receive him into thy holy protection, declaring thyself to be his God and Saviour, remitting to him the original sin of which the whole lineage of Adam is guilty, and then afterwards sanctifying him by thy Spirit, so that *when he comes to the age of understanding,* he may know and adore thee as his only God, glorifying thee all through his life, so as to obtain evermore from thee remission of his sins. And so that he can obtain such graces, may it please thee to incorporate him in the fellowship of our Lord Jesus to be a partaker of all his benefits, as one of the members of his body. Grant us, Father of mercy, that the baptism which we minister to him according to thine ordinance may bring forth its fruit and virtue."[60]

[59] Ibid., 114; emphasis added.
[60] Ibid., 115–6; emphasis added.

It is difficult not to see a continuity with the theologies of Zwingli and Bucer here. There is no question but that Calvin has clearly restored baptism as a public rite of Christian *initiation* or incorporation into the Church. In fact, one of Calvin's emphases in the administration of the rite was to insist:

". . . that the baptismal 'stones' be placed before the congregation so that the baptism of infants could be a fully congregational event. Usually this meant moving the font to a position near the pulpit and eventually using basins placed in a metal hoop attached to the pulpit. All were to see the actions of worship, however simplified they became. Thus, while ceremonial was limited to what was edifying, a special effort was made to ensure that everything done was both seen and heard by the entire congregation."[61]

Nevertheless, it is hard not to interpret the overall focus of Calvin's rite as a solemn "pledging" or "dedication" of the infant to God. For, in spite of his emphasis on the gifts which are *conferred* in baptism, the rite itself *sounds* more like a solemn enrollment in the catechumenate. Based on circumcision, the belief that the children of the elect are sanctified "from their mother's womb," and on Jesus' blessing of children,[62] one is left with the distinct impression that baptism itself for Calvin was primarily an outward "sign" of what was true internally on other grounds and, as such, there was no necessary causal relationship between the two. The baptismal washing, for example, may "signify to us that, as by this element the bodily defilements are cleansed, so he [God] wishes to wash and purify our souls," but that does not mean that it is by *this* baptismal washing that God does, in fact, do this.

Calvin's sacramental theology, of course, cannot be separated from his views on divine election. For Calvin, as noted above, human "perversity and stupidity can be overcome only by God's grace, and God out of mercy has chosen to liberate a select number from the limitations of their humanity. God has gathered all the chosen in the church." But this does not mean that *all* who are members of the visible Church through baptism are necessarily part of that "select number" whom God has liberated from their human limitations. That is,

[61] White, *Protestant Worship*, 67.
[62] See Fisher, *Christian Initiation*, 115.

255

the "select number" does not equal the sum total of the Church's official membership. Rather, even within the visible Church itself only that invisible Church, that "select number" of those whom God has elected, are the "saved," their number and identity known to God alone.

In such a way, then, Calvin's apparent ambiguity with regard to his theology of baptism becomes clarified. For the "elect," baptism *is* effective and, hence, *does* "perform what it symbolizes."[63] For those less fortunate, however, baptized or not, catechized or not, faithful or not, nothing can change God's just and eternal decree. But, since it cannot be known who truly constitutes the "select number" of the invisible Church, baptism and membership in the visible Church are required of all.

It is sometimes suggested that had Calvin and Luther known each other the Lutheran and Reformed movements would not have been separated, on the basis of sacramental theology at least, into distinct Christian bodies. But, while Calvin may have had a higher appreciation of the role of sacramental signs than Zwingli, there is still a fundamental disagreement with the sacramental approach of Luther and that fundamental disagreement is related to Calvin's distinction between the external sign and interior reality signified. Like Luther, Calvin too could speak of the comforting nature of baptism, saying that if troubled by sin, we need only remind ourselves of our baptism to be assured of the cleansing of our sins by Christ's blood.[64] But unlike Luther, for whom the Holy Spirit is inseparably *bound* to the *external* Word and sacraments as the very "instruments," "means," or "vehicles" of God's grace, Calvin, like Zwingli, made a careful distinction between the sacraments and the working of the Holy Spirit. He wrote:

"If the Spirit be lacking, the sacraments can accomplish nothing more in our minds than the splendor of the sun shining upon blind eyes, or a voice sounding in deaf ears. Therefore, I make such a division between Spirit and the sacraments that the power to act rests with the former, and the ministry alone is left to the latter—a ministry empty and trifling, apart from the action of the Spirit; but charged with great effect when the Spirit works within and manifests his power."[65]

[63] White, *A Brief History of Christian Worship*, 114.
[64] See Calvin, *Institutes*, 4.15.3.
[65] LCC, XXI, as cited in White, *Documents of Christian Worship*, 133.

Indeed, apart from Calvin's strong appreciation for the anthropological need for sacramental signs, one wonders just how different Calvin's theology of baptism actually is from that of Zwingli. Since, for Calvin, it is also the interior baptism which is important, that interior "washing and purification" of Christ to which the sign of baptism *points,* an interior "washing" of salvation already promised and given to the elect, it remains questionable whether Calvin's theology is so different from Zwingli's "dualism between nature and spirit" after all. What *is* different from Zwingli, of course, is that Calvin's theology of "visible words" offered the *possibility* of a united Protestantism moving in a different theological direction together. But, by separating Spirit and sacrament from each other and by relating the fruitfulness of the sacraments to predestinarian divine election in the first place, such possibilities could not be considered. Had Luther and Calvin known each other, they probably would have debated and fought over sacramental theology quite fiercely.

Thomas Cranmer. In order to understand the reforms of the baptismal rite in England under Thomas Cranmer, the reform-minded Archbishop of Canterbury from 1532 until his execution as a Protestant "heretic" during the short-lived restoration of Roman Catholicism under Queen Mary in 1556, we must return briefly to the work of Martin Bucer in southern Germany. At the invitation of Hermann von Wied, Archbishop of Cologne (1515–46) and Lutheran sympathizer, Bucer and Philip Melanchthon (one of Luther's close colleagues, who authored both the *Augsburg Confession* and its *Apology),* went to Cologne to assist in the reformation of the Church there. Composed principally by Bucer and accepted by Hermann in 1543 was a German *Church Order* containing, among other liturgical services, the rites for baptism and confirmation. This *Einfaltigs Bedencken,* translated into Latin in 1545 as the *Pia Deliberatio,* and into English in 1548 as *A simple and religious consultation of us Hermann by the grace of God Archbishop of Cologne . . . ,* or, simply, the *Consultation,* was to play a role in the English Reformation as well as at Cologne.

The rite of baptism in this *Consultation* was divided into two parts: *A Form of Catechism that is to say of Institution Exhortation and Demands made to the Godfathers and All Them that Bring Infants to Holy Baptism,*[66] to be done on the day before baptism was to take place (i.e., on Saturdays);

[66] Fisher, *Christian Initiation,* 58–67.

and *Of Administration of Baptism,*[67] the baptismal rite itself, which was to take place during the Sunday celebration of the Eucharist after the reading of the Gospel and the singing of the Creed. While clearly expressing an overall *Lutheran* theology of baptism and its generally conservative approach to reforming the rites, with the *Form of Catechism* retaining many of the traditional catechetical or prebaptismal ceremonies (e.g., three-fold renunciation of Satan, three-fold interrogative profession of faith, an exorcism, signing of the forehead and breast with the cross, and Luther's own Flood Prayer), Bucer's own prebaptismal emphasis on the postbaptismal catechesis that godparents are to provide is also very apparent. The baptismal rite itself is relatively brief and consists of an opening exhortation, readings from Titus 3 and Matthew 28, a prayer, baptism with the trinitarian formula, the traditional presbyteral postbaptismal anointing prayer (but without anointing, as in Luther's 1526 *Taufbüchlein*), and a concluding greeting of peace. Perhaps the most significant element within this *Consultation* is Bucer's emphasis on the location of baptism within the Sunday Eucharist. J.D.C. Fisher writes:

"Bucer, recognizing that the old custom of baptizing only at Easter and Pentecost could not be restored, ordered baptism to be administered on Sundays or holy days when a congregation would be present, except in the case of children who might not survive till the next holy day, *so that the sacrament called Eucharist might be joined with baptism, as in the manner of the primitive church.*"[68]

It is this element which proved to be the least influential.

In the First Prayerbook of King Edward VI, or the *Book of Common Prayer* (hereafter, BCP), 1549,[69] Thomas Cranmer, certainly under Lutheran theological influence, made use both of Hermann's *Consultation* and the *Sarum Rite,* the traditional usage of Canterbury, for his own reforms of baptism. Following Bucer, the 1549 BCP required baptism to be administered on "Sundays and other holy days when the most number of people may come together," with the exception that the baptismal party was ordered to be ready at the church door,

[67] Ibid., 67–9.
[68] Fisher, "Lutheran, Anglican, and Reformed Rites," 156; emphasis added.
[69] The relevant texts are in Fisher, *Christian Initiation,* 89–95, from where they will be cited.

not at the beginning of the Eucharist, but before the last canticle at either Morning or Evening Prayer. The first part of the rite, a remnant of the old order for the making of catechumens, took place at the church door and consisted of an explanatory preface; a free version of Luther's Flood Prayer; the signing of the child with the cross on the forehead and breast; an exorcism; the reading of Mark 10:13-16; a brief exhortation; the Our Father and Apostles' Creed recited by all present; a concluding prayer taken directly from Hermann's *Consultation;* and the leading of the candidate by the right hand to the font.

Within this introductory rite, two elements are to be noted especially: (1) the explanatory preface to the rite and (2) the formula accompanying the signing of the cross on the candidate's forehead and breast. With regard to the first of these, Cranmer drastically shortened the preface of Hermann's *Consultation* from its several pages of instruction to one carefully worded *sentence:*

"Dear[ly] beloved, forasmuch as all men be *conceived and born in sin,* and that no man born in sin can enter into the kingdom of God (except he be regenerate and born anew of water and the Holy Ghost) I beseech you to call upon God the Father through our Lord Jesus Christ, that of his bounteous mercy he will grant to these children that thing, which by nature they cannot have, that is to say, they may be baptized with the Holy Ghost, and received into Christ's holy church, and be made lively members of the same."

This explanatory introduction was to remain unchanged in subsequent editions of the BCP.

The second element, the signing of the cross on the candidate's forehead and breast with its accompanying formula, was a revision of the prebaptismal anointing from the *Sarum Rite.* But, while the formula for the anointing in the *Sarum Rite* stated "N. I also anoint thee *upon the breast* with the oil of salvation, *between the shoulders,* in Christ Jesus our Lord that thou mayest have eternal life and live for ever and ever. Amen,"[70] Cranmer's version read:

"N., receive the sign of the holy cross, both in thy forehead, and in they breast, in token that thou shalt not be ashamed to confess thy faith in Christ crucified, and manfully to fight under his banner

---

[70] DBL, 246.

against sin, the world and the devil, and to continue his faithful soldier and servant unto thy life's end. Amen."

Here Cranmer combined into one prebaptismal ceremony the signing of the candidate's forehead and breast with the cross, which occurred at the very beginning of the *Sarum Rite* without anointing, and the later prebaptismal anointing of the forehead and breast, although for Cranmer this signing no longer included an anointing. Precedent for such a move had already been provided in Hermann's *Consultation*, where a similar prebaptismal signing without anointing appeared: "Take the figure of the holy cross in thy forehead, that thou never be ashamed of God and Christ thy Saviour or of his gospel: take it also on thy breast, that the power of Christ crucified may be ever thy succour and sure protection in all things."[71] While the precise language of the formula in the 1549 BCP is due, undoubtedly, to Cranmer's own creative genius and reminds us of the kind of battle and conflict imagery associated with the prebaptismal anointing in the fourth- and fifth-century Christian East, it is, thus, actually Martin Bucer, via Hermann's *Consultation,* who stands behind such a combined prebaptismal ceremony. But, as we shall see shortly, this prebaptismal ceremony in the 1549 BCP will actually become a *postbaptismal* ceremony in subsequent editions.

The baptismal rite itself in the 1549 BCP closely followed the traditional *Sarum Rite* with two interesting exceptions. Before the traditional three-fold renunciation of Satan and three-fold interrogative profession of faith, expanded by Cranmer to include all of the Apostles' Creed in question and answer form, the Reformation emphasis on catechesis was expressed to the godparents in the following words: "Wherefore, after this promise made by Christ, these infants must also faithfully for their part promise by you that be their sureties, that they will forsake the devil and all his works, and constantly believe God's holy word and obediently keep his commandments."

Following the three-fold baptismal "dipping" (first the right side of the infant, then the left, then face down into the font) with the trinitarian formula and the giving of the white baptismal robe (or *chrisom*), the newly baptized were anointed with chrism. While all of this was

---

[71] Fisher, *Christian Initiation,* 65.

traditional and rather conservative, it is important to note the specific formula that Cranmer used for the postbaptismal anointing itself:

"Almighty God, the Father of our Lord Jesus Christ, who hath regenerated thee by water and the Holy Ghost, and hath given unto thee remission of all thy sins, he vouchsafe to anoint thee *with the unction of his Holy Spirit,* and bring thee to the inheritance of everlasting life. Amen."

Clearly, Cranmer revised and adapted the traditional presbyteral postbaptismal anointing of Western Christianity so that it was related explicitly to the gift of the Holy Spirit. Similarly, this anointing, for Cranmer, was not an anointing on the crown of the head, the traditional presbyteral practice, but on the *forehead,* as in Roman episcopal confirmation! Since no Western precedent existed for associating the Holy Spirit with the presbyteral anointing in Cranmer's time, and, for that matter, anointing itself by 1549 had already tended to disappear from Reformation baptismal rites in general, it is quite possible that Cranmer was influenced here by Eastern liturgical sources, where, since the time of Cyril of Jerusalem, the gift of the Holy Spirit had been associated with the single postbaptismal anointing. Some have called this anointing a "presbyteral confirmation," that is, the application by Cranmer of the medieval Western theology of confirmation as the "anointing of the Spirit" to this presbyteral postbaptismal anointing.[72] Yet, since, as we shall see, Cranmer also prepared a rite of confirmation for the 1549 BCP which was virtually identical to the late medieval rites of confirmation themselves, calling the postbaptismal anointing a "presbyteral confirmation" may be rather deceptive. Similarly, it is important that one *not* assume that *a* postbaptismal anointing associated with the Holy Spirit is always to be called "confirmation." It is certainly not so within the Christian East. Nevertheless, given the fact that Cranmer was a product of the Western Middle Ages, and was himself, after all, a *bishop,* it is hard not to see some kind of "confirmation" theology operative and perpetuated here in this rite, whether due to Cranmer's own theology of baptism or gleaned from other sources at his disposal.[73] In any case,

---

[72] See Fisher, "Lutheran, Anglican, and Reformed Rites," 156.

[73] See Marion J. Hatchett, *Commentary on the American Prayer Book* (New York: Seabury Press, 1981) 261ff.

however, this interesting and compelling revision of the postbaptismal anointing in England would not continue beyond the 1549 rite.

The baptismal rite of the 1549 BCP concluded with a final exhortation to the godparents, charging them to remember that it is

"your parts and duty to see that these infants be taught, so soon as they shall be able to learn, what a solemn vow, promise, and profession they have made by you. And that they may know these things the better, ye shall call upon them to hear sermons, and chiefly you shall provide that they may learn the creed, the Lord's prayer and the ten commandments in the English tongue."

And to this exhortation was attached a rubric which directed that "the children be brought to the bishop to be confirmed of him, so soon as they can say in their vulgar tongue the articles of faith, the Lord's prayer and the ten commandments, and be further instructed in the catechism, set forth for that purpose."

In a separate section of the 1549 BCP, Cranmer also included a series of prayers for the blessing of the baptismal font to be used whenever it was necessary to replace the water in the font (ideally, once a month in accord with traditional *Sarum* rubrics). Based on various Mozarabic and Gallican sources at Cranmer's disposal,[74] this blessing consisted of an initial prayer of "sanctification" of the waters with a signing of the cross and an epiclesis of the Holy Spirit: "send down, we beseech thee . . . thy Holy Spirit to assist us, and to be present at this our invocation of thy holy name: Sanctify + this fountain of baptism."[75] And, after eight short petitions for all who would be baptized in this water, the concluding prayer referred to the baptismal water as having been "prepared for the ministration of thy holy sacrament." Like the postbaptismal anointing itself, however, such a prayer of "consecration" was not to remain in subsequent editions of the BCP. And the reason for their omissions was due, once again in large part, to the influence of Martin Bucer.

At Cranmer's invitation, Martin Bucer, by this time a professor at Cambridge, England, wrote a critique of the 1549 BCP. This 1551 document, known as the *Censura*, or *The Judgment of Martin Bucer*

---

[74] See Fisher, "Lutheran, Anglican, and Reformed Rites," 158; and Hatchett, *Commentary on the American Prayer Book*, 275.

[75] Fisher, *Christian Initiation*, 154.

upon the Book of Sacred Rites or of the Ordering of the Church and Ecclesi-astical Ministration in the Kingdom of England written at the Request of the Reverend Archbishop Thomas Cranmer, was based on a translation of the 1549 BCP from Cranmer's English into Latin so that Bucer, unable to speak or read English, might be able to analyze the BCP rites. With regard to the baptismal rite specifically, Bucer was generally satisfied. Indeed, since via Hermann's *Consultation* he had already been influential in its overall shape, how could he not be pleased? At the same time, however, he did have several criticisms of it and several suggestions for its further improvement. J.D.C. Fisher summarizes Bucer's overall critique:

"(1) Baptism should not take place during morning or evening prayer, but 'when the congregation is still present in the greatest numbers, before the administration of the Holy Supper is begun.' (2) The service at the church door is 'possessed of enough decency, order and edification' for it to take place inside the church in the hearing of the congregation. (3) The prayer at the signing of the child, the questions concerning the renunciation, and the Creed are all addressed to the child, who cannot understand. (4) Inanimate objects such as water ought not to be blessed. (5) Exorcism is appropriate only in the case of demoniacs. (6) The giving of the chrisom and the anointing, though ancient signs, are no longer edifying but promote superstition."[76]

That Bucer's critique was taken seriously by Cranmer is obvious when looking at the baptismal rite in next edition of the BCP, published in 1552.[77] Although baptisms still took place within the context of Morning or Evening Prayer, the preliminary rites were revised and shortened with the retention of only Cranmer's introductory exhortation and Luther's Flood Prayer. Both of these, however, now took place at the baptismal font rather than at the church door, with baptismal fonts in England, still large enough to submerge infants, remaining in their previous location near the main entrance to churches. After the reading of Mark 10:13-16 and an exhortation and prayer, the godparents were asked to make a single renunciation and single interrogative profession of faith in response to the complete Apostles' Creed. Next followed a series of four short petitions and a

---

[76] See Fisher, "Lutheran, Anglican, and Reformed Rites," 158
[77] The text of this rite appears in Fisher, *Christian Initiation*, 106–11.

concluding prayer, based on the blessing of the font from the 1549 BCP, but without any reference to either the "sanctification" of the waters or their having "been prepared for the ministration of thy holy sacrament." After asking the name of the candidate(s), baptism itself was administered by what appears to have been now a *single* dip accompanied by the trinitarian formula. In place of the postbaptismal giving of the garment and chrismation, Cranmer put a signing of the cross on the neophytes' forehead together with the formula, slightly revised, which had previously accompanied the *prebaptismal* signing of the forehead and breast:

"We receive this child into the congregation of Christ's flock, and do sign him with the sign of the cross, in token that hereafter he shall not be ashamed to confess the faith of Christ crucified, and manfully to fight under his banner against sin, the world and the devil, and to continue Christ's faithful soldier and servant unto life's end. Amen."

In other words, a prebaptismal *catechumenal* rite became in 1552 a postbaptismal signation! Even so, it is difficult not to see here, even without anointing, the classic medieval theology of "confirmation" as being "confirmed for battle" and becoming a "soldier of Christ."[78] Similarly, this rite was itself followed by another former prebaptismal rite, the praying of the Our Father. Finally, after a newly added prayer of thanksgiving, the catechetical exhortation to godparents with the rubrical directions concerning catechesis and confirmation from the 1549 BCP concludes the rite.

As with Luther's 1526 *Taufbüchlein,* so it was Cranmer's 1552 BCP which was to play the most influential role within the Anglican liturgical tradition. Although a history of the BCP itself is well beyond the scope of this study, it should be noted that it went through several subsequent editions in relationship to various political and ecclesiastical crises in England from 1552 until its final edition in England in 1662. With regard to baptism, however, the 1662 BCP, with the exception of regulating the number of godparents (two of the same sex as that of the candidate, one of the opposite), the addition of another question to the godparents before baptism was administered ("Wilt thou then obediently keep God's holy will and commandments, and walk in the same all the days of thy life?"), and the inclusion of a pe-

---

[78] See Hatchett, *Commentary on the American Prayer Book,* 264.

264

tition for the "sanctification" of the waters in the last prayer before baptism, remained the same as Cranmer's 1552 edition.

The 1662 BCP remains the official prayer book of the Church of England even today, although there were some minor revisions made in the eighteenth and nineteenth centuries (e.g., permission for parents to serve as baptismal sponsors and the making of the postbaptismal signation and formula optional).[79] As such, Cranmer's 1552 rite in its 1662 version would come even to serve as the baptismal rite for the Methodist movement in England during the eighteenth century under John Wesley (1703–09), an Anglican priest, who cherished the sacramental and liturgical tradition of the Church and sought to make that tradition normative in his experiential approach to Christianity. Wesley's own "methodical" focus on sacraments and prayer as contained within the BCP, however, in the words of James White, "sank somewhere while crossing the Atlantic" on the way toward the establishment of Methodism in its American forms.[80]

It is difficult to make a theological assessment of the Anglican reforms as they are presented in Cranmer's 1549 and 1552 editions of the BCP. Anglicanism, of course, has understood and presented itself as a *via media,* a "middle way," between Roman Catholicism and Protestantism. Certainly the rite of baptism in the 1549 BCP can be interpreted in that way with the retention of many of the traditional pre- and postbaptismal ceremonies, an overall Reformation focus on catechesis, the attention paid to the rites of Hermann's *Consultation,* and, with that, Bucer's own emphasis on the public and "edifying" nature of baptism. The rite of 1552, however, appears to have gone beyond the "middle way" in a more Reformed or Protestant direction altogether. But even here, it should be noted, Cranmer's revision of the prebaptismal signing of the forehead and breast into a postbaptismal signing of the forehead retains by gesture and formula something quite different than what is contained in the rites of other Reformation traditions at this point.

Concerning the theological interpretation of baptism, this same ambiguity or comprehensiveness, depending upon one's perspective, appears also in the Church of England's *Articles of Religion* (1563), where Article 29 states:

[79] Ibid., 265.
[80] White, *A Brief History of Christian Worship,* 145.

"Baptism is not only a sign of profession, and mark of difference, whereby Christian men are discerned from others that be not christened, but it is also a sign of Regeneration or New-Birth, whereby, as by an instrument, they that receive Baptism rightly are grafted into the Church; the promises of the forgiveness of sin, and of our adoption to be the sons of God by the Holy Ghost, are visibly signed and sealed; Faith is confirmed, and Grace increased by virtue of prayer unto God. . . . The Baptism of young Children is in any wise to be retained in the Church, as most agreeable with the institution of Christ."[81]

Luther, for example, would have been happy with the focus therein on baptism as "an instrument" of God's grace in which "faith is confirmed and grace increased." Calvin too would have liked the focus on the "promises . . . visibly signed and sealed." The "confirmation of faith" and the emphasis on prayer would have been pleasing to Calvin and Bucer alike. Zwingli and Calvin together would have liked the emphasis on being "grafted into the Church." All of the Reformers would have appreciated the emphasis on the "promises" and certainly all of them could have agreed on what is said here concerning the desirability of infant baptism. And, depending upon how one interpreted the use of "sign" throughout this statement, even a sixteenth-century Catholic would have found little in this article with which to disagree. But if one asks which of the various positions reflected is *the* doctrinal position, a single answer cannot be given. Such is the way in which diverse theological and doctrinal emphases are held together in synthesis. An Anglican of Zwinglian orientation and one of Catholic orientation, for example, can and could interpret the baptismal rite according to their own theological understandings.

The Anabaptist movement. In spite of the distinct theological approaches and various attempts at the reform of the baptismal rites within the Lutheran, Reformed, and Anglican traditions, very little actually changed with regard to baptismal *practice* at all within Reformation Protestantism in general. While the rite itself may have been "reformed" according to various theological positions on how much or how little of traditional ceremony was to be retained in the rite, the fact remains that Lutherans, Reformed, and Anglicans in the six-

[81] *Articles of Religion* (1563) in the *Book of Common Prayer* (Oxford 1784), as cited in White, *Documents of Christian Worship,* 174.

teenth century and beyond did scarcely little to change the practice of baptism they had inherited from the late medieval Church, other than to insist more strongly on, and make more provision for, post-baptismal catechesis. Even if the baptismal rite was now transferred to Sundays and generally administered in the context of public worship, infant baptism, as it had been practiced for centuries, was still the accepted norm, with Lutherans and Anglicans even retaining the practice of "emergency" or "private" baptisms in situations of severe illness or the possibility of death.

One of the major reasons for the strong defense and continuation of infant baptism among the major Protestant Reformers was, of course, their encounter with and rejection of the Anabaptist ("rebaptism") movement of the sixteenth century, another reforming movement often identified as the "Radical Reformation" or "left wing" of the Protestant Reformation.[82] Present in Luther's Wittenburg as early as 1521, under Thomas Münzer (1490–1525); in Zwingli's Zurich and throughout southwestern Germany with the Swiss Brethren in 1525, under the leadership of Balthasar Hübmaier (1485–1528); in Moravia under Jacob Hutter (+ 1536), who founded the Hutterite Brethren (or "Hutterites"); in Holland under Menno Simons (the "Mennonites") after 1535; and, to some extent, in Cranmer's England as early as 1534, Anabaptism was widespread and provided an alternative approach to a reform of the medieval Church. Rejected and frequently persecuted to the point of martyrdom by Protestant and Catholic alike, the overall theological approach of the Anabaptist movement may be summarized as follows:

"In the eyes of the Anabaptists . . . the church is not a natural community living a continuous life from generation to generation. Certainly the church should be independent of the political order; it receives no legitimation from the state and cannot justly be controlled by the state. Rather, the church is called into being by the act and summons of God. This act is not just an historical founding: it is a fresh act, renewed in every age. *The church is formed by believing persons freely coming together in mutual covenant in response to the call of*

---

[82] On Anabaptist worship and theology in relationship to baptism, see Old, *The Shaping of the Reformed Baptismal Rite,* 77–109; and White, *Protestant Worship,* 79–93. For a select bibliography see D. Tripp, "The Radical Reformation," *The Study of Liturgy,* 166–7.

God. Infant baptism had been a sign of the old organic conception of the church. The radical sectarian critique of ecclesiology *broke with the pattern of infant baptism and introduced . . . 'believer's baptism.' . . .* Baptism, by this account, is a public act witnessing to one's faith and made in obedience to Christ. *One is constituted a Christian by conscious faith.* Baptism belongs not to the economy of salvation but to the economy of obedience. It is not something that is done *for* one by the Church as part of becoming a Christian; rather, it is something done *by* one who has *already* become a Christian *by conversion.* In such a context, *true* baptism is impossible for an infant. . . . Baptism must wait until a person can, on his own, give an account of faith; otherwise the rite becomes magical, a mechanization of grace."[83]

Within such a "sectarian" view of Christianity, infant baptism would, in some Anabaptist communities, at least, be replaced by a rite of infant dedication, with baptism itself postponed until conscious faith and conversation were attained and one could thus make a personal decision to accept and follow Christ. The rite of baptism itself, then, was a consequence of this decision and done in obedience to Christ's baptismal "ordinance" or command as a public witness or testimony to that decision. Because infant baptism was not *true* baptism, it also became a common practice that those who had already been baptized in infancy would be rebaptized when they had experienced such a necessary adult conversion to Christ. Of course, this was not interpreted as a "rebaptism" at all, but in a manner somewhat similar to both Cyprian of Carthage and the Donatists of centuries before, the only baptism that truly mattered. Indeed, like the Donatists, the Anabaptists considered themselves to be the ideal and pure church; unlike them, the entrance into this community was by deliberate choice.

Both Scripture and reason provided Anabaptists with the grounds for such an approach. According to Menno Simons, for example,

[83] D. B. Stevik, "Christian Initiation: Post-Reformation to the Present Era," *Made, Not Born: New Perspectives on Christian Initiation and the Catechumenate,* from the Murphy Center for Liturgical Research (Notre Dame, Ind.: University of Notre Dame Press, 1976) 105; emphasis added. See also George H. Williams, *The Radical Reformation* (Philadelphia: Westminster Press, 1962); and Rollin S. Armour, *Anabaptist Baptism: A Representative Study* (Scottdale, Pa.: Herald Press, 1966).

there was "not a single command in the Scriptures that infants are to be baptized, or that the apostles practiced it," and, further, "young children are without understanding and reason."[84] Although some Anabaptists argued that "believer's baptism" should be postponed until, in strict imitation of Christ himself, one reached the age of thirty years, the general age for baptism appears to have been at least the traditional "age of reason," the same "canonical age" required for confirmation in the Roman rite.

It is often assumed that Anabaptists required "believer's baptism" by full submersion, but this is simply not true. English Baptists, coming out of the Puritans in seventeenth-century England, were the first to make such a requirement as a visible sign of obedience to and in imitation of Christ's ordinance. For the Anabaptists themselves, however, affusion or pouring was generally employed as the mode of baptismal administration, although the amount of water used in pouring was substantially greater than would have been the case in the average Protestant or Catholic parish church in the same time period. One of our first descriptions of an Anabaptist baptismal rite, in fact, relates that a milking pail was the vessel used for the pouring of the water and reports that at this service, led by Balthasar Hübmaier on Easter Sunday in 1525, over three hundred were (re)baptized.[85]

As noted above, it is, to a large degree, against the Anabaptists that the preceding defenses of infant baptism offered by Lutherans, Reformed, and Anglicans were primarily directed. Indeed, it is due to the Anabaptist movement that Lutherans, Reformed, and Anglicans were forced to spend as much time and energy on baptism as they did in their writings and liturgical reforms. Whether Anabaptism received a fair hearing from either Protestants or Catholics can be, and certainly is, a matter for serious debate. Nevertheless, in spite of their individually distinct theological positions, the Lutheran, Reformed, and Anglican traditions were one in their perception that the Anabaptists had exchanged an Augustinian theology of salvation rooted in grace for a form of Pelagianism which emphasized baptism as a human rather than divine act and as the consequence of a deliberate,

[84] Menno Simons, "Foundation of Christian Doctrine," *The Complete Writings of Menno Simons*, trans. J. C. Wenger (Scottdale, Pa.: Herald Press, 1956) 126–7; as cited by White, *A Brief History of Christian Worship*, 113.

[85] See White, *A Brief History of Christian Worship*, 112.

free, and salvific choice or human decision. In response to this, infant baptism continued to be defended and advocated. Indeed, it was only in the 1662 BCP that, in response to a growing need on the part of adults converted overseas by Anglican missionaries, a separate rite for adult baptism, based on the infant rite itself, was provided for the Church of England.[86] As Hughes Oliphant Old writes of the Reformers' defense of infant baptism:

"Above all, the Reformers were devoted to celebrating baptism in such a way that the sacrament be a sign of the richness of God's grace. If the early Reformed theologians rejected the Anabaptist approach to reform it was above all because the Anabaptists had failed to appreciate the primacy of grace. An appreciation of the Augustinian doctrine of grace was one of the fundamental insights of classical Protestantism. It was this appreciation for grace which led the Reformers out of late medieval scholasticism, and the Reformers were not about to be charmed back into it by the Anabaptists. The Anabaptists were Pelagian and just as voluntaristic as the late medieval scholastic theologians. In continuing to baptize infants the Reformers were only confirming their original Augustinianism. The baptismal rites they developed bore witness to a strong doctrine of grace. They were confident that the God who had so graciously made them members of the covenant community would be just as gracious to their children, and so they baptized their children. It was not because of a superstitious belief that their children would be saved by some sort of magical ceremony, but out of faith in the covenant promises of God."[87]

"Confirmation" and First Communion Among the Protestant Reformers
One of the great ironies of the Protestant Reformation is that, in spite of the Reformers' almost unanimous deletion of confirmation from the list of sacraments in the Church, Lutheranism, Reformed Protestantism, and Anglicanism all ended up with some form of "confirmation" as a preliminary rite leading to the reception of first communion.[88] This becomes all the more ironic when the severe and

[86] See Fisher, "Lutheran, Anglican, and Reformed Rites," 165.

[87] Old, *The Shaping of the Reformed Baptismal Rite,* 77–109.

[88] One of the best guides to confirmation in the context of the Protestant Reformation is Paul Turner, *The Meaning and Practice of Confirmation: Perspectives from a Sixteenth-Century Controversy* (New York: P. Lang, 1987).

harsh criticisms of confirmation raised especially by Luther and Calvin in their anti-Roman polemics are noted. According to Luther, the sacrament and rite of confirmation as it existed in the late medieval Church was nothing more than *Affenspiel* ("monkey business"), *Lügentand* ("fanciful deception"), and *Gaukelwerk* ("mumbo jumbo").[89] Calvin's assault on confirmation was even stronger:

"I hasten to declare that I am certainly not of the number of those who think that confirmation, as observed under the Roman papacy, is an idle ceremony, inasmuch as I regard it as one of the most deadly wiles of Satan. Let us remember that this pretended sacrament is nowhere recommended in Scripture, either under this name or with this ritual, or this signification. . . . Let the Romanists produce the word, if they wish us to contemplate in the oil anything beyond the oil itself. . . . Even if they could prove themselves to imitate the apostles in the imposition of hands, . . . whence do they derive their oil, which they call the oil of salvation? Who has taught them to seek salvation in oil? Who has taught them to attribute to it the property of imparting spiritual strength? . . . And with this they joined detestable blasphemy, because they said that sins were only forgiven by baptism, and that the Spirit of regeneration is given by that rotten oil which they presumed to bring in without the word of God."[90]

Indeed, for all of the Reformers, baptism as "new birth in water and the Holy Spirit" was complete in and of itself. Nothing additional was needed to "complete" or "perfect" it. Not surprisingly, then, neither Luther nor Calvin produced any rite to replace it. Nor, for that matter, did Zwingli, who also believed that confirmation was to be "deservedly abolished"[91] from the Church.

At the same time, however, most of the Reformers were open to the possibility of some kind of reformed rite, done in relationship to an examination of the faith of children after a period of catechetical instruction. Luther wrote of this, saying that, as long as it did not infringe upon the gift and promise of baptism, some kind of reformed rite would be appropriate. He stated that: "Confirmation as the bishops

---

[89] See Arthur Repp, *Confirmation in the Lutheran Church* (St. Louis, Mo.: Concordia Publishing House, 1964) 15.

[90] Fisher, *Christian Initiation*, 254.

[91] Ibid., 260.

want it should not be bothered with. Nevertheless we do not fault any pastor who might scrutinize the faith from children. If it be good and sincere, he may impose hands and confirm."[92] And Calvin actually thought that such was the original practice of confirmation in the early Church, a practice which had degenerated into the episcopal chrismation only after this earlier practice died out. He wrote:

"This was once the custom, that the children of Christians after they had grown up were stood up before the bishop that they might fulfill that duty which was required of those adults who were offering them for baptism. . . . Therefore, those who had been initiated at baptism as infants, because they had not then performed a confession of faith before the Church towards the end of childhood—or as adolescence was beginning—were again presented by the parents, were examined by the bishop according to a formula of catechism which people held definite and universal. But so that this action, which otherwise deservedly ought to have been weighty and holy, might have all the more of reverence and dignity, the ceremony of the imposition of hands was also being used."[93]

While the need for postbaptismal catechesis and some kind of profession of faith on the part of those baptized in infancy was thus considered desirable by both Luther and Calvin, it was, not surprisingly, Martin Bucer himself, the "Father of Protestant Confirmation," who was to produce reformed rites for use especially among Lutherans. Among some Lutherans and, at least, the Reformed in Calvin's Geneva, a service with an examination of the faith of children based on various Reformation catechisms (Luther's and others), but without any kind of "confirmation" ceremony included, often served as a preparation for admission to first communion on the day before principal feasts such as Christmas, Easter, and Pentecost, with the catechism itself being taught during the seasons preceding those feasts.[94] It was, however, more than "first communion instruction" with a public examination that Bucer produced.

[92] Paul Turner, *Sources of Confirmation: From the Fathers through the Reformers* (Collegeville: The Liturgical Press, 1993) 22.

[93] Ibid., 22.

[94] See Fisher, "Lutheran, Anglican, and Reformed Rites," 161–2; and Old, *The Shaping of the Reformed Baptismal Rite*, 216–26.

Already in 1522, Erasmus of Rotterdam, Holland, the great Humanist, had suggested a reform of the Roman rite of confirmation, in which those having arrived at puberty "be asked whether they ratify what their godparents promised in their name in baptism"[95] within a catechetical examination by the bishop to be included as part of the confirmation rite. Consistent with Erasmus' concern, Bucer himself was to make this kind of approach influential in the development of confirmation rites within several of the Lutheran *Church Orders* throughout sixteenth-century Germany.[96] Such rites, taking place on the great festivals of Christmas, Easter, and/or Pentecost, included a presentation of the children; an examination on the catechism, conducted by the parish pastor, or, ideally, by a visiting pastor; prayers of intercession by the assembled congregation; an individual laying on of hands by the pastor(s), in which the Holy Spirit was invoked to "strengthen" the candidates in faith, or, surprisingly enough, in some *Orders* the candidates themselves were addressed with a formula that appeared still to "give" the Holy Spirit (i.e., "Receive the Holy Spirit . . .");[97] and, finally, the newly confirmed were admitted to first communion. Eugene Brand summarizes the various ways in which confirmation thus continued among Lutherans, saying:

"Arthur Repp has distinguished six different major types of confirmation within the Lutheran churches: catechetical (as instructional preparation for Holy Communion, often without liturgical form), hierarchical (derived from Bucer; emphasis upon confession of faith and vow of obedience to the Church), sacramental (accents from Roman tradition retained; gift of the Spirit through laying on of hands, conferral of fuller membership), traditional (relating only to Baptism, not a rite of admission to the Eucharist), pietistic (moment for personal confession and witness; acceptance of obligation to lead the Christian life), and rationalistic (exaltation of confirmation over Baptism; declaration of allegiance to a local congregation, a religious oath). The first four types emerged in the 16th century; the pietistic and rationalistic types emerged in the 17th and 18th centuries. Not until the 19th century was confirmation accepted in the Church of

---

[95] Cited by Fisher, "Lutheran, Anglican, and Reformed Rites," 162.
[96] For examples of Lutheran confirmation rites see Fisher, *Christian Initiation*, 174–84.
[97] Ibid., 180.

Sweden and only then 'as the rite for the admission to the Lord's Supper.'"[98]

Bucer's overall influence on confirmation rites within Protestantism, especially within Lutheranism and Anglicanism, however, is again best seen in Hermann von Wied's *Consultation* and in Thomas Cranmer's two editions of the BCP in 1549 and 1552. Within the *Consultation*,[99] the rite of confirmation was preceded by a lengthy explanation of the meaning of confirmation and its necessity for those baptized in infancy "when they be meetly well instructed of religion, and when they somewhat understand those great benefits that be given in baptism." The first part of the rite, then, consisted of a detailed catechetical examination by the bishop (or other minister) in question and answer form, including a recitation and explanation of each section of the Apostles' Creed, the meaning of baptism and Eucharist, and the implications of Christian faith and participation in the life of the Church. A lengthy prayer of invocation followed and was concluded by an individual handlaying rite and prayer addressed to Christ, in which the following was requested: "Confirm this thy servant with thy Holy Spirit, that he may continue in the obedience of thy gospel, and strongly resist the devil and his own weakness." The use of chrism, consistent with Bucer's emphasis against the use of symbols not explicitly referred to in Scripture, was abolished from the rite in favor of the imposition of hands alone. Such an omission was explained here by saying that "the sign of laying on of hands shall be sufficient in this ministration, which the apostles and old fathers thought sufficient."

As in the 1549 BCP rite of baptism, so was the *Consultation* somewhat influential in the 1549 BCP rite of confirmation.[100] This influence, however, appears to have been limited to the absence of chrism and to the fact that a short catechism has been placed immediately before the rite. The catechism was in question and answer form to be used by the bishop in catechizing the candidates; it contained the Apostles' Creed, the Our Father, and an abbreviated version of the Ten Commandments together with some other

[98] E. Brand, "New Rites of Initiation and Their Implications: In the Lutheran Churches," LWSS, 294.

[99] Fisher, *Christian Initiation*, 194–203.

[100] Ibid., 236–43.

instruction on their meanings. Attached to this catechism was a rubric, which stated that:

"So soon as the children can say in their mother tongue the articles, the Lord's prayer, the ten commandments and also can answer to such questions of this short catechism as the bishop (or such as he shall appoint) shall by his discretion appose them in, then shall they be brought to the bishop by one that shall be his godfather or god-mother, that every child may have a witness of his confirmation."

The rite of confirmation itself in the 1549 BCP included the traditional Western "confirmation prayer" for the sevenfold gift of the Holy Spirit (". . . send down from heaven . . . upon them thy Holy Ghost"). After a short petition, in which the bishop asked that the candidates might be signed and marked "by the virtue of [Christ's] holy cross and passion," and be confirmed and strengthened "with the inward unction" of the Holy Spirit, the bishop was directed to sign the candidates' foreheads with the cross and then lay hands on their heads, saying: "N. I sign thee with the sign of the cross, and lay my hand upon thee, in the name of the Father and of the Son and of the Holy Ghost. Amen." The rite concluded with the traditional greeting of peace between the bishop and confirmand, a final prayer and blessing, and a rubric which underscored the necessity of parish priests offering catechetical instruction at least once every six weeks on a given Sunday or holy day. And, in order to impress upon all the importance of both catechesis and confirmation, this rubric concludes: "and there shall none be admitted to holy communion, until such time as he be confirmed."

It has often been noted that, with the exception of chrism and the Reformation emphasis on catechizing, the confirmation rite of the 1549 BCP was little other than an English translation of the late medieval Latin *Sarum Rite* itself. As such, confirmation in England not only remained a rite reserved exclusively to the bishop, but its theological emphasis on the gift of the Holy Spirit also enabled a sacramental understanding of this rite to continue. In fact, among English bishops at the time of Cranmer there was not agreement on whether confirmation was to be included as one of the sacraments or not.[101]

---

[101] See *The Questionnaire of 1540* sent to a group of bishops and theologians by the king, in Fisher, *Christian Initiation*, 223–7.

Bucer's critique of the 1549 rite of confirmation, in his *Censura*,[102] was again effective in Cranmer's revision of the rite in 1552.[103] Bucer's concerns, however, were directed primarily toward increased catechesis. Hence, a more complete catechism was attached at the beginning of the rite. In addition, in 1552 the concluding rubric of the 1549 rite directing public catechesis once every six weeks became a requirement for *every* Sunday and holy day. Bucer's insistence on catechetical understanding and knowledge also became expressed in the final sentence of the above-noted rubric about confirmation and first communion, where ability to "say the catechism" has also been made, together with confirmation, as a prerequisite for admission to first communion.

Most striking in the 1552 rite of confirmation is the shift of language regarding the Holy Spirit. Whereas the 1549 rite had simply continued the traditional Western prayer for the sevenfold gift of the Spirit, i.e., "send down from heaven . . . upon them thy Holy Ghost," this prayer, although retained, was significantly revised by Cranmer in 1552 to read, "strengthen them . . . with the Holy Ghost . . . and daily increase in them thy manifold gifts of grace." At the same time, even the signing with the cross and the formula of 1549 was omitted in favor of a handlaying alone during the following petition: "Defend, O Lord, this child with thy heavenly grace, that he may continue thine for ever, and daily increase in thy Holy Spirit more and more, until he come unto thy everlasting kingdom. Amen." If the 1549 rite was essentially the medieval Roman rite in English, that of 1552 (continuing, of course, in the 1662 BCP and to the present day in the Church of England) was clearly a "Lutheran," or, at least, Reformation rite from start to finish. Apart from the requirement that the bishop be the minister of this rite, which did, certainly, give it a more "Catholic" flavor, there is little to distinguish it from the kinds of catechetical exams and connected rites regularly used among the other Protestant traditions in preparation for the reception of first communion.

Whether such rites were called "confirmation" or not, with Lutherans and Anglicans tending to retain the term and Reformed Protestants avoiding it strongly, by the development of such rites of

---

[102] For Bucer's critique, see Fisher, *Christian Initiation*, 244–50.
[103] Ibid., 251–3.

profession based on extended catechesis, and by making such catechesis and profession a prerequisite for the reception of first communion, the Protestant Reformation did restore something akin to the rites associated with the *redditio symboli* in the ancient catechumenate,[104] although, properly speaking, the term "catechumen" is to be reserved for one who is being catechized but not yet baptized. Nevertheless, whatever the particular profession rite is called, since it was the *baptized* who, by these "confirmation replacement rites," were generally admitted to first communion sometime near the traditional "age of reason," it cannot be ignored that the traditional Western initiatory sequence of baptism, "confirmation," and first communion, in that order, was actually maintained by the Protestant Reformation with a greater tenacity than it had been among the late medieval Roman Church itself. Even among the Anabaptists, the denial of infant baptism tended to mean that, at the age of reason, baptism, the postbaptismal "laying on of hands," and first communion were reunited in a single event. If the traditional *theology* of confirmation as a special sacrament of the Holy Spirit for strength and the augmentation of grace was denied, the rite itself was still deemed important, even if primarily revised into a catechetical ceremony. Similarly, if the Reformers themselves were incorrect in their understanding of the origins of confirmation as a catechetical rite by which those baptized in infancy, after instruction, had made their adolescent and public profession as an owning of their baptismal faith, and if they were also incorrect about the origins and history of the use of chrism within the baptismal rites in general, one cannot but be struck with how their biblical literacy regarding the use of handlaying alone may have actually placed them closer to the earlier Western liturgical tradition in relationship to the postbaptismal ritualization of the gift of the Holy Spirit altogether.

The fact that this catechetically-based profession rite was not considered to be a necessary part of Christian initiation for the Protestant Reformers, however, raises the question about the relationship between baptism and first communion among the Reformers other than the Anabaptists. Along with considering baptism itself as *full* initiation

---

[104] On this, see Old, *The Shaping of the Reformed Baptismal Rite*, 201–26. See also, L. Mitchell, "Christian Initiation: The Reformation Period," *Made, Not Born*, 83–98.

"in water and the Holy Spirit," it is well known that among the Eucharistic reforms within Protestantism was the restoration of the cup to the laity in the reception of communion. The Hussites, an earlier and ultimately suppressed reforming movement in fifteenth-century Bohemia, centered in Prague, restored not only the cup but frequent and regular communion reception, and, together with this, the communion of baptized infants as well. Justified by appeal to John 3:5; 1 Corinthians 10:17; and John 6:53, infant communion became not only a common practice within their communities but one upon which they would not compromise.[105] In his *Large Catechism,* Luther too had said, "since [children] are baptized and received into the Christian church, they should also enjoy this fellowship of the sacrament so that they may serve us and be useful."[106] And, from the late sixteenth through the seventeenth century the question of infant communion was hotly debated between Anglicans and Puritans in England, although the practice of excluding infants did not change.[107]

Apart from the Hussites in the previous century, none of the major reform movements of the sixteenth century restored this traditional and ancient practice. What Old calls the Reformers' "original Augustinianism," upon which was based the retention and defense of infant baptism, then, can only be called a *selective* Augustinianism when one remembers that for Augustine himself the infant was the ideal sacramental subject for *both* baptism and Eucharist.[108] To be fair, of course, such selectivity on the part of the Reformers with regard to the postponement of communion reception was the practice they had inherited from the medieval period itself, a practice they now would perpetuate through the centuries with the addition of a strong doctrinally-based catechesis.

CHRISTIAN INITIATION
IN THE CATHOLIC REFORMATION

It was not only the various forms of Protestantism that emerged as the result of the sixteenth-century Reformation, nor was it only those

---

[105] On this movement and its demise see Holeton, *Infant Communion—Then and Now,* 9–15.

[106] Tappert, *The Book of Concord,* 456–7.

[107] See Holeton, *Infant Communion,* 9–15.

[108] See above, chapter 4.

known as the "Protestant" Reformers who were concerned about reform and renewal within the Western Church. As much as the Lutheran, Reformed, Anglican, and other Protestant Churches owe their immediate origins to the various sixteenth-century reforming movements, so also does the particular shape and self-understanding of the Roman Catholic Church itself as it emerged from the late Middle Ages. As Gary Macy states so clearly:

"Different churches retained different customs of the old medieval church, to be sure, and some of the churches, especially the Roman Catholic and Anglican churches, treasured their continuity with the medieval centuries. Yet it is important to remember that none of the churches which emerged from this great upheaval can claim the past exclusively their own. *The modern Roman Catholic Church started in the sixteenth century just as surely as the Lutheran and Calvinist churches.* . . . Before the reformation there were no Protestants, no Anglicans, no Roman Catholics. Christians were simply Christians—eastern and western Christians sometimes, but mostly simply Christians."[109]

It is thus important to note that just as there was a "Protestant" Reformation so also was there a decidedly "Catholic" Reformation, that is, an internal reform of the Roman Church itself apart from the challenges of the various Protestant movements. While a significant part of this Catholic Reformation was what has been often called the Counter Reformation,[110] in response to Protestantism, the mere fact that among Roman Catholic concerns was the reform of liturgical books, liturgical and devotional life, and the catechetical education of clergy and laity alike demonstrates that far more was at stake than simply responding to Protestantism.

Both Counter Reform and Catholic Reform were the concerns of the Council of Trent, which met in some twenty-five sessions and over three separate historical periods (1545–47, 1551–52, and

---

[109] Gary Macy, *The Banquet's Wisdom: A Short History of the Theologies of the Lord's Supper* (New York: Paulist Press, 1992) 135.

[110] This helpful distinction between "Catholic" and "Counter" Reformations is that of Hubert Jedin. See his four-volume *A History of the Council of Trent*, trans. Ernest Graf (St. Louis, Mo.: Herder, 1957) as well as his *Ecumenical Councils of the Catholic Church*, trans. Ernest Graf (New York: Herder and Herder, 1960).

1562–63). Concerning the rites of Christian initiation themselves, however, it is quite clear that the primary concern at Trent, in fact, was not so much with the internal reform of those rites and their theological interpretation as it was with defending traditional teaching and practice against what it perceived to be the attacks of the various Reformers themselves.

The Canons and Decrees on Initiation at the Council of Trent

At its seventh session, March 3, 1547, under the presidency of Pope Paul III, the Council of Trent approved and adopted a total of thirteen condemnatory propositions or canons on the "Sacraments in General," fourteen "On Baptism," and three "On Confirmation."[111] In every case, the negative proposition was stated with the result that any who found their position included under the proposition in question were summarily condemned by the famous concluding formula, "anathema sit," that is, "let him be condemned." In no case, however, was any attempt made to clarify the Roman Catholic doctrinal position on any of these issues, nor is it always certain that what was condemned was clearly the complete theological positions of the Reformers rather than an unnuanced caricature of those positions.

Within the Tridentine canons "On the Sacraments in General," strongly-worded propositions appeared in defense of all seven sacraments against the Protestant reduction to the two "dominical" sacraments. Along with this, these canons also pointed to the salvific necessity of the sacraments versus "faith alone," to the belief that the sacraments contained and conferred *ex opere operato* the grace they signified and were not to be regarded only as "outward signs of grace," and to the position that sacramental grace was not limited by God only to some recipients but given to all who received the sacraments rightly. Indeed, without specifying any Protestant Reformer in particular, these first thirteen canons did little more than affirm the late medieval Catholic sacramental position against what the Council Fathers believed the Protestant Reformers had attacked.

Within the fourteen canons "On Baptism," faith "alone" was, again, a target for attack (Cann. 6, 7, and 10) as was, against the Anabaptists

---

[111] For texts of these canons and decrees see H. J. Schroeder, trans., *The Canons and Decrees of the Council of Trent* (1941; reprint Rockford, Ill.: Tan Books, 1978).

in particular, the repeatability of baptism in adulthood (Can. 11) or the postponement of baptism until either the "age of discretion" (Can. 13) or the "age at which Christ was baptized" (Can. 12). Similarly condemned was the making of baptism optional and so not necessary for salvation (Can. 5), as well as the spiritualizing of John 3:5 into a metaphor of "baptism in the Holy Spirit" without the necessary and connected use of real water (Can. 2). At the same time, the three canons "On Confirmation" not only defended confirmation as "a true and proper sacrament" (Can. 1), but condemned those who taught that it was merely an adolescent profession of faith after catechesis in Christian antiquity (Can. 1), affirmed the use of chrism for its administration (Can. 2), and merely repeated the traditional understanding that the bishop was the "ordinary minister" of the rite.

Along with the above canons, issues relating to Christian initiation were also treated in the fifth session of the council on June 17, 1546, where in the Decree Concerning Original Sin[112] infant baptism continued to be justified on this basis, and in the twenty-first session on July 16, 1562, where infant communion was treated briefly. With regard to infant communion specifically, the Council Fathers stated in chapter IV of The Doctrine of Communion under Both Kinds and the Communion of Little Children that:

"little children who have not attained the use of reason are not by any necessity bound to the sacramental communion of the Eucharist; for having been regenerated by the laver of baptism and thereby incorporated with Christ, they cannot at that age lose the grace of the sons of God already acquired. Antiquity is not therefore to be condemned, however, if in some places it at one time observed that custom. For just as those most holy Fathers had acceptable ground for what they did under the circumstances, so it is certainly to be accepted without controversy that they regarded it as not necessary to salvation."[113]

To this a condemnatory canon was attached, which read: "if anyone says that communion of the Eucharist is necessary for little children before they have attained the years of discretion, let him be anathema."

By the inclusion of this statement and canon it is quite obvious that still in 1562, in some places in the West at least, infant communion

[112] See paragraphs 3, 4, and 5 in ibid., 22–3.
[113] Ibid., 134.

was being practiced on occasion and the concern of Trent was not really to abolish it altogether but to point out that it was not a necessary practice. Nonetheless, as J.D.C. Fisher notes:

"[the] Council was hard put to explain away the practice of the past without appearing to condemn it. Antiquity, it said, was not to be condemned if it maintained that custom in certain places for a time—an extraordinary statement in view of the fact that all Churches in the West admitted infants to communion until the 12th century, and this practice had been generally approved for a thousand years. Nor is this all: for the Council . . . went on to allege that the holy Fathers of antiquity found an adequate reason for what they did in the situation of that time, and without treating communion as necessary to the salvation of infants, a claim which is not in accordance with the facts."[114]

What is most surprising, of course, is that it is not only the practice of the *past* that "appears to have been condemned" here but the traditional and continued practice of the Christian East as well. And yet, it should be noted that the Council of Trent actually left open the possibility that Roman Catholics could at some future point reconsider this issue. That is, by saying that little children "are not by *necessity* bound to the sacramental communion of the Eucharist," this statement did *not* say that baptized children before the "age of discretion" *can* not, *ought* not, or even *must* not receive communion; only that they *need* not. While that itself certainly contradicted the theologies of Cyprian and Augustine, as well as the common tradition and interpretation in both East and West for centuries, its rather careful language provides an interesting loophole for those who might seek to restore the authentic tradition of the Western Church in this regard.

The "Tridentine" Liturgical Books

If, in response to the Protestant Reformers, the Council of Trent did nothing more than defend the shape and theological interpretation of the rites of Christian initiation as they had developed in the medieval West, so the "new" liturgical books called for by that council tended simply to codify and standardize in official *Roman* books the late medieval liturgical texts and rubrics for the celebration of those rites.

[114] J.D.C. Fisher, *Christian Initiation: Baptism in the Medieval West* (London: SPCK, 1965) 106–7.

None of the "Tridentine" liturgical books were finished or promulgated at the Council of Trent itself, with the *editio typica* (typical or normative edition) of the *Breviarium Romanum (Roman Breviary)* for the Divine Office, or Liturgy of the Hours, appearing in 1568 and the *editio typica* of the *Missale Romanum (Roman Missal)* for the celebration of the Mass in 1570. Official liturgical books containing the rites of Christian initiation, however, did not appear until much later with the universally mandatory *Pontificale Romanum (Roman Pontifical)* containing all the particular rites needed by bishops, including confirmation, in 1596, and with the *Rituale Romanum (Roman Ritual)*, containing all the rites needed by priests, including baptism, not being printed until 1614, although the *Ritual* did not become universally mandatory at this time and local diocesan usages continued. The *Pontifical* and *Ritual*, of course, did not represent "reformed" rites but, rather, the codification and uniformity of the sacraments of initiation throughout the Roman Catholic Church as they had come to be celebrated and interpreted. To further this cause of liturgical uniformity, Pope Sixtus V in 1588 established the Congregation of Sacred Rites (later renamed the *Sacred* Congregation of Rites) for the direction of the liturgy throughout the Latin church, based on uses in Rome itself.

In this way not only was the pattern of Christian initiation in its disordered and separated sequence inherited by the Council of Trent, it was received, defended, advocated, and perpetuated by the Tridentine liturgical books, the same books which continued to shape the Roman Catholic understanding of Christian initiation until the Second Vatican Council of the early 1960s. Also, like the Protestant Reformers, the Council Fathers at Trent were greatly concerned about catechesis and Christian education. Again like, and undoubtedly influenced by, the popularity of catechisms written by the Protestant Reformers themselves, they called for an official catechism of Catholic teaching entitled the *Catechism of the Council of Trent for Parish Priests*.[115] This lengthy and detailed catechism (containing about six hundred pages of text in English translation) on the Apostles' Creed in twelve articles, the seven sacraments, the ten commandments, and the Our Father appeared in 1566, two years before the first new liturgical

---

[115] Various editions of this catechism are available, having been reprinted several times. See *Catechism of the Council of Trent for Parish Priests* (New York: Joseph F. Wagner, Inc., 1923).

book was printed. This order of appearance is itself indicative of the surpassing value that the Fathers of Trent placed on education. Indeed, it may be said, in relationship to the strong emphasis placed on Christian education of laity and clergy by both Protestants and Catholics in this time period, that the Reformations of the sixteenth century represent the first successful "Christianization" or "evangelization" of Europe itself. Such a statement may seem to be a rather harsh judgment until it is remembered that, prior to this emphasis, catechesis in general had tended to be limited to the memorization of the Apostles' Creed, the Our Father, and the Hail Mary.

While it is certainly clear that the dominant candidate for baptism in the mind of the Fathers of the Council of Trent remained the infant, the *Catechism* did refer to the possibility of adult baptism, saying that

"with regard to those of adult age who enjoy the perfect use of reason, persons, namely, born of infidel parents, the practice of the primitive Church points out that a different manner of proceeding should be followed. To them the Christian faith is to be proposed; and they are earnestly to be exhorted, persuaded and invited to embrace it."

Furthermore, it continued:

"On adults . . . the Church has not been accustomed to confer the Sacrament of Baptism at once, but has ordained that it be deferred for a certain time. . . . The candidate for Baptism is thus better instructed in the doctrine of the faith which he is to profess, and in the practice of the Christian life. Finally, when Baptism is administered to adults with solemn ceremonies on the appointed days of Easter and Pentecost only greater religious reverence is shown to the Sacrament."[116]

In spite of these statements, it has often been assumed that the adult catechumenate itself was essentially nonexistent in the sixteenth century. In making this assumption scholars have pointed to early-sixteenth-century missionary work by the Jesuits in India and other religious orders such as the Franciscans, Augustinians, and Dominicans throughout Latin America. Whatever catechesis may have been

---

[116] Ibid., 178–80.

given, it has been assumed that it was either of a very rudimentary sort, or later based on the *Catechism of the Council of Trent* itself, and took place only after baptism, often in preparation for confirmation and/or first communion.[117]

While it is certainly true that the ancient adult catechumenate was not restored officially by Rome in the sixteenth century, a recent article by Jaime Lara suggests that the standard assumption about its nonexistence within missionary contexts is in need of serious revision today.[118] Lara himself demonstrates that in Mexico, as early as 1540, a *Manual for Adults* was published which, in fact, did restore an adult catechumenate, beginning either in mid-Lent for Easter baptism or in the middle of the Easter season for baptism at Pentecost. An early attempt at liturgical inculturation, this manual also directed that the parts of the various rites directed to the catechumens, including the profession of faith, be done in the native Aztec language of Náhuatl. Although this manual was shortlived, being replaced in 1560 by another ritual in which such catechumenal rites were not present, Lara's work demonstrates that liturgical research in the sixteenth-century missionary contexts and often-ignored liturgical texts and references might yet reveal further evidence for catechumenal experimentation.

Finally, if the *Catechism* referred to adult baptism, it also referred to the possibility of infant confirmation. "It is to be observed," it stated:

"that after Baptism, the Sacrament of Confirmation may indeed be administered to all; but that, until children shall have reached the age of reason, its administration is inexpedient. If it does not seem well to defer (Confirmation) to the age of twelve, it is most proper to postpone this Sacrament at least to that of seven years."[119]

Similarly, the following rubric appeared in the *Pontificale Romanum* of 1596: "Infants are to be held in their right arms by their godparents before the bishop when he is ready to confirm them with chrism. But let adults or other older persons place their foot on the right foot of their godparent."[120] Since, as we saw in the previous chapter, the

[117] On this see L. Mitchell, "Christian Initiation," 83–4.

[118] J. Lara, "'Precious Green Jade Water': A Sixteenth-century Adult Catechumenate in the New World," *Worship* 71:5 (1997).

[119] *Catechism of the Council of Trent for Parish Priests*, 208.

[120] Fisher, *Baptism in the Medieval West*, 183.

Pontifical of 1596 was based on the thirteenth-century *Pontifical of William Durandus* and its subsequent editions, the inclusion of this rubric could have been an editorial oversight. Nevertheless, it is interesting to note that the choreography of the rite of confirmation in the Tridentine *Pontifical,* in spite of the Roman insistence on the age of discretion for the reception of confirmation, still makes infants the regular candidates. Indeed, if it is not a sign of somehow being held by a sponsor, what else can the placing of the foot of the adult candidate on the foot of the sponsor possibly signify? Again, therefore, as with the possibility of restoring infant communion and the adult catechumenate, neither the *Catechism of Trent* nor the Tridentine *Pontifical* stand in the way of a Roman Catholic reconsideration of infant confirmation.

CONCLUSION

It was suggested above in chapter 4 that within Augustine of Hippo's response to Donatism and Pelagianism in the late fourth and early fifth centuries there was the beginning of a "reduction to sacramental minimalism" that would be quite influential in Western Christianity. Perhaps nowhere is the result of that "minimalism" more clearly expressed than in the sixteenth-century Protestant and Catholic reforms of the rites of Christian initiation. Among the Protestant Reformers, the systematic excision of what Hughes Oliphant Old calls the "heavy overlay of supplementary rites" in baptism led to an overall ritual shape of baptism in which only what was considered to be the "essential ceremony" of the rite, that is, the administration of the water with the trinitarian formula, remained. Not surprisingly, justification for this "reduction to essentials" was not only the New Testament based, dominical institution of the "two" sacraments of baptism and Eucharist, but the often quoted sacramental "definition" of Augustine himself that when a "word" is added to an "element" there results a "visible word." Word plus element, which, via medieval scholasticism, had become "matter" and "form," of course, was the common theological vocabulary and common inheritance of Protestants and Roman Catholics alike in the sixteenth century, although Roman Catholics did not draw the same conclusions from this vocabulary for the reform of the ritual shape of initiation that the Protestant Reformers did.

The reduction to sacramental minimalism among some of the Protestant Reformers, however, was to go beyond a simple reduction to "essentials." While the early Protestant Reformers wanted the essential rite of baptism to be a literal bath or submersion and sought to make that normative so that baptism could be a true "sign of what it signified," a further reduction even here was to develop. As James White notes of this development:

"The decline in baptism by immersion is reflected in the gradual shrinking of fonts. The massive medieval fonts gave way to smaller pedestal fonts and for the moderate traditions these often yielded to portable basins. With remarkable tenacity, Roman Catholics and Anglicans clung to having the font situated near the main entrance. By the seventeenth century, many Lutheran fonts had migrated to the front of the church where they stood next to altar-table and pulpit, uniting word and sacrament. Reformed and Puritan churches usually used a portable basin, always near the pulpit as Calvin dictated: '. . . in order that there be better hearing for the recitation of this mystery and practice of baptism.'"[121]

And, as he notes further, even within the Anglican and Roman Catholic Churches, where rubrics still directed the "dipping" of the baptismal candidate, the practice itself gradually gave way to baptism by affusion.[122] Hence, even the essential baptismal ceremony was increasingly reduced to the bare essence of that essential rite.

This Reformation reduction to sacramental minimalism in overall ritual shape and practice along with the retention and defense of infant baptism appears to have brought to a logical conclusion the ritual and theological tradition of the late Middle Ages in which, as we have seen, infant baptism itself was a form of "clinical" baptism, a rite for the dying to be administered *quamprimum*. Similarly, in emergency situations all that was necessary for baptism was the pouring or sprinkling of water with the trinitarian formula. Although, to their credit, the Protestant Reformers did restore the administration of baptism to the public, Sunday liturgical assembly, and so did challenge, in part, the medieval *quamprimum* emphasis, the rites themselves, so drastically reduced and increasingly filled with didactic materials, were little more than public forms of clinical baptism. And with this, neither Protestantism nor Catholicism did much to change the late medieval

---

[121] White, *A Brief History of Christian Worship*, 111.
[122] See ibid., 109–10.

situation of baptizing infants but not "fully" initiating them until they reached the "catechetical" age of discretion or reason.

Perhaps the greatest contribution of Protestants and Roman Catholics alike in this period of reform was the renewed emphasis on catechesis and, with that, at least the possibility of the restoration of the catechumenate itself. For Protestants, in particular, such a recovery was related to the necessity of faith development in the baptized so that a profession of faith might be made in response to the promises of God and the vows made on one's behalf by godparents in baptism. For both Protestants and Catholics, however, this catechesis was highly doctrinal and cerebral in nature.

"Behind much of the reforming program of both the Protestant Reformation and the Catholic Reformation, was the emerging modern concept of the person as an autonomous individual. Whereas earlier and non-Western concepts of the person tended to identify the person in terms of his or her place in the community, the modern concept of the autonomous individual makes the individual self the source of its values and its own identity. Hence we have the emphasis on individual conversion and commitment and on the education which would shape each individual to take his place in the Church or in society. Through diligent training of intellect and will, Catholics and Protestants alike believed, a new generation of committed individuals could be formed."[123]

In such a way, even in spite of denying the "sacramentality" of confirmation, the Protestant Reformation traditions clung to some form of that rite for catechetical purposes, much as the medieval separation of baptism, confirmation, and first communion into intervals of several years enabled Roman Catholics to adopt a similar educational or catechetical basis for their administration and/or reception. One of the great ironies in all this, of course, is that in practice Protestants and Roman Catholics differed very little here and, hence, in spite of all the polemics on both sides, both continued to baptize in early infancy and then catechize in preparation for "confirmation," or some other rite named differently, and first communion. However, for Roman Catholics the placement of confirmation itself in this initiatory sequence would still depend upon the availability of bishops.

[123] Mark Searle, "Infant Baptism Reconsidered," LWSS, 377.

Even here, however, by not fully initiating people, or at least not permitting them to receive first communion until they were at the proper age at which they could respond in faith, a greater irony is the parallel established between Protestants and Catholics with the Anabaptist tradition altogether. Indeed, while Anabaptists might have "dedicated" their children to God in infancy and then baptized, imposed hands, and communed them after catechesis, Protestants and Roman Catholics continued to baptize in infancy, catechize, and only then, by means of "confirmation" or first communion rites, fully welcome them into membership around the same age. Although there may be a world of difference in the theological claims made about infant baptism, in practice there is a commonality between these traditions not often noted. That is, in spite of the theological understanding, all were, in practice, fully initiating only "responsible" and faith-professing "adult" individuals whose intellect and will had been shaped by catechetical education.[124] In other words, except for some isolated instances, infant *initiation* was not restored in the sixteenth century.

Finally, whatever one's overall assessment of the sixteenth-century Reformation and the resultant division of Western Christianity may be, there is at least one major contribution that ought to be noted. Although largely for polemical purposes in attempting to expose the doctrinal "errors" of one another, the sixteenth-century Reformation began to set in motion a return to the sources of the Christian tradition, especially Scripture and the writings of the patristic period. Indeed, the Reformers thought that the reformed rites they had created were nothing other than a restoration of early Christian practice. John Calvin's *The Form of Prayers and Ecclesiastical Chants with the Manner of Administering the Sacraments and Solemnizing Marriage, according to the Custom of the Ancient Church, 1542,* is certainly indicative of this Reformation intent, as is the fact that the official Roman rites, in the words of Pope Pius V in the 1570 *Missale Romanum,* were understood to have been compiled "ad pristinam . . . sanctorum Patrum normam" ("according to the norm of the holy Fathers").[125] While impossible to

---

[124] See ibid., 371, 376–8.

[125] Pius V, the papal bull, *Quo Primum,* the promulgation of the 1570 *Missale Romanum,* appearing at the beginning of every edition of the pre-Vatican II Missal.

do in the historical context of the sixteenth century, due to the unavailability of several of those writings, this Reformation "return to the sources," aided by advances in scholarship in the following centuries, would ultimately make possible in the modern world the critical recovery of the rites of Christian initiation in early Christianity and so enable the contemporary churches to move beyond the Reformation deadlock toward a more thoroughgoing reform of those rites today. Here the Council Fathers of Trent are to be commended in that, rather than calling for a complete reform of the Roman rites themselves, they preserved for the following centuries much of the classic Western liturgical tradition, even if in its late medieval form.

Chapter 8

Christian Initiation in the Churches Today

The second half of the twentieth century has witnessed unprecedented change, recovery, renewal, and ecumenical convergence in the rites of Christian initiation and their interpretation within several churches throughout the world. In response to the mandate of the Constitution on the Sacred Liturgy of the Second Vatican Council (1963–65) that "the rite for the baptism of infants is to be revised, and should be adapted to the circumstance that those to be baptized are, in fact, infants," and that "the roles of parents and godparents, and also their duties, should be brought out more sharply,"[1] the Roman Catholic Church in 1969, under Pope Paul VI, produced a new *Ordo Baptismi Parvulorum* (Rite of Baptism for Children, RBC). The mandate of this same Constitution regarding confirmation, that "the rite of confirmation is to be revised and the intimate connection which this sacrament has with the whole of Christian initiation is to be more lucidly set forth," and should be preceded by "the renewal of baptismal promises,"[2] led in 1971 to a new *Ordo Confirmationis* (Rite of Confirmation). And, in response to the Liturgy Constitution's call for the revision of the rites for adult baptism[3] and the related restoration of the adult catechumenate, "comprising several distinct steps" and "sanctified by sacred rites to be celebrated at successive intervals,"[4] the *Ordo Initiationis Christianae Adultorum* (Rite of Christian Initiation of Adults, RCIA), a rite which actually restored for adults the primitive Western unity and sequence of baptism, confirmation, and first communion, celebrated together at the Easter Vigil, was published in 1972.

Other churches prepared and adopted similar new initiation rites in the years following the publication of the current Roman rites. In 1976 the Episcopal Church, USA (ECUSA), after a series of various

---

[1] *Constitution on the Sacred Liturgy*, 67.

[2] Ibid., 71.

[3] Ibid., 66.

[4] Ibid., 64.

Prayer Book Studies, including rites for trial use, in the early 1970s,[5] produced a new *Book of Common Prayer* (BCP),[6] with rites for baptism and confirmation. This book was approved in 1979. In 1979 they also published a *Book of Occasional Services,*[7] with rites for the adult catechumenate. The Church of England published an *Alternative Service Book 1980,*[8] to be used in conjunction with the official BCP (1662), in which, similar to the Roman RCIA, baptism, confirmation, and first communion were restored for the initiation of adults, and new separate rites of baptism and confirmation were provided for others. Other member churches of the worldwide Anglican communion have been involved with similar projects of liturgical revision.[9]

In close relationship to and dependency on the Episcopal *Prayer Book Studies* and the then-proposed BCP of ECUSA, in 1978 the major North American Lutheran bodies, after a similar series of trial rites,[10] produced the *Lutheran Book of Worship* (LBW),[11] with rites for baptism, and "Affirmation of Baptism: Confirmation." In 1982 they produced the *Occasional Service Book,*[12] including a "Rite of Enrollment of Candidates for Baptism." Although the Lutheran Church–Missouri Synod (LC–MS) was the original catalyst in forming the Inter-Lutheran Commis-

---

[5] See *Holy Baptism with the Laying-on-of-Hands,* Prayer Book Studies 18, *On Baptism and Confirmation* (New York: Church Pension Fund, 1970); and *Holy Baptism: Together with a Form for Confirmation or the Laying on of Hands by the Bishop with the Affirmation of Baptismal Vows, as Authorized by the General Convention of 1973,* Prayer Book Studies 26 (New York: Church Hymnal Corp., 1973).

[6] *The Book of Common Prayer and Administration of the Sacraments and Other Rites and Ceremonies of the Church: Together with the Psalter or Psalms of David: According to the Use of the Episcopal Church* (New York: Church Hymnal Corp., 1979).

[7] *The Book of Occasional Services,* 2d ed. (New York: Church Hymnal Corp., 1988).

[8] *The Alternative Service Book 1980: Services Authorized for Use in the Church of England in Conjunction with the Book of Common Prayer* (Cambridge: Cambridge University Press, 1980).

[9] See the Anglican Church of Canada, *The Book of Alternative Services* (Toronto: Anglican Book Centre, 1985).

[10] See *Holy Baptism,* Contemporary Worship 7 (Minneapolis: Augsburg, 1973); and *Affirmation of the Baptismal Covenant,* Contemporary Worship 8 (Minneapolis: Augsburg, 1975).

[11] Minneapolis: Augsburg, 1978.

[12] Minneapolis: Augsburg, 1982.

sion on Worship which was to produce LBW, and while a number of its congregations do, in fact, use the LBW as their worship book, the LC–MS withdrew from this project near the completion date. Citing the theology of LBW's postbaptismal rites as one problem among many,[13] the LC–MS rejected the LBW altogether and in 1982 produced its own worship book, *Lutheran Worship*,[14] with rites for both baptism and confirmation that differ significantly from those in the LBW. As such, the LBW and *Occasional Service Book* remain the worship books only of the recently formed Evangelical Lutheran Church in America (ELCA) and the Evangelical Lutheran Church in Canada (ELCIC).

At the same time, joint ventures with regard to the restoration and introduction of the adult catechumenate among North American Lutherans and Episcopalians have continued to produce results, with three new resources for the catechumenate, including a collection of ritual texts, published as recently as 1997.[15] And, just as other member churches of the Anglican communion, beyond ECUSA, have produced new initiation rites, so also has liturgical revision of Christian initiation been a concern for Lutherans throughout the world.[16] In fact, so ecumenically widespread has the modern revision of Christian initiation been that even those churches not usually considered among the traditional "liturgical" churches have published new liturgical resources for their own, at least optional, use. In the United States, for example, both Methodists and Presbyterians have also produced new liturgical texts containing similar rites of Christian initiation,[17] including resources for the adult catechumenate.[18]

[13] See Lutheran Church–Missouri Synod, "Report and Recommendations of the Special Hymnal Review Committee" (December 1977) 27.

[14] St. Louis: Concordia Publishing House, 1982.

[15] See below, 332–3.

[16] On this see M. Johnson, "The Shape of Christian Initiation in the Lutheran Churches: Liturgical Texts and Future Directions," *Studia Liturgica* 27:1 (1997) 33–60.

[17] *The United Methodist Hymnal* (Nashville: United Methodist Pub. House, 1990) 32–54; and *Book of Common Worship* (Philadelphia: n.p., 1993) 403–88. See also Laurence Stookey, *Baptism: Christ's Act in the Church* (Nashville: Abingdon Press, 1982); and K. Watkins, "Baptism and Christian Identity: A Presbyterian Approach," *Worship* 60 (1986) 55–63.

[18] See for the United Methodist Church, Daniel Benedict, *Come to the Waters: Baptism and Our Ministry of Welcoming Seekers and Making Disciples* (Nashville: Discipleship Resources, 1996).

So common are the rites of Christian initiation in several churches today that the Faith and Order Commission of the World Council of Churches, in its significant 1982 document Baptism, Eucharist, Ministry, could point to a widespread contemporary convergence both in baptismal theology and the overall shape of Christian initiation rites. That shape, easily recognizable from the initiation rites in the modern liturgical books of several churches, contains the following agreed upon structural elements:

"the proclamation of the scriptures referring to baptism; an invocation of the Holy Spirit; a renunciation of evil; a profession of faith in Christ and the Holy Trinity; the use of water; a declaration that the persons baptized have acquired a new identity as sons and daughters of God, and as members of the Church, called to be witnesses of the Gospel. Some churches consider that Christian initiation is not complete without the sealing of the baptized with the gift of the Holy Spirit and participation in holy communion."[19]

Such convergence and commonality in the theology and rites of Christian initiation across ecclesial boundaries in the second half of the twentieth century are due to a number of factors. The "return to the sources" of Scripture and early Christian tradition brought about initially, as we have seen, by the Protestant and Catholic Reformations of the sixteenth century was given further impetus by the rise of the historical-critical reading of biblical and other texts in the eighteenth-century Enlightenment, the period of Romanticism and restoration mentality of the nineteenth century, and not least by the development of patristic scholarship at the University of Tübingen and elsewhere. Such a patristic focus brought with it the increasing desire to move behind medieval scholasticism and a narrow institutional understanding of the Church toward the recovery of a richer sacramental world view, an understanding of the Church corporately as the Body of Christ and People of God, and the rediscovery of the theology and spirituality of the Christian East by the West. So also the various and related "movements" taking shape throughout the Church (e.g., the Anglo-Catholic Oxford Movement in England; the beginnings of the Benedictine-based Liturgical Movement in the

---

[19] Baptism, Eucharist, Ministry (Geneva: World Council of Churches, 1982) par. 20.

monasteries of Germany, France, and Belgium; the confessional revival among Lutherans in North America; and the Mercersburg Movement among some of the American Reformed churches), the continued discovery of long-lost early Christian liturgical texts (e.g., the *Didache* and the *Apostolic Tradition*), and, not least, the devastating European experience of two world wars in the first half of the twentieth century all contributed to setting the stage for renewed attention to the liturgy and its role in Christian formation. In a recent article, Paul Bradshaw summarizes further the various causes for what he calls the "homogeneity" of Christian worship throughout the churches today. He writes that:

"This twentieth-century phenomenon stemmed from a number of different causes. The rise of modern liturgical scholarship was, of course, a major factor, particularly in its earlier—primarily historical—phase, which revealed the changing past that existed behind current forms of public worship. This not only demonstrated how very different were the liturgical practices of all churches today from those of the first few centuries of Christians, but also appeared to point towards a unified way of worship among those early Christians that contrasted sharply with the diverse traditions of contemporary denominations. . . . Historical scholarship both gave birth to, and in turn was stimulated by the Liturgical Movement, which sought to bring renewal to Christian worship in large measure by a return to what was thought to be the pattern of worship in the early Church. But the movement also provided a common theology of worship to undergird the changes and supply a rationale for them. . . . One other great movement of the twentieth century—ecumenism—must be counted as both cause and effect of the phenomenon that we are considering. The desire to overcome the barriers that had for centuries divided one denomination from another inevitably led to an examination of the differences in liturgical customs that existed between the churches, and to the wish not to do separately what we could do together in the area of liturgical revision. . . . Nor must we forget that—just as in the fourth century—the causes of liturgical reform were not located solely within the churches. At least in the developed nations of the western world (which was where the agenda for official liturgical revision was primarily determined), the different denominations were strongly influenced by the same socio-cultural factors around them. They were subject to the same challenges and pressures from the post-Christian society that was beginning to emerge from the 1960s onwards, and so it is hardly surprising that from their embattled position they would look to one another for guidance or that they tended to come up with similar solutions to their common problems."[20]

There is no question but that the dominant and most ecumenically influential of the modern reforms of the rites of Christian initiation have been those of the Roman Catholic Church, especially the RCIA. Understood by many as the most mature fruit of all the liturgical reforms mandated by the Second Vatican Council, it is this Roman Catholic restoration of the adult catechumenate and especially the recovery of the integral and unitive sequence and sacramental connection of baptism, confirmation, and first communion in the RCIA which clearly underlie all of the modern liturgical revisions of Christian initiation in other churches. Since this is the case, this chapter provides a descriptive overview of the current Roman Catholic rites and *some* of the rites in other modern churches within, primarily, a North American context, that is, the Episcopal and Lutheran churches, whose current liturgical books provide the closest parallels to the Roman Catholic rites and whose rites have been decidedly influential throughout the rest of North American Protestantism. Indeed, it is primarily the 1979 BCP that provides the best window for viewing the liturgical reforms of North American Protestantism in general. Thus, without intending to minimize the importance of modern liturgical development within other Protestant traditions or to gloss over any distinctive elements, the fact remains that if one knows the current Episcopal and Lutheran initiation rites one has at hand an appropriate model for studying other Protestant rites as well. Such is one of the gifts of ecumenism today.

After describing the current rites of Christian initiation and their development in these churches, the final section of the chapter is con-

---

[20] Paul Bradshaw, "The Homogenization of Christian Liturgy—Ancient and Modern: Presidential Address," *Studia Liturgica* 26 (1996) 6–8. On the ecumenical liturgical movement see also John R. K. Fenwick and Bryan Spinks, *Worship in Transition: Highlights of the Liturgical Movement: The Liturgical Movement in the Twentieth Century* (New York: Continuum, 1995); and James White, *Christian Worship in North America, A Retrospective: 1955–1995* (Collegeville: The Liturgical Press, 1997).

cerned with various theological questions and problems of interpretation in these rites. For, as we shall see, in spite of the remarkable achievement in liturgical celebration that these new rites represent, several theological issues remain either unresolved or in need of further revision and clarification.

CHRISTIAN INITIATION
IN CONTEMPORARY ROMAN CATHOLICISM

At the risk of drastic oversimplification, it can be said generally that from the publication and promulgation of the Tridentine liturgical books in the sixteenth and seventeenth centuries to those brought about by the Second Vatican Council in the late 1960s and early 1970s, very little actually happened to the shape, liturgical texts, structure, or theological interpretation of the rites of Christian initiation within the Roman Catholic Church. The Tridentine liturgical books and their rubrics were followed closely and, hence, no real changes in the rites could be made. There were, however, a number of changes in pastoral practice and theology during these years which were to have long-lasting effects both on the process of Christian initiation and its perception.

Changes in Pastoral Practice and Theology
Leading to the Reforms of Vatican II

French liturgical scholar Robert Cabié notes that, following the post-Tridentine focus on religious education, when the catechetical instruction of children was given an organized form in the seventeenth century, there developed a tendency to correlate years of catechetical instruction with the reception of the initiation sacraments.[21] Thus, an educational model corresponding to development and chronological age, rather than a sacramental model of Christian formation, was increasingly adopted. This catechetical teaching began at about the age of seven and was correlated, it seems, with the reception of confirmation. Meanwhile, first communion itself, which was prepared for by futher catechesis and concluded this cycle of Christian instruction, was received at the age of eleven or twelve. It became an especially festive day in local parishes, even including a

---

[21] R. Cabié, "Christian Initiation," *The Church at Prayer,* ed. A. G. Martimort et al., vol. 3, *The Sacraments* (Collegeville: The Liturgical Press, 1988) 75ff.

profession of faith on the part of the candidates, and was celebrated with a great degree of solemnity. Although such a process theoretically preserved the sacramental sequence of baptism, confirmation, and first communion, even if separated by a number of intervening years, this process itself was to be reversed, especially in France during the eighteenth century, with the result that first communion would now normally be received *before* confirmation. Since catechesis itself was oriented more toward the reception of first communion than to confirmation, the *Instructions of the Ritual of Toulon* in 1748, for example, stated that: "in order to be sure that children presented for confirmation in this diocese are adequately instructed, it has been decided that they are to be confirmed only *after* having received their first communion."[22]

While Cabié himself suggests that this custom was to become widespread only throughout France, especially after the French Revolution, largely unstudied evidence for similar diocesan legislation also exists for the same time period in Austria, Belgium, and eastern Europe.[23] So problematic and obviously common was this practice in the minds of the Roman authorities that a preparatory document, *De Administratione Sacramentorum*, prepared for discussion at the First Vatican Council (1870), stated: "we absolutely want to correct the custom that is opposite to the perpetual practice of the Church, but that is practiced here and there. It concerns the practice that follows an inverse order by administering confirmation to those who have previously been admitted to communion."[24] Even after 1910 when Pope Pius X issued his now famous *Quam singulari*, in which he underscored, reinforced, and so "restored" the reception of first communion to the traditional canonical age of the "years of discretion," that is, age seven,[25] this pastoral situation did not really change. If anything, the postponement of confirmation until *after* first

[22] Ibid., 76; emphasis added.
[23] On this see R. Levet, "L'age de la confirmation dans la législation des diocéses de France depuis le Concile de Trente," *La Maison-Dieu* 54 (1958) 142.
[24] As cited by H. Vinck, "Sur l'age de la confirmation: Un projet de décret au Concile Vatican I," *La Maison-Dieu* 132 (1977) 137. Unfortunately, this document apparently was never discussed at the council itself.
[25] *Acta Apostolicae Sedis* 1 (Vatican City: Typis Polyglottis Vaticanis, 1910) 625ff.

communion (and first confession) became even more pronounced. While Pius did not deal with confirmation explicitly in *Quam singulari* (indeed, given the consistent Roman tradition that it was also to be conferred at the age of seven, he did not have to!), some dioceses did, in fact, reverse their previous practice and lower the age for confirmation to correspond more closely to his decree. But several others merely followed the letter of the law by legislating first communion at age seven and instituting what came to be known as "first *solemn* communion" at age eleven or twelve, followed by confirmation either shortly thereafter or by an interval of some years.[26] Such a practice was quite common also within some dioceses of the United States throughout the early twentieth century.

Official Roman legislation against such pastoral practices, however, has been consistent through the years. The 1917 Code of Canon Law, for example, stated clearly that:

"Although the administration of the sacrament of confirmation should preferably be postponed in the Latin Church until about the seventh year of age, nevertheless it can be conferred *before* that age if the infant is in danger of death or if its administration seems to the minister justified for good and serious reasons."[27]

Similarly, in 1932, the Sacred Congregation for the Sacraments said that is was more in conformity with the nature of the sacrament of confirmation that children should *not* come to first communion until they had received confirmation. And, Gerard Austin notes as late as 1952, "the Commission for Interpreting the Code of Canon Law *denied* to bishops the power to defer confirmation until children were ten years old."[28]

As has often been the case with confirmation throughout history, such official legislation was again, often for "pastoral reasons," largely ignored. Consequently, the Roman Catholic pastoral practice of confirmation rapidly became, as it was, ironically, in much of Protestantism as well, a rite of maturity and adulthood, a sacrament which tended to overshadow baptism in importance and become

---

[26] On this see Levet, "L'age de la confirmation," 135.

[27] Gerard Austin, *Anointing with the Spirit: The Rite of Confirmation: The Use of Oil and Chrism* (New York: Pueblo, 1985) 52; emphasis added.

[28] Ibid., 52; emphasis added.

connected to the assumption of adult responsibilities in church and society on the part of adolescents. Aidan Kavanagh summarizes the results of such pastoral practice throughout the Roman Catholic Church, noting that:

"confirmation in adolescence or early adulthood as the sacrament peculiar to one's mature assumption of public responsibilities in Church and society had the effect of reenforcing the presumption that baptism was the sacrament peculiar to birth and infancy. In that position, baptism was the wholly necessary exorcism of original sin and the occasion of the infant's being lent sufficient faith by the Church, through the good offices of godparents and parents, to see it through to the critical stage when, as an individual on the verge of 'maturity,' that faith could be appropriated by the former infant in his or her own right—namely, in confirmation. Liturgical practice validated this perception on the peoples' part. Baptism was done by a simple priest or even layperson as soon after birth as feasible, in the parish church or hospital, privately and apart from regular community worship with only family and a few friends present. Confirmation, however, was a high point of the parish year, presided over by the bishop at a major event of public worship and prepared for weeks or months in advance by intensive instruction of the recipients. Confirmation could not but seem at least on a par with baptism. In such a context, further ideological emphasis on confirmation as the sacrament of Christian maturity *par excellence* made it a baptismal surrogate in practice if not in theory."[29]

Given this common pastoral practice, emphasis, and perception, along with traditional Roman legislation, it is no wonder that among the reforms desired in the Constitution on the Sacred Liturgy of Vatican II was that "the rite of confirmation is to be revised and the intimate connection which this sacrament has with the whole of Christian initiation is to be more lucidly set forth."

Another development in pastoral practice which contributed to the modern call for liturgical reform was the attempt made toward the recovery and restoration of the adult catechumenate. Jesuit theologian Donald Gelpi summarizes the history of this development, saying:

[29] Aidan Kavanagh, *The Shape of Baptism: The Rite of Christian Initiation* (New York: Pueblo, 1978) 86.

"The explosion of missionary activity in the Church during the six-teenth century refocused pastoral attention on the need for adequate adult preparation prior to sacramental initiation. In 1534 Augustin-ian missionaries to Latin America petitioned to restrict the celebra-tion to only four times a year: on Easter, Pentecost, the feast of St. Augustine [August 28], and the Epiphany. In 1538 a Latin American bishops' synod required that adult converts undergo prior to bap-tism a forty-day catechumenate that included fasting, instruction, and the scrutiny and exorcism of candidates. In practice, such legis-lation seems to have had little pastoral impact. . . . In the early days of missionary activity in Asia and Africa, little was required of Christian neophytes prior to baptism. In 1552, however, St. Ignatius of Loyola required his Jesuit missionaries in India to establish houses in which candidates for baptism would be gathered for three months of preparation prior to initiation. The Indian bishops eventu-ally endorsed his recommendation. . . . The seventeenth century saw the beginning of more serious pastoral efforts to retrieve the catechumenate. Missionary bishops in Asia instituted a catechetical preparation that unfortunately lacked a liturgical dimension and failed to advance in clearly defined stages. . . . From the eighteenth century on, the Holy Ghost missionaries in Africa intensified their efforts to ensure a thorough program of catechesis prior to adult baptism. Largely through the efforts of Cardinal Lavigerie, the African Church successfully established a catechumenate that not only advanced in stages but also lasted long enough to ensure the likelihood of perseverance in the faith. The African catechumenate required a postulancy of two years, a two year catechumenate, and a prebaptismal retreat."[30]

Not to be overlooked here is the fact that in 1951 Pope Pius XII re-stored the Easter Vigil to Holy Saturday night, a vigil which since the time of Pope Pius V in 1566 had actually migrated to Holy Saturday morning. Although the restoration of this vigil in the early 1950s did not yet include the celebration of the rites of Christian initiation as part of its overall official structure and shape, it did include a re-newal of baptismal vows in the context of the traditional Easter vigil

[30] Donald Gelpi, *Committed Worship: A Sacramental Theology for Converting Christians*, vol. 1, *Adult Conversion and Initiation* (Collegeville: The Liturgical Press, 1993) 188–9.

readings and, hence, began to restore a "paschal" or Easter, rather than "original sin," focus for the celebration of baptism. Aidan Kavanagh notes that "this event, a highwater mark of the modern liturgical movement . . . brought back to the attention of theologians and injected forcibly into the popular consciousness the pre-Augustinian Roman liturgical formulas touching baptism in its paschal context."[31] In the Latin Quarter of Paris in 1957, Kavanagh notes further, experiments with an adult catechumenate during Lent, where the focus of baptismal catechesis was the theme of water in creation, the flood, and the crossing of the Red Sea, included also baptism by immersion at the Easter vigil, followed immediately by confirmation and first communion.[32]

Similarly, in 1962, the Congregation of Rites, in large part responding to the success of the African catechumenate, decreed that adult baptism was to be carried out in stages.[33] To accomplish this the 1962 *Collectio Rituum* merely divided the introductory catechetical portions of the rite for baptism into seven stages corresponding to the seven scrutinies of *Ordo Romanus XI*.[34] Although the rites and prayers in this *Collectio Rituum* were not modified and, hence, were rather repetitive, this shift also helped to open the door for the renewal and restoration of the adult catechumenate at Vatican II.

Rooted firmly in modern missionary contexts and other experiments for the full Christian initiation of adults through baptism, confirmation, and first communion, therefore, the RCIA itself is concerned with and was designed for the preparation and catechetical formation of *unbaptized* adults. These origins and explicit intent of the RCIA ought not be forgotten.

A third development in modern Roman Catholicism that must be noted before moving into a description of the current rites themselves is what some have called today a "Copernican Revolution" in theology, a revolution both in sacramental theology and ecclesiology which led to, and in turn was fostered by, the Second Vatican Council. Concerning these changes, Mark Searle wrote in 1987:

[31] Kavanagh, *Shape*, 91.

[32] Ibid., 95.

[33] See Gelpi, *Adult Conversion and Initiation*, 189.

[34] See *The 1964 English Ritual: Collectio Rituum* (Collegeville: The Liturgical Press, 1964) 44–183.

"During the past twenty or thirty years sacramental theology has undergone an enormous transformation. Undoubtedly the leading indicator if not the cause of this transformation is the abandonment of the questions and vocabulary of Scholasticism in favor of more existentialist and personalist approaches to understanding what sacraments are and how they function in the Christian life. What began as a recovery of the ecclesial dimension of the sacraments quickly led to further shifts: from speaking of sacraments as 'means of grace' to speaking of them as encounters with Christ himself; from thinking of them primarily as acts of God to thinking of them mainly as celebrations of the faith community; from seeing sacraments as momentary incursions from another world to seeing them as manifestations of the graced character of all human life; from interpreting them as remedies for sin and weakness to seeing them as promoting growth in Christ."[35]

Central to this transformation, both prior to and as a result of Vatican II, has been a renewed emphasis on Christ as the "primordial," or primary and fundamental, "Sacrament" of God and the Church itself as the "sacrament" of Christ. J. D. Crichton summarizes this emphasis, saying:

"The ultimate subject of the liturgical celebration . . . is . . . Christ who acts in and through his Church. Obviously his action is invisible, but the people of God, his body, is a visible and structured community and over the whole range of its liturgical action, which . . . consists of both word and sacrament, manifests Christ's presence, shows forth the nature of his activity, which is redemptive, and by his power makes his redeeming work effectual and available to men and women today. It is for these reasons that the Church is called the 'sacrament of Christ.' Like him it is both visible and invisible, and its sole *raison d'être* is to mediate his saving love to humankind. . . . From Christ, the sacrament of the Father and of his saving purpose, to the Church, which is the sacrament of Christ, and then to the liturgy, which exists to manifest and convey the redeeming love of God, the line is clear. The liturgy then is essentially and by its nature sacramental. . . . It addresses a word to us but it *embodies* this word in actions, gestures and symbols; . . . [and] the gesture or thing

---

[35] Mark Searle, "Infant Baptism Reconsidered," LWSS, 365.

(water, bread, wine) forces us to attend to the word, enables us to grasp its import and to appropriate its content."[36]

Such a renewed emphasis in sacramental theology and ecclesiology within Roman Catholicism led to even greater attention to liturgical action, gesture, and symbol as the liturgical self-expression and self-actualization of the sacramental nature and identity of the Church itself. While medieval scholastic sacramental theology had always maintained that "sacraments cause grace by signifying *(significando causant),*" theological emphasis had customarily been placed on the sacramental "cause" and "effects" of grace for and in the recipient rather than on the signifying dimension of the sacramental signs themselves within the liturgical celebration of the Church. With the recovery of the notion of Christ as the "primordial sacrament" of God and the Church as the "sacrament of Christ," however, the door was also opened to renewed attention to this phenomenon as well. Not surprisingly, then, with specific regard to the rites of Christian initiation, special attention to patristic theology and rite, especially as both were known from the recovery of the prebaptismal and mystagogical catecheses of the great "mystagogues" of the fourth and fifth centuries, where the various elements associated with the prebaptismal catechumenate and the meaning of the different ritual acts and gestures within the rites of Christian initiation themselves provided the subjects for detailed theological commentary and exposition, was highly influential in the modern liturgical revision of these rites.[37] The shape and contents of the modern RCIA, in fact, are so indebted to this so-called "Golden Age" of the great eastern and western mystagogues that a frequent complaint of graduate students in courses on Christian initiation throughout the 1970s and 1980s was that such courses seldom, if ever, proceeded beyond the fourth and fifth centuries. Indeed, it is no coincidence that the second edition of E. Yarnold's wonderful collection of fourth- and fifth-century cate-

---

[36] J. D. Crichton, "A Theology of Worship," *The Study of Liturgy,* rev. ed., ed. Chelsyn Jones et al. (New York/London 1992) 23. A very helpful and readable summary of contemporary Roman Catholic sacramental theology appears in Adolf Adam, *Foundations of Liturgy: An Introduction to Its History and Practice* (Collegeville: The Liturgical Press, 1992) 103–13.

[37] See Jean Daniélou's classic study, *The Bible and the Liturgy* (Notre Dame, Ind.: University of Notre Dame Press, 1956) 1–126.

chetical and mystagogical homilies, the *Awe-Inspiring Rites of Initiation*, is subtitled: *The Origins of the R.C.I.A.*

This contemporary Roman Catholic transformation of sacramental theology and ecclesiology, long associated with names like Henri du Lubac, Yves Congar, Otto Semmelroth, Odo Casel, Edward Schillebeeckx, and Karl Rahner, many of whom were themselves *periti* ("theological experts" or "consultants") at Vatican II, has been ecumenically fruitful as well. If, for example, the determination of the concrete form and number of the sacraments themselves is seen increasingly in relationship to the self-expression and celebration of the Church as it seeks to be faithful to the saving will of God in Christ within changing historical periods and circumstances, then the relationship of all the "sacraments" to an explicit dominical word becomes less of a theological issue. That is, together with the primary biblical-dominical sacraments of baptism and Eucharist, the existence of other "sacraments" in the Church can be attributed to the sacramental nature of the Church itself as it "addresses itself to the whole human being, whom it seeks to draw into union with God by means that are consonant with human nature." In other words, it is the Church itself as the sacrament of Christ in history that has developed various sacraments and rites for proclaiming the gospel of Christ to human beings as through word, gesture, and ritual act it celebrates the ongoing presence of Christ. As such, while contemporary Protestant theology has yet to articulate a clear and precise ecclesiology, some Protestant sacramental theologians have drawn upon contemporary Roman Catholic insights in such a way that, along with baptism and Eucharist, the other traditional "Roman Catholic" sacraments are often included either as "apostolic" or "ecclesial" sacraments in their overall approaches.[38] Similarly, if the sacraments are increasingly understood as grace-filled "encounters"

---

[38] See James White, *Sacraments as God's Self Giving: Sacramental Practice and Faith* (Nashville: Abingdon Press, 1983); C. Braaten, *Visible Words* (Philadelphia: n.p., 1978); and Gordon Lathrop, *Holy Things: A Liturgical Theology* (Minneapolis: Fortress Press, 1993), where Protestant sacramental theology or the number of the sacraments are not limited to baptism and Eucharist alone. Lutheran theologian Paul Tillich, in fact, called the loss of an overall "sacramental principle" within theology "the Protestant pitfall," and called for the recovery of this in christology, ecclesiology, and theology in general. See M. Johnson, "The Place of Sacraments in the Theology of Paul Tillich," *Worship* 63:1 (1989) 17–30. At the time of this writing it is interesting to note that both

with Christ, which manifest the "graced character of all human life" and are designed to "promote growth in Christ," then an overly narrow, almost magical understanding of the scholastic phrase *"ex opere operato,"* coined originally to safeguard the objective role of Christ in the sacraments against a Donatist approach, is avoided in favor of underscoring the necessity of active faith in this "encounter" both on the part of the celebrating community and the individual "recipient." And, if the sacraments themselves are not abstracted theologically from the actual liturgical doing of them in the liturgical assembly, then attention to the overall shape, contents, and structure of the rites, and the "significance" of such words, gestures, actions, and signs in their liturgical performance, will be of paramount importance. Here as well, the contemporary Roman Catholic patristic-based recovery of the importance of sacramental signs as signs has been influential in the liturgical revision of Christian initiation rites among modern Protestants. Ritual actions, ceremonies, and gestures, especially elements often omitted from the rites of the Reformers in the sixteenth century as "superstitious human ceremonies," and contrary or even "repugnant" to the Word of God, in favor of the "essentials" of water and trinitarian formula, have been restored today as parts of richer and more full liturgical-sacramental rites.

While the Copernican Revolution in sacramental theology today has been primarily a Roman Catholic phenomenon, the influence of this revolution has gone far beyond the confines of the contemporary Roman Catholic Church. Indeed, there is a sense in which this contemporary recovery is highly consistent with and brings to expression one of the early sacramental insights of Martin Luther himself, one who certainly knew the available writings of the Fathers well. After all, it was Luther, in his polemical 1520 *Babylonian Captivity of the Church,* in language similar to that of modern Roman Catholic theologians, who said that "if I were to speak according to the usage of the Scriptures, I should have only one single sacrament [Christ, 1 Tim 3:16], but with three sacramental signs, of which I shall treat more fully at the proper time."[39] Unfortunately, while neither Luther

---

Braaten and Lathrop are preparing theological studies of ecclesiology, *Holy Mother Church* and *Holy People* respectively, that will appear from Augsburg-Fortress Press in 1998 or 1999.

[39] LW 36, 18.

nor his theological heirs ever found the "proper time" to treat this insight "more fully," it is precisely the theological recovery of this "one single sacrament," Christ himself, that has shaped and continues to shape modern sacramental theology in Roman Catholicism and, at least through the wide influence of the Roman Catholic liturgical rites, across ecclesial lines.

The Roman Catholic Rite of Christian Initiation of Adults

The RCIA was published in Latin in 1972 and first translated into an interim English edition in 1974. With the final approved English version appearing in 1985, it was then mandated for regular use in the dioceses of the United States in 1988. This rite, actually a collection of liturgical rites, directs that the Christian initiation of adults is to be carried out in accord with a ritual process involving four distinct periods of time with three primary liturgical "steps" correlated closely with each of these periods. These periods and liturgical steps are:

Period of Evangelization and Precatechumenate;

First Step: Acceptance into the Order of Catechumens;

Period of the Catechumenate;

Second Step: Election or Enrollment of Names;

Period of Purification and Enlightenment;

Third Step: Celebration of the Sacraments of Initiation; and

Period of Postbaptismal Catechesis or Mystagogy.[40]

Each of these periods and steps calls for comment.

The preparatory period of evangelization and precatechumenate has no particular structure or fixed length. Rather, this is merely the time in which inquirers are evangelized by the Christian community in a variety of different ways, given a basic introduction to Christian teaching, and invited to embrace a Christian manner of living "so

---

[40] *The Rites of the Catholic Church as Revised by the Second Vatican Ecumenical Council* (hereafter, *Rites*), vol. 1 (Collegeville: The Liturgical Press, 1990) 48–9. To avoid unnecessary notes, the paragraph numbers of the particular rites in question will be indicated in parentheses throughout the main body of the text.

that the genuine will to follow Christ and seek baptism may mature"
(no. 37). When those responsible for catechumenal formation in the
local community—clergy, sponsors, catechists, and others—have determined that adult inquirers have demonstrated the beginnings of
faith, an initial conversion, and a commitment to follow the way of
Christ in the Church, they are accepted into the Order of Catechumens by means of the first liturgical step in this process. This rite of
acceptance, which takes place publicly in the liturgical assembly, contains several traditional and optional ceremonies: the acceptance of
the Gospel; the signing(s) of the catechumens with the cross (at least
the forehead but possibly all of the senses); the presentation of a Bible
and a cross; and, depending upon locale and cultural context, exorcism with exsufflation (breathing); the giving of a new name; and
even, if appropriate, the renunciation of false worship on the part of
the catechumens.[41] Although these newly accepted catechumens are
not yet fully initiated sacramentally into the Church they are,
nonetheless, now reckoned as "joined to the Church" and as "part of
the household of Christ."

"From this time on the Church embraces the catechumens as its own
with a mother's love and concern. Joined to the Church, the catechumens are now part of the household of Christ, since the Church nour-
ishes them with the word of God and sustains them by means of
liturgical celebrations. The catechumens should be eager, then, to
take part in celebrations of the word of God and to receive blessings
and other sacramentals. When two catechumens marry or when a
catechumen marries an unbaptized person, the appropriate rite is to
be used. One who dies during the catechumenate receives a Christian
burial" (no. 47).

While the ensuing period of the catechumenate may last for several
years, the National Statutes for the Catechumenate, approved by the
American Catholic Bishops for the dioceses of the United States in
1986, require a minimum of "one year of formation, instruction, and
probation" (no. 6). During this period, through ongoing instruction,
participation in the Liturgy of the Word at the Sunday Eucharistic
Liturgy, and involvement with other Christians in the life and mission of the Church, catechumens are led progressively on a spiritual

[41] Ibid., 54–69.

journey toward greater conversion, deeper faith, and commitment to Christ and the Church. While in the years since the Council of Trent and its *Catechism* catechesis had often been quite doctrinal or cerebral in nature, the manner of catechesis envisioned throughout this process

"should be of a kind that while presenting Catholic teaching in its entirety also enlightens faith, directs the heart toward God, fosters participation in the liturgy, inspires apostolic activity, and nurtures a life completely in accord with the spirit of Christ" (RCIA, no. 78).

That is, the catechumenate as envisioned and structured in the RCIA is not a series of classes in Christian doctrine. Without ignoring doctrine or the conversion of the intellect, it is a kind of apprenticeship or ongoing formation in becoming a disciple of Christ.

Several liturgical rites are provided in the RCIA for use during this period of the catechumenate: "first, celebrations held specially for the catechumens; second, participation in the liturgy of the word at Sunday Mass; third, celebrations held in connection with catechetical instruction" (no. 81).[42] In addition, various prayers, exorcisms, anointings with the oil of catechumens, and blessings are also included. In accord with early Christian tradition, catechumens are regularly and solemnly dismissed with special prayers and blessings from the Sunday liturgical assembly after the homily and before the general intercessions are offered. While such may strike moderns as a bit of liturgical-historical romanticism, especially given the fact that any person today—believer and nonbeliever alike—is usually welcome to attend any and every liturgy of the Church from beginning to end, the purpose of this solemn dismissal for ongoing instruction and preparation is to underscore in a dramatic manner the fact that catechumens themselves are not yet fully initiated into the Church and its eucharistic communion through baptism.

At the end of this period, and again at the discretion of all involved with the catechumenal process, including the individual catechumens themselves, the second liturgical step, the rite of election or enrollment of names, takes place. In this rite, normally taking place on the First Sunday in Lent in the context of a special Liturgy of the Eucharist held at the local diocesan cathedral and presided over by

---

[42] On the various rites themselves see ibid., 73–93.

the bishop as the chief pastor of the local diocese, the catechumens are now solemnly "elected" by the Church for the sacraments of initiation and write their names in a "book of the elect."[43] No longer catechumens, those elected and enrolled for Christian initiation are now known as the elect, *competentes* (those who "co-petition" for initiation), or *illuminandi* (those to be enlightened by baptism).[44] As such, this second liturgical step concludes the period of the catechumenate and inaugurates the third period of the RCIA, the period of purification and enlightenment, a period coinciding with the season of Lent that will lead ultimately to the celebration of Christian initiation itself at the Easter vigil.

Of particular note in this lenten period of purification and enlightenment, this time understood by the RCIA to be one of "more intense spiritual preparation, . . . interior reflection, . . . [purification of] the minds and hearts of the elect, . . . [and enlightenment] of the minds and hearts of the elect with a deeper knowledge of Christ the Savior" (nos. 138–9), are the various liturgical rites celebrated throughout this time of final preparation. As in the Old Gelasian Sacramentary, three public "scrutinies" are celebrated, one each on the Third, Fourth, and Fifth Sundays in Lent. These scrutinies, consisting of intercessions, prayers of exorcism, and dismissals from the liturgical assembly, "are meant to uncover, then heal all that is weak, defective or sinful in the hearts of the elect; to bring out, then strengthen all that is upright, strong, and good" (no. 141).[45] Similarly, at special celebrations held within the third and fifth weeks of Lent, the elect are solemnly presented *(traditio)* with either the Nicene or Apostles' Creed (no. 148) and the Our Father (no. 149), and are expected to be able to recite them back *(redditio)* at a later appropriate time, with the recitation of the Creed as part of the prebaptismal rites and the recitation of the Our Father within the context of the Easter Vigil Eucharist.

At the conclusion of this period, the third liturgical step, the celebration of the sacraments of initiation, takes place normally at the Easter Vigil on Holy Saturday night, with several of the prebaptismal preparatory rites such as the recitation *(redditio)* of the Creed, and the

---

[43] See ibid., 94ff.

[44] Ibid., par. 124, 95–6.

[45] For the ritual texts of these scrutinies see ibid., 112–37.

effeta or *apertio* on the ears and mouths of the elect, assigned to a special celebration on Holy Saturday morning (nos. 185–92). After the Liturgy of the Word and homily at the Easter Vigil the rites of Christian initiation are celebrated in the following manner:

Celebration of Baptism

Presentation of the Candidates for Baptism

Invitation to Prayer

Litany of the Saints

Blessing of the Water

Profession of Faith (in question and answer form)

1. Renunciation of Sin

2. Profession of Faith

Baptism (with the trinitarian formula)

Explanatory Rites

1. Anointing after Baptism [omitted if confirmation is to follow immediately]

2. Clothing with a Baptismal Garment

3. Presentation of a Lighted Candle

Celebration of Confirmation

Invitation

Laying on of Hands

Anointing with Chrism

Liturgy of the Eucharist

Several elements in this rite are noteworthy. The preferred mode for the conferral of baptism itself, for example, is clearly indicated as being that of a three-fold immersion (i.e., submersion), either of the whole body or head of each candidate, as the baptismal formula, "N., I baptize you in the name of the Father, and of the Son, and of the Holy Spirit," is recited (no. 226). Indeed, along these lines there is no question but that the RCIA itself, as a product of the Roman Catholic recovery of the theological and symbolic importance of rich and full sacramental signs, has contributed greatly to the contemporary liturgical architectural renovation of baptismal fonts and pools throughout much of modern Christianity in general.[46]

Theoretically, baptism itself is followed immediately by three rites called "explanatory rites," that is, rites intended to "explain" further the baptism just received: an anointing with chrism on the crown of the head of the neophyte; the clothing of the neophyte in a baptismal garment by the godparents (sponsors); and the lighting of a baptismal candle from the Easter candle and its presentation to the neophyte by the godparents. The prayer preceding the anointing is particularly rich in its symbolic associations. It reads:

"The God of power and Father of our Lord Jesus Christ has freed you from sin and brought you to new life through water and the Holy Spirit. He now anoints you with the chrism of salvation, so that, united with his people, you may remain for ever a member of Christ who is Priest, Prophet, and King" (no. 228).

The first part of this prayer, through the words "chrism of salvation," is recognizable as the standard and classic postbaptismal anointing prayer of Western Christianity since the time of Ambrose of Milan. The second and concluding part is a new formulation which expresses the very identity of the baptized in their assimilation to Christ, the classic biblical associations of the anointing of priests, prophets, and kings in ancient Israel, and the christological and ecclesiological implications of these associations. This rich prayer and anointing, however, are regularly omitted from the rite when, as is normally the case, confirmation is also to be conferred on newly baptized adults during the Easter Vigil. In that case, the following rite replaces this traditional postbaptismal anointing:

[46] For examples of several ancient and contemporary baptismal fonts, cf. Regina Kuehn, *A Place for Baptism* (Chicago: Liturgy Training Publications, 1992).

Celebration of Confirmation[47]

232. If the bishop has conferred baptism, he should now also confer confirmation. If the bishop is not present, the priest who conferred baptism is authorized to confirm. . . .

Invitation

233. The celebrant first speaks briefly to the newly baptized in these or similar words:

My dear newly baptized, born again in Christ by baptism, you have become members of Christ and of his priestly people. Now you are to share in the outpouring of the Holy Spirit among us, the Spirit sent by the Lord upon his apostles at Pentecost and given by them and their successors to the baptized.

The promised strength of the Holy Spirit, which you are to receive, will make you more like Christ and help you to witness to his suffering, death, and resurrection. It will strengthen you to be active members of the Church and to build up the Body of Christ in faith and love.

[The priests who will be associated with the celebrant as ministers of the sacrament now stand next to him.]

With hands joined, the celebrant next addresses the people:

My dear friends, let us pray to God our Father, that he will pour out the Holy Spirit on these newly baptized to strengthen them with his gifts and anoint them to be more like Christ, the Son of God.

All pray briefly in silence.

Laying on of Hands

234. The celebrant holds his hands outstretched over the entire group of those to be confirmed and says the following prayer.

[In silence the priests associated as ministers of the sacrament also hold their hands outstretched over the candidates.]

---

[47] *Rites*, vol. 1, 162–4.

All-powerful God, Father of our Lord Jesus Christ, by water and the Holy Spirit you freed your sons and daughters from sin and gave them new life.

Send your Holy Spirit upon them to be their helper and guide.

Give them the spirit of wisdom and understanding, the spirit of right judgment and courage, the spirit of knowledge and reverence. Fill them with the spirit of wonder and awe in your presence.

We ask this through Christ our Lord.

R. Amen.

Anointing with Chrism

235. A minister brings the chrism to the celebrant. . . .

Each candidate, with godparent or godparents, goes to the celebrant (or to an associated minister of the sacrament); or, if circumstances require, the celebrant (associated ministers) may go to the candidates.

Either or both godparents place the right hand on the shoulder of the candidate and either a godparent or the candidate gives the candidate's name to the minister of the sacrament. During the conferral of the sacrament a suitable song may be sung.

The minister of the sacrament dips his right thumb in the chrism and makes the sign of the cross on the forehead of the one to be confirmed as he says:

N., be sealed with the Gift of the Holy Spirit.

Newly confirmed:

Amen.

The minister of the sacrament adds:

Peace be with you.

Newly confirmed:

Amen.

At least four things should be noted here about this confirmation rite. First, the section entitled "Laying on of Hands" is surely a misnomer since no hands are laid on anyone in the rite. Beginning with the eighteenth-century edition of the Tridentine *Roman Pontifical*, the *Pontifical of Benedict XIII*, the custom of the bishop—or delegated priest—imposing his right hand on the top of the candidate's head, while anointing the forehead with the thumb of the same hand, became a common practice in the conferral of confirmation.[48] But no such practice is indicated here in connection with either the prayer for the sevenfold gifts of the Spirit or to the anointing with chrism.

Second, in spite of the historical connection between confirmation and bishops in the Roman rite, a connection at least as old as the famous letter of Pope Innocent I to Decentius of Gubbio (416 C.E.),[49] presbyters (priests) are actually now authorized by the RCIA itself to confer confirmation on adult candidates. In other words, while it is certainly desirable for bishops themselves to preside at the rites of Christian initiation in their entirety, the RCIA has actually restored the practice of the patristic, Eastern, and early medieval non-Roman Western liturgical traditions, where presbyters themselves functioned as the presiding ministers for all of the initiation rites.

Third, and closely related, is the fact that the unity of the rites in their primitive and integral sequence is given, obviously, a much higher value than is the need for the physical presence of the bishop at confirmation. Paragraph 215 of the introduction to the rites themselves could not be more precise about the connection between baptism and confirmation:

"The conjunction of the two celebrations signifies the unity of the paschal mystery, the close link between the mission of the Son and the outpouring of the Holy Spirit, and the connection between the two sacraments through which the Son and the Holy Spirit come with the Father to those who are baptized."[50]

---

[48] On this see Austin, *Anointing*, 22–3.

[49] See above, 127–30.

[50] *Rites*, no. 215, 146–7. The Latin text of this paragraph is even stronger, actually calling what the official English translation describes as the "close link between the mission of the Son and the outpouring of the Holy Spirit" a "necessity that obtains" (*necessitudo*) between the mission of the Son and the Holy Spirit. On this see Aidan Kavanagh, "Christian Initiation in Post-Conciliar Catholicism: A Brief Report," LWSS, 2, n. 2.

Similarly, it is also clearly indicated that both baptism and confirmation lead to the reception of the Eucharist as the very "culminating point in their Christian initiation" (no. 217).

The fourth and final point to be noted here concerns the formula now used for the confirmation anointing: "N., be sealed with the Gift of the Holy Spirit." As we have seen before in this study, the traditional confirmation anointing formula in the Roman Church was "I sign you with the sign of the cross and confirm you with the chrism of salvation in the name of the Father, and of the Son, and of the Holy Spirit." And, while the "matter" and "form" of confirmation associated with the gift of the Holy Spirit was understood as consisting of the anointing with chrism and this formula, this new formula was consciously adopted and adapted in 1971 from the *single*, postbaptismal chrismation inseparably connected to baptism of the Byzantine liturgical tradition.[51] Never before had the Roman confirmation anointing been this explicitly pneumatic in language and orientation and, with the omission of the traditional Roman postbaptismal anointing in the RCIA in favor of this confirmation anointing alone, an interesting new parallel between Roman confirmation and Byzantine postbaptismal chrismation has been decidedly established.

With the culminating reception of first communion at the Easter Vigil Eucharist the specific rites of Christian initiation for adults come to their close. Nevertheless, the process itself is not yet concluded. The fourth period of the RCIA, the period of postbaptismal catechesis or mystagogy, now begins and, according to the *National Statutes on the Catechumenate*, is to last for at least one year.[52] This period, although again largely unstructured like the period of evangelization and precatechumenate, is to be one in which "the community and the neophytes together . . . grow in deepening their grasp of the paschal mystery and in making it a part of their lives through meditation on the Gospel, sharing in the eucharist, and doing the works of charity" (no. 244). Similarly, through this postbaptismal mystagogy, "the neophytes, with the help of their godparents, should experience a full and joyful welcome into the community and enter into closer ties with the other faithful. The faithful, in turn, should derive from it a

[51] See Paul VI, Apostolic Constitution on the Sacrament of Confirmation, in *Rites*, vol. 1, 474–8.

[52] See *Rites*, vol. 1, no. 24, 345.

316

renewal of inspiration and of outlook" (no. 246). Such mystagogy for both the neophytes and the community is to form the core of the Sunday eucharistic liturgies of the fifty days of the Easter Season with a special celebration for them to be held near Pentecost. Until the next Easter, according to the *National Statutes on the Catechumenate*, monthly gatherings of the neophytes, godparents, and others are to be held "for their deeper formation and incorporation into the full life of the Christian community" (no. 24).

A second section of the RCIA, "Rites for Particular Circumstances,"[53] includes various adaptations of the above ritual process for: the full "Christian Initiation of Children who have Reached Catechetical Age" (age seven); the "Christian Initiation of Adults in Exceptional Circumstances"; the "Christian Initiation of a Person in Danger of Death"; and the "Preparation of Uncatechized Adults for Confirmation and Eucharist," that is, those who have been baptized, but who were neither catechized nor received confirmation and first communion. In addition to these adaptations, the RCIA also provides a rite of "Reception of Baptized Christians into the Full Communion of the Catholic Church," either during or outside of Mass, including the conferral and reception of confirmation and, at least within Mass, the preferred occasion for this rite, the reception of first communion.

Although this revised rite of reception, also mandated by the Constitution on the Sacred Liturgy at Vatican II, appears within the RCIA materials, it is not to be seen necessarily as part of the RCIA process leading to Easter initiation. Nevertheless, within an appendix to the RCIA approved for the dioceses of the United States, and often imitated elsewhere around the world, a series of rites called "Additional (Combined) Rites" regularly places real catechumens (unbaptized adults), candidates for confirmation and first communion (uncatechized but baptized adults), and candidates for reception into full communion together into the same overall ritual process of catechumenal formation with the respective initiation rites then celebrated at the Easter Vigil.[54] While the attempt to be so inclusive of people at differing stages in their spiritual journeys may be laudable, these combined rites, especially with regard to the rite of reception into full

[53] Ibid., 170–286.
[54] See ibid., 287–356.

communion, as we shall see below, present particular problems still needing to be resolved.

The Roman Catholic Rites of Baptism for Children and Confirmation
If in the RCIA the contemporary Roman Catholic Church has restored for adults—and children of catechetical age—the primitive fullness and ritual sequence of Christian initiation all the way from inquiry and catechesis through mystagogy, the general practice of the Christian initiation of children has remained that of infant baptism with their confirmation and first communion still separated by intervals of several years. Even here, however, the current revisions of these rites display some noteworthy shifts and changes.

The RBC. As we have already seen, the RBC, published in 1969, was the first of the revised initiation rites coming from the Second Vatican Council and was to be "adapted to the circumstance that those to be baptized are, in fact, infants," with "the roles of parents and godparents, and also their duties . . . brought out more sharply." While the RBC does provide several adaptations for different occasions, such as a "Rite of Baptism for One Child," a "Rite of Baptism for a Large Number of Children," wherein even the postbaptismal anointing with chrism *may* be omitted, a "Rite of Baptism for Children Administered by a Catechist when no Priest or Deacon Is Available," a "Rite of Baptism for Children in Danger of Death when no Priest or Deacon Is Available," and, in relationship to these last two, a "Rite of Bringing a Baptized Child to the Church,"[55] the primary rite, called the "Rite of Baptism for Several Children,"[56] has the overall following ritual structure and content:

Reception of the Children

Liturgy of the Word

Scripture Readings and Homily

Intercessions (Prayer of the Faithful)

Prayer of Exorcism and Anointing before Baptism

[55] Ibid., vol. 1, 394–458.
[56] Ibid., 376–93.

Celebration of the Sacrament

Blessing and Invocation of God over Baptismal Water

Renunciation of Sin and Profession of Faith

Baptism

Explanatory Rites

Anointing After Baptism

Clothing with White Garment

Lighted Candle

Effeta or Prayer over Ears and Mouth

Conclusion of the Rite

Lord's Prayer

Blessing and Dismissal

Although in general this baptismal rite closely parallels that in the RCIA, there are at least four primary differences or distinctions to be noted. First of all, in this rite designed explicitly for *infant* candidates, the role and duties of parents and godparents is, indeed, underscored sharply throughout the rite. During the reception of the children, the parents are addressed and told that, in asking to have their children baptized, it will be their "duty to bring them up to keep God's commandments as Christ taught us, by loving God and our neighbor," and the godparents are similarly asked to "help these parents in their duty as Christian mothers and fathers" (nos. 39–40). At the renunciation of sin and profession of faith such a charge is again repeated and it is made clear that it is their *own* faith, "the faith of the Church . . . the faith in which these children are about to be baptized," that the parents and godparents are now to renew. Hence, the following questions of the renunciation of Satan and the profession of faith themselves are addressed directly to them alone, rather than to the children as mute adults (nos. 56–9). And, again, at the postbaptismal presentation of the lighted candle, the parents and godparents are told: "this light is entrusted to you to be kept burning brightly" (no. 64).

Second, although explicit language about "original sin" appears nowhere in the RCIA, both options provided for the "Prayer of Exorcism and Anointing Before Baptism" make clear reference to it. The first option states: "We pray for these children: set them free from original sin . . ."; the second asks that "By [Christ's] victory over sin and death, cleanse these children from the stain of original sin" (no. 49). While such a theology is not dominant throughout the rite, its presence here certainly underscores the traditional inheritance of the Augustinian rationale *for* infant baptism itself.

The third distinctive element to be noted in this rite is the curious inclusion of the *effeta* or *apertio* among the "explanatory rites" after baptism. Although it is only an option in the current rite to be performed at the discretion of the minister, this *effeta* or *apertio*, as we have seen, is traditionally either a catechumenal rite administered before the *traditio* of the Gospels or the Creed during the period of the catechumenate, or, as in the RCIA, as part of the prebaptismal rites. Its presence at this *postbaptismal* location in the RBC, however, might seem to suggest that, in the case of infants, baptism itself is also a kind of enrollment in the catechumenate, where, at some point in the development of future faith, the ears of the baptized might "receive [God's] word," and their mouths might "proclaim his faith" (no. 65).

Also to be noted in the RBC are the significant changes regarding the time and place for the baptism of children and the conscious attempt to avoid the practice of indiscriminate infant baptism altogether. Although the introduction to the RBC states that "an infant should be baptized within the first weeks after birth" (no. 3), it further directs that:

"to bring out the paschal character of baptism, it is recommended that the sacrament be celebrated during the Easter Vigil or on Sunday, when the Church commemorates the Lord's resurrection. On Sunday, baptism may be celebrated even during Mass, so that the entire community may be present and the relationship between baptism and eucharist may be clearly seen" (no. 9).

And along with this, the General Introduction to Christian Initiation also indicates that "as far as possible, all recently born babies should be baptized at a common celebration on the same day" (no. 27).

The significance of this change should not be overlooked. In the past, while the *quamprimum* baptism of infants led to a regular practice of individual baptisms in private with only a few people present, often not even including the presence of the mother who was still recovering from childbirth and would need to undergo herself a rite of purification—*The Churching of Women*—before reentering the church, the RBC has attempted to make the public celebration of infant baptism in the context of the liturgical assembly, the local community into which the infant is initiated, the modern norm for sacramental practice. Such a focus on the public nature of the rite, as we have seen, was one of the emphases of the sixteenth-century Protestant reforms of baptism, and one which has now been accepted as well by the Roman Catholic Church in its recovery of the ecclesial and corporate nature of the sacraments themselves.

Together with this, as well as with the emphasis on the faith of the Church into which one is baptized, the RBC also directs that the indiscriminate baptism of infants is to be avoided. In fact, "in the complete absence of any well-founded hope that the infant will be brought up in the Catholic religion, the baptism is to be delayed, in conformity with particular law . . . , and the parents are to be informed of the reasons" (no. 3). Such a restriction is intended to underscore the necessity of faith within the celebration of the sacraments and to invite unprepared parents themselves to a greater conversion and commitment in undertaking the duties and responsibilities for the faith development of their children that the rite itself implies and for which it expressly asks. Hence, a longer delay between birth and baptism than the usual "first weeks after birth" might surely be expected in some cases today.

The Rite of Confirmation. The *Rite of Confirmation,* published in 1971[57] and intended primarily for those who were baptized previously as infants, is essentially the same rite used for adults after the celebration of baptism in the RCIA, so it need not be outlined here in full. There are, however, three significant differences. First, consistent with the mandate of Vatican II, in order to make more explicit the relationship between baptism and confirmation, the actual confirmation rite itself is preceded by a renewal of baptismal promises including the renunciation of Satan and profession of the Apostles' Creed in question and answer form. But of particular interest here is the shape of the question concerning the Holy Spirit. Here, instead of

[57] Ibid., 469–512.

simply asking for a renewal of baptismal faith according to the language of the Apostles' Creed, the specific theology and sacramental understanding of confirmation becomes, inexplicably, part of the very contents of the faith to which assent is now to be given: "Do you believe in the Holy Spirit, the Lord, the giver of life, who came upon the apostles at Pentecost *and today is given to you sacramentally in confirmation*?" (no. 23).[58]

Second, while in the RCIA the conferral of confirmation is preceded by a brief invitation given the celebrant, here the renewal of baptismal promises is preceded by a homily or instruction delivered by the bishop, the normal minister of this sacrament, "in these or similar words":

"On the day of Pentecost the apostles received the Holy Spirit as the Lord had promised. They also received the power of giving the Holy Spirit to others and so completing the work of baptism. This we read in the Acts of the Apostles. When Saint Paul placed his hands on those who had been baptized, the Holy Spirit came upon them, and they began to speak in other languages and in prophetic words.

"Bishops are successors of the apostles and have this power of giving the Holy Spirit to the baptized, either personally or through the priests they appoint.

"In our day the coming of the Holy Spirit in confirmation is no longer marked by the gift of tongues, but we know his coming by faith. He fills our hearts with the love of God, brings us together in one faith but in different vocations, and works within us to make the Church one and holy.

"The gift of the Holy Spirit which you are to receive will be a spiritual sign and seal to make you more like Christ and more perfect members of the Church. At his baptism by John, Christ himself was anointed by the Spirit and sent out on his public ministry to set the world on fire.

"You have already been baptized into Christ and now you will receive the power of his Spirit and the sign of the cross on your forehead. You must be witnesses before all the world to his suffering,

---

[58] Emphasis added.

death, and resurrection; your way of life should at all times reflect the goodness of Christ. Christ gives varied gifts to his Church, and the Spirit distributes them among the members of Christ's body to build up the holy people of God in unity and love.

"Be active members of the Church, alive in Jesus Christ. Under the guidance of the Holy Spirit give your lives completely in the service of all, as did Christ, who came not to be served but to serve.

"So now, before you receive the Spirit, I ask you to renew the profession of faith you made in baptism or your parents and godparents made in union with the whole Church" (no. 22).

Almost everything we have seen associated with confirmation as a sacrament separate from baptism throughout its long and complex evolution and interpretation is here woven together into one instructional statement: (1) the presumed normative status of the problematic and exceptional situations in the Acts of the Apostles (chapters 8 and 19) as constitutive of confirmation; (2) the explicit association of the gift of the Holy Spirit with the role of the bishop as the successor to the apostles as in the *Letter of Innocent I to Decentius of Gubbio*; and (3) the relationship of confirmation to Christian vocation and witness. About the only thing missing from this homily is the emphasis in the famous fifth-century Pentecost homily ascribed to Faustus of Riez, wherein the gift of the Holy Spirit is associated with "strengthening for battle." Nevertheless, even this emphasis appears in both Pope Paul VI's Apostolic Constitution on the Sacrament of Confirmation, 1971, and in the *Introduction* to the rite itself. Paul VI wrote that "through the sacrament of confirmation those who have been born anew in baptism receive the inexpressible Gift, the Holy Spirit himself, by whom 'they are endowed . . . with special strength.'"[59] And in the *Introduction* we read that "this giving of the Holy Spirit conforms believers more fully to Christ and strengthens them so that they may bear witness to Christ for the building up of his Body in faith and love" (no. 2). Similarly, such an emphasis on "strengthening" appears throughout the language of the rite itself.

The third major difference from the RCIA follows upon these rather traditional theological emphases. While in the RCIA confirmation

[59] *Rites*, vol. 1, 474.

functions clearly as the postbaptismal "seal of the Holy Spirit" by drawing baptism itself to completion with the gift of the Holy Spirit, in the case of those baptized in infancy this postbaptismal gift of the Spirit still remains separated by an interval of several years. Consistent with traditional confirmation legislation in the Roman Catholic Church, the *Introduction* states that "in the Latin Church the administration of confirmation is generally delayed until about the seventh year." But even in saying this the *Introduction* goes on to direct that:

"For pastoral reasons . . . especially to implant deeply in the lives of the faithful complete obedience to Christ the Lord and a firm witnessing to him, the conferences of bishops may set an age that seems more suitable. This means that the sacrament is given, after the formation proper to it, when the recipients are more mature" (no. 11).

With regard to this option, an option which has become the accepted norm at least in the dioceses of the United States, where the "age" of confirmation varies all the way from age seven in some dioceses to age eighteen in others, Gerard Austin writes:

"This option of delaying the conferring of confirmation to a later age changes the whole focus of the question from the baptismal grace to the baptized person; from who we are (those loved gratuitously by God) to what we do (respond to that love). . . . In choosing a later age, an age 'which appears more appropriate,' one wonders if more is not being demanded for confirmation than is demanded for the apex of Christian initiation, the eucharist itself. While young children are allowed to receive the greatest of all the Christian sacraments, the eucharist, they are denied the right to be confirmed. More important, by delaying the age of confirmation, has not the church turned the sacrament from the purpose for which it was instituted? The church changed confirmation from its original role as the completion and perfection of baptism (and as the gift of the fullness of the Spirit preparing for the reception of the body and blood of Christ) into something totally new: namely, a personal, mature ratification of one's earlier baptism."[60]

[60] Austin, *Anointing*, 53–4.

Such a shift in emphasis, of course, is precisely what happened to the rite and theology of "confirmation" in the sixteenth-century Protestant traditions, which, while denying the sacramentality of *Roman* confirmation, nevertheless, through Martin Bucer and others, developed new catechetical rites in adolescence for the ratification or affirmation of baptism. Such later "owning" of one's infant baptism, as we have seen, was viewed as necessary in the theology of some of the Protestant Reformers. If, in spite of official legislation to the contrary, pastoral practice had been moving in this direction for some time within Roman Catholicism as well, never before had an *official* liturgical document permitted such a decisive shift. And, for that matter, even in the current 1983 Code of Canon Law, while permitting conferences of bishops to set later or, presumably, *earlier,* ages for confirmation's conferral,[61] no reference to confirmation as a "mature ratification of one's earlier baptism" is made.

Although this concession is certainly made, it is tempered significantly by the expectation both in the *Introduction* and in Paul VI's Apostolic Constitution that confirmation will normally *precede* the reception of first communion. Paul VI could not be clearer when he writes that "confirmation is so closely linked with the holy eucharist that the faithful, *after* being signed by baptism *and confirmation,* are incorporated fully into the Body of Christ by participation in the eucharist."[62] Similarly, the *Introduction,* even after referring to the possibility of postponing confirmation until a "more suitable" age, states that "Christian initiation reaches its *culmination* in the communion of the body and blood of Christ. The newly confirmed therefore participate in the eucharist, which *completes* their Christian initiation" (no. 13).[63] Hence, in spite of the various—and significant—differences between both the RBC and the separate *Rite of Confirmation* with the RCIA, the traditional ritual *sequence* of baptism, confirmation, and first communion of the RCIA is also here to be the normal and expected sacramental sequence for *all* who are initiated into Christ and the Church, even if, in the case of infants, confirmation and first communion—in *that* order!—are to be "generally delayed until about the seventh year."

---

[61] Canon 891 in *The Code of Canon Law: Latin-English Edition* (Collegeville: The Liturgical Press, 1983) 335.

[62] *Rites,* vol. 1, 474; emphasis added.

[63] Emphasis added.

CHRISTIAN INITIATION IN CONTEMPORARY ANGLICANISM AND LUTHERANISM

As indicated previously, the dominant and most ecumenically influential of the modern reforms of the rites of Christian initiation have been those of the Roman Catholic Church, especially the RCIA. This, however, should not be taken to imply that the revisions of the rites of Christian initiation in other churches today are simply carbon copies or mere and deliberate imitations of Roman Catholic sacramental and liturgical rites and practice. Rather, due in large part to ecumenical involvement in the Liturgical Movement in the early and mid twentieth century, the close parallels which exist between modern Protestant rites with the Roman rites are primarily based on similar appropriations of the ritual and sacramental patterns of early Christianity and, for Protestants, at least, on the recovery of some of the earlier, rather than later, sacramental-liturgical reforms of the sixteenth-century Reformers themselves. For modern Anglicans and Lutherans, concretely, this has meant that the 1549 (rather than 1552) BCP and Luther's 1523 (rather than 1526) *Taufbüchlein*, respectively, have been seen as providing rich models for the contemporary revision of liturgical rites. And, along with this, various internal discussions and debates, as well as the same cultural and social challenges facing modern Roman Catholicism, have also helped in setting the agenda for change in these churches today.

Among Anglicans, the years between 1928 and 1970 were marked by intense debate over Christian initiation in general and the relationship between baptism and confirmation in particular.[64] At issue,

---

[64] The best guide to the modern development of the rites of Christian initiation throughout Anglicanism is Ruth A. Meyer's 1992 Notre Dame doctoral dissertation, "The Renewal of Christian Initiation in the Episcopal Church 1928–1979," recently revised and published as *Continuing the Reformation: Re-Visioning Baptism in the Episcopal Church* (New York: n.p., 1997). Much of the following, especially as it concerns the rites of Christian initiation in the ECUSA, is based upon Meyers' excellent and detailed studies. See also Marion Hatchett, *Commentary on the American Prayer Book* (New York: Seabury Press, 1981) 251–88; Leonel Mitchell, *Praying Shapes Believing: A Theological Commentary on the Book of Common Prayer* (Minneapolis: Winston Press, 1985); and Michael Moriarty, *The Liturgical Revolution: Prayer Book Revision and Associated Parishes: A Generation of Change in the Episcopal Church* (New York: Church Hymnal Corp., 1996).

of course, was the fact that the Church of England had inherited from the various editions of the BCP in the sixteenth and seventeenth centuries a rite of confirmation, still administered by the bishop with the laying on of hands, but following an extended period of catechesis and serving as a rite of baptismal ratification or "owning" of one's previous baptism in preparation for the reception of communion. Sparked initially by Gregory Dix,[65] who argued that from the very beginning Christian initiation had been a two-stage ritual process with water baptism as preparatory for the seal of the Holy Spirit in confirmation, and opposed strongly by G.W.H. Lampe,[66] who argued to the contrary that, according to the New Testament, baptism itself conveyed the seal of the Spirit, a relationship that had become corrupted in the early Church and turned into a two-stage affair, this debate was to continue for some time. As Ruth Meyers notes:

"By the late 1960s, there was a growing understanding of Christian initiation as a complex of rites. However, there was no clear consensus as to the meaning of confirmation or the action of the Holy Spirit in Christian initiation. . . . Confirmation was understood variously as an initiatory bestowal of the Holy Spirit and as a public affirmation of faith. The debate between Dix and Lampe had not been resolved in the Anglican communion. . . . As the debate continued, there was growing awareness of the unity of Christian initiation in the early church and desire to restore this unity as much as possible. This led to proposals to restore an anointing to baptism, emphasizing the objective conferral of the Spirit as integral to Christian initiation. Several of these proposals continued to link the bestowal of the Spirit to the postbaptismal ceremonies, in effect maintaining a distinction between water baptism and Spirit baptism. Other reports and proposals stressed that the Spirit is active throughout the initiatory process."[67]

[65] Gregory Dix, *The Theology of Confirmation in Relation to Baptism* (London: Dacre Press, 1946).

[66] Gregory W. H. Lampe, *The Seal of the Spirit: A Study in the Doctrine of Baptism and Confirmation in the New Testament and the Fathers*, 2d ed. (London: SPCK, 1967).

[67] Meyers, "The Renewal of Christian Initiation in the Episcopal Church," 193.

At the same time, she continues:

"There was continuing emphasis on the importance of a personal profession of faith, but no agreement as to how this was to be implemented for those baptized as infants. In the Episcopal Church there was increasing frustration with the use of confirmation as an admission ticket to communion and a sort of 'graduation' from Sunday school. While this led to proposals to admit children to communion prior to confirmation, most of these required some instruction before admission to communion. . . . There was great reluctance to consider infants as appropriate candidates for full Christian initiation, including admission to communion."[68]

While in the Church of England itself very little was to come of these debates, with confirmation by the bishop, even in the 1980 *Alternative Service Book,* still serving regularly as a prerequisite for the reception of communion even today, the ECUSA was eventually able to break the traditional Anglican connection between this catechetical rite of ratification or affirmation of baptism and the participation of the baptized in the Eucharist. In fact, in a significant collection of trial rites for Christian initiation, published by the Standing Liturgical Commission of the Episcopal Church in 1971,[69] not only were rites of handlaying and anointing, associated with the gift and seal of the Holy Spirit, added as postbaptismal rites within the rite of baptism itself, but confirmation by a bishop was entirely eliminated. While this move to eliminate confirmation met with vigorous opposition, especially on the part of Episcopal bishops, and had to be revised prior to the 1979 BCP, the connection between confirmation and first communion in the ECUSA was broken once and for all. Similarly, since no particular age was specified for the reception of first communion, the door was also opened to the possibility that, as in early Christianity, *all* who were baptized, whether infants, children, or adults, would be welcomed to participation in the Eucharist.[70]

During the same time period that the ECUSA was preparing a new BCP so also were the majority of North American Lutheran churches,

[68] Ibid., 194.
[69] *On Baptism and Confirmation.*
[70] See Meyers, *Continuing the Reformation,* 132–57, 234–6.

through the Inter-Lutheran Commission on Worship, preparing new rites for the eventual publication of the LBW.[71] As in the ECUSA, the new Lutheran rite for baptism itself would include a postbaptismal handlaying and signing and (optional) anointing for the "seal" of the Spirit.[72] Similarly, the link between first communion and confirmation was also broken for American Lutherans in the late 1960s. In a 1968 report of a Joint Commission on the Theology and Practice of Confirmation, those Lutherans now comprising the ELCA initiated a practice which placed both preparation for and reception of first communion during the fifth grade (age ten) of elementary school education.[73] Together with this, and based on the then-proposed rites of the ECUSA, *Contemporary Worship 8: Affirmation of the Baptismal Covenant*[74] also omitted the term "confirmation" altogether and was met

[71] No comprehensive or detailed account of the modern development and revision of the rites of Christian initiation in North American Lutheranism yet exists. The following studies should be consulted: D. Armentrout, "The New Lutheran and Episcopal Baptismal Rites," *Lutheran Quarterly* 27 (1975) 295–311; Hans Boehringer, "Baptism, Confirmation, and First Communion: Christian Initiation in the Contemporary Church," *Christian Initiation: Reborn of Water and the Spirit*, ed. Daniel Brockopp et al., Institute of Liturgical Studies Occasional Papers 1 (Valparaiso, Ind.: Institute of Liturgical Studies, 1981) 73–98; Eugene Brand, *Baptism: A Pastoral Perspective* (Minneapolis: Augsburg, 1975); Eugene Brand, "New Rites of Initiation and Their Implications in the Lutheran Churches," LWSS, 292–309; Eugene Brand, "Toward the Renewal of Christian Initiation in the Parish," *Christian Initiation: Reborn of Water and the Spirit*, 120–38; T. A. Droege, "The Formation of Faith in Christian Initiation," *Cresset* (April 1983) 16–23; Maxwell Johnson, "The Shape of Christian Initiation in the Lutheran Churches: Liturgical Texts and Future Directions," *Studia Liturgica* 27:1 (1997) 33–60; F. Senn, "A New Baptismal Rite: Toward Revitalizing the Whole Community," *Currents in Theology and Mission* 2 (1975) 206–14; F. Senn, "End for Confirmation?" *Currents in Theology and Mission* 3 (1976) 45–52; and F. Senn, "Shape and Content of Christian Initiation: An Exposition of the New Lutheran Liturgy of Holy Baptism," *Dialog* 14 (1975) 97–107. I am pleased to announce, however, that my doctoral student, the Rev. Jeffrey Truscott, is preparing to undertake such a study for his doctoral dissertation at the University of Notre Dame.

[72] See *Holy Baptism*.

[73] Frank Klos, *Confirmation and First Communion: A Study Book* (Minneapolis: Augsburg, 1968).

[74] *Affirmation of the Baptismal Covenant*.

with similar opposition from Lutherans. According to Eugene Brand, then project director of the LBW, "Lutheran self-consciousness [was and] is not yet able to tolerate the idea of an unconfirmed Lutheran."[75]

Again, as in the ECUSA, the trend toward a lower first communion age has continued almost everywhere throughout Lutheranism around the world with the result that first communion before confirmation is acknowledged almost universally today. Especially significant in this regard is the 1991 decision of the ELCIC, which, in adopting a statement on sacramental practices, boldly went where no Lutheran church had gone before by affirming the participation of *all* the baptized in the reception of communion in the following words:

"In Baptism we are incorporated into the Body of Christ, the Church. In Holy Communion the Church is nourished and strengthened. Therefore we speak of and practise Communion of the baptized. . . . The Lord's supper is God's meal for the baptized. Admission to the Supper is by Christ's invitation, offered through the church to the baptized."[76]

What is most significant in this ELCIC decision is that the Canadian Lutheran church bodies forming the ELCIC, like the ELCA in the United States, had inherited a 1978 "Common Statement on Communion Practices."[77] This statement, endorsed again by the ELCA in 1989 but *not* by the ELCIC, noted that Lutheran congregations might have a concern for the admission to communion of baptized children under the age of ten, but nevertheless "precluded" the communion of baptized infants altogether. Unfortunately, it did this without providing a firm theological rationale against what in some places had been taking place already. Significantly, this 1978 statement also reaffirmed the fifth grade (or age ten) level as the most appropriate time for communion reception.

---

[75] Brand, "New Rites of Initiation," 308. Of the contemporary reformed rites of initiation in North American Protestantism, only the 1993 Presbyterian *Book of Common Worship,* consistent with Calvin himself, has been successful in avoiding the terminology of confirmation altogether.

[76] *Statement on Sacramental Practices,* ELCIC, 1991, 5.8, 6.9.

[77] *Common Statement on Communion Practices* (Minneapolis/Philadelphia: n.p., 1978).

As recent as 1997, however, the ELCA followed its Lutheran neighbors to the north and adopted *The Use of the Means of Grace: A Statement on the Practice of Word and Sacrament,* in which it is stated that "infants and children may be communed for the first time during the service in which they are baptized."[78] Unlike either the statement of the ELCIC or the practice of ECUSA,[79] however, this ELCA statement qualifies admission to communion by adding that:

"Baptized children begin to commune on a *regular basis* at a time determined through mutual conversation that includes the pastor, the child, and the parents or sponsors involved, within the accepted practices of the congregation. *Ordinarily* this beginning will occur only when children can eat and drink, and can start to respond to the gift of Christ in the Supper."[80]

It is really no surprise that contemporary Christians should have a concern for the communion of baptized children in general when it is noted that one of the great and most successful intentions of the Liturgical Movement was the recovery of "full, conscious, and active participation" in the Eucharist itself. From Pius X's *Quam singulari* in 1910 through Vatican II's Constitution on the Sacred Liturgy (1963) and the Missal of Paul VI (1969) to the present, Roman Catholics in the twentieth century have experienced the eucharistic liturgy and participation in the Eucharist once again, as in the early Church, as being the very center and source of all Christian life and activity. In such a context, as other Christians also moved the Eucharist from an "occasional" service to a more frequent—increasingly, every Sunday—celebration, it was only inevitable that the question of who may fully participate in the Eucharist and when would be raised anew. As David Holeton says:

"Any church that begins to encourage frequent communion among the laity in the context of a piety that sees the eucharist as a communal

---

[78] ELCA, *The Use of the Means of Grace* (Minneapolis: n.p., 1997) 42.

[79] On the restoration of infant communion in contemporary Anglicanism see Ruth Meyers, ed., *Children at the Table: The Communion of All the Baptized in Anglicanism Today* (New York: Church Hymnal Corp., 1994). For a Lutheran approach see Eugene Brand, "Baptism and Communion of Infants: A Lutheran View," LWSS, 350–64.

[80] *The Use of the Means of Grace,* 41; emphasis added.

action rather than as an action done on the behalf of a collection of individuals cannot help but pose new questions as to who is to be included in the eucharistic community. Once the community becomes one in which all are accepted in its corporate life despite age, or intelligence, or social status, the question of universal participation in the eucharist becomes a real one. Once the community shares in the eucharist the experience becomes a conversion. You can never be as you were before."[81]

Such "conversion" is exactly what has happened throughout much of contemporary American Protestantism.

Finally, before looking briefly at the current rites of baptism and confirmation in the 1979 BCP and LBW themselves, attention must also be given to the contemporary restoration of the adult catechumenate among Episcopalians and Lutherans. In response to the need for the evangelization and baptismal preparation of the increasing number of unbaptized and uncatechized adults in a so-called "post-Christendom" world, Episcopalians and Lutherans, like Roman Catholics in the earlier published RCIA, have attempted to recover the historic catechumenal process. The catechumenate itself appears in neither the BCP nor the LBW. But, as noted at the beginning of this chapter, in 1979 the ECUSA published a *Book of Occasional Services* containing the "Preparation of Adults for Holy Baptism: The Catechumenate,"[82] together with various prayers, rites, and instructions for its implementation. In 1982 the ELCA published an *Occasional Service Book* with a rite of "Enrollment of Candidates for Baptism" and a very brief description of the catechumenal process.[83]

Such attempts, however, were only the beginning. In 1988, a second edition of the *Book of Occasional Services* was published, which, much like the "Additional (Combined) Rites" in the U.S. version of the RCIA, contained additional "parallel rites" to be used in preparing baptized people for confirmation, reception, and/or reaffirma-

[81] David Holeton, *Infant Communion: Then and Now,* Grove Liturgical Study 27 (Bramcote, Nottingham: Grove Books, 1981) 15.

[82] *The Book of Occasional Services,* 112–26. See also, Office of Evangelism Ministries, The Episcopal Church, *The Catechumenal Process: Adult Initiation & Formation for Christian Life and Ministry* (New York: Church Hymnal Corp., 1990).

[83] *Occasional Service Book* (Minneapolis/Philadelphia: n.p., 1982) 13–5.

tion, as well as for the preparation of parents and godparents for the baptism of their children.[84]

Since the late 1980s, Episcopalians and North American Lutherans have been working together toward the implementation of the adult catechumenate. Since 1995 they have collaborated together with several Protestant groups in the North American Association for the Catechumenate. Not surprisingly, then, current Lutheran adaptations of the catechumenate tend to parallel quite closely the overall approach of the ECUSA rites. In 1992, the ELCIC published a series of booklets and a manual designed to introduce the catechumenate to Canadian Lutherans.[85] And, in 1997, the ELCA, the ELCIC, and the LC–MS together published a series of three catechumenal resources under the general title *Welcome to Christ*.[86] Unlike either the rites of the ECUSA or the ELCIC, *Welcome to Christ* does not provide an adaptation of the catechumenal process for the preparation of parents and sponsors for the baptism of their children. However, like the rites of the ECUSA and the ELCIC, as well as the "Additional (Combined) Rites" of the RCIA, it does provide various adaptations for those seeking to affirm their baptism at the Easter Vigil.

With the publication of these new Lutheran resources for the catechumenate, contemporary Roman Catholics, Episcopalians, and Lutherans, at least in North America, have converged greatly toward a common ritual process designed for the initiation of adults, either

---

[84] *The Book of Occasional Services,* 132–41, 155–6. See also the 1987 essay by Gail Ramshaw, "Celebrating Baptism in Stages: A Proposal," *Alternative Futures for Worship,* ed. Mark Searle, vol. 2, *Baptism and Confirmation* (Collegeville: The Liturgical Press, 1987) 137–55.

[85] See ELCIC, *Living Witnesses: The Adult Catechumenate: A Manual for the Catechumenal Process* (Manitoba: n.p., 1994); Gordon Lathrop, *Living Witnesses: The Adult Catechumenate (ELCIC): Congregational Prayers to Accompany the Catechumenal Process* (Minneapolis: n.p., 1994); and F. Ludolph, *Living Witnesses: The Adult Catechumenate (ELCIC): Preparing Adults for Baptism and Ministry in the Church* (Minneapolis: n.p., 1994).

[86] *Welcome to Christ: A Lutheran Catechetical Guide* (Minneapolis: n.p., 1997); *Welcome to Christ: A Lutheran Introduction to the Catechumenate* (Minneapolis: n.p., 1997); and *Welcome to Christ: Lutheran Rites for the Catechumenate* (Minneapolis: n.p., 1997). For a study of the recovery of the catechumenate among Lutherans see M. Strobel, "Adaptation of the Catechumenate among North American Lutherans," *Worship* (1998) forthcoming.

by the rites of Christian initiation themselves (baptism, "confirmation," and first communion), or, in the case of those already baptized, by "confirmation" or some kind of rite of affirmation or reception. Along with this convergence and commonality in overall ritual structure and process, however, also come similar problems needing further resolution. These will be considered after looking at the current Episcopal and Lutheran rites themselves.

The Rites of Christian Initiation in the 1979 BCP of the ECUSA

Holy baptism. According to the 1979 BCP, "Holy Baptism is *full initiation* by water and the Holy Spirit into Christ's Body the Church . . . [and] is appropriately administered with the Eucharist as the chief service on a Sunday or other feast."[87] Along with Sundays, or at any time the diocesan bishop might be present, the Easter Vigil, Pentecost Sunday, All Saints (Nov. 1 or the Sunday following), and the Feast of the Baptism of Our Lord (the Sunday after January 6, the Epiphany) are indicated as "especially appropriate" occasions for its celebration.[88] Rooted firmly in the public and corporate liturgical life of the Church, then, the *single* rite of holy baptism, including various options for adults and infants, is itself placed after the sermon and has the following overall structure:[89]

Presentation and Examination of the Candidates

Adults and older children

Infants and younger children

Questions to parents and godparents

Renunciation of Satan (three-fold)

Act of adherence to Christ (three-fold)

[Presentation and examination of candidates for confirmation, reception, and reaffirmation]

Questions to the congregation

[87] BCP, 298.
[88] Ibid., 312.
[89] Ibid., 298–313.

334

The Baptismal Covenant

Interrogatory Apostles' Creed

Questions of commitment

Prayers for the candidates

Thanksgiving over the water

[Consecration of the chrism]

The Baptism

Immersion or pouring with indicative formula

Prayer over the newly baptized for the sevenfold gift of the Holy Spirit

Handlaying with signing of the newly baptized and (optional) anointing

Welcome of the newly baptized

[Confirmation, reception, and reaffirmation]

Exchange of peace

Eucharist

Since everything in brackets in the above outline is reserved to the bishop, it is important to note that what the BCP considers to be "full initiation by water and the Holy Spirit" for *both* infants and adults is expressed ritually in the rite of holy baptism itself. That means, concretely, that the rites of confirmation, reception into membership, and reaffirmation, although connected to the ministry of bishops alone, are *not* considered to be rites of Christian *initiation* but other kinds of rites altogether.

While several elements in this baptismal rite could be addressed in detail (e.g., the presence of an early Syrian-type act of adherence [*syntaxis*] or the rich prayer of thanksgiving over and sanctification of the baptismal waters),[90] perhaps the most striking are the postbaptismal

---

[90] For a detailed analysis of the entire rite see Meyers, *Continuing the Reformation*, 192–213.

prayer related to the sevenfold gift of the Holy Spirit and the hand-laying prayer with its consignation and optional anointing:[91]

"When [Baptism] has been completed for all candidates, the Bishop or Priest, at a place in full sight of the congregation, prays over them, saying

"Let us pray.

"Heavenly Father, we thank you that by water and the Holy Spirit you have bestowed upon *these* your *servants* the forgiveness of sin, and have raised *them* to the new life of grace. Sustain *them*, O Lord, in your Holy Spirit. Give *them* an inquiring and discerning heart, the courage to will and to persevere, a spirit to know and to love you, and the gift of joy and wonder in all your works. Amen.

"Then the Bishop or Priest places a hand on the person's head, marking on the forehead the sign of the cross [using Chrism if desired] and saying to each one

"N., you are sealed by the Holy Spirit in Baptism and marked as Christ's own for ever. Amen."

Although the language of the prayer and the formula which accompanies the optional anointing are not completely identical to the confirmation prayer and chrismation of the current Roman rite, the parallels are close enough to make that connection quite obvious. Even if the prayer does not specifically request a separate postbaptismal *gift* of the Spirit ("*Sustain* them . . . in your Holy Spirit"), and even if the formula for the "seal" of the Spirit appears to refer back to baptism itself ("you are sealed by the Holy Spirit *in* Baptism"), the mere postbaptismal location of this prayer and consignation, and the obvious literary connections between the prayer with the traditional Western confirmation prayer, clearly indicate that the 1979 BCP has attempted to restore the traditional Western "confirmation rites" to baptism itself. That is, at the very place where the medieval Western liturgical rites—including Cranmer's own 1549 reform—all contained the classic postbaptismal anointing prayer and its references to having been begotten through water and the Holy Spirit, the 1979 BCP, like the Roman RCIA, simply placed the prayer and consignation of

[91] BCP, 308.

Western confirmation. But, interestingly enough, the formula for this consignation and optional anointing in the BCP is neither the traditional Western formula for the postbaptismal anointing nor for the confirmation anointing. Instead, like the 1971 *Roman* formula, it makes use of the Byzantine postbaptismal language of the "seal of the Holy Spirit." While the attempt to give explicit ritual expression to the gift of the Holy Spirit in a postbaptismal context may be laudable, one wonders why Cranmer's own compelling 1549 revision of the traditional postbaptismal anointing prayer, with the addition of the words "vouchsafe to anoint thee with the unction of his Holy Spirit,"[92] was not given closer consideration. Attention to that, it would seem, may have provided an obvious model for contemporary baptismal revision which would have been faithful to the classic Anglican tradition itself.

Nevertheless, the rite of baptism in the 1979 BCP, along with the addition of those Western postbaptismal "confirmation rites" traditionally associated with the gift of the Holy Spirit, has accomplished for all baptismal candidates, adults and infants alike, what the RCIA was able to accomplish only for adults: a single, unitive, and integral rite constituting "full initiation by water and the Holy Spirit," with baptism in the trinitarian name and the postbaptismal "seal" of the Holy Spirit combined closely together as in the initiation rites of early Christianity. In doing so, holy baptism in the 1979 BCP provided American Protestantism, in general, with a highly influential paradigm for similar revisions of baptismal rites within other traditions.

Confirmation with forms for reception and for the reaffirmation of baptismal vows. As we have seen, one of the characteristics of the modern liturgical reforms both in the ECUSA and among North American Lutherans was the eventual breaking of the traditional Protestant Reformation connection between some form of "confirmation," understood catechetically, and the participation of the baptized in the Eucharist. Both Episcopalians and Lutherans tried, with little success, to avoid the term confirmation entirely. Nevertheless, some form of confirmation, together with rites for reception into membership and the reaffirmation of baptismal vows, not only remains in the 1979 BCP but also remains connected in a special way with the ministry of bishops. As expressed in the introduction to these rites, called

[92] See above, chapter 7, 261.

"Confirmation with forms for Reception and for the Reaffirmation of Baptismal Vows":

"those baptized at an early age are expected, when they are ready and have been duly prepared, to make a mature public affirmation of their faith and commitment to the responsibilities of their Baptism and to receive the laying on of hands by the bishop. . . . Those baptized as adults, unless baptized with laying on of hands by a bishop, are also expected to make a public affirmation of their faith and commitment to the responsibilities of their Baptism in the presence of a bishop and to receive the laying on of hands."[93]

Placed either within the context of baptism itself, if the bishop is present, or as a separate service following a renewal of baptismal vows, on other occasions, these rites include optional forms for the laying on of the bishop's hands in the following manner:[94]

For Confirmation

The Bishop lays hands upon each one and says

Strengthen, O Lord, your servant N. with your Holy Spirit; empower *him* for your service; and sustain *him* all the days of *his* life. *Amen.*

or this

Defend, O Lord, your servant N. with your heavenly grace, that *he* may continue yours for ever, and daily increase in your Holy Spirit more and more until *he* comes to your everlasting kingdom. *Amen.*

For Reception

N., we recognize you as a member of the one holy catholic and apostolic Church, and we receive you into the fellowship of this Communion. God, the Father, Son, and Holy Spirit, bless, preserve, and keep you. *Amen.*

For Reaffirmation

N., may the Holy Spirit, who has begun a good work in you, direct and uphold you in the service of Christ and his kingdom. *Amen.*

---

[93] BCP, 412.
[94] Ibid., 418–9.

The Bishop concludes with this prayer

Almighty and everliving God, let your fatherly hand ever be over *these* your servants; let your Holy Spirit ever be with *them;* and so lead *them* in the knowledge and obedience of your Word, that *they* may serve you in this life, and dwell with you in the life to come; through Jesus Christ our Lord. *Amen.*

The Peace is exchanged

While specified for these three occasions in particular, the rite for reaffirmation is not necessarily limited to a one time "public affirmation of . . . faith and commitment to the responsibilities of . . . Baptism," but may be a repeatable rite associated with various moments in a Christian's life (e.g., restoration of membership, renewal of faith, entrance into certain forms of lay ministry, various changes in life circumstances, or other "crisis" and passage moments) that seem to call for some ritually appropriate way to connect these new beginnings to the foundational baptismal gift and faith of the Church.[95] Such multiple uses for these rites underscore the theology clearly expressed in holy baptism that "Confirmation with forms for Reception and for the Reaffirmation of Baptismal Vows" are *not* to be understood as rites of Christian initiation, the fullness of which is given in baptism itself, but, rather, in traditional Reformation fashion, as rites of ratification or "owning" of a previous baptism. Indeed, although almost 50 percent of ECUSA bishops surveyed in 1986 indicated that they used chrism for the confirmation "handlaying," and so, have tended to foster a rather ambiguous understanding of confirmation in the BCP,[96] the placing of the "seal of the Holy Spirit" as an inseparable part of the baptismal rite was a deliberate attempt to express the absolute and integral unity of baptism itself as a single rite of Christian initiation in "water and the Holy Spirit." Nevertheless, given the historical connotations of the term "confirmation" in the Roman Catholic and Anglican traditions, and by continuing to mandate for "those baptized at an early age" a reaffirmation rite called "confirmation," especially as it remains connected to the rite of handlaying by bishops, theological ambiguity about the meaning and importance of this rite in modern Episcopalianism will continue.

[95] See Meyers, *Continuing the Reformation,* 238–48.
[96] Ibid., 239.

The Rites of Christian Initiation Among Lutherans
  According to Episcopal liturgist Daniel Stevick:

"The design of new rites for Christian Initiation in the *Lutheran Book of Worship* (1978); in the baptismal texts issued by the Methodist Church ("We Gather Together," 1980); in *Holy Baptism and Services for the Renewal of Baptism* (1985), a liturgical resource for Presbyterian churches; and in *The Book of Alternative Services* (1985) of the Anglican Church of [Canada] . . . all seem to take a direction pioneered in the Episcopal Church's work of the early 1970s."[97]

Nowhere is that "direction pioneered in the Episcopal Church" more clearly demonstrated than in the LBW, and, to a lesser extent, by the LC–MS 1982 rejection of LBW in its own publication of *Lutheran Worship.* Prior to the work of the Inter-Lutheran Commission on Worship leading ultimately to these current publications, Lutheran baptismal rites in general had tended to follow the overall pattern of Luther's 1526 *Taufbüchlein*,[98] with the traditional post-baptismal ceremonies of anointing, the giving of the baptismal garment, and the presentation of a baptismal candle no longer included in the rite. Similarly, as we have seen, a rite of confirmation had continued to function among Lutherans until 1968 as a non-sacramental rite of baptismal ratification with handlaying as a means of admission to first communion following an extended period of catechesis.

Contemporary Lutheran rites for baptism. Often defended by appeal to Luther's 1523 *Taufbüchlein*,[99] the rite called holy baptism in the LBW has restored for the majority of Lutherans in North America many of the traditional rites and ceremonies of the classic Western baptismal rite omitted in the later stages of liturgical revision during the Protestant Reformation. Closely parallel to and obviously dependent upon

[97] Daniel Stevick, *Baptismal Moments: Baptismal Meanings* (New York: Church Hymnal Corp., 1987) xv–xvi. See also F. Senn, "Lutheran and Anglican Liturgies: Reciprocal Influences," *Anglican Theological Review* 64 (1982) 60ff.; and Laurence Stookey, "Three New Initiation Rites," LWSS, 274–91.
  [98] See the *Service Book and Hymnal* (Minneapolis: Augsburg; Philadelphia: Board of Publication, Lutheran Church in America, 1958) 242–4.
  [99] See the literature cited above in n. 71.

holy baptism in the 1979 BCP, the baptismal rite in LBW has the following shape:[100]

Introductory address

Presentation of candidates

Address to sponsors and parents

    Young children

    Older children and adults

The prayers

Thanksgiving over the waters (a version of Luther's Flood Prayer)

Renunciation of evil (single)

Profession of faith (triple)

Baptism (by pouring; two formulas provided)

Postbaptismal rites

    Handlaying prayer for the sevenfold gift of the Holy Spirit

    Sealing and (optional) anointing

    Clothing (optional)

    Presentation of baptismal candle

Prayer for parents of the baptized

Welcome

Peace

This rite, however, is not simply a restoration of the baptismal rite in Luther's 1523 *Taufbüchlein*. The thanksgiving over the waters, for example, including a rather ambiguous invocation of the Holy Spirit

---

[100] LBW, Minister's Edition (Minneapolis: Augsburg, 1978) 308–12. The optional postbaptismal rite of clothing with the baptismal garment, together with its accompanying formula ("Put on this robe, for in Baptism you have been clothed in the righteousness of Christ, who calls you to his great feast") does not even appear in the rite itself but only in the rubrics elsewhere. See p. 31.

("pour out your Holy Spirit . . ."), without specifying either where or upon what that Spirit is to be poured, makes use of some of the imagery in Luther's Flood Prayer, but functions here, as in both the Roman and BCP rites, as a kind of blessing or sanctification of the baptismal waters, even if explicit language of blessing and/or sanctification does not appear.[101] Similarly, in the administration of baptism itself LBW provides as an option the passive formula of the eastern Christian traditions, "N. is baptized in the name of the Father, and of the Son, and of the Holy Spirit. Amen." But the most notable distinction by far between this rite and Luther's 1523 rite is, again as in the 1979 BCP, the addition of the following postbaptismal rite at the very place where Luther had originally retained the traditional Western postbaptismal prayer and anointing:

. . . The minister lays both hands on the head of each of the baptized and prays for the Holy Spirit:

P. God, the Father of our Lord Jesus Christ, we give you thanks for freeing your sons and daughters from the power of sin and for raising them up to a new life through this holy sacrament. Pour your Holy Spirit upon ___name___: the spirit of wisdom and understanding, the spirit of counsel and might, the spirit of knowledge and the fear of the Lord, the spirit of joy in your presence.

C. Amen.

The minister marks the sign of the cross on the forehead of each of the baptized. Oil prepared for this purpose may be used. As the sign of the cross is made, the minister says:

P. ___name___, child of God, you have been sealed by the Holy Spirit and marked with the cross of Christ forever.

The sponsor or the baptized responds: "Amen."[102]

Here in the LBW baptismal rite the specifically Roman *confirmation* prayer for the sevenfold gift of the Spirit and the chrismation, refor-

[101] The earlier version of this prayer in *Holy Baptism*, 27, was clearer, asking that the Spirit might be poured out on the baptismal water itself in order "to make this a water of cleansing."
[102] LBW, Minister's Edition, 311.

mulated—as in the current Roman Rite of confirmation itself, in language more akin to the single postbaptismal chrismation of the Byzantine rite—to refer to being "sealed by the Holy Spirit," is even more pronounced than it is in the BCP version. And, at the same time, if the BCP rite is ambiguous as to whether or not this postbaptismal rite constitutes an explicit conferral of the Spirit, the LBW rite, in asking for a postbaptismal "pouring of the Holy Spirit" upon the newly baptized, could certainly be interpreted in such a way. Even the language of the formula for the signing and optional anointing in the LBW is rather unclear and suggests various possible interpretations. Because it refers to the sealing of the Holy Spirit in the perfect tense (i.e., "you have been sealed"), for example, it is not certain whether it is baptism (as in the BCP formula) or the handlaying prayer which, supposedly, has constituted this "sealing" of the Spirit.

Since, as we have seen, Lutheran theology has always been adamant in its assertion that baptism in the trinitarian name, with or without additional rites and gestures, constitutes *full* Christian initiation in water *and* the Holy Spirit, *the* theological question, then, is what LBW intends by a postbaptismal rite such as this. Given the traditional Lutheran theological position on this issue perhaps the best answer is that this unit, together with the giving of the garment and candle, constitute what the current Roman Catholic initiation rites call "explanatory rites," or what the recent ELCA statement on the practice of word and sacrament, *The Use of the Means of Grace,* calls "symbolic acts,"[103] that is, acts or rites which merely explain, underscore, or symbolically express further what the Church believes happens and is given in baptism itself.

Nevertheless, the insertion of this specific unit with its long history of particular sacramental content and meaning within the Roman Catholic tradition does raise an important theological question. As noted at the beginning of this chapter, it is precisely this postbaptismal rite that was cited as problematic for the official adoption of the LBW baptismal rite within the LC–MS. In the December 1977 LC–MS "Report and Recommendations of the Special Hymnal Review Committee" the following critical note appeared in relationship to this unit: "Both the rubric and the prayer imply that the Spirit comes after (apart from?) the new life through this sacrament. One wonders why

---

[103] *The Use of the Means of Grace,* 33.

the traditional prayer with its clear connection of water and the Spirit was dropped for this doubtful one."[104] Questioning even an *optional* postbaptismal anointing, the final rite prepared and accepted by the LC–MS, appearing in *Lutheran Worship,* contains a postbaptismal section which consists of Luther's own 1526 revision of the anointing prayer with handlaying, followed by the giving of the baptismal garment and lighted candle. What *Lutheran Worship* does, therefore, is to restore partially the postbaptismal rites and formulas of Luther's 1523 *Taufbüchlein,* without, however, the anointing. Only then does the baptismal group assemble before the altar for a concluding prayer and welcome.[105]

Contemporary Lutheran rites for "confirmation." If the baptismal rite of the 1979 BCP was highly influential in the development of contemporary Lutheran baptismal rites so also did its "Confirmation with forms for Reception and for the Reaffirmation of Baptismal Vows" play a significant role in the development of Lutheran "confirmation" rites. Here, however, that influential role is clear and obvious in the LBW and non-existent in *Lutheran Worship.*

Like the 1979 BCP, in a rite entitled "Affirmation of Baptism" the LBW also provides three different options for use: (1) confirmation, (2) reception into membership, and (3) restoration to membership.[106] In all three of these options the rite contains the renunciation of evil and the profession of faith from the baptismal rite, followed by prayers of intercession, a short address to those making affirmation and their response, and a version of the postbaptismal prayer for the Spirit, with the phrase "pour out your Holy Spirit" replaced by "continue to strengthen them with the Holy Spirit." Of the three uses intended for the rite for affirmation of baptism in the LBW, only confirmation itself, in distinction to the BCP, includes a concluding laying on of hands with the following prayer: "Father in heaven, for Jesus' sake, stir up in __name__ the gift of your Holy Spirit; confirm *his/her* faith, guide *his/her* life, empower *him/her* in *his/her* serving, give *him/her* patience in suffering, and bring *him/her* to everlasting life."[107]

---

[104] LC–MS, "Report and Recommendations of the Special Hymnal Review Committee" (December 1977) 27.

[105] *Lutheran Worship* (St. Louis, Mo.: Concordia Publishing House, 1982) 203–4.

[106] LBW, Minister's Edition, 324–7.

[107] Ibid., 327.

While the use of an affirmation rite for restoration to membership was not included specifically in the BCP, it is clear that the BCP rite of reaffirmation has been used in this way in the ECUSA as well. Indeed, Lutherans and Episcopalians alike have viewed such affirmation of baptism rites as repeatable rites adaptable to a variety of circumstances marking significant transition moments in life. And they do this "by connecting these significant transitions with the baptismal understanding of our dying and rising with Christ. These rites mark moments when the faith given in Baptism finds new expression, and the spiritual gifts given in Baptism are stirred up to meet new challenges."[108] As such, confirmation is only one of many possible applications.

Theologically speaking, confirmation in the LBW, as in the BCP, is not understood to be part of the rites of Christian initiation per se but as a rite in which, after a period of catechetical instruction, the "confirmands" publicly affirm God's past baptismal action on their behalf. Among Lutherans, even the term "confirmation" itself, then, tends to be interpreted not in a liturgical or ritual manner but, consistent with classic Lutheran theology, in catechetical ways. That is, as current ELCA policy states, confirmation is seen less as a particular *rite* than it is "a pastoral and educational *ministry* of the church that helps the baptized through Word and Sacrament to identify more deeply with the Christian community and participate more fully in its mission."[109] Or, as the introduction to the rite itself says, "confirmation marks the completion of the congregation's program of confirmation ministry, a period of instruction in the Christian faith as confessed in the teachings of the Lutheran Church."[110] Seen in this way, the LBW rite of confirmation, while including handlaying and prayer for the Holy Spirit's *continued* gifts of presence and grace, is to be interpreted not as an initiatory rite *completing* baptism at all, "for Baptism is already complete through God's work of joining us to Christ and his body, the Church."[111]

---

[108] Ibid., 9.
[109] ELCA, "The Confirmation Ministry Task Force Report" (September 1993) 1.
[110] LBW, Minister's Edition, 324.
[111] ELCA, "The Confirmation Ministry Task Force Report," 4.

If the confirmation rite of LBW is viewed in this way as a public celebration of mature ratification or present owning of one's previous baptism and marking the completion of the Church's ministry *to* those being "confirmed," one must note, by way of contrast, the unique confirmation rite of *Lutheran Worship.* The LC–MS, as noted above, rejected the baptismal rite of LBW partly because its post-baptismal rites supposedly separated the gift of the Holy Spirit from the water bath of baptism itself. How surprising then that the confirmation rite of *Lutheran Worship* has what can clearly be interpreted as an explicit conferral of the Holy Spirit to those being confirmed! What is referred to as the "blessing" in this rite reads: "__Name__, God, the Father of our Lord Jesus Christ, *give* you his Holy Spirit, the Spirit of wisdom and knowledge, of grace and prayer, of power and strength, of sanctification and the fear of God."[112]

This apparent inconsistency between the baptismal and confirmation rites in *Lutheran Worship* presents a serious theological problem about the gift of the Holy Spirit in baptism and in the life of the baptized. And, when this confirmation conferral of the Holy Spirit is related to the specific questions addressed to those being confirmed—inexplicably called catechumens—even greater problems arise. For, not only do these catechumens acknowledge the gifts they received in baptism by reciting a renunciation of evil and a profession of faith, they also are asked specific questions about their acceptance of doctrine (biblical interpretation and Lutheran confessional doctrine) and their desire for church membership (both in the Evangelical Lutheran Church and this particular congregation), and, subsequently, are invited and welcomed to "share . . . in all the gifts our Lord has for his Church and to live them out continually in his worship and service."[113] In other words, unlike the LBW rite, the confirmation rite of *Lutheran Worship* can be interpreted not so much as a rite of baptismal *affirmation* but as a rite of *reception* or initiation *into* the LC–MS and one of its congregations. And, when combined with the explicit language about the gift of the Holy Spirit in this context, one wonders, indeed, whether this rite has not become the *real* rite of initiation itself with the gift of the Holy Spirit related explicitly to *Lutheran* Church membership.

[112] *Lutheran Worship,* 206–7; emphasis added.
[113] Ibid., 206–7.

With the notable exception of the baptism and confirmation rites in *Lutheran Worship,* the rites of Christian initiation in several churches today, as we have seen, show a remarkable degree of commonality and homogeneity with regard to ritual structure, gesture, liturgical texts, and theology. In the attempts to recover and restore to the modern Church both the adult catechumenate and the integral fullness of baptism as new birth in water and the Holy Spirit leading to the Eucharist, either by the restoration of the "seal of the Holy Spirit" to baptism itself (RCIA, BCP, and the LBW) or by the revision of confirmation itself so that its connection to baptism is underscored more clearly, initiation rites in modern Western Christianity have transcended the splits of the Reformation to achieve a degree of ecumenical convergence unparalleled in the history of the Church since the aftermath of Constantine's conversion in the fourth and fifth centuries.

At the same time, however, and in spite of these remarkable achievements, several theological and unresolved issues, especially with regard to various practices associated with adult initiation, with infant baptism versus infant initiation, and, still, with the practice and interpretation of confirmation, remain. It is to these three issues that the following section is devoted.

Christian *Initiation of Adults or the* Conversion *of Other Christians?*

The overall importance of the modern restoration of the adult catechumenate for the faith and life of the contemporary Church cannot be overestimated. "What the Roman documents contain," writes Aidan Kavanagh of the RCIA, "are not merely specific changes in liturgical rubrics, but a restored and unified vision of the Church." He continues:

"One may turn an altar around and leave *reform* at that. But one cannot set an adult catechumenate in motion without becoming necessarily involved with *renewal* in the ways a local church lives its faith from top to bottom. For members of an adult catechumenate must be secured through evangelization; they must be formed to maturity in ecclesial faith through catechesis both prior to baptism and after it; and there must be something to initiate them into that will be correlative to the expectations built up in them throughout their whole initiatory process. This last means a community of lively faith in Jesus

Christ dead, risen, and present actually among his People. In this area, when one change occurs, all changes."[114]

In short, because of the need for the active involvement of the whole faith community in the process of adult initiation, the RCIA, as well as all other attempts at restoring the adult catechumenate, do not so much offer a new way to do the rites as much as they offer a new way to be and do Church.

It must not be forgotten here that the origins of the adult catechumenate are to be found within the various attempts of missionaries in the late nineteenth and early twentieth centuries to prepare adult converts for the full rites of Christian initiation. Similarly, with regard to the RCIA itself, as we have seen, the intent of this restored catechumenate is also for the conversion of the unbaptized. In other words, the adult catechumenate as envisioned by the RCIA is *prebaptismal* in nature and orientation and *not* designed with the reception or transfer of Christians from one ecclesial tradition to another in mind.

Nevertheless, in the "Additional (Combined) Rites" of the RCIA, the 1979 BCP, and the various attempts at restoring the adult catechumenate among Lutherans and others, both real catechumens and other "candidates," including those for reception into membership— and occasionally those seeking restoration to membership[115]—are often joined together within the same catechumenal process. Hence, while adult catechumens receive baptism, confirmation, and first communion at the Easter Vigil, other candidates are often received into membership with some form of confirmation or affirmation of baptism rite, and receive their first communion at the same time.

To be fair, attempts are certainly made in all of these combined situations to make clear distinctions between catechumens and candidates so that the dignity of baptism itself is not compromised. In the RCIA, for example, candidates are not exorcized, neither do they sign the book of the elect, nor do they receive other rites designated for catechumens alone. But, by placing various groups together in the same catechumenal process, and by celebrating both Christian initiation and

[114] Aidan Kavanagh, "Christian Initiation in Post-Conciliar Catholicism: A Brief Report," LWSS, 8–9.

[115] For such a category of people some sort of restoration of the classic "order of penitents" would certainly be more desirable with their reconciliation, as in the traditional Roman liturgy, taking place on Holy Thursday.

reception with some form of "confirmation" together at the Easter Vigil, it is not always clear if the distinctions between these groups is all that clear either to the liturgical assembly or the catechumens and candidates themselves. Such confusion, in fact, becomes even more problematic when the number of candidates becomes greater than the number of catechumens in a given parish, a regular phenomenon in several places today. Such has led some to suggest that the *real* intent of the restored catechumenate in today's churches is but a new way to make "converts" out of already baptized Christians, who seek to be received or transferred into another church. Indeed, I have heard parish RCIA directors describe the RCIA itself in precisely this way, that is, as a "program people go through to become Catholics."

What are often neglected in Roman Catholic dioceses and parishes in this regard are the norms for the rite of "Reception of Baptized Christians into the Full Communion of the Catholic Church" in the *National Statutes on the Catechumenate*. In the rite itself, following the profession of the Nicene Creed in the context of the eucharistic liturgy, those being received into full Roman Catholic communion state simply, "I believe and profess all that the holy Catholic Church believes, teaches, and proclaims to be revealed by God,"[116] and are then confirmed and receive their first communion. According to the *National Statutes on the Catechumenate*, not only are those received into full communion from other Christians *never* to be designated as "converts," a term strictly reserved for those who convert "from unbelief to Christian belief,"[117] but it is also clearly stated that:

[116] *Rites*, vol. 1, par. 491, 280. This rite of reception represents a radical departure from previous rites for the reception of "converts." Prior to 1962, those "converting" from a variety of other religious traditions were required to make an abjuration either of "Hebrew superstition," the Islamic "sect of the infidel," or the "heretical errors" of the particular "evil" Protestant "sect" they were leaving. See *Rituale Parvum* (Turin: Maison Mame, 1949) 35–6. In addition to this, a detailed profession of faith, still used in 1964, including explicit doctrinal assent to the existence of seven sacraments, the teaching of the Council of Trent on original sin, the sacrificial nature of the Mass, the doctrine of transubstantiation, the existence of purgatory, the veneration of images, the salutary use of indulgences, an oath of obedience to the pope, and the teaching of Vatican Council I on the infallibility of the pope, was also made. See *The 1964 English Ritual: Collectio Rituum*, 193–5.

[117] *Rites*, vol. 1, par. 2, 341.

"It is preferable that reception into full communion *not* take place at the Easter Vigil lest there be any confusion of such baptized Christians with the candidates for baptism, possible misunderstanding of or even reflection upon the sacrament of baptism celebrated in another Church or ecclesial community, or any perceived triumphalism in the liturgical welcome into the Catholic eucharistic community."[118]

It is lamentable that such a powerful and ecumenical statement about the theology of baptism and the common identity and dignity of all the baptized has not been taken more seriously in the pastoral adaptations made of the RCIA today. Equally lamentable is the fact that in restoring the adult catechumenate in other churches today the same dynamic of combining rites and people has also been at work. Such is a problem that will need continual and increased attention among all the churches in the future.

A related issue in this context, especially in the Roman Catholic Church, is the use of confirmation as a part of the rite of reception into full communion. Confirmation, in fact, is mandated for the reception into full communion of all baptized Christians from other traditions, with the notable exception of Eastern Orthodox Christians for whom no liturgical rites whatsoever are required. While the recognition of the fullness of Christian initiation in the rites of the Eastern churches is ecumenically worthy of praise, one wonders why the same recognition cannot be given to the rites of other Christians today. Here, at least, as the current rites of the BCP and LBW demonstrate, it is, essentially, the equivalent to the Roman rite of confirmation, that is, the handlaying prayer for the sevenfold gift of the Holy Spirit and a signing rite for the seal of the Spirit, that has been added to baptism. Almost all modern Protestant reforms of Christian initiation have restored some kind of postbaptismal rite giving symbolic and ritual expression (handlaying, anointing, or both) to the initiatory gift of the Holy Spirit.[119] Without recognizing the theological full-

---

[118] Ibid., par. 33, 347. While the following paragraph makes a concession "for pastoral reasons," it asserts, nevertheless, that "a clear distinction should be maintained during the celebration between candidates for sacramental initiation and candidates for reception into full communion, and ecumenical sensitivities should be carefully respected."

[119] Most interesting here among current Protestant revisions of Christian initiation rites is that in the postbaptismal rites even Presbyterians have

ness of Christian initiation in the rites of other Western churches, then, the current Roman Catholic use of confirmation in the rite of reception into full communion remains open to the critique that *the* gift of the Holy Spirit in Christian initiation appears to be tied to membership in the Roman Catholic Church alone, much as the confirmation rite of *Lutheran Worship* tends to suggest, similarly, that the gift of the Holy Spirit is connected to membership in the LC—MS. This, too, is a problem needing increased attention in today's ecumenical context. Perhaps, if any kind of rite of reception above a tradition-specific profession of faith is needed, a rite like the reception in the 1979 BCP could serve as a fitting model even for Roman Catholics: "*N.*, we recognize you as a member of the one holy catholic and apostolic Church, and we receive you into the fellowship of this Communion. God, the Father, Son, and Holy Spirit, bless, preserve, and keep you. *Amen.*"

Infant Baptism or Infant Initiation?

As we have seen, the breaking of the connection between a catechetically understood rite of "confirmation" with first communion among North American Episcopalians and Lutherans; the subsequent addition of the seal of the Holy Spirit to adult and infant baptism alike in the BCP, LBW, and other modern Protestant rites; and the restoration of the Sunday Eucharist in several Protestant traditions have raised the possibility of recovering infant *initiation* in full, including infant participation in the Eucharist, within several churches today. Such, however, was not a primary focus in the modern Roman Catholic reforms of Christian initiation. If anything, in fact, the great enthusiasm brought about by the 1972 publication of the RCIA tended to make infant baptism itself a subject of intense discussion and debate among Roman Catholics.

In the 1982 article "The Postconciliar Infant Baptism Debate in the American Catholic Church,"[120] Paul F. X. Covino summarizes four

---

provided for an optional anointing with oil in relationship to the "seal" of the Holy Spirit. See *Book of Common Worship*, 413–4. If this appears to be a long way from Calvin, who considered chrism to be "that rotten oil" (see above, 271), it is also a strong indication of the power of contemporary ecumenical liturgical convergence.

[120] In LWSS, 327–49.

theological and pastoral approaches to the question of infant baptism within American Catholicism between 1965 and 1980. These approaches include, first, what Covino calls the "mature adulthood school," in which the RCIA, with its emphasis on catechesis and mature adult faith and commitment, is interpreted as the absolute "norm" for modern Christian initiation. Infant baptism, if allowed at all, is seen as permissible, if abnormal (i.e., a departure from the norm), only for the children of mature and committed adult believers, but discouraged in all other situations. As an alternative practice, adherents of this school often suggest that infants be enrolled in a kind of catechumenate and then receive all three of the initiation sacraments together after the possibility of making a commitment of faith is assured.

The second is called the "environmentalist school," an approach which, while strongly supporting the tradition of infant baptism, looks at the overall environment provided both by the family of the infant and the local Christian community for the formation and development of faith. If the mature adulthood school makes the profession of mature, personal faith a primary emphasis, the environmentalist school places its emphasis on the Christian community and corporate faith of the Church into which infants are initiated, and on the corporate responsibility that the Christian community bears in relationship to the future faith development of those baptized infants.

The third school identified by Covino is called the "initiation unity school." Simply put, this school of thought argues that the unitive celebration and integral sequence of baptism, confirmation, and first communion in the RCIA be normative for *all* who are initiated, regardless of age. That is, if infant *baptism* is permitted, then, adherents of this school argue, there is no compelling reason why the other sacraments of initiation cannot also be conferred at the same time.

Finally, the fourth school, the "corresponding practice school," takes neither the RCIA nor the RBC and *Rite of Confirmation* as single or exclusive norms for modern Christian initiation. Rather, adherents of this school claim that all three rites together are to be seen as constituting Roman Catholic initiatory polity since these rites have been formed to correspond closely to the various and multiple ways and times in life in which people come to Christian faith.

The various debates and discussions on infant baptism among Roman Catholics after Vatican II, both in the United States and Europe, led eventually to an *Instruction on Infant Baptism* issued by the Sacred Congregation for the Doctrine of Faith in 1980.[121] Much to the disappointment of those in the mature adulthood school, this *Instruction* underscored traditional Roman Catholic teaching on the necessity of infant baptism and, in support of that, made appeal to the doctrine of original sin. It must be noted, however, that the understanding of original sin itself had been undergoing further development in Roman Catholic theological circles for some time. That is, a rather narrow interpretation of original sin as a personal or individual inheritance needing the washing away of baptism to ensure the individual's salvation had been broadened and reinterpreted to include other categories more related to the social nature of human life and the overall existential and relational context in which an individual human life is actually lived. As early as 1968, Dominican theologian Christopher Kiesling summarized this new approach to original sin, writing:

"Conception and birth into the human race is assurance that one's personality development will not be what God intends it to be morally and religiously. This failure is not through one's personal fault, his own deliberate sinning, but results from being born into a human race caught in the web of sin. It is a condition of estrangement from God's ideal for [hu]man[kind] and from God which affects the person through his inheritance of human nature from a race of sinners and through his humanization and socialization by sinners. As estrangement from God, this condition precludes communion and life with God and any presuppositions which may be necessary for that communion and life. . . . [People] born into the human race are destined to egoism, alienation, and isolation which reach their term in the condition called eternal death or hell. Unless the creator of [hu]mankind intervenes to rectify this situation, to justify [people], they cannot escape this sad destiny."[122]

If, in such a context, original sin is "social," so also is the "forgiveness" of this sin received and known in social relationships. According to Covino, "the grace that is imparted in baptism is not some

---

[121] Vatican City: Vatican Polyglot Press, 1980.
[122] C. Kiesling, "Infant Baptism," *Worship* 42:10 (1968) 617–26.

kind of magic metaphysical change in the infant, but the acceptance into a community of people living in reversal of the sinful orientation which constitutes original sin."[123] Infant baptism in contemporary Roman Catholic theology, therefore, appears to have less to do with the individual inheritance of sin or guilt and much to do with the process of initiation into and subsequent socialization by the Christian community itself. As a result, the narrative of the fall of Adam and Eve into sin in Genesis 3 has been rescued from its almost biological use as a "proof text" for the reproductive transmission of sin and restored as a paradigm for the universal human condition of sin, a condition overcome by the death and resurrection of Jesus Christ and celebrated in the rites of Christian initiation.

Neither the mature adulthood nor corresponding practice schools have many adherents among Roman Catholic or Protestant liturgists in the United States today. Rather, it is the initiation unity school, together with the overall emphases of the environmentalist approach, that has been on the rise. So much is this the case today that, along with the above noted attempts of Episcopalians and Lutherans to restore the communion of baptized infants, the Roman Catholic Federation of Diocesan Liturgists (FDLC) adopted the following statement at its 1992 annual meeting:

"It is the position of the delegates . . . that the Board of Directors of the [FDLC] and the Bishops' Committee on the Liturgy urge the National Conference of Catholic Bishops to take the initiative to propose to the Apostolic See a discussion on the restoration of the ancient practice of celebrating confirmation and communion at the time of baptism, including the baptism of children who have not yet reached catechetical age, so that through connection of these three sacraments, the unity of the Paschal Mystery would be better signified and the eucharist would again assume its proper significance as the culmination of Christian initiation."[124]

Although only time will tell whether such a proposal will achieve its desired aim or not, one other significant development occurring in contemporary Roman Catholic liturgical practice in the United States

[123] Paul F. X. Covino, "The Postconciliar Infant Baptism Debate in the American Catholic Church," LWSS, 337.
[124] *FDLC Newsletter* 22:4 (December 1995) 45.

does point in a similar direction. As we have seen, the age for the reception of confirmation in the Roman Catholic dioceses of the United States today varies from age seven, the traditional "canonical" age, all the way to age eighteen, with the majority of dioceses somewhere in the middle of these two.[125] What has been happening, however, is that several dioceses in recent years have lowered the age for confirmation to the age of seven and, with that shift, have also restored the traditional location and reception of confirmation as coming *before* the reception of first communion.[126] While this is not the restoration of infant initiation by any means, it is certainly a step in that direction and, at the same time, it is also a *significant* step away from using sacramental confirmation itself as a catechetical rite of maturity or an adolescent rite of passage to adulthood. Most important for now in the history of the Church is that such a move restores the traditional Western sequence of the initiation rites, a sacramental sequence clearly underscored and expected by the contemporary Roman rites themselves.

Not since the time of the Gelasian Sacramentary and *Ordo Romanus XI* has Western Christianity been so close to the possibility of restoring full infant *initiation* to its liturgical and sacramental life. Indeed, if children who have not yet reached the catechetical age of seven can be baptized, and if confirmation is properly restored as nothing other than the concluding ritualization and sacramentalizing Spirit-gift and seal of baptism, then there is absolutely no reason, theological or otherwise, why such children should not be communed as well. As a Greek Orthodox woman once explained to a youth group I brought to her parish to experience Byzantine Liturgy: "We feed our small children regular food without expecting them to know yet about vitamins and nutrition. So also we Orthodox feed them the spiritual food of the Eucharist without expecting them to know yet the meaning of this Gift. Both foods are necessary for life." But perhaps it was Mark

---

[125] See the National Conference of Catholic Bishops, *Report of the Ad Hoc Committee for the Canonical Determination of the Age of Confirmation* (Washington, D.C.: n.p., 1993). The American Catholic Bishops have yet to reach a consensus on the "age" for confirmation in the dioceses of the United States.

[126] See for the diocese of Portland, Maine, the brief comments by Bishop Gerry, "Confirmation: A Sacrament of Initiation," *Origins* 27:21 (1997) 358–62. The diocese of Saginaw, Michigan, has also moved in this direction in recent years.

Searle who best summed up the rationale for restoring both confirmation and communion to the baptism of young children when he said that:

"At a time when the Church is so intent on rescuing the humane values of Christianity and is concerned to do greater justice to the role of the family . . . and a time when the role of the nonrational and prerational dimensions of the life of faith is being recovered, perhaps infant initiation ought to be seen less as a problem to be grappled with than as an opportunity to be grasped. Far from barring children from the font, the chrism, and the altar, the Church should welcome their participation in these sacraments as a reminder both of the catholicity of the Church and of the fact that, no matter how informed or committed we might be as adults, when we take part in the sacramental liturgies of the Church we are taking part in more than we know."[127]

Together with the issues raised above by the various practices associated with the Christian initiation of adults, so too is the question of the full Christian initiation of children in need of continued and increased attention among all the churches today.

Confirmation or Chrismation?

The modern reforms of the rites of Christian initiation throughout several Western churches across denominational lines—in liturgical texts, in the overall ritual pattern, and in theological interpretation—are largely indebted to a recovery of what has been the regular initiation practice of the churches of the East for several centuries. Nowhere is this recovery more prominent or obvious than in the current formula for confirmation in the Roman rite ("N., be sealed with the Gift of the Holy Spirit."), and in the postbaptismal signings (with optional anointing) in the BCP ("N., you are sealed by the Holy Spirit in Baptism and marked as Christ's own for ever. Amen.") and in the LBW ("___Name___, child of God, you have been sealed by the Holy Spirit and marked with the cross of Christ forever."). Such attention to the postbaptismal rites of the Christian East here has been deliberate.

In his Apostolic Constitution on the Sacrament of Confirmation of August 15, 1971, Pope Paul VI decreed that, in its essence, *"the Sacrament of Confirmation is conferred through the anointing with chrism on the*

---

[127] Searle, "Infant Baptism Reconsidered," 408–9.

forehead, which is done by the laying on of the hand, and through the words: be sealed with the gift of the Holy Spirit."[128] And, while Paul VI refers to the "dignity of the respected formulary used in the Latin Church" for this anointing, that is, the formula first appearing in the twelfth-century Roman Pontifical ("I sign you with the sign of the cross and confirm you with the chrism of salvation. In the name of . . .") and continuing in use until 1971, he makes a deliberate choice for the single (and *presbyteral!*) chrismation formula of the Byzantine Rite.

Why, however, was this done? According to him, this Byzantine formula, "expresses the Gift of the Holy Spirit himself and calls to mind the outpouring of the Spirit on the day of Pentecost."[129] But did not the Roman tradition of the handlaying prayer with its invocation of the sevenfold gifts of the Holy Spirit upon the newly baptized do the same for centuries in a legitimately distinct, and, at least, more obvious biblical-apostolic manner? Indeed, in the Gelasian Sacramentary it is this handlaying prayer itself that was understood as constituting the baptismal seal ("to seal *[ad consignandum]* then he imposes his hand on them with these words . . .").

The further justification for the dominance of chrismation, that "the most important place [in confirmation] was occupied by the anointing, *which in a certain way represents the apostolic laying on of hands,*"[130] simply defies logic and is based, ultimately, upon the words of Pope Innocent III (+1216), who, as we saw above in chapter 6, similarly claimed that "the anointing . . . with chrism *signifies* the laying on of hands."[131] But why and how does the episcopal chrismation as opposed to an actual laying on of hands do this? If something "signifying" or "representing the apostolic laying on of hands" was desired, would not an actual imposition of hands themselves have been a fuller and clearer sacramental sign of this?

The operating assumption in Paul VI's Apostolic Constitution is that Byzantine chrismation *is* the same thing as Roman confirmation, an assumption repeated in the current *Catechism of the Catholic Church.*[132] But this assumption is questionable, to say the least. Byzantine

---

[128] *Rites,* vol. 1, 477; emphasis added.

[129] Ibid., 477.

[130] Ibid.; emphasis added.

[131] Ibid., 475; emphasis added.

[132] *Catechism of the Catholic Church* (Collegeville: The Liturgical Press, 1994) 327ff.

chrismation, as we have seen, is an integral part of the *baptismal* rite itself and is located not at the equivalent place of Western confirmation but at the very place of the traditional presbyteral postbaptismal anointing of the Roman rite. The current Roman rite of confirmation, therefore, especially in the RCIA, where this confirmation chrismation has simply replaced the traditional Western postbaptismal anointing, has created an unprecedented liturgical and theological connection between Western confirmation and Byzantine postbaptismal chrismation. Aidan Kavanagh refers to this correctly as the "Byzantinization of western confirmation."[133] But, by omitting the traditional Western postbaptismal anointing prayer from their rites, and by similarly placing a version of this Eastern formula for the "seal of the Holy Spirit" in its place, modern Protestant rites of baptism have also been "Byzantinized" to some extent.

While ecumenical attention to the liturgical riches of Eastern Christianity on the part of the West is to be welcomed, the recovery of a richer pneumatological focus in the sacramental rites of the West does not automatically necessitate the Western adoption of Eastern formularies. That is, East and West need not ritualize the gift of the Holy Spirit in exactly the same way, especially when, as in the case of both the traditional postbaptismal anointing prayer and the confirmation prayer, the West already has a long standing, pneumatologically-oriented tradition of its own. In this context, the omission of the traditional postbaptismal prayer in the RCIA, BCP, and LBW, a Western baptismal prayer at least as old as the *De Sacramentis* of Ambrose of Milan, is, indeed, a lamentable loss. Not only is the connection between water and the Holy Spirit in baptism clearly and unambiguously articulated by this prayer, as the LC–MS critique of the LBW noted strongly, but the reference in this prayer to baptism as "new birth" (John 3) provides a fitting and necessary complement to what has been an almost exclusive Western theological emphasis upon baptism as death and resurrection in Christ (Romans 6). If only *one* postbaptismal anointing is desired for the RCIA, or for the current Protestant rites, the traditional anointing with its comparatively richer christic, ecclesiological, and thus, implicitly, pneumatic imagery, especially as it appears in the "explanatory rites" of the current

---

[133] Aidan Kavanagh, *Confirmation: Origins and Reform* (New York: Pueblo, 1988) 92ff.

Roman texts, may have been a better choice. If a more pronounced pneumatology in such an anointing prayer is desired, then, either the precedent established by Thomas Cranmer in his 1549 BCP or the following formula, suggested by Bryan Spinks from the ecumenical chapel at Churchill College, Cambridge, England, might provide models for further revision today:

"Jesus the Anointed One anoints you with grace and signs you as one of his flock. You are a member of a chosen race, a royal priesthood, a holy nation, God's own people. May the Holy Spirit which is poured out upon you sanctify and preserve you. N., you are signed with the oil of Anointing in the Name of the Father, and of the Son, and of the Holy Spirit. Amen."[134]

The current reform of confirmation in the Roman rite reflects a mere continuation of what has been an unfortunate medieval theological trajectory in the West, a theological interpretation focused on what was a secondary (the episcopal anointing) rather than primary and more traditional element (the pneumatic handlaying prayer). The origins and development of the episcopal chrismation in the Roman rite, as we have seen throughout this study, are by no means clear. There is really no hard evidence for it as an integral part of the Roman postchrismational rites before Innocent I in the early fifth century. And, in spite of the scholastic theological interpretation emphasizing the episcopal chrismation as the true "matter" and "form" of confirmation, the fact is that the formula for its administration was never clearly pneumatic in orientation until the 1971 reform.

By focusing so exclusively on the chrismation, by defining that as the essence of confirmation, and especially by adopting the Byzantine formula for its administration, however, the Roman rite of confirmation is subject to losing the richness and evocative power of the biblical gesture of handlaying in Christian initiation. Therefore, instead of "reforming" the *rite* of confirmation by turning the chrismation formula itself into the *seal* of the Spirit and, thus, bringing to an unfortunate conclusion the medieval theological focus on episcopal chrismation as bestowing the gift of the Spirit, it would have been

[134] Bryan Spinks, "Vivid Signs of the Gift of the Spirit? The Lima Text on Baptism and Some Recent English Language Baptismal Liturgies," LWSS, 318.

preferable to do two things. First, as in the case of the modern revision of Roman Catholic ordination rites, the imposition of hands and the prayer for the sevenfold gift of the Spirit should have been restored theologically as constituting confirmation's "matter" and "form." Such a reform or restoration of the essential nature of the handlaying prayer would have allowed the traditional Western post-baptismal anointing in baptism to remain an integral component of *all* baptisms and not just those of infants or others unfortunate enough not to be confirmed in the same celebration. Second, a true "reform" of confirmation would have simply restored it to its ancient Western location immediately following baptism and anointing in *all* cases, as, indeed, the final pneumatic blessing and ecclesial ratification of Christian initiation and public welcome to the eucharistic communion of the Church. Here I can only underscore the comment made by Frank Quinn some years ago that "today . . . an emphasis upon the classic rite of handlaying with prayer for the Spirit would be quite healthy. Not only does the prayer offer much food for thought to the preacher; it is absolutely necessary for understanding the rite."[135]

CONCLUSION

In the contemporary reform of the rites of Christian initiation throughout several of the churches in the West, much has been accomplished in a relatively short period of time. The last thirty years, for example, have witnessed a recovery of baptismal immersion or submersion as the desired norm for the conferral of baptism and, along with that, significant changes in baptismal fonts and spaces have been and continue to be made. Similarly, the celebration of baptism itself, even that of infants, has been recovered as a *public* celebration taking place within the liturgical assembly of the Church. In those places where the adult catechumenate leading to full Christian initiation in water, oil, and eucharistic table has been restored, and along with it the immense variety of lay ministries needed (e.g., catechists, sponsors, and the role of the entire faith community in general) to lead and accomplish such a process of conversion, parishes themselves have experienced a renewal in faith and life, the recovery

[135] Frank Quinn, "Confirmation Reconsidered: Rite and Meaning," LWSS, 235–6.

of the dignity of baptism, and a renewed sense of their own identity as Church, as the Body of Christ in the world. At the same time, a renewed emphasis on the need for catechesis and continual formation in faith has accompanied the introduction of the new rites of baptism and confirmation for children across denominational boundaries. Attention to the *necessary* connection between baptism and confirmation has led almost all churches today as well to restore (or add), partially at least, those traditional postbaptismal rites that became confirmation historically to the rites of baptism itself. If among some churches within Protestantism this has also brought with it the possibility of restoring Christian initiation in full to infants, it has also meant for Roman Catholics the possibility, at least, of moving in this direction as well by recovering the traditional canonical age for confirmation and first communion. Indeed, as all of the current rites demonstrate, a liturgical-ecumenical consensus has been reached today on the normativity of the classic ritual sequence of baptism, "confirmation," or some kind of rite giving symbolic-sacramental expression to the sealing gift of the Holy Spirit, and Eucharist as constituting, in that order, the fullness of Christian initiation itself. For Protestants, in general, this has meant a revision of former confirmation rites themselves so that new and repeatable rites of baptismal affirmation or renewal could meet the need for postbaptismal catechesis leading to a later profession of faith or a personal and public owning of the baptismal gift. If the Roman Catholic Church as a whole has yet to move in this direction and still continues to use confirmation as a rite expressing the Spirit-gift in initiation (as in the RCIA), a rite of baptismal affirmation for adolescents, and as a rite of reception into full communion, recent moves in some dioceses of the United States to restore confirmation to the canonical age of seven before first communion may eventually lead to further questions about the need for other kinds of repeatable rites of affirmation or new rites of reception into full communion.

In response to such profound, rich, and broad-sweeping ecumenical changes in initiatory theology and practice, one can only stand in grateful awe. If much has changed, however, much, unfortunately, remains the same. In spite of the clarity in the current Roman liturgical documents that the reception of the Eucharist is the *culmination* of Christian initiation, that it is to *follow* confirmation, and that baptism and confirmation together signify "the unity of the paschal mystery, the close link between the mission of the Son and the outpouring of the Holy Spirit, and the [necessary] connection between the two sacraments through which the Son and the Holy Spirit come with the Father to those who are baptized," the pattern of infant initiation in Roman Catholic pastoral practice often still follows what was established as an accident of history in the Middle Ages. That is, baptism in infancy is followed by first reconciliation and first communion at age seven with the entire sacramental process culminating at a later age in confirmation. The association of sacramental reconciliation and the reception of communion, a problem since Lateran IV (1215), not only makes four distinct sacraments out of Christian initiation, but continues to raise the theological question of the relationship between reconciliation and initiation itself. That is, if, according to current Roman Catholic theology, one is fully initiated into the Church by baptism, confirmation, and Eucharist together, it is hard to speak of being "reconciled" to a community in which one is not yet initiated. Similarly, if reception of the Eucharist constitutes the *culmination* of Christian initiation, it is extremely difficult to speak of the need for confirmation for those who have already received their first communion.

Remaining issues in Christian initiation, however, are not simply Roman Catholic problems. As we have seen, for example, the ELCA statement on Word and sacrament, *The Use of the Means of Grace,* while permitting the *first* communion of infants at the baptismal Eucharist, goes on to state that their "regular" eucharistic participation may commence later in their lives, *"ordinarily . . .* only when children can eat and drink, and can start to respond to the gift of Christ in the Supper." Such appears theologically inconsistent. If *first* communion is allowed for baptized infants, then their *regular* participation in the Eucharist would seem naturally to follow. Similarly, the great discrepancy in the understanding of confirmation as expressed in the rite of affirmation of baptism in the LBW and the rite for confirmation in *Lutheran Worship* suggests also that no consensus has yet been reached on the meaning, rite, and role of confirmation among North American Lutherans. And, in spite of the clear theology in the 1979 BCP that "Holy Baptism is *full initiation* by water and the Holy Spirit into Christ's Body the Church," the continued practice of confirmation, reception, and reaffirmation administered by Episcopal bishops (!), expected even in the case of recently baptized adults, cannot but be perceived as being part of Christian initiation itself.

The current rites of Christian initiation and their theology, therefore, present several challenges for the continued reform of Christian initiation in general today. But among these, perhaps, the greatest challenge is also the greatest gift. That is, the current rites and their theology offer to modern Christians, as never before in history, the opportunity to recover a profound Christian spirituality, a way of living in Christ which is consciously and intentionally rooted in Christian initiation in water and the Holy Spirit itself. It is to this challenge and gift that the final chapter of this study is directed.

Chapter 9

Back Home to the Font:
The Place of a Baptismal Spirituality and
Its Implications in a Displaced World

Paragraph 10 of Vatican II's Constitution on the Sacred Liturgy states clearly that the very center of the Church's life in all of its aspects is the liturgy:

"The liturgy is the summit toward which the activity of the Church is directed; at the same it is the fountain from which all her power flows. . . . From the liturgy . . . as from a fountain, grace is channeled into us; and the sanctification of [people] in Christ and the glorification of God, to which all other activities of the Church are directed as toward their goal, are most powerfully achieved."[1]

While it is to the Eucharist primarily that this paragraph refers, it must not be forgotten that the Eucharist itself is both the culmination and *repeatable* portion of the rites of Christian initiation themselves. And because this is the case, the particular focus upon the role of liturgy in the spiritual journey emphasized in this chapter is not the eucharistic *culmination* of initiation but the very *beginnings* of that initiation in the sacrament of baptism. For baptism itself is the liturgical and sacramental center out of which we live; it is the watery Spirit-filled womb and tomb to which we are called to return time and time again to find a welcome place in our displaced lives. Indeed, the spiritual journey in Christ is a journey of both place and displacement, a journey of death and resurrection, of birthing pangs and the bringing forth of new life, and the paradigm for all this is most certainly baptism. Baptism places into the world a community of displaced people, people on a pilgrimage who really belong nowhere except where they are led, a people sure of their identity as the Body of

---

[1] Constitution on the Sacred Liturgy, par. 10.

365

Christ, as those who always walk wet in the baptismal waters of their origin. This final chapter, then, is an invitation, a call for a recovery of a baptismal spirituality and its implications, for a renewed sense of a foundational "baptismal consciousness" which might guide us ecumenically as we rapidly approach the third Christian millennium. There are eight points I want to make.

A RECLAIMING OF BAPTISM AS THE GREAT AND RADICAL EQUALIZER

The recovery of a baptismal spirituality calls us to a rediscovery and a reclaiming of the radical implications of baptism as St. Paul describes them in Galatians 3:27-28 and 4:6:

"As many of you as were baptized into Christ have clothed yourselves with Christ. There is no longer Jew or Greek, there is no longer slave or free, there is no longer male and female; for all of you are one in Christ Jesus. . . . And because you are children, God has sent the Spirit of his Son into our hearts, crying 'Abba! Father!'"

Who are the displaced in our world today if not those separated by race, by social and economic status, or by gender? Who are the displaced even, at times, in the Church if not those separated by race, by social and economic status, or by gender? But, says Paul, in a statement that was too radical for the Church of his own day, too radical for the Church of subsequent centuries, and probably too radical for himself to realize as well, these common distinctions mean absolutely *nothing* in relationship to being clothed with Christ in baptism. Indeed, baptism into Christ—like death itself, the central Pauline metaphor for baptism—is the "Great Equalizer." It transcends all such distinctions and, as such, provides us with a perspective and foundational basis from which we might address any and all forms of racism, classism, and sexism. For here in baptism—as on the day of Pentecost itself (one of the great New Testament paradigms for Christian baptism)—are the divisions of the Tower of Babel reversed and all again become initiated into Christ as one people, speaking a common language of prayer, thanksgiving, and witness. Here in baptism is the paradise of Genesis 1 and 2 restored where God is most appropriately imaged by the unity of both male and female. Here rich and poor come together as equals, clothed in the baptismal garments of Christ, and take their place together at the banquet table.

When we speak of multiculturalism, for example, we dare not forget that by baptism in the Church we are quite literally plunged already into a multicultural[2] ecclesial reality in which all the baptized, by the gift and power of the indwelling baptismal Spirit, are enabled to address God with Christ as "Abba" and recognize one another in Christ as common brothers and sisters by that watery sacramental bond, which, in this case at least, is thicker than blood. Not only do we recognize our common baptismal relationship, but because of the one Spirit of baptism we rejoice in the variety of Spirit-given charisms that such diverse cultures, ethnic groups, and races bring to the whole Christian community. Multiculturalism is not merely a social challenge or issue to be addressed in our rapidly changing and shrinking world, even within rural America. Rather, because of the place of baptism multiculturalism already is a given in the Church, a reality and a gift to be cherished, a place where all the displaced are welcomed by a common bath into a common home. The challenge before us then is to allow this baptismal reality to develop and grow in our ecclesial consciousness that we may become more fully what and who our baptism has made us to be already, a richly diverse people of God, the Body of Christ, indeed Christ himself existing as community in the world. Here there is neither Jew nor Greek, neither German nor Irish, Scandinavian nor Pole, neither African American nor Native American, neither Hispanic nor Anglo, but in Christ Jesus one richly diverse ecclesial reality, a multicultural "stew" in the words of Virgilio Elizondo,[3] having a common origin, a common home in the Spirit-generated font of death, birth, and new life.

A similar point can be made in reference to Paul's statement that there is neither male nor female in this baptismal unity. Paul, of course, is speaking here primarily about equal access to salvation in Christ and not ministry per se, but there are implications for ministry in what he says. Here again we dare not forget that when we speak of issues related to gender or sex-based distinctions and roles—whether those issues concern public ministry or other types of leadership in the Church—we have already received a preliminary

[2] Note that I did not say "into a *polycentric* ecclesial reality" because there is room for only one center in the Church, namely, Christ himself!

[3] See Virgilio Elizondo, "A Bicultural Approach to Religious Education," *Religious Education* 76 (1981) 261–2.

baptismal answer that must be taken with the utmost seriousness. Paragraph 18 of the section on ministry in the Faith and Order document Baptism, Eucharist, and Ministry produced by the World Council of Churches in 1982 reads:

"Where Christ is present, human barriers are being broken. The Church is called to convey to the world the image of a new humanity. There is in Christ no male or female (Gal. 3:28). Both women and men must discover together their contributions to the service of Christ in the Church. The Church must discover the ministry which can be provided by women as well as that which can be provided by men. A deeper understanding of the comprehensiveness of ministry which reflects the interdependence of men and women needs to be more widely manifested in the life of the Church. . . . Though they agree on this need, the churches draw different conclusions as to the admission of women to the ordained ministry. An increasing number of churches have decided that there is no biblical or theological reason against ordaining women, and many of them have subsequently proceeded to do so. Yet many churches hold that the tradition of the Church in this regard must not be changed."[4]

However such issues are decided in the various churches today and whatever those decisions may be, ultimately, it is baptism and the resulting image of Christ that the baptized bear and reflect that must be at the heart and center of the discussion. If so, the conversation will never be about rights, status, and privilege as it may be elsewhere. In the Church the conversation will always be about the *baptismal* imaging of Christ, about the God-given dignity of *all* the baptized, and about discerning the charisms imparted to the baptized by the Spirit for the sake of Christ's Body in the world. That in Christ there is neither male nor female comes to all, then, as a baptismal word of both judgment and good news. And, again, the challenge here as well is to become more fully who and what baptism has made us to be already, a people of God in which sex roles have no role.

The recovery of a baptismal spirituality, of the central, foundational, and ongoing role of baptism in our spiritual journeys, brings with it

[4] "Ministry," *Baptism, Eucharist, Ministry* (Geneva: World Council of Churches, 1982) par. 18 (pagination varies in the different editions of this document).

an agenda for the churches of today, an agenda that constantly calls us back home to the font where over and over again we might learn what it means to be an inclusive, or better, a truly "catholic," universal image of Christ in the world. Here, among these radical implications of Paul, is where the questions of inclusive language, particular lectionary translations, the use of other languages in liturgy, the nature of the assembly and its ministers, and even the architectural prominence (or lack thereof) given to baptism within worship spaces find their appropriate context. To all of this the churches are called to pay serious attention for no other reason than because of what and who they have been made to be by water and the Holy Spirit.

A REEVALUATION OF THE RELATIONSHIP BETWEEN BAPTISM AND "CONFIRMATION"

The recovery of a baptismal spirituality calls us today to a reevaluation of that other initiatory rite known as "confirmation," especially in its inseparable relationship to baptism itself. In the current Roman RCIA, where confirmation follows baptism immediately as part of the unified complex of initiation rites, the connection between these two sacramental moments is explicit and clear. As we have seen above, paragraph 215 states:

"The conjunction of the two celebrations [baptism and confirmation] signifies the unity of the paschal mystery, the close link between the mission of the Son and the outpouring of the Holy Spirit, and the connection between the two sacraments through which the Son and the Holy Spirit come with the Father to those who are baptized."[5]

In spite of this, however, confusion reigns with regard to confirmation in the churches of today. For if the joining of baptism and confirmation does "signify the unity of the paschal mystery," the very unity of our Trinitarian God in the saving economy of grace, then what mystery can possibly be signified in the situation of those only *baptized* in infancy, with confirmation separated from baptism by an interval of time that, according to the American Catholic bishops, can last from as few as seven (the traditional canonical age) to as many as *eighteen* years?

[5] *The Rites of the Catholic Church as Revised by the Second Vatican Ecumenical Council* (hereafter, *Rites*), vol. 1 (Collegeville: The Liturgical Press, 1990) 146–7.

It is the separation of these two ritual moments within what the early Church called by the inclusive term of "baptism"—a definite *liturgical* displacement to be sure—which has caused the confusion both historically and theologically, a confusion which continues to form and shape the members of the churches today. Whenever I teach courses on the rites of Christian initiation to Roman Catholics, my experience tends to be similar each time. That is, coming out of their own experience, for the most part, of baptism in infancy, first communion (and first confession) at age seven, and confirmation in early or later adolescence after an extensive period of "catechesis," most view confirmation not as a sacrament, gift, seal, or pneumatic completion of their baptismal initiation into Christ and the Church, but rather as an independent rite of maturity, growth, adult commitment, adult membership, adult decision, or even as a rite of adult vocation and ministry. As a member of a Reformation Christian tradition I am always amazed at these common answers and how much they reveal the influence that the theologies of the sixteenth-century Protestant Reformers have had among contemporary Roman Catholics. For, as we have seen, such an understanding of "confirmation" is precisely the view these Reformers held and the view according to which they sought to "reform" confirmation according to a catechetical, educational model, a model they believed to be the ultimate origins of confirmation in the early Church.

In his recent study of confirmation, Paul Turner notes that what is called "confirmation" today has functioned and continues to function in three distinct ways in the life of the Church. Turner writes:

"Our liturgies tell us we have three separate needs: the need to emphasize the gift of the Spirit in the rites of initiation, the need to mark a transfer of membership from another Christian church . . . , and the need for children baptized in infancy to affirm their baptism and strengthen their faith and commitment. . . . A rite of initiation is not the same as a rite of transfer or of commitment. Rites of transfer only heighten the intolerable situation of Christian disunity. And the need to recommit and celebrate the strengthening of faith is a need best ritualized by a repeatable celebration. . . . If we could start all over and imagine a day when our ancestors devised these rituals, if we could say, 'We need a rite of initiation, a rite of transfer, and a rite of maturity,' would we choose the *same* rite and the *same* name for all three events? Of course not, yet this is the burden we have laid on the sacrament of confirmation."[6]

Similarly, Gerard Austin states:

"Confirmation is not a reaffirmation of a previous baptism; it is not the ritualization of a key moment in the human life cycle. It is, rather, the gift of the Spirit *tied intimately to the water-bath* that prepares one for the reception of the body and blood of Christ as a full member of the church."[7]

Indeed, the recovery of a baptismal spirituality calls for reuniting confirmation with baptism in all cases, not just in those rites designed for *adult* initiation. For baptism is the only context in which "confirmation" makes any liturgical, ecclesiological, trinitarian, and sacramental sense as the ritualization of the Spirit-gift in Christian initiation.

In spite of the fact that the initiation rites in the *Lutheran Book of Worship* (LBW) and the American Episcopal *Book of Common Prayer* (BCP) have done precisely that by placing within baptism itself the traditional Western *confirmation* prayer for the seven-fold gift of the Spirit with handlaying, followed by a sealing of the Spirit rite (with or without the use of chrism), confusion about confirmation itself is by no means a problem only for Roman Catholics. In fact, one could argue that by retaining also a rite for adolescents called "confirmation" following a period of catechesis, Lutherans and Episcopalians actually practice a *double* confirmation: once according to the classic sacramental initiation model, where the Spirit gift *is* tied to the water bath, and once according to a catechetical, educational model, having its roots in the Reformation traditions. Of course, the wonderful irony in this is that those traditions which have historically denied the sacramentality of confirmation now end up with two "confirmations" in practice, both related in some way to the Holy Spirit. And in both liturgical traditions even the medieval scholastic focus on confirmation as a rite of "strengthening" continues to make its appearance.

---

[6] Paul Turner, *Confirmation: The Baby in Solomon's Court* (New York: Paulist Press, 1993) 128. See also, Paul Turner, "Forum: Confusion Over Confirmation," *Worship* 71:6 (1997) 537–45.

[7] Gerard Austin, *Anointing with the Spirit: The Rite of Confirmation: The Use of Oil and Chrism* (New York: Pueblo, 1985) 146; emphasis added.

At the same time, however, such rites of baptismal affirmation and renewal present in the BCP and LBW could be adapted for Roman Catholics as well. The anthropological need for passage rites, or the need for rites of faith commitment and baptismal affirmation, needs currently met for Roman Catholics by first communion and confirmation, is a need that must be acknowledged and met in some way. With a restored unitive initiation practice for all ages, would it not be possible for Roman Catholics similarly to develop new, and repeatable, rites of faith commitment and baptismal affirmation, rites which mark significant transition moments in life? Such rites, as the BCP demonstrates clearly, could even be celebrated under the presidency of the local diocesan bishop, if so desired.

Given the increasing number of Hispanic-Latino peoples within the American Catholic Church, for example, certainly one occasion for such a rite of renewed commitment and affirmation could be the celebration of *quinceañeras,* the traditional rite of transition to adulthood for fifteen-year-old Hispanic females, which, customarily, has included a renewal of baptismal vows in the context of a special Liturgy of the Eucharist.[8] Similarly, since first reconciliation, sometimes understood as even a fourth sacrament of initiation, would no longer occur in the immediate context of first communion, this sacrament could now be given renewed attention, finally, as the sacrament of reconciliation with the Church into which one, in fact, *has* been fully initiated. And, further, American Catholics are not really strangers to additional rites related to the initiation sacraments at all. As we saw in the previous chapter, there was a time not that long ago where, in a number of places in the United States, as in France and Germany, a distinction was made between "first communion" at about age seven, of course, and "first *solemn* communion" at a later age. Is there any reason why some kind of special eucharistic celebration marking the culmination of specific catechesis on the Eucharist could not be reclaimed today as well, even if that celebration did not function as and was not called *first* communion?

Nevertheless, for all of the churches today, the goal is not simply the liturgical-sacramental rejoining of what has been separated, al-

---

[8] The current ELCA worship resource, *Libro de Liturgia y Cántico,* (Minneapolis: Augsburg, 1998) 119–20, has such a rite. Please note, however, that I am suggesting *quinceañeras* as one occasion for such an affirmation rite, not as a model for creating such rites.

though this is a crucial and important liturgical step. The primary goal, rather, is to take with the utmost seriousness that Christian baptism *is* full initiation in water *and* the Spirit, and that, theologically, "confirmation," or whatever we might call it, is but the ritualizing or sacramentalizing of the Spirit gift inseparably connected to the water bath itself. Such a unitive realization of initiation has vast implications for our spirituality, for our life *in the Spirit*. Again, Austin writes:

"Viewing the sacrament [of confirmation] as a unique and isolated moment in the Christian life can create a letdown later on, or even worse, a failure to recognize continued gifts of the Spirit. The Christian life is one of mission to the world and this involves frequent moments of commitment and even more frequent movements of the Spirit. This life begins with the sacraments of initiation. . . . The Spirit cannot be separated from the Christian life. Why, then, separate the sacrament of confirmation, the gift of the Spirit, from the sacraments that celebrate initiation into the Christian life? Do we not give the impression that the Spirit is dormant until we take the initiative to commit ourselves? Do we not imply that the gift of the Spirit is not part of incorporation into the body of Christ? . . . Confirmation . . . must ever be viewed in the larger context—the Christian life as a life of the Spirit, a Pentecost life. The future of the church is that of the future of the Spirit, a Spirit urging all to become one in Christ to the glory of God."[9]

Confirmation should be placed back where it belongs—as the inseparable concluding seal of the baptismal rite itself whenever baptism takes place. As a consequence, all the debates about knowledge, preparation, and age for confirmation should be terminated. Perhaps then the churches can get busy on life-long *mystagogy* and the life-long return to the font as Christians seek to live out in the Spirit the implications of their new birth!

AN ADVOCACY FOR AND THE PRACTICE OF THE COMMUNION OF ALL THE BAPTIZED

Closely related to the issue of the intimate relationship between baptism and confirmation, of course, is the question of communion reception; the recovery of a baptismal spirituality calls the churches to a thorough reevaluation of communion practices. If it is nothing

[9] Austin, *Anointing*, 155.

other than the inseparable unity of water and the Holy Spirit that makes Christians, that initiates people into the Body of Christ, the Church, then it should be clear that the very means by which the Church sacramentally and liturgically expresses its self-identity *as* Church, that is, in the Eucharist, is for *all* the baptized, *all* who are initiated into the Christian community, which, at heart, is nothing other than the continuation of the table companionship of Jesus himself. The recovery of such a foundational understanding of baptism as entry to the eucharistic companionship of the Church then calls rightly to an advocacy for and practice of the communion participation of all the baptized, along the lines of the pristine tradition of the Orthodox East from as far back as we can go and along the lines of the tradition of Rome and the West for at least the first Christian millennium. As Benedictine liturgist Aidan Kavanagh says, "Although no person has a right to baptism, the baptized *do* possess rights to confirmation and the eucharist."[10] Or, in the words of the LBW, "Holy communion is the birthright of the baptized."[11]

As we have seen, such a recovery of the intimate connection between initiation and Eucharist, in fact, is currently happening throughout the ecumenical Church with several in our own day calling explicitly for the restoration of confirmation and communion reception to baptism at whatever age baptism is conferred. Closely parallel to this central theological orientation of the inseparable unity of the three initiation rites are the insights of a number of contemporary educators and social scientists, who assert that it is precisely within what some have called the "first stage of faith," that is, ages two to six, where children possess the greatest and most lasting responsiveness to images, rituals, and symbols.[12] Given this, it should become increasingly clear as well that the denial of the Eucharist to the youngest of baptized children is nothing other than the denial of the *primary* way in which they actually *can* participate in the symbolic,

---

[10] Aidan Kavanagh, "Initiation: Baptism and Confirmation," *The Sacraments: Readings in Contemporary Sacramental Theology*, ed. Michael Taylor (New York: Alba House, 1981) 93.

[11] LBW, Minister's Edition (Minneapolis: Augsburg, 1978) 31.

[12] See the work of James Fowler, *Stages of Faith: The Psychology of Human Development and the Quest for Meaning* (San Francisco: Harper & Row, 1981); and John H. Westerhoff, III, *Building God's People in a Materialistic Society* (New York: Seabury Press, 1983) esp. 59–78.

ritual, and image-laden liturgical self-expression of the faith community. If we wait until age seven or later to introduce them to eucharistic participation, that is, until a time in which they can be catechized, prepared, and begin to "understand" the implications of the Eucharist cognitively and rationally, we have waited too long. Eucharistic faith is not equal to cognitive understanding. Faith is not only rational but unrational and prerational as well. In the Pauline New Testament sense, faith is not intellectual acceptance of or assent to propositional revelation, but trust. And such trust develops, it seems, only in relationship, only in an environment, in a community of trust such as the family or the church. Recall the words of James Fowler here:

"We are endowed at birth with nascent capacities for faith. How these capacities are activated and grow depends to a large extent on how we are welcomed into the world and what kinds of environments we grow in. Faith is interactive and social; it requires community, language, ritual, and nurture. Faith is also shaped by initiatives from beyond us and other people, initiatives of spirit and grace. How these latter initiatives are recognized and imaged, or unperceived and ignored, powerfully affects the shape of faith in our lives."[13]

My own experiences of children and Eucharist have convinced me completely not only of the desirability but of the sheer rightness of communing all the baptized. My own daughter, age two at the time, who had been a regular communicant—although secretly—from the time of her infant baptism, surprised me greatly during dinner one Sunday noon. After we worshiped at a nearby parish that used a style of bread for Eucharist closely resembling mid-eastern pita bread, our dinner that day, although unintentionally, included pita bread as well. I remember my daughter holding a piece of bread in her hand, and, pointing both to a Byzantine icon of Christ above our table and to that piece of bread, she said something like, "Christ Jesus there, Christ Jesus right here." In her own way, she had made some rather interesting and proper theological-liturgical-sacramental connections. Similarly, in a parish I once served, where we had moved from once-a-month to every Sunday Eucharist, I remember a young mother

---

[13] James Fowler, as cited by Ruth Meyers, *Children at the Table: The Communion of All the Baptized in Anglicanism Today* (New York: Church Hymnal Corp., 1995) 160. See above, 237.

telling me of the influence this had begun to have on her own pre-school daughter, who, without any prompting, had suddenly begun to recite the words of institution aloud as she rode along in the car. Alternatively, I was recently told by one of my graduate students of her experience where a young child she knew had flatly refused to go forward any longer for a "blessing" at the time of communion distribution. When asked why, the child responded that the last time he had gone he had been "Xed" out by the communion minister, who, instead of giving him bread, had traced an "X" over him (obviously the sign of the cross in blessing), telling him by this gesture that he did not belong. Children are formed by symbol, by image, by ritual. Even when we adults think that we are being inclusive in our communion practices by giving children a blessing, or, as in one case I know of, giving a *grape* (!) to non-communing children, we may, in fact, be only reenforcing their *exclusion* from Jesus' table. When children stayed in the pews and did not come forward during communion distribution at all, we were, at least, being consistent in our exclusionary practices.

The recovery and restoration of first communion to Christian initiation, even within the rites of initiation for infants, is not coming about because of sacramental romanticism or from any attempt at a liturgical repristination of a supposed, normative "Golden Age" of the Church of the first few centuries. Far from it. Rather, such a move is coming about, ultimately, because of the spirituality of initiation itself, because of the rootedness of all Christian initiation and life in the very graciousness of God, the God who through both Word and sacrament always acts first, always acts in love prior to our action, leading us by the Holy Spirit to the response of faith, hope, and love within the community of grace. As Gerard Austin says:

"Such a practice [i.e., the uniting of all three sacraments whenever baptism takes place] would underscore the reality that God takes the initiative, that baptism-confirmation-eucharist form an essential unity, and that admission to eucharist is built on incorporation into Christ and not upon something extrinsic such as knowledge or age. . . . Such an approach would not destroy programs of religious catechesis; rather it would base such programs on personal development and needs and would be ongoing, rather than coming to a halt after the reception of confirmation."[14]

[14] Austin, *Anointing,* 145.

This reality of God always taking the initiative in the order of salvation, especially as that is expressed in the unitive ritual fullness of Christian initiation, brings me to my next point.

A RENEWED STANCE AGAINST CREEPING PELAGIANISM

The recovery of a baptismal spirituality as the center out of which the Church lives and the center to which it constantly returns by the repeatable sacrament of initiation, the Eucharist, calls the churches, perhaps today more than ever, to a renewed stance against that sort of creeping Pelagianism which affects much of what today is generically called "spirituality" in especially an American context. God's gracious initiative, concretized and mediated as sheer *gift* in the font and in the assembly around the eucharistic table, should give the churches a firm basis from which to critique and shun so much of contemporary Gnosis and individualism that passes before our eyes constantly and influences so many in our churches. Indeed, a clear baptismal spirituality places the theological emphasis where it should be; on God, the great author and initiator of salvation. Because of this we can and must say, boldly, in the words of Daniel Erlander:

"[We are not saved] by: . . . proving [God's] existence by the wonder of nature or the power of logic; validating God's presence by visible blessings; having a prescribed religious experience; . . . building glorious religious institutions; reaching a high level of personal morality; [or] saving ourselves through status, wealth, knowledge, consumption, chemicals, positive thinking, correct religious doctrine, self help groups, health foods, or exercise plans."[15]

Rather, he continues:

"In the baptismal water we died with Christ. We were crucified and buried in order that we might be raised with Christ to live the new life, to dwell in a new reality, a new order of existence. Because of Baptism we *are* Christians. Never does our status before God depend on . . . how we feel, having the right experience, being free of doubts, what we accomplish, our success or our position. We are

[15] Daniel Erlander, *Baptized, We Live: Lutheranism as a Way of Life* (Chelan, Wash.: Holden Village, 1981) 4.

Christians because God surprised us. Coming in water, God washed us and grafted us into Christ. Our identity for all the days of our life is set! We are children of God, priests of the King, disciples of Christ, a servant people, a holy nation, the communion of saints, the followers of the Way, proclaimers of the wonderful deeds of God. Jesus' story becomes our story. Baptized into his death, we are raised to live as the Body of Christ in the world today."[16]

A baptismal spirituality rooted in God's gracious initiative and activity calls us to be especially careful with how the rites of initiation are celebrated and presented. Especially in an American context of individualism, with its focus on self-actualization, and an understanding of life based on a system of achievement and reward, even the grace-filled sacraments of Christian initiation can become interpreted in a rather Pelagian manner, that is, viewed as particular rewards to be received by individuals as a result of their so-called "free choice," their "decision for Christ," or their somehow "earning" them through a program of required catechesis and preparation. In saying this, I am critizing neither the current Roman RCIA nor the recent attempts underway to restore the adult catechumenate among Lutherans, Episcopalians, and other Christian churches. No, the pastoral situation of the church in today's world calls for such serious attention to the liturgical evangelization of adults! What I am saying is this. Designed primarily for missionary contexts, with the initiation of *unbaptized* adults in mind, the RCIA is not a program but a sacramental *process* designed to "seal" conversion to Christ and the Church, a conversion always rooted in the prior activity of the Holy Spirit, a Spirit who, as the RCIA makes abundantly clear, is active prior, during, and after the sacramental rites themselves.[17] And it is this gracious activity of the Holy Spirit in the Word and sacramental life of the faith community that always must be stressed. For it is the Holy Spirit and none other that leads to conversion. It is, says Paul, only in the Holy Spirit that one can confess Jesus as Lord (see 1 Cor 12:3). As such, in spite of the great debates in the last thirty years or

---

[16] Ibid., 7.

[17] On the meaning of conversion in relationship to the RCIA see Donald Gelpi, *Committed Worship: A Sacramental Theology for Converting Christians,* vol. 1, *Adult Conversion and Initiation* (Collegeville: The Liturgical Press, 1993) 3–181.

so among especially Roman Catholic liturgical scholars about whether or not infant baptism is still a desirable or even defensible practice, the words of Eugene Brand, written in 1975, call for particular attention:

"Though a response of faith may antedate Baptism and lead someone to request it, Baptism is largely a prelude to faith, standing, as it does, at the inception of the life in Christ. In regard to faith, almost everyone is baptized in infancy. Baptism has an inescapable proleptic character because it is tied to the future of one's life for its completion."[18]

What this means is that the churches need to be just as concerned, if not *more*, with postbaptismal mystagogy as they are with the prebaptismal catechumenate; that, at the very least, the one-year period of extended mystagogy, that extended incorporation of the newly initiated into the liturgy, life, and mission of the community, expected by the National Conference of Catholic Bishops in the *National Statutes for the Catechumenate*, be followed closely. If Brand is correct that "in regard to faith, almost everyone is baptized in infancy," such a necessary focus on lifelong postbaptismal catechesis merely reinforces that for *all* in the faith community—infants, children, and adults—new life *begins* in initiation and it is to this new life begun in water and the Holy Spirit that all are invited to return constantly for refreshment, renewal, and reorientation in life.

One of the ways to keep a focus on what is central is, instead of debating the initiation of infants, to continue to celebrate it *publicly*. For what could be more countercultural, more against the prevailing tide of modern American culture, and still more anti-Pelagian and grace filled than doing something so apparently foolish and silly as to celebrate God's salvific activity, God's choice, God's adoption of children into God's reign as it is known and celebrated in the faith community through the initiation of infants? And who, I would ask, are more displaced in today's world than children, innocent victims of poverty, violence, hunger, and crime? As the late Eugene Maly put it:

"Through infant Baptism we *initiate* a person into a faith-community long before he or she can choose whether to belong. And through

[18] Eugene Brand, *Baptism: A Pastoral Perspective* (Minneapolis: Augsburg, 1975) 38.

infant Baptism we also *celebrate* a person's salvation long before he or she consciously experiences the need to be saved or can take any responsibility for turning self toward God. Something about this flies in the face of very basic notions in our culture about individual freedom and the importance of personal choice—in short, our insistence on individualism. We want to believe that we choose God (rather than that God chooses us). We want to believe that we can and should save ourselves (rather than that we are saved). . . . Biblical faith challenges our basic human temptation to individualism. Infant Baptism is . . . one way we have institutionalized our conviction that community is central to Christian life, to God's plan of salvation."[19]

Indeed, I would go so far as to say that how we think of *infant* initiation speaks volumes about our understanding of grace, the role of the Holy Spirit, and the Christian community itself in the Christian life.

Along these lines, perhaps it is time for Roman Catholics, Episcopalians, and Lutherans, at least, to think about some further revision of the rites for infant baptism themselves. As noted in the previous chapter, one of the clear intentions of Vatican II for the liturgical reform of infant baptism was that "the roles of parents and godparents, and also their duties, should be brought out more sharply." The Roman *Rite of Baptism for Children* (RBC) has certainly done this, as have the BCP and LBW. But in all three, emphasis on these parental and godparental roles, duties, and responsibilities has been placed *before* the actual rite and conferral of baptism itself in a manner quite inconsistent with the classic Western Roman Catholic tradition, with Luther's 1523 and 1526 rites, and with Cranmer's 1549 rite. Instead, this emphasis in the RBC, BCP, and LBW is highly consistent with the various sixteenth-century rites of the Reformed tradition as they developed in southern Germany and Switzerland, where such promises and obligations on the part of parents, sponsors, and the community appear to have been the very condition *for* the giving of baptism to infants in the first place. As Bryan Spinks has recently written:

"[A] bilateral covenant has infiltrated most modern baptism rites. Parents are given a crucial role in the rite, prior to the baptism. It

[19] Eugene Maly, "Still a Case for Infant Baptism?" *The Sacraments: Readings in Contemporary Sacramental Theology*, ed. Michael Taylor (New York: Alba House, 1981) 95.

might be argued that such preliminaries are simply a modern counter-part to the enrolling of the old catechumenate, giving the candidates into the care of the church, and taking seriously the responsibility of those who present them. However, parents and sponsors are not simply asked whether they want baptism for the child, asked to renounce evil, and confess the Catholic creed; now words such as responsibility, duty, and obligation, and 'you for your part,' *precede* the act of infant baptism."[20]

And, as he continues, with specific regard for the "unilateral" or unconditional theology of Luther:

"Although responsible parishes and pastors may well have a baptismal policy which involves visiting, instructing, and exhorting, Luther teaches us that in the baptismal liturgy the structure and contents must witness only to the work of God. Any admonitions to godparents or parental duties—any covenantal response—if they are to be included at all, ought to be placed after the baptismal act. But this is true of adult baptism too. Renunciation and the *fides* [faith] of the Christian church may come before, but duties and promises ought only to come after the baptism as a response to the unmerited grace of God."[21]

In the interest of a renewed and firm stance in favor of unconditional and unmerited grace against creeping Pelagianism, perhaps such further revision in this part of the current rites would be highly desirable.

A RENEWED SENSE OF THE BAPTISMAL FOCUS AT THE CENTER OF THE LITURGICAL YEAR

The recovery of a baptismal spirituality invites today's churches as well to develop a renewed understanding of the baptismal focus which is at the heart and center of the liturgical year, the ongoing celebration of baptismal identity in Jesus Christ. For the most part, the contemporary churches have done very well in recapturing the baptismal import and implications of both Lent and Easter, especially the Paschal Vigil, as the Church's prime time for both the initiation

[20] Bryan D. Spinks, "Luther's Timely Theology of Unilateral Baptism," *Lutheran Quarterly* 9 (spring 1995) 26.

[21] Ibid., 42.

sacraments themselves and for the renewal of all the baptized. Indeed, such a paschal or Easter focus in the current reformed liturgies of the churches has strongly underscored the characteristic Western theological interpretation of baptism as sacramental participation in the paschal mystery, the dying and rising of Christ along the lines of Romans 6.

Neither Easter nor the image of death and resurrection in Christ, however, exhaust the variety of rich images associated with initiation in Scripture and our liturgical traditions. Over the past twenty years or so, contemporary liturgical scholarship, as we saw in chapter 5 above, has helped us understand that, while there was an early *preference* for initiation at Easter in the churches of North Africa and Rome, other churches—e.g., those of Syria, Egypt, and the non-Roman Western churches in Gaul and Spain—tended to focus on other occasions like Epiphany, understood, of course, as the great theophany of Christ in the Jordan, and that a Romans 6 theology of baptism came to the forefront of sacramental theology universally only within a fourth-century post-Nicene context. Prior to that, the dominant interpretation and paradigm of initiation appears to have been that of Jesus' own baptism in the Jordan and the rebirth imagery of John 3. And from such a focus in this equally ancient and biblical tradition comes a whole cluster of initiation images which have little to do with passing from death to life, or with sharing in the dying and rising of Christ through baptism. Such images include seeing the font as *womb*, rather than tomb, literally called the "Jordan" itself in some traditions, images like "adoption, divinization, sanctification, gift of the Spirit, indwelling, glory, power, wisdom, rebirth, restoration, [and] mission."[22]

We would do well to rediscover such rich images today as complementary with our customary Romans 6 emphasis. And one way to do that is to broaden our understanding of other feasts and seasons besides Easter as equally fitting occasions for the initiation rites—even the RCIA in its fullness. There is absolutely no reason, given the contents, at least, of the current Roman books, why all four of the optional Old Testament readings for the Vigil of Pentecost could not constitute part of another full baptismal vigil in which the dominant imagery of the celebration would become that of the Pentencostal

---

[22] Mark Searle, "Infant Baptism Reconsidered," LWSS, 385.

and, hence, *baptismal* gift of the Holy Spirit. There is no reason, given the dominant importance of Jesus' own baptism in the theology and liturgy of the early Church, why the feast of his baptism on the Sunday after Epiphany could not be given its own initiation-oriented vigil with a final catechumenate that begins on the first Sunday in Advent.

Another way to expand our appreciation for the richness of baptismal imagery is to pay attention to the entire liturgical year itself as the hermeneutical key for ongoing liturgical catechesis, ongoing mystagogy in the meaning and significance of our initiation. Contrary to popular belief, the liturgical year is neither a kind of Hellenistic mystery religion's reenactment of the life of Jesus nor an annual recurring cyclic meditation on and devotion to the historical life of Jesus. Rather, the liturgical year through feast and fast, through festival and preparation, celebrates the presence of the already crucified and risen Christ among us "now!" as we remember *(anamnesis)* what he did "once for all" in history (Heb 10:10) and as we await his coming again.[23] But it is always one and the same Christ we remember and expect as we celebrate his abiding presence in the Spirit and as we behold what that presence means for us here and now through the multifaceted prism of Advent, Christmas, Epiphany, Lent, Easter, Pentecost, or through the lives of his saints throughout the ages. Awareness and respect for the integrity of the liturgical year helps us enter into it more deeply. For it is the means by which we are allowed, invited, and privileged to celebrate the reality that the Gospel of Jesus Christ, mediated to us by Word, Sacrament, and community, declares us, forms us, and calls us to be Easter people, Lenten people, Christmas people, and Advent people who live in hope and expectation for the Day of His Coming. The issue is our baptismal identity in Christ as his people, his Body in the world. It is precisely this identity we celebrate in the liturgical year.

Christmas, then, is not about baby Jesus in the manger "back there and then." It is about *our* baptismal birth in the adult Christ as he is born anew in us through the Spirit who brings the "glad tidings" of salvation—the one salvation—to us now. Easter and Pentecost are

---

[23] On this see Robert Taft, "Toward a Theology of the Christian Feast," *Beyond East and West: Problems in Liturgical Understanding* (Washington, D.C.: Pastoral Press, 1984) 1–13.

about *our* death and resurrection in Christ, our passover from death to life in his passover, through water and the Holy Spirit in baptism. Lent is about *our* annual retreat, our annual reentry into the catechumenate and order of penitents in order to reflect on, affirm, remember, and reclaim that baptism. And Advent is about *our* hope for fulfillment in Christ when "he will come to judge the living and the dead," a hope solidly grounded in the baptismal Spirit-gift who is the very downpayment and seal of our redemption.

I am constantly amazed at how this integral understanding was a characteristic of the preaching and teaching of the Fathers. In one of his Christmas sermons, for example, Pope St. Leo the Great in mid-fifth-century Rome, while speaking of the incarnation, concludes:

"Christian, remember your dignity, and now that you share in God's own nature, do not return by sin to your former base condition. Bear in mind who is your head and of whose body you are a member. Do not forget that you have been rescued from the power of darkness and brought into the light of God's kingdom. Through the sacrament of baptism you have become a temple of the Holy Spirit. Do not drive away so great a guest by evil conduct and become again a slave to the devil, for your liberty was bought by the blood of Christ."[24]

The making of such connections in our preaching and catechesis is precisely what a foundational baptismal spirituality suggests to us not only in the Sundays, solemnities of our Lord, and seasons of the year, but in the celebration of other feasts as well. What else is Trinity Sunday than the celebration of God's drawing close to us in divine three-fold saving activity, the mystery of God into whose inner trinitarian life we are graciously initiated and made to become partakers? What else is All Saints Day if not the celebration of the Church's very identity as a community of grace that transcends both space and time, that great cloud of witnesses into which we are initiated as brothers and sisters? How can we celebrate the feast of the Presentation of Our Lord on February 2, the "Candle-Mass" of Christ, the light of the world, without making the connection between the candles that are blessed and our own baptismal "illumination"? Or, for Roman Catholics in particular, what else is the solemnity of the Immaculate Con-

[24] *Sermo 1 in Nativitate Domini.* ET from *The Liturgy of the Hours,* vol. 1 (New York: Catholic Book Pub. Co., 1975) 405.

ception of Mary if not parallel to our own "immaculate conceptions" and new births solely by God's unmerited grace in the baptismal womb of the Church? Or, what is Mary's Assumption if not a concrete eschatological sign of our own baptismal hope in "the resurrection of the dead and the life everlasting"?

The recovery of a baptismal spirituality calls us to the liturgical year itself as the ongoing celebration and continued formation in our baptismal identity. The year provides liturgical catechesis of the highest order, mystagogy, continual formation in who we are and who we are called to be in Christ.

A RENEWED SENSE
OF BOTH LAY AND ORDAINED MINISTRY

The recovery of a baptismal spirituality invites us to a renewed sense of both lay and ordained ministry in the life of the Church. By water and the Holy Spirit *all* are, we might say, "ordained" as priests, initiated into that royal, prophetic, and communal priesthood of the baptized in which, of which, and for which the specially ordained serve as the sacramental sign not to *do* the ministry of the baptized, but to lead the baptized in their collaborative ministries of proclamation, service, prayer, and witness in the world. Indeed, to put it in traditional theological language, it is not just the ordained but the *Church* as the Body of Christ in the world which acts *in persona Christi*.[25] In an article devoted in large part to precisely the relationship between Christian initiation and ministry, Aidan Kavanagh writes:

"A baptismal element needs to be introduced into our contemporary discussion of ministry. . . . But while one cannot discuss baptism without ministerial implications arising, it has unfortunately become usual to discuss ministries without ever feeling it necessary to enter into the implications of this discussion for baptism. That holy orders are rooted in baptism never seems to cross our minds. I suggest that it must. . . . [T]he Church baptizes to priesthood: it ordains only to executive exercise of that priesthood in the major orders of ministry. Indeed *Ordo Romanus XI* of the ninth century has the baptized and anointed neophytes vested in stole and chasuble as they are presented

[25] On this see S. K. Wood, "Priestly Identity: Sacrament of the Ecclesial Community," *Worship* 69:3 (1995) 109–27.

to the Bishop of Rome for consignation prior to the beginning of the Easter Eucharist. The point being that *sacerdotium* [priesthood] in orthodox Christianity is not plural but single. It is that of Christ, shared among those in solidarity with whom . . . he was himself baptized in the Jordan, and also in solidarity with whom he now stands as both sacrifice and sacrificer in heaven. . . . While every presbyter and bishop is therefore a sacerdotal person, not every sacerdotal person in the Church is a presbyter or bishop. Nor does sacerdotality come upon one for the first time, so to speak, at one's ordination. In constant genesis in the font, the Church is born there as a sacerdotal assembly by the Spirit of the Anointed One himself. *Laos* ['laity'] is a priestly name for a priestly person."[26]

He continues:

"In baptism by water and the Holy Spirit . . . one is anointed with as full a sacerdotality as the Church possesses in and by the Anointed One himself. Ordination cannot make one more priestly than the Church, and without baptism ordination cannot make one a priest at all. Becoming a Christian and becoming a sacerdotal being are not merely correlative processes, they are one and the same."[27]

We often hear it said today, especially within Roman Catholic circles, that there is a great crisis in vocations. I know that this is painfully true with regard to specific vocations to ordained ministry and religious life. But I also know that such a crisis was inevitable. "The greatest achievement of Vatican II," said Fr. Godfrey Diekmann, O.S.B., to me recently, "was the restoration of the baptismal dignity of the laity, an achievement even greater than episcopal collegiality."[28] And with such a restoration comes an inevitable crisis. No longer is a sense of religious vocation, a call to ministry within the Church, specifically tied to entering a particular ordained office or religious community. Rather, the primary vocation of all Christians is that very call of baptism itself to share in the one priesthood of Jesus Christ in a great variety of ways through a variety of Spirit-given charisms. There's something downright biblical, Pauline, about that and we

---

[26] Aidan Kavanagh, "Unfinished and Unbegun Revisited," LWSS, 267–9.
[27] Ibid., 270–1.
[28] Godfrey Diekmann, personal conversation.

would do well to pay attention to this fundamental baptismal reality whenever we think of ministry.

There may be, indeed, a crisis in particular kinds of vocations in the Church today but, on another more basic level, there is no vocational crisis whatsoever, a fact brought out by the increasing numbers of laity today seeking pastorally-oriented theological degrees and serving in an ever greater variety of pastoral ministries. Where else but in contemporary Roman Catholicism do we see the "royal priesthood of the faithful," the "priesthood of all believers," better expressed in liturgy, in pastoral ministries of witness and service? I am convinced that it is Roman Catholicism which will teach us "Protestants" what this baptismal "priesthood of all believers" really means. If, then, there is a crisis it may be that this is a crisis of *discernment,* a crisis in failing to recognize and celebrate the rich ministerial charisms given by the baptismal Spirit, a crisis remedied only by continual returning to the common source of all ministry, the watery womb of the Church's very life.

A RENEWED SENSE OF AND ZEAL FOR ECUMENISM

A baptismal spirituality, by definition, can be nothing other than an ecumenical spirituality as well. The language of the New Testament could not be more clear here: "There is one body and one Spirit, just as you were called to the one hope of your calling, one Lord, one faith, one baptism, one God and Father of all, who is above all and through all and in all" (Eph 4:4-6). Through water and the Spirit in baptism all are incorporated into the *one* Christ, the *one* Church, the *one* Body of Christ. And because of this, Christian unity is, above all, not a demand, not a call, but already a gift of baptism itself to be received and further realized gratefully. Although we are baptized within particular ecclesial communities, according to the liturgical rites of those communities, and although we live out our baptism in those particular ecclesial manners of life, we are not baptized "Catholic," "Lutheran," "Episcopalian," or anything else. We are baptized into Christ and, thus, into the *one* Church of Jesus Christ; i.e., all the baptized, in a very real way, already belong to the same Church! It is this sacramental bond of "Real" communion that must be on the forefront of any discussion of visible Christian unity today.

While Vatican II was quite clear that baptism and Eucharist are the two premiere sacraments, and while recent Roman Catholic documents on ecumenism have certainly given pride of place to the "sacramental bond of unity" that exists among all the baptized, I fear that we have not taken baptism and its implications seriously *enough* in this regard. Between our displaced churches we often seem to want there to be something *more,* to place other obstacles in the way to unity at a common eucharistic table. We often call that something more "confirmation." But listen to the words of Paul Turner in a Roman Catholic context:

"We can only hope that the need for a rite of transferring membership will become minimized. Progress in the ecumenical movement should help us move toward a single eucharistic table for all Christian families. This would reduce the need for a separate rite of 'Reception of Baptized Christians into the Full Communion of the Catholic Church' and purify the purpose of confirmation. . . . Current pastoral practice sadly initiates such candidates in much the same way as catechumens. The two groups are catechized together, and pass through either the same rituals or ponderous adaptations which struggle to challenge the non-baptized without offending non-Catholic Christians. Frequently, candidates are disappointed that they cannot be baptized like catechumens, that they should not sign the book of the elect like catechumens, that they are not called to scrutinies like catechumens, that they are not anointed with the oil of catechumens like catechumens. . . . By making candidates imitate the path of catechumens we have too often made it too difficult for Christians who share one baptism to share one eucharistic table. The ecumenical movement longs for the day when the rites which prepare baptized Christians for full communion will be ripped from our books, and the catechumenate now so freely adapted for the *baptized* may become again the proper province of the unbaptized. . . . When the disciples warned Jesus that some who were not of their company were exorcising demons in his name they expected him to put a stop to it. Jesus tolerated strange exorcists with the simplest of aphorisms: 'If they're not against us, they're for us.' The church tolerates baptisms. Is it too much to ask that we tolerate confirmations as well? Our churches are irresponsibly dawdling toward a common table."[29]

A baptismal-ecumenical spirituality or way of life calls us, indeed, to stop "irresponsibly dawdling toward a common [eucharistic] table." I am not so naive as to think that there are no significant differ-

[29] Turner, *Confirmation,* 129.

ences between the churches of today. Nor do I think that there should not be particular tradition-specific catechesis for those seeking to enter fully into a particular ecclesial tradition. But if the past thirty years or so of ecumenical dialogue have taught us anything, at least those dialogues between Roman Catholics, Episcopalians, and Lutherans, it should be that such traditional differences are not *necessarily* church-dividing any longer, but rather legitimate, distinctive, and complementary emphases and traditions within the one Body of Christ and the common ecumenical faith of the Church, emphases and traditions which can, indeed, enrich one another in a greater communion.

By "common ecumenical faith of the Church," I do not mean some kind of generic acknowledgment that Jesus is Lord, but an *explicit* profession of faith rooted in the common ecumenical *baptismal* creeds and confessions (i.e., the Apostles' and Nicene Creeds) of the Church—the centrality of the one faith in God, Jesus Christ, and the Holy Spirit which is shared and confessed within and across particular faith communities. As such, the "common ecumenical faith of the Church" is a common *faith* professed in those creeds, a real communion, a oneness in faith, constituted by "one baptism" in which *all* the baptized are united already.

It is crucial for the sake of ecumenism, I believe, that a baptismal spirituality, a baptismal understanding of life, a baptismal ecclesiology be recovered and/or reemphasized in our own day. Don't we get it? Ecumenically, because of baptism we already belong to the same Church, the one, holy, catholic, and apostolic Church of Jesus Christ. According to the 1993 *Directory for Ecumenism* and Pope John Paul II's *Ut unum sint*, we already share in the *real* presence of Christ in the modes of assembly, word, prayer, and the sacramental baptismal bond. Now, given this, how much more time and effort do we need to spend on figuring out who is permitted and who is not permitted to be seated at Jesus' *one* eucharistic table in our legitimately diverse liturgical assemblies? I am convinced that baptismal unity in the *one* faith far outweighs any other distinctions, be they cultural, social, sexual, age-related, or ecclesial.

A RENEWED SENSE OF ALL CHRISTIAN LIFE AS A LIVING OUT OF BAPTISM

Finally, the recovery of a baptismal spirituality calls us to a renewed sense of all Christian life as nothing other than a continual, day-after-day living out of our baptism. And that, of course, means a life of continual conversion and reconversion, a life of death and resurrection, of continual claiming that new birth and Spirit of our baptism. Such conversion, of course, is a key and necessary element in all of what I have been saying in this chapter, but especially so regarding our recovery of the baptismal inclusiveness of Paul, a renewed baptismal understanding of ministry, and a renewed zeal for ecumenism.

If ever there was a person who made baptism the very center of Christian life it was Luther, ecumenically called by some today, "our common teacher." It is said that when plagued by doubt or tempted to despair Luther would trace the sign of the cross on his forehead and say, "I have been baptized!" No matter what he felt, experienced, doubted, or perceived, remembering his baptism reminded him that God had spoken the promise of salvation and life in that baptism. In his *Small Catechism,* as we saw in chapter 7 of this study, he wrote of the lifelong implications of baptism saying:

"What does such baptizing with water signify?

"Answer: It signifies that the old Adam in us, together with all sins and evil lusts, should be drowned by daily sorrow and repentance and be put to death, and that the new man should come forth daily and rise up, cleansed and righteous, to live forever in God's presence."[30]

And in his *Large Catechism* he wrote:

"In Baptism . . . every Christian has enough to study and to practice all his life. He always has enough to do to believe firmly what Baptism promises and brings—victory over death and the devil, forgiveness of sin, God's grace, the entire Christ, and the Holy Spirit with his gifts. . . . No greater jewel . . . can adorn our body and soul than Baptism, for through it we obtain perfect holiness and salvation, which no other kind of life and no work on earth can acquire."[31]

The spiritual journey in Christ is a journey of both place and displacement, a journey of death and resurrection, of birthing pangs and the bringing forth of new life, the paradigm for which is baptism itself. For baptism places us into the world as a community of dis-

---

[30] Cited from Theodore Tappert, ed., *The Book of Concord* (Philadelphia: Muhlenberg Press, 1959) 349.
[31] Ibid., 441–2.

placed people ourselves, people on a pilgrimage who really belong nowhere except where they are led, a people sure of their identity as the Body of Christ, as those who always walk wet in the baptismal waters of their origin.

But back again to this origin, back to the font, back home, this people is invited over and over again. And there at home flow the life-giving and renewing waters, the healing oil, the illuminating Light in the darkness, the royal festal garments, abundant clothing for all so that together they may be seated at that great and luxurious banquet table of the kingdom. The liturgy is a welcome place in our constant experience of displacement, inviting us home always, always back home to reclaim, renew, reaffirm, and reappropriate our baptism so that we might learn again to become who we are, the people God has already made us to be in Jesus Christ by water and the Spirit. Not only *can* we go home again. We *must* go home again! Our very identity depends upon it.

CONCLUSION

At the end of his 1977 article "Christian Initiation in Post-Conciliar Catholicism: A Brief Report," Aidan Kavanagh writes:

"I shall take confidence that the restored Roman rites of Christian Initiation have begun to come alive when I read a treatise on Christian ethics that begins with baptism into Christ; when I see episcopal meetings deciding on Church discipline from a baptismal perspective; when I partake in ecumenical discussions that begin not with Luther or Cranmer or Calvin or Trent, but with baptism; when I am lectured on ministry in terms not of modern sexual roles but of baptism; when I can worship in a parish that consummates its corporate life through Lent at the paschal vigil, gathered around the font where all new life begins. . . . In the meantime, there is much work to be done."[32]

Today, well over twenty years later, there is still "much work to be done." Indeed, with this blessed sacrament of baptism there will be always be much work to be done, "enough to study and to practice" all our lives.

[32] Cited from LWSS, 10.

A Select Bibliography

* = The essay is also included in Maxwell Johnson, ed. *Living Water, Sealing Spirit: Readings on Christian Initiation.* Collegeville: The Liturgical Press, 1995.

RITUAL AND SYMBOL

Eliade, Mircea. *Birth and Rebirth: The Religious Meanings of Initiation in Human Culture.* Trans. Willard Trask. New York: Harper, 1958. Also published under the title *Rites and Symbols of Initiation.* New York: Harper & Row, 1965.

Gennep, Arnold van. *The Rites of Passage.* Trans. Monika B. Vizedom and Gabrielle L. Caffee. Chicago: University of Chicago Press, 1960.

Mitchell, Leonel. *The Meaning of Ritual.* New York: Paulist Press, 1977.

Turner, Victor. "Passages, Margins and Poverty: Religious Symbols of Communitas," *Worship* 46 (1972) 390–412, 482–95.

____. *The Ritual Process: Structure and Anti-Structure.* Chicago: Aldine Pub. Co., 1969.

GENERAL HISTORIES/TEXTS

Davies, J. G. *The Architectural Setting of Baptism.* London: Barrie and Rockliff, 1962.

Finn, Thomas M. *Early Christian Baptism and the Catechumenate.* Vol. 5, *West and East Syria.* Vol. 6, *Italy, North Africa, and Egypt.* Message of the Fathers of the Church. Collegeville: The Liturgical Press, 1992.

Johnson, Maxwell, ed. *Living Water, Sealing Spirit: Readings on Christian Initiation.* Collegeville: The Liturgical Press, 1995.

Kuehn, Regina. *A Place for Baptism.* Chicago: Liturgy Training Publications, 1992.

Murphy Center for Liturgical Research. *Made, Not Born: New Perspectives on Christian Initiation and the Catechumenate.* Notre Dame: University of Notre Dame Press, 1976.

Scheer, A. "The Influence of Culture on the Liturgy as Shown in the History of the Initiation Rite," *Christian Initiation*. London: n.p., 1969.

Stauffer, S. Anita. *On Baptismal Fonts: Ancient and Modern*. Alcuin/GROW Liturgical Study 29–30. Bramcote, Nottingham: Grove Books, 1994.

_____, ed. *Worship and Culture in Dialogue: Reports of International Consultations, Cartigny, Switzerland, 1993, Hong Kong, 1994*. Geneva: Department for Theology and Studies, Lutheran World Federation, 1994.

Turner, Paul. *Sources of Confirmation: From the Fathers Through the Reformers*. Collegeville: The Liturgical Press, 1993.

Wainwright, Geoffrey. *Christian Initiation*. Richmond, Va.: John Knox Press, 1969.

_____. "The Rites and Ceremonies of Christian Initiation: Developments in the Past." *Studia Liturgica* 10 (1974) 2–24.

Whitaker, Edward Charles. *The Baptismal Liturgy*. 2d ed. London: SPCK, 1981.

_____. *Documents of the Baptismal Liturgy*. London: SPCK, 1960.

_____. "The History of the Baptismal Formula." *Journal of Ecclesiastical History* 16 (1965) 1–12.

NEW TESTAMENT

Beasley-Murray, George R. *Baptism in the New Testament*. Grand Rapids, Mich.: Eerdmans, 1973.

Brown, Raymond. "We Confess One Baptism for the Remission of Sins." *Worship* 40 (1966) 260–71.

*Collins, A. "The Origin of Christian Baptism." *Studia Liturgica* 19:1 (1989) 28–46.

Cullmann, Oscar. *Baptism in the New Testament*. Trans. J.K.S. Reid. London: SCM Press, 1950.

Flemington, William F. *The New Testament Doctrine of Baptism*. London: SPCK, 1964.

George, A., ed. *Baptism in the New Testament: A Symposium*. Trans. David Askew. Baltimore: Helicon, 1964.

Lathrop, Gordon. "Baptism in the New Testament and Its Cultural Settings." *Worship and Culture in Dialogue: Reports of International Consultations, Car-*

tigny, Switzerland, 1993, Hong Kong, 1994. Ed. S. Anita Stauffer, 17–38. Geneva: Department for Theology and Studies, Lutheran World Federation, 1994.

Manson, T. W. "Entry into Membership of the Early Church." *Journal of Theological Studies* 48 (1947) 1964.

Tripp, D. H. *"Eperotema* (1 Peter 3.21). A Liturgist's Note." *Expository Times* 92 (1981) 267–70.

Wagner, Günter. *Pauline Baptism and the Pagan Mysteries.* Edinburgh: Oliver & Boyd, 1967.

White, Reginald Ernest Oscar. *The Biblical Doctrine of Initiation.* Grand Rapids, Mich.: Eerdmans, 1960.

EARLY CHRISTIAN RITES

Benoit, André. *Le baptême au second siècle.* Paris: Presses Universitaires de France, 1953.

Botte, Bernard. "Post-Baptismal Anointing in the Ancient Patriarchate of Antioch." *Studies in Syrian Baptismal Rites.* Ed. Jacob Vellian, 63–71. The Syrian Churches Series. Kottayam: n.p., 1973.

Bradshaw, Paul. *Early Christian Worship: A Basic Introduction to Ideas and Practice.* London: n.p., 1996.

____, ed. *Essays in Early Eastern Initiation.* Alcuin/GROW Liturgical Study 8. Bramcote, Nottingham: Grove Books, 1989.

Brock, Sebastian P. "Some Early Syriac Baptismal Commentaries." *Orientalia Christiana Periodica* 46 (1980).

____. "Studies in the Early History of the Syrian Orthodox Baptismal Liturgy." *Journal of Theological Studies* 23 (1972) 16–64.

____. *The Holy Spirit in the Syrian Baptismal Tradition.* Syrian Churches Series 9. Bronx, N.Y.: Available at John XXIII Centre, Fordham University, 1979.

____. "The Syrian Baptismal Ordines." *Studia Liturgica* 12 (1977) 177–83.

____. "The Syrian Baptismal Rites." *Concilium* 122 (1979) 98–104.

____. "The Transition to a Post-baptismal Anointing in the Antiochene Rite." *The Sacrifice of Praise.* Ed. Bryan Spinks, 215–25. Rome: C.L.V.-Edizioni Liturgiche, 1981.

Burnish, Raymond. *The Meaning of Baptism: A Comparison of the Teaching and Practice of the Fourth Century with the Present Day*. London: SPCK, 1985.

_____. "The Role of the Godfather in the East in the Fourth Century." *Studia Patristica* 17 (1982) 558–64.

Burns, J. P. "On Rebaptism: Social Organization in the Third Century." *Journal of Early Christian Studies* 1:4 (1993) 367–403.

_____. "Salvation: Two Patristic Traditions." *Theological Studies* 37 (1976) 598–611.

Chalassery, Joseph. *The Holy Spirit and Christian Initiation in the East Syrian Tradition*. Rome: Mar Thoma Yogam, 1995.

Cross, F. L., ed. *St. Cyril of Jerusalem's Lectures on the Christian Sacraments: The Procatechesis and the Five Mystagogical Catecheses*. London: SPCK, 1951.

Cunningham, A. "Patristic Catechesis for Baptism: A Pedagogy for Christian Living." *Before and After Baptism: The Work of Teachers and Catechists*. Ed. J. A. Wilde. Chicago: n.p., 1988.

Daniélou, Jean. *The Bible and the Liturgy*. Notre Dame, Ind.: University of Notre Dame Press, 1966.

Driscoll, M. "The Baptism of Clovis and French Baptismal Consciousness." *Proceedings of the North American Academy of Liturgy*. Valparaiso: The Academy, 1997. Pp. 133–46.

Dujarier, Michel. *A History of the Catechumenate*. New York: Sadlier, 1979.

Duncan, Edward Joseph. *Baptism in the Demonstrations of Aphraates the Persian Sage*. Washington, D.C.: Catholic University of America Press, 1945.

Field, Anne. *From Darkness to Light. What It Meant to Become a Christian in the Early Church*. Ann Arbor, Mich.: Servant Books, 1978.

Finn, Thomas M. *From Death to Rebirth: Ritual and Conversion in Antiquity*. New York: Paulist Press, 1997.

_____. "It Happened One Saturday Night: Ritual and Conversion in Augustine's North Africa." *Journal of the American Academy of Religion* 58 (1990) 589–616.

_____. *The Liturgy of Baptism in the Baptismal Instructions of St. John Chrysostom*. Studies in Christian Antiquity 15. Washington, D.C.: Catholic University of America Press, 1967.

Fisher, J.D.C. "The Consecration of Water in the Early Rites of Baptism." *Studia Patristica* 2 (1957) 41–6.

Harmless, William. *Augustine and the Catechumenate.* Collegeville: The Liturgical Press, 1995.

Jackson, P. "The Meaning of 'Spiritale Signaculum' in the Mystagogy of Ambrose of Milan." *Ecclesia Orans* 7:1 (1990) 77–94.

Jeanes, Gordon, ed. *The Day Has Come! Easter and Baptism in Zeno of Verona.* ACC 73. Collegeville: The Liturgical Press, 1995.

Johnson, Maxwell. *Liturgy in Early Christian Egypt.* Alcuin/GROW Liturgical Study 33. Bramcote, Nottingham: Grove Books, 1995.

____. "The Postchrismational Structure of *Apostolic Tradition* 21, the Witness of Ambrose of Milan, and a Tentative Hypothesis Regarding the Current Reform of Confirmation in the Roman Rite." *Worship* 70:1 (1996) 16–34.

Kretschmar, Georg. "Beiträge zur Geschichte der Liturgie, insbesondere der Taufliturgie, in Ägypten." *Jahrbuch für Liturgik und Hymnologie* 8 (1963) 1–54.

____. "Die Geschichte des Taufgottesdienstes in der alten Kirche." *Leitourgia: Handbuch des evangelischen Gottesdienstes.* Vol 5. Kassel: J. Stauda-Verlag, 1970. 1–348.

*____. "Recent Research on Christian Initiation." *Studia Liturgica* 12 (1977) 87–106.

Lampe, Geoffrey William Hugo. *The Seal of the Spirit: A Study in the Doctrine of Baptism and Confirmation in the New Testament and the Fathers.* London: SPCK, 1967.

Lanne, E. "La confession de foi baptismale à Alexandrie et à Rome." *La liturgie, expression de la foi: Conférences Saint-Serge XXVe Semaine d'études Liturgiques Paris, 27–30 juin 1978.* Ed. A. M. Triacca and A. Pistoia, 213–28. Bibliotheca "Ephemerides liturgicae" 16. Rome: C.L.V.-Edizioni liturgiche, 1979.

Latte, R. de. "Saint Augustin et le baptême: Étude liturgico-historique du rituel baptismal des adultes chez saint Augustin." *Questions Liturgiques* 56 (1975) 177–223.

____. "Saint Augustin et le baptême: Étude liturgico-historique du rituel baptismal des enfants chez saint Augustin." *Questions Liturgiques* 57 (1976) 51–5.

Ligier, L. "The Biblical Symbolism of Baptism in the Fathers and in the Liturgy." *Concilium* 22 (1967) 16–30.

Mazza, Enrico. *Mystagogy.* Trans. Matthew J. O'Connell. New York: Pueblo, 1989.

397

McDonnell, Kilian. *The Baptism of Jesus in the Jordan: The Trinitarian and Cosmic Order of Salvation.* Collegeville: The Liturgical Press, 1996.

_____, and George T. Montague. *Christian Initiation and Baptism in the Holy Spirit: Evidence from the First Eight Centuries.* Collegeville: The Liturgical Press, 1991.

Murray, R. "The Exhortations to Candidates for Ascetical Vows at Baptism in the Ancient Syrian Church." *New Testament Studies* 21 (1974) 59–80.

Pocknee, C. E. "The Archaeology of Baptism." *Theology* 74 (1971) 309–11.

Quasten, Johannes. "The Blessing of the Font in the Syriac Rite of the Fourth Century." *Theological Studies* 7 (1946) 309–13.

Ratcliff, E. C. "The Old Syrian Baptismal Tradition and Its Resettlement under the Influence of Jerusalem in the Fourth Century." *Studies in Church History* 2 (1965) 19–37. This also appears in *Liturgical Studies [of] E. C. Ratcliff.* Ed. A. H. Couratin and D. H. Tripp, 135–54. London: SPCK, 1976.

Riley, Hugh M. *Christian Initiation: A Comparative Study of the Interpretation of the Baptismal Liturgy in the Mystagogical Writings of Cyril of Jerusalem, John Chrysostom, Theodore of Mopsuestia and Ambrose of Milan.* Studies in Christian Antiquity 17. Washington, D.C.: Catholic University of America Press, 1974.

Rusch, W. R. "Baptism of Desire in Ambrose and Augustine." *Studia Patristica* 15 (1984) 374–8.

Stenzel, A. "Temporal and Supra-Temporal in the History of the Catechumenate and Baptism." *Concilium* 22 (1967) 31–44.

Verghese, P. "Relation between Baptism, 'Confirmation,' and Eucharist in the Syrian Orthodox Church." *Studia Liturgica* 4 (1965) 81–93.

Wainwright, G. "The Baptismal Eucharist before Nicea: An Essay in Liturgical History." *Studia Liturgica* 4 (1965) 9–36.

Wilkinson, John, trans. *Egeria's Travels.* London: SPCK, 1971.

Willis, G. G. "What Was the Earliest Syrian Baptismal Liturgy?" *Studia Evangelica* 6 (1973) 651–4.

Winkler, Gabriele. *Das Armenische Initiationsrituale: Entwicklungsgeschichtliche und liturgievergleichende Untersuchung der Quellen des 3. bis 10. Jahrhunderts.* Orientalia Christiana Analecta 217. Rome: Pont. Institutum Studiorum Orientalium, 1982.

*____. "The Original Meaning of the Prebaptismal Anointing and Its Implications." *Worship* 52 (1978) 24–45.

Yarnold, Edward. *The Awe-Inspiring Rites of Initiation: The Origins of the R.C.I.A.* Collegeville: The Liturgical Press, 1994.

____. "Baptism and the Pagan Mysteries in the Fourth Century." *Heythrop Journal* 13 (1972) 247–67.

____. "Initiation: Sacrament and Experience." *Liturgy Reshaped.* Ed. Kenneth Stevenson, 17–31. London: SPCK, 1982.

Ysebaert, Joseph. *Greek Baptismal Terminology.* Nijmegen: Dekker & Van de Vegt, 1962.

MEDIEVAL/REFORMATION RITES

Akeley, T. C. *Christian Initiation in Spain, c. 300-1100.* London: Darton, Longman & Todd, 1967.

Arranz, M. "Les Sacrements de l'ancien Euchologe constantinopolitain" (9 articles). 1, *Orientalia Christiana Periodica* (hereafter OCP) 48 (1982) 284–335. 2, OCP 49 (1983) 42–90. 3, OCP 49 (1983) 284–302; 4, OCP 50 (1984) 43–64; 5, OCP 50 (1984) 372–97. 6, OCP 51 (1985) 60–86. 7, OCP 52 (1986) 145–78. 8, OCP 53 (1987) 59–106. 9, OCP 55 (1989) 33–62.

____. "Evolution des rites d'incorporation et de réadmission dans l'église selon l'Euchologe byzantin." *Gestes et paroles dans les diverses familles liturgiques.* Ed. A. Pistoia and A. Triacca, 31–75. Rome: Centro liturgico vincenziano, 1978.

Beraudy, R. "Scrutinies and Exorcisms." *Concilium* 22 (1967) 57–61.

Buchem, L. A. van *L'Homelie pseudo-Eusebienne de Pentecôte: l'origine de la confirmation in Gaule Méridionale et l'interprétation de ce rite par Fauste de Riez.* Nijmegen: Drukkerij Gebr. Janssen, 1967.

Cramer, Peter. *Baptism and Change in the Early Middle Ages, c. 200-c. 1150.* Cambridge Studies in Medieval Life and Thought, Fourth Series, vol. 20. Cambridge: Cambridge University Press, 1993.

Davies, J. G. "The Disintegration of the Christian Initiation Rite." *Theology* 50 (1947) 407–12.

Finnegan, Eugene M. "The Origins of Confirmation in the Western Church: A Liturgical-dogmatic Study of the Development of the Separate Sacrament of Confirmation in the Western Church prior to the Fourteenth

Century." 4 vols. Ph.D. diss., Theological Faculty of Trier, West Germany, 1970.

Fisher, John Douglas Close. *Christian Initiation: Baptism in the Medieval West.* ACC 47. London: SPCK, 1965.

____. *Christian Initiation: The Reformation Period.* ACC 51. London: SPCK, 1970.

Gy, P.-M. "La formule 'Je te baptise' (Et ego te baptizo)." *Communio Sanctorum: Melanges offerts à Jean-Jacques von Allmen.* Ed. B. Bobrinskoy et al., 65–72. Geneva: Labor et Fides, 1982.

*Kavanagh, Aidan. "Confirmation: A Suggestion from Structure." *Worship* 58 (1984) 386–95.

____. *Confirmation: Origins and Reform.* New York: Pueblo, 1988.

Lara, J. "'Precious Green Jade Water': A Sixteenth-Century Adult Catechumenate in the New World." *Worship* 71:3 (1997) 415–28.

*Levesque, J. "The Theology of the Postbaptismal Rites in the Seventh and Eighth Century Gallican Church." *Ephemerides Liturgicae* 95 (1981) 3–43.

Mitchell, Leonel L. *Baptismal Anointing.* ACC 48. London: SPCK, 1966.

____. "The Thanksgiving over the Water in the Baptismal Rite of the Western Church." *The Sacrifice of Praise.* Ed. Bryan Spinks, 229–44. Rome: C.L.V.-Edizioni Liturgiche, 1981.

Old, Hughes Oliphant. *The Shaping of the Reformed Baptismal Rite in the Sixteenth Century.* Grand Rapids, Mich.: Eerdmans, 1992.

*Quinn, F. C. "Confirmation Reconsidered: Rite and Meaning." *Worship* 59 (1985) 354–70.

Ramis, G. "La Iniciación Cristiana en la Liturgia Hispánica: El Domingo 'in Vicesima.'" *Ecclesia Orans* (1994) 189–206.

Ratcliff, E. C. "The Relation of Confirmation to Baptism in the Early Roman and Byzantine Liturgies." *Theology* 49 (1946) 258–65, 290–5. This also appears in *Liturgical Studies [of] E. C. Ratcliff.* Ed. A. H. Couratin and D. H. Tripp, 118–34. London: SPCK, 1976.

Schmemann, Alexander. *Of Water and the Holy Spirit: A Liturgical Study of Baptism.* Crestwood, N.Y.: St. Vladimir's Seminary Press, 1974.

Serra, D. "The Blessing of Baptismal Water at the Paschal Vigil in the *Gelasianum Vetus:* A Study of the Euchological Texts, Ge 444–448." *Ecclesia Orans* 6 (1989) 323–44.

Shepherd, M. H. "Confirmation: The Early Church." *Worship* 46 (1972) 15–21.

Spinks, Bryan D. "Luther's Timely Theology of Unilateral Baptism." *Lutheran Quarterly* 9 (1995) 23–45.

Turner, Paul. *Confirmation: The Baby in Solomon's Court.* New York: Paulist Press, 1993.

____. *The Meaning and Practice of Confirmation: Perspectives from a Sixteenth-Century Controversy.* New York: P. Lang, 1987.

*____. "The Origins of Confirmation: An Analysis of Aidan Kavanagh's Hypothesis." *Worship* 65 (1991) 320–36.

*Winkler, Gabriele. "Confirmation or Chrismation? A Study in Comparative Liturgy." *Worship* 58:1 (1984)

INFANT BAPTISM AND COMMUNION

Aland, Kurt. *Did the Early Church Baptize Infants?* Trans. G. R. Beasley-Murray. London: SCM Press, 1963.

*Brand, Eugene. "Baptism and Communion of Infants: A Lutheran View." *Worship* 50 (1976) 29–42.

Bretscher, P. "First Things First: The Question of Infant Communion." *Una Sancta* 20 (1962) 34–40.

Brusselmans, C. "Christian Parents and Infant Baptism." *Louvain Studies* 2 (1968) 29–48.

*Covino, Paul F. X. "The Postconciliar Infant Baptism Debate in the American Catholic Church." *Worship* 56 (1982) 240–60.

Crawford, C. "Infant Communion: Past Tradition and Present Practice." *Theological Studies* 31 (1970) 523–36.

Holeton, David. *Infant Communion, Then and Now.* Bramcote, Nottingham: Grove Books, 1981.

Instruction on Infant Baptism. Vatican City: Vatican Polyglot Press, 1980.

Jeremias, Joachim. *Infant Baptism in the First Four Centuries.* Trans. David Cairns. Philadelphia: Westminster Press, 1960.

____. *The Origins of Infant Baptism: A Further Study in Reply to Kurt Aland.* Naperville, Ill.: A. R. Allenson, 1963.

Kiesling, C. "Infant Baptism." *Worship* 42:10 (1968) 617–26.

Maly, E. "Still a Case for Infant Baptism?" *The Sacraments: Readings in Contemporary Sacramental Theology.* Ed. Michael Taylor, 95–103. New York: Alba House, 1981.

Marsh, T. "Infant Baptism: The Role of the Community." *The Furrow* 22:1 (1971) 4–12.

McKenna, J. "Infant Baptism: Theological Reflections." *Worship* 70 (1996) 192–210.

Meyers, Ruth, ed. *Children at the Table: The Communion of All the Baptized in Anglicanism Today.* New York: Church Hymnal Corp., 1994.

Mitchell, N. "The Once and Future Child: Towards a Theology of Childhood." *The Living Light* 12:3 (1975) 423–37.

Muller-Fahrenlolz, Geiko, ed. *—and do not hinder them: An Ecumenical Plea for the Admission of Children to the Eucharist.* Faith and Order Paper 109. Geneva: World Council of Churches, 1982.

Redmond, R. X. "Infant Baptism: History and Pastoral Problems." *Theological Studies* 30 (1969) 79–89.

Searle, Mark. *Christening: The Making of Christians.* Collegeville: The Liturgical Press, 1980.

*____. "Infant Baptism Reconsidered." *Alternative Futures for Worship.* Vol. 2, *Baptism and Confirmation.* Ed. Mark Searle, 15–54. Collegeville: The Liturgical Press, 1987.

____. "Response: The RCIA and Infant Baptism." *Worship* 56:4 (1982) 327–32.

Taft, R. "On the Question of Infant Communion in the Byzantine Catholic Churches of the U.S.A." *Diakonia* 17 (1982) 201–14.

Vanbergen, P. "Baptism of the Infants of 'non satis credentes' Parents." *Studia Liturgica* 12 (1977) 195–200.

CONFIRMATION

Austin, Gerard. *Anointing with the Spirit: The Rite of Confirmation: The Use of Oil and Chrism.* New York: Pueblo, 1985.

____. "The Essential Rite of Confirmation and the Liturgical Tradition." *Ephemerides Liturgicae* 86 (1972) 214–22.

Banting, H. "Imposition of Hands in Confirmation: A Medieval Problem." *Journal of Ecclesiastical History* 7 (1956) 147–59.

Botte, Bernard. "Apropos de la confirmation." *Nouvelle Revue Théologique* 88 (1966) 848–52.

Breuning, W. "Baptism and Confirmation: The Two Sacraments of Initiation." *Concilium* 22 (1967) 95–108.

Browning, Robert L., and Roy A. Reed, eds. *Models of Confirmation and Baptismal Affirmation: Liturgical and Educational Issues and Designs.* Birmingham, Ala.: Religious Education Press, 1995.

Buchem, L. A. van *L'Homelie pseudo-Eusebienne de Pentecôte: l'origine de la confirmation in Gaule Méridionale et l'interprétation de ce rite par Fauste de Riez.* Nijmegen: Drukkerij Gebr. Janssen, 1967.

Buckley, F. J. "What Age for Confirmation?" *Theological Studies* 27 (1965) 635–66.

Finnegan, Eugene M. "The Origins of Confirmation in the Western Church: A Liturgical-dogmatic Study of the Development of the Separate Sacrament of Confirmation in the Western Church prior to the Fourteenth Century." 4 vols. Ph.D. diss., Theological Faculty of Trier, West Germany, 1970.

Fisher, J.D.C. *Confirmation Then and Now.* ACC 60. London: SPCK, 1978.

_____. "Gifts of the Spirit and a Confession of Faith: The Age for Confirmation." *The Sacrifice of Praise: Studies on the Themes of Thanksgiving and Redemption in the Central Prayers of the Eucharistic and Baptismal Liturgies, in Honour of Arthur Hubert Couratin.* Ed. Bryan D. Spinks, 247–57. Rome: C.L.V.-Edizioni Liturgiche, 1981.

Gaupin, L. "Now Confirmation Needs its Own *Quam Singulari.*" *When Should We Confirm? The Order of Initiation.* Ed. J. A. Wilde, 85–93. Chicago: Liturgy Training Publications, 1989.

Johnson, Maxwell. "The Postchrismational Structure of *Apostolic Tradition* 21, the Witness of Ambrose of Milan, and a Tentative Hypothesis Regarding the Current Reform of Confirmation in the Roman Rite." *Worship* 70:1 (1996) 16–34.

*Kavanagh, Aidan. "Confirmation: A Suggestion from Structure." *Worship* 58 (1984) 386–95.

_____. *Confirmation: Origins and Reform.* New York: Pueblo, 1988.

Levet, R. "L'age de la confirmation dans la législation des diocèses de France depuis le Concile de Trente." *La Maison-Dieu* 54 (1958) 118–42.

National Conference of Catholic Bishops. *Report of the Ad Hoc Committee for the Canonical Determination of the Age of Confirmation.* Washington, D.C.: United States Catholic Conference, 1993.

Nocent, Adrian. "La Confirmation: Questions posées théologiens at aux pasteurs." *Gregorianum* 72:4 (1991) 689–704.

*Quinn, F. C. "Confirmation Reconsidered: Rite and Meaning." *Worship* 59 (1985) 354–70.

Ratcliff, E. C. "The Relation of Confirmation to Baptism in the Early Roman and Byzantine Liturgies." *Theology* 49 (1946) 258–65, 290–5. This also appears in *Liturgical Studies [of] E. C. Ratcliff.* Ed. A. H. Couratin and D. H. Tripp, 118–34. London: SPCK, 1976.

Repp, Arthur. *Confirmation in the Lutheran Church.* St. Louis, Mo.: Concordia Publishing House, 1964.

Senn, F. "End for Confirmation?" *Currents in Theology and Mission* 3 (1976) 45–52.

Shepherd, M. H. "Confirmation: The Early Church." *Worship* 46 (1972) 15–21.

Turner, Paul. *Confirmation: The Baby in Solomon's Court.* New York: Paulist Press, 1993.

____. *The Meaning and Practice of Confirmation: Perspectives from a Sixteenth-Century Controversy.* New York: P. Lang, 1987.

*____. "The Origins of Confirmation: An Analysis of Aidan Kavanagh's Hypothesis." *Worship* 65 (1991) 320–36.

Vinck, H. "Sur l'age de la confirmation: Un projet de décret au Concile Vatican I." *La Maison-Dieu* 132 (1977) 136–40.

MODERN RITES
(See also under Infant Baptism/Communion and Confirmation above)

Roman Catholic

Bryce, M. C. "The Catechumenate: Past, Present, Future." *American Ecclesiastical Review* 160 (1969) 262–73.

Chapman, M. E. "RCIA and the Making and Sustaining of Christians." *Dialog* 31 (1992) 62–5.

*Covino, Paul F. X. "The Postconciliar Infant Baptism Debate in the American Catholic Church." *Worship* 56 (1982) 240–60.

Duggan, R. "Conversion in the *Ordo Initiationis Christianae Adultorum:* An Analysis and Critique." *Ephemerides Liturgicae* 96 (1982) 57–83, 209–52; 97 (1983) 141–223.

_____. "Mystagogia and Continuing Conversion: RCIA Success Stories." *Christian Initiation Resource Reader.* Vol. 4, *Mystagogia and Ministries.* Ed. Moya Gullage, 19–30. New York: Sadlier, 1984.

Dunning, J. "The Stage of Initiation IV: The Sacraments of Initiation and Afterwards." *Becoming a Catholic Christian.* Ed. William J. Reedy, 141–2. New York: Sadlier, 1979.

Dujarier, M. "Sponsorship." *Concilium* 22 (1967) 45–50.

Fischer, B. "Baptismal Exorcism in the Catholic Baptismal Rites after Vatican II." *Studia Liturgica* 10 (1974) 48–55.

Frohlich, M. "Toward a Modern Mystagogy." *Liturgy* 4:1 (1983) 51–9.

Gelineau, J. "The Symbols of Christian Initiation." *Becoming a Catholic Christian.* Ed. William J. Reedy, 190–6. New York: Sadlier, 1979.

Gelpi, Donald. *Committed Worship: A Sacramental Theology for Converting Christians.* 2 vols. Collegeville: The Liturgical Press, 1993.

Jackson, Pamela. *Journeybread for the Shadowlands: The Readings for the Rites of the Catechumenate, RCIA.* Collegeville: The Liturgical Press, 1993.

*Kavanagh, Aidan. "Christian Initiation in Post-Conciliar Roman Catholicism: A Brief Report." *Studia Liturgica* 12 (1977) 107–15.

_____. "The New Roman Rites of Adult Initiation." *Studia Liturgica* 10 (1974) 35–47.

*_____. "Unfinished and Unbegun Revisited: The Rite of Christian Initiation of Adults." *Worship* 53 (1979) 327–40.

_____. "Symbolic Implications of Christian Initiation in Roman Catholicism since the Second Vatican Council." *I Simboli dell' Iniziazone Cristiana.* Studia Anselmiana 87. Rome: Pontificio Ateneo S. Anselmo, 1983. 223–41.

Kemp, R. "Mystagogical Principle in the Rite and in Catechesis." *Christian Initiation Resources* 2:1 (1981) 1–7.

_____. "The Rite of Christian Initiation of Adults at Ten Years." *Worship* 56 (1982) 309–26; see also responses, 327–43.

Küng, H. "Confirmation as the Completion of Baptism." *Concilium* 99 (1974) 79–102.

405

Lengeling, J. "The Blessing of the Baptismal Water in the Roman Rite." *Concilium* 22 (1967) 62–8.

Lewinski, R. "Recovering Christian Mystagogy for Contemporary Churches." *Before and After Baptism: The Work of Teachers and Catechists.* Ed. J. A. Wilde. Chicago: n.p., 1988.

Manders, H. "The Relationship between Baptism and Faith." *Concilium* 22 (1967) 4–15.

Mitchell, Nathan. *Eucharist as Sacrament of Initiation.* Chicago: Liturgy Training Publications, 1994.

National Conference of Catholic Bishops. *Christian Initiation of Adults: A Commentary.* Study Text 10. Washington, D.C.: United States Catholic Conference, 1985.

Neunheuser, Burkhard. *Baptism and Confirmation.* New York: Herder and Herder, 1964.

Palliard, C. "The Place of Catechesis in the Catechumenate." *Concilium* 22 (1967) 88–94.

Quinn, F. "The Sacraments of Initiation and Christian Life." *Spirituality Today* 34:1 (1982) 27–38.

Searle, Mark, ed. *Alternative Futures for Worship.* Vol. 2: *Baptism and Confirmation.* Collegeville: The Liturgical Press, 1987.

Serra, D. "The Blessing of Baptismal Water at the Paschal Vigil: Ancient Texts and Modern Revisions." *Worship* (1990) 142–56.

_____. "The Blessing of Baptismal Water at the Paschal Vigil in the Post-Vatican II Reform." *Ecclesia Orans* 7 (1990) 343–63.

Tufano, Victoria, ed. *Celebrating the Rites of Adult Initiation: Pastoral Reflections.* Chicago: Liturgy Training Publications, 1992.

Other Christian Traditions

Armentrout, D. "The New Lutheran and Episcopal Baptismal Rites." *Lutheran Quarterly* 27 (1975) 295–311.

Benedict, Daniel. *Come to the Waters.* Nashville: Discipleship Resources, 1996.

Boehringer, H. "Baptism, Confirmation, and First Communion: Christian Initiation in the Contemporary Church." *Christian Initiation: Reborn of Water and the Spirit.* Ed. Daniel Brockopp et al., 73–98. Institute of Liturgical

Studies Occasional Papers 1. Valparaiso, Ind.: Institute of Liturgical Studies, 1981.

Brand, Eugene. *Baptism: A Pastoral Perspective.* Minneapolis: Augsburg, 1975.

*____. "New Rites of Initiation and Their Implications in the Lutheran Churches." *Studia Liturgica* 12 (1977) 151–65.

____. "Toward the Renewal of Christian Initiation in the Parish." *Christian Initiation: Reborn of Water and the Spirit.* Ed. Daniel Brockopp et al., 120–38. Institute of Liturgical Studies Occasional Papers 1. Valparaiso, Ind.: Institute of Liturgical Studies, 1981.

Browning, Robert L., and Roy A. Reed, eds. *Models of Confirmation and Baptismal Affirmation: Liturgical and Educational Issues and Designs.* Birmingham, Ala.: Religious Education Press, 1995.

Droege, T. A. "The Formation of Faith in Christian Initiation." *Cresset* (April 1983) 16–23.

Evangelical Lutheran Church in America. *Welcome to Christ: A Lutheran Catechetical Guide.* Minneapolis: Augsburg Fortress, 1997.

____. *Welcome to Christ: A Lutheran Introduction to the Catechumenate.* Minneapolis: Augsburg Fortress, 1997.

____. *Welcome to Christ: Lutheran Rites for the Catechumenate.* Minneapolis: Augsburg Fortress, 1997.

Evangelical Lutheran Church in Canada. *Living Witnesses: The Adult Catechumenate: A Manual for the Catechumenal Process.* Winnipeg: n.p., 1994.

Frederick, J. "The Initiation Crisis in the Church of England." *Studia Liturgica* 9 (1973) 137–57.

Holeton, David. "Confirmation in the 1980's." *Ecumenical Perspectives on Baptism, Eucharist, and Ministry.* Ed. Max Thurian, 68–89. Faith and Order Paper 116. Geneva: World Council of Churches, 1983.

Johnson, Maxwell. "The Shape of Christian Initiation in the Lutheran Churches: Liturgical Texts and Future Directions." *Studia Liturgica* 27:1 (1997) 33–60.

Jasper, R.C.D. "Christian Initiation: The Anglican Position." *Studia Liturgica* 12 (1977) 116–25. In that same issue see also L. Weil, "Christian Initiation in the Anglican Communion: A Response," 126–8; David Holeton, "Christian Initiation in Some Anglican Provinces," 129–50.

G. Lathrop, *Living Witnesses: The Adult Catechumenate (ELCIC): Congregational Prayers to Accompany the Catechumenal Process.* Minneapolis: n.p., 1994.

F. Ludolph, *Living Witnesses: The Adult Catechumenate (ELCIC): Preparing Adults for Baptism and Ministry in the Church.* Minneapolis: n.p., 1994.

McElligott, A. *The Catechumenal Process: Adult Initiation and Formation for Christian Life and Ministry.* New York: Church Hymnal Corp., 1990.

Mitchell, Leonel L. "Revision of the Rites of Christian Initiation in the American Episcopal Church." *Studia Liturgica* 10 (1974) 25–34.

Meyers, Ruth A. *Continuing the Reformation: Re-Visioning Baptism in the Episcopal Church.* New York 1997.

Pfatteicher, Philip H. *Commentary on the Occasional Services.* Philadelphia: Fortress Press, 1983.

____, and C. Messerli. *Manual on the Liturgy: Lutheran Book of Worship.* Minneapolis: Augsburg, 1979.

Schlink, Edmund. *The Doctrine of Baptism.* Trans. Herbert J. A. Bouman. St. Louis, Mo.: Concordia Publishing House, 1972.

Schmemann, Alexander. *Of Water and the Spirit: A Liturgical Study of Baptism.* Crestwood, N.Y.: St. Vladimir's Seminary Press, 1974.

Senn, F. "A New Baptismal Rite: Toward Revitalizing the Whole Community." *Currents in Theology and Mission* 2 (1975) 206–14.

____. "Shape and Content of Christian Initiation: An Exposition of the New Lutheran Liturgy of Holy Baptism." *Dialog* 14 (1975) 97–107.

*Spinks, Bryan D. "Vivid Signs of the Gift of the Spirit? The Lima Text on Baptism and Some Recent English Language Baptismal Liturgies." *Worship* 60 (1986) 232–46.

Stookey, Laurence. *Baptism: Christ's Act in the Church.* Nashville: Abingdon Press, 1982.

*____. "Three New Initiation Rites." *Worship* 51 (1977) 33–49.

Strobel, M. "Adaptation of the Catechumenate among North American Lutherans." *Worship* (1998) forthcoming.

Watkins, K. "Baptism and Christian Identity: A Presbyterian Approach." *Worship* 60 (1986) 55–63.

World Council of Churches. *Baptism, Eucharist & Ministry.* Faith and Order Paper 111. Geneva: World Council of Churches, 1982.

Index

John 3 and, 19, 30–1, 38–9, 47, 59,
87, 107, 116, 119, 198, 358
Pentecost and, 22, 64, 145–7, 202,
213, 317, 322, 357, 382–3
proselyte, Jewish, 7–10
Romans 6 and, 27, 30–1, 57, 64, 87,
102, 107–11, 121, 123, 175, 358,
382
spirituality of, 236, 365–91
Baptism, Eucharist, and Ministry, 294,
368
bishop(s), 42, 66, 81, 123–4, 128–9,
143, 158, 199–200, 203, 315, 386
Bobbio Missal, 197–8
Book of Common Prayer (England),
258, 261–5, 274–5, 326
Book of Common Prayer (USA, 1979),
292, 296, 334–9, 351, 362, 371
Book of Common Worship, 293, 351
Bucer, Martin, 246–9, 258, 261–2,
272–4, 276, 325
Byzantine, 222–5, 316

C
Cappadocia, 111, 168
Calvin, John, 249–57, 271
candle, 31, 233, 243, 247, 311–2, 319,
341, 384
Canon Law, 299, 325
Canones ad Gallos, 127
Canons of Hippolytus, 52, 58, 90,
116–7, 120, 170
Carthage, 61, 66, 148–50, 155
catechesis, 36, 48–9, 51, 98, 131, 216,
232, 240, 248, 253, 288, 301, 345
catechism(s), 240, 283–5, 357, 390
catechumen(s), 73, 173, 180
catechumenate
length of, 49, 52, 59, 73, 87, 90–1,
101, 117, 215–20, 301, 308
(*see also* Lent, season of)
Charlemagne, Emperor, 177–9
chrism
consecration of, 23, 143, 144, 224
chrismation, 23, 143–4, 224
(*see also* confirmation, consignation)
Christ–Messiah, 15, 47, 149, 192–3

Christmas (*see* baptism, Christmas
and)
Chrysostom, John, 102–4, 122, 173
Church, 150–1, 153, 255–6, 267, 294,
303, 347, 374, 385
Clement of Alexandria, 51–6
Clovis, 141–2
Communion (*see also* Eucharist)
as completion of initiation, 37, 39,
42, 77, 104, 196, 114, 122, 134,
157, 185, 258, 311, 316, 361
first, 187, 217, 218, 221, 299, 328,
372
infant, 68, 155–6, 185, 218–20, 223,
278, 281–2, 286, 328, 330, 331,
354–6, 362, 373–7
competentes, 122, 131, 133–5, 159,
195, 310
confession, first, 218, 221
confirmation (*see also* handlaying)
affirmation of baptism as, 324–5,
338, 344, 362
age(s) for, 210–2, 285, 299, 324–5,
369
as completion or perfection of initiation, 185, 324, 346
as sacrament or rite of maturity,
210–1, 213, 299–300, 370
baptism and, 24, 130, 146, 189,
194, 203–13, 296, 300, 321, 345,
361, 369–73
before first communion, 207, 212,
220, 270, 277, 288, 298–9, 355
bishops and, 83, 130, 142, 144, 157,
193–4, 204, 276, 313, 323, 362
(*see also* bishop(s), *and* handlaying)
catechetics and, 272–3, 275–6, 297,
370–1
(*see also* catechesis)
chrismation and, 83, 139, 205, 311,
356–60
(*see also* anointing(s), postbaptismal, *and* chrismation)
development of, 139, 158, 188,
197, 210–21
(*see also* handlaying)

Roman (Rome), 34, 71–87, 125–35, 157, 179–89